A WRITER'S
RHETORIC

A WRITER'S RHETORIC

Suzanne Britt
Meredith College

HARCOURT BRACE JOVANOVICH, PUBLISHERS

San Diego   New York   Chicago   Austin   Washington, D.C.

London   Sydney   Tokyo   Toronto

Preface

What has been lost in student essays, according to college admissions committees quoted in the *New York Times,* is the invigorating voice of a regular human being. When pressed to define "bad" writing, I say that it is, first of all, the writing that sounds like an echo. *A Writer's Rhetoric* reminds students that their voices are their own, that they must claim them and use them. Competent writers are imitators; compelling writers are originals. And this book challenges students to be the latter.

The models, activities, and discussions in this textbook use anything, everything, to stimulate the writing apprentice—newspapers, jokes, movies, literature, family fights, Sunday rests, magazines, street scenes, facts, fiction, colors, voices, science, sighs. And the "everything" is not sterile, isolated, theoretical. Writing is not a laboratory exercise, though it yields many of its simpler secrets to careful practitioners. Divorcing writing from immediate experience and isolating it in theory and technique will not work. Meanings suffocate. Passion dies.

A fine piece of writing relies on the particular. No matter how far the imagination flies, it must alight, finally, on a concrete detail. *A Writer's Rhetoric* urges students to pay attention to everything because everything is potentially significant: tall tales on a Sunday porch, trees black with rain, Mother's fierce eye, algebra's balanced certainties. Philosopher Simone Weil promises that "one day a light will dawn in exact proportion to the amount of attention paid." The promise is heartening when students are looking at an ordinary moment and wondering how to find their way through its slick surfaces to the textured insides where good writing begins.

Students must begin with passion and particularity and advance to precision. Strategies and techniques have their secure and worthy place in the creation of a polished essay. To this end, *A Writer's Rhetoric* discusses the whole essay—the thesis; the well-ordered parts of the essay; the creation of well-developed paragraphs, full of purpose and order; the subtle demands of transition, logic, and point of view; the delicate refinements of style, grammar, and punctuation; the importance of correct spelling—as well as research papers and the handling of literary analysis, which includes the specialized language of literature.

The title *A Writer's Rhetoric* indicates a dual perspective: the student writer's, of course, and also my own. I am a composition teacher and a professional writer. What I preach, I mostly practice. Small boxes scattered throughout the text highlight my own doubts and insights—lessons learned on the long journey from talking about writing to writing. In addition to many fine essays and paragraphs by respected writers, several of my own published essays appear. In my professional writing career, now over a decade long, I have never abandoned the strategies and techniques of the classroom: clear thesis and topic sentences, enticing introduction, solid middle, snappy conclusion, concrete details and examples, pleasing style. Ingenuity and originality reside not in revolutionary approaches to writing but, rather, in the particular and fresh angle a writer brings to a topic.

Experience as a "real" writer has taught me humility and flexibility. Both the astute instructor and the beginning student can appreciate this delicate difference between lofty principles and enlightened practice. I have learned, whether in writing or life, that you can do everything right and still be wrong. This paradox is a liberating tribute to the complex, satisfying activity we call writing.

I owe special thanks to respected friends, colleagues, and relatives who read the manuscript in all or several stages, commented, sighed amiably, and read it again: Dr. Catherine E. Moore and Dr. Elliot Engel, North Carolina State University; Dr. Jean Bauso, Peace College; Martha Stephenson Clarke, kind and canny critic; and my parents, Suzanne and Don Britt, who took an editorial, not merely a proprietary interest in the work.

In addition, I would like to express my appreciation to the following reviewers who contributed their time and their insights to the development of the manuscript: Ruth Dorgan, University of Wisconsin, Stevens Point; Jeffrey Duncan, Eastern Michigan University; Henrik Eger, University of Illinois, Chicago; Eileen Evans, Western Michigan University; Vicki Goldsmith, Northern Michigan University; Adrienne Robins, Occidental College; John Snapper, Calvin College (retired). Thanks also to Jim Owen, who contributed the section on documentation for research papers; to N. Charlene Turner, who typed anything I asked her to, except on her bowling night; and to head librarian Janet L. Freeman and other staff members of the Carlyle Campbell Library at Meredith College, who provided research materials.

Suzanne Britt

Contents

CHAPTER 4

CHAPTER 5

CHAPTER 6

PART III   Refining the Essay

CHAPTER 7

CHAPTER 8

CHAPTER 9

CHAPTER 10

PART IV   Special Assignments

CHAPTER 11

CHAPTER 12

PART

I

About Writing

1

The Writer's Life

Consider the importance of written words.

Ours is surely an audiovisual society. We ride to work or school humming along with Bruce or Barry on the car radio. We spend an hour around the conference table or the classroom watching a filmstrip on interpersonal relationships. We catch 15 minutes of headlines on CNN. Nowadays, even simple directions, instructions, and warnings are delivered more and more in pictures, not words. The word "empty" on the dashboard of the car has been replaced by a little gas pump. The sign reading "Deer Crossing" now pictures a buck or doe in midlope. "No Smoking" is signaled by a big red slash across a lighted cigarette.

Where do you stand in the middle of all that you see or hear? Are you *there*—reacting, thinking, taking action, developing a critical ear and eye? Of course you are, especially if you have the skill and energy and confidence to use written and spoken words to respond to the fast-moving pictures roaring past you in a fast-lane culture. One of the megatrends of this century is talk. The strong, silent heros and heroines of the frontier are gone forever. The laconic "Yeps" and "Nopes" are inadequate to a technologically sophisticated, fast-paced society. Now, whether you are destined for careers in business, law, medicine, education, entertainment, sports, politics, science, or fashion, someone is bound to step up sooner or later, stick a microphone in your face, and ask you what you think and know about what you have seen and heard. Someone will surely tell you, when you get a bright idea, to put it in writing. Someone may ask you to write a report, get out a memo, send a letter to the editor, or compose a script for a television pilot.

You can not now imagine all the connections writing will have to your life, but you can be sure that your ability to write well and clearly will put you in control of the images and sounds of the 1980s and 1990s. You are not going to be felling trees, building log cabins, and making quilts (except for fun, of course). You are going to be acting as an interpreter of the modern world. After you have watched and listened for a while, you will step back to read, study, and think about what is going on inside you and all around you. And you can act as a responsible interpreter of major and minor events when you understand the importance of written words and how to use them effectively.

You will discover, if you have not already, that even the best-stocked electronics store in America can provide you with only a bit of the equipment you need to be fully educated, mature, competent, and effective as a public citizen and as a private human being. Sometimes a quiet hour with the *New York Times* can teach you more than a whole year of *60 Minutes*. Sometimes one carefully worded letter to the utility company can get better results than a month of frantic phone calls. Sometimes a poem or story you wrote in an idle hour can bring more clarity and health to your emotional life than 20 sessions with a therapist.

Reading and writing engage you actively. They give you pleasure and perspective. They are time machines, enabling you to travel back and forth in time and space, to see the connections between yesterday and today, between the present and, as playwright Tennessee Williams put it, the "perhaps." When writer Flannery O'Connor's mother invited her to go to the movies to see *The Ten Commandments*, O'Connor quipped, "I read the book." If you understand the importance of written words, you can read the book of Life—and maybe write it, too.

Writing heightens consciousness.

When you write, you find yourself using every part of your being—your polished surfaces and your rough insides; your cool head and your pounding heart; your bitterest memories and your brightest dreams. If you work at writing, you will be continually surprised to discover what is *really* going on inside of you. The pen has a way, after awkward starts, of taking off and carrying you to places you did not expect to visit. Writing engages all your senses, demands all your ingenuity, asks nothing less than your total attention and your very best effort.

Writing pushes you to responsible action.

Often in discussions, words fly around, but no one listens very closely or remembers *exactly* what is said. But when you express your opinion *in writing*, you expose yourself for all to see. You may find yourself in the crossfire of an unpopular position or in the quicksand of an unsupported assertion.

Having written something that is important to you, you have no choice now but to accept responsibility for your opinions and even to act on it. If you have *said*, for example, that you "hate" the medical profession or the utility companies, you might be on safe ground among friends. But if you *write* those words, and you want a newspaper to print them, you will have to support your statement with facts and credible arguments. You will need to present the source of the problem and to suggest ways to clean up the system. Having gotten our attention, you will need to offer solutions. And you will have to commit yourself to one of them.

Writing carries risks because it is permanent. It is there for everyone to read and reread. But it can also be the touchstone for your actions, forcing you to a higher standard and a steadier course than the person who simply hurls an insult or makes a complaint in an idle conversation.

Writing helps you define yourself.

Most family albums are filled with snapshots of grinning relatives and friends on various important occasions, from birth onward. You can see what you wore to an eighth-grade dance, how fat you were in the summer of 1984, what you looked like in purple hair or in diapers. What is missing from these pictures? Though you may have been saying "cheese" for the class picture, you may have been trembling, on the edge of tears. A picture provides only images, surfaces. The thoughts and feelings, when put into words, complete the story and give color and meaning to it. One word from the heart, recorded right then, might have told more than a thousand pictures.

Even if most of your writing tasks are academic or occupational, you will still have an opportunity to observe your personality taking shape on the written page. Through writing you will learn to present a true impression of yourself about your identity, habits, flaws, talents, eccentricities. You will get to know yourself, perhaps for the first time, when you write. And over weeks or months or years, you will have, in effect, a personal record, a portfolio of your progress toward maturity.

Writing is a conversation with the world.

You may, at times, feel cut off from national, local, or private events, powerless to change or influence the actions and thoughts of others. But you have a voice. You can use it. Writing can propel you to the center of life, restore you to your rightful and responsible place in society. When you write a letter to the editor, deliver a valedictory address at a graduation, submit a report to the boss, or present a scholarly paper at a meeting, you are conversing with an audience. Be assured that your readers or listeners will talk or write back. And you will gain mastery over the conditions of isolation and powerlessness that lead to apathy, indifference, or glum hostility.

Writing helps you advance in your career.

Studies show that people who write well and speak well have wider choices in the job market and greater chances for promotion and salary increases. Writing *is* important to professional advancement, even though you may suspect that you will never need to write seriously again once you pass this course. Our society depends on communication; we use words to settle matters of law, to negotiate an end to strikes, to establish relations with other companies and other countries. We sell products, images, political candidates with words. Those who can speak and write effectively are promoted to positions of management and leadership. They have careers. Those who cannot communicate as well often find themselves doing chores.

Writing is a highly practical activity.

One of the common misconceptions about writing is that it has very little to do with the "real" world. The real world is taxes and shopping and budgets and bosses and boredom and résumés and hardware stores and rainy days and trash cans and quarrels and death. But writing is certainly a vital part of everyday living. Writing uses life to make sense of life. Above all, writing is a very practical activity, enabling people to get jobs, make proposals, keep up with the activities of friends and relatives. Writing can save a romance, sell a product, assist a scientific discovery, win an argument, help a refugee family, support an embattled politician. Writing is thinking and communicating.

◆

Questions for discussion

1. Is anybody in your family a "closet" writer, forever shoving poems and stories and journals into the sock drawer? What motivates some people to write down what happens to them or to create a fictional world? Do you consider their writing to be a healthy activity? Why or why not?

2. What good reasons have you heard for improving your writing, whether from teachers, parents, or friends? Were the reasons practical or impractical? Why?

3. Business people have, in recent years, lamented the alleged decline in writing skills among college students. Do you agree with this gloomy assessment? Why or why not? If you had the difficult task of improving students' writing skills, how would you go about it? What techniques and strategies would you suggest? Be specific.

4. Recall several of your writing experiences. Were they useful? Exhilarating? Tedious? Confidence building? Did you feel better or worse for having written? Why? Did you ever write simply because you wanted to? What compelled you to turn out a poem, keep a diary, create a story?

5. Would you recommend writing as a way to get something off your chest? A therapeutic activity? A way to advance in a career? A means of settling disputes? A method of instruction? Why or why not? Have you used writing in any of these ways? Would you say that writing is as important as

seeing sunrises? Eating balanced meals? Selling real estate? Making a killing on the stock market? Why or why not?

6. What kinds of reading do you enjoy? Are you more likely to read newspapers, high-tech magazines, scientific articles, how-to books, romances, mysteries, comic books, histories, or biographies? Why? Do your reading choices vary with your moods? If so, what genres do you prefer reading when you are happy, depressed, angry, or fearful?

7. If you have no interest in reading or writing, can you remember who or what influenced you to think negatively about those activities?

Activities

1. Write a few paragraphs explaining your political convictions. Were they shaped by your own experiences, by your mentors, or by various political figures, including members of national or local government? Have television or newspaper journalists had a significant impact on your thinking? How? Why?

2. Begin a journal in which you record personal impressions, moods, values, philosophies. Keep a daily or weekly record of your self throughout the semester or year. Place your feelings and personality in context, being careful to use specific details, description, and examples of the circumstances that make you act and think the way you do. Later, you may find the journal useful as a source for possible topics for essays.

3. If you had a library consisting of only one book, what would that book be? What is the most important book you have ever read? Write a short essay explaining why the book had such a profound influence on you.

Develop a professional attitude toward writing.

What images come to mind when you hear the word "professional"? Pinstripe-suited women and men toting briefcases? A sports figure paid to endorse a brand of cereal? Six-figure salaries and gold credit cards? These are outward signs of a person who is a professional, but *being* a professional is different from *looking* like a professional. Professionalism is not an image at all; rather, it is a state of mind, a way of working, a way of thinking about work.

Most students would agree that a professional attitude is useful in their chosen careers. If they are heading toward engineering, business, law, or medicine, they have no trouble seeing themselves in a professional role, with all the habits, disciplines, and strategies their career choices require. But, very likely, only a small percentage of your classmates will major in English, and an even smaller percentage will end up as professional writers. Most will consider themselves writing "amateurs," even after they have successfully completed one or more writing courses. What is an amateur? Someone who writes only for fun and not for profit? Someone who is not expected to achieve high standards of competency and quality? Someone who takes few risks, accepts few challenges, retains the "right" to be average, is only half-heartedly committed, and just barely gets by?

If you think of yourself as an "amateur" simply because you are not planning to be another Saul Bellow or Alice Walker, you may be risking more than you realize. To repeat: good writing ability is often the cornerstone of many professional pursuits. What use is a great discovery if you cannot report it? Or a legal position if you cannot defend it? Or a policy if you cannot implement it? Or a product if you cannot advertise it? What is a salary raise if you do not know how to ask for it?

What is a professional attitude toward writing?

Call yourself a writer.

Don't laugh. You have to begin somewhere, and what you call yourself is a good place to start. Names matter. Ask a secretary whose title has been changed to "administrative assistant." Ask an actor who dares to think of herself as a star. The psychological effect is invigorating, even though you may feel a bit silly the first time you think of yourself as a writer. But consider the facts: you are taking a course in writing; you are writing regularly; you are meeting deadlines; you are submitting your work to an editor or teacher; you are learning to accept criticism and rejection. Therefore, you are a writer.

Take professional responsibility for your work.

The moment you finish writing and sign your name to the essay, memo, business report, or letter, you are accepting responsibility for the truth, accuracy, and quality of your written communication. There is no place to hide when you write. Putting your name on your work is a bit scary, but it also pushes you to a higher level of performance. And readers will hold you to what you have written, both on small points and large ones. Professionals wait to put their bylines on newspaper articles or their signatures on documents and letters until they have read and reread their work. They ask the critical questions: Do I agree with what I wrote? Did I express my ideas in a convincing way? Have I used reputable sources? Have I unwittingly offended anyone? Will I be ashamed or embarrassed tomorrow or next week or next year by what I wrote in haste or anger? Will the writing hold up over time? Is the information clear, precise? Is the writing surface marred by pesky errors, silly typos, uneven margins, smudgeprints, or inkblots? If my written communication represents my company or legal firm, will my colleagues be proud to claim me as their spokesperson?

Remember that your name is still—even in these more casual, sometimes unethical, times—your word. And your words are, in turn, a reflection of your responsible, professional attitude.

Learn from others.

You are becoming a professional when you admit that you do not know everything about writing, when you willingly accept a period of apprenticeship with experienced writers and teachers, when you seek out other writers of all kinds for guidance, when you can accept possible rejection or even harsh criticism with as much grace as possible, when you feel a genuine kinship with peers who are also learning to write well, and when you are not ashamed to admit that you have problems with spelling or coherence or creativity.

In fact, your apprenticeship in writing may extend for a lifetime. Writing, unlike riding a bicycle or solving a math problem, is not something you learn thoroughly and all at once and never have to learn again. Experienced writers daily learn more and more about perfecting their prose. The prose is never perfect. And so, though they proceed with confidence, they rarely become arrogant. They remain teachable, willing to be taught, going continually back and forth between the roles of teacher/ expert and student/novice.

Maintain your integrity, convictions, values, and voice.

A good critic or editor or teacher wants you to write well in the context of who you are, where you come from, what you believe in, and how you act. Your writing voice is your own. The ideal teacher will help you improve the quality, strength, beauty, harmony, and technical level of whatever you write. Experienced writers welcome assistance and criticism but do not hesitate to stand up for their work and defend it against unnecessary manipulation.

Always strive to improve your writing.

If you like right answers, immediate results, instant recognition, you will remain a writing amateur. Experienced writers have written entire novels not once but 10 times. They rely on careful research, not guesswork and memory. They know that, like athletic prowess or stock market savvy, writing improves only by doing, not by theorizing. Finally, they keep on writing, even when they feel an overwhelming desire to clean out the kitchen junk drawer or visit their in-laws. Just when they think the essay is finished, they see, with a sigh, that it is not.

Give your writing the tinkering and time it deserves. Pause in the doorway to the classroom for one last look before you relinquish your paper to the teacher. Do not lightly assume that "alot" is one word, that what you found boring will entertain others, that your razzle-dazzle language and style will disguise dull content. Until the clock runs out and the writing must go public, look again—and again.

◆

Activity

Write an essay describing your professional goals. Explain in detail the steps you hope to take to achieve these goals. Discuss the relationship that improved writing skills will have to your particular career advancement.

Create your work environment.

No one can tell anyone else how best to work, to create, to conceive an idea and successfully deliver it to the written page. Writing, at least in its early stages, is a very personal activity. As you go through various drafts, your essay will go public, so to speak, inviting more and more outside critical comment from teacher, classmates, friends. But at the beginning, as one professional writing friend commented, "It's just me and that frightening blank page."

Professional writers share certain habits and philosophies that apply equally well to students. Flannery O'Connor advised a struggling writer to go to the typewriter and sit there for three hours—not reading, not listening to music, not answering letters, just waiting. Anthony Trollope demanded of himself a certain number of words per hour every morning, and then went off to his "real" job as a post office employee. Even the businessperson, faced with a stack of unanswered mail, will likely find that writing tasks are best handled first thing in the morning, when the head is clear and the busy demands of the working day do not intrude.

The daily workout is essential for physical fitness and weight control. The daily practice is necessary for the violinist or the voice student. And time and again, if you read about how writers get their work done, you will see that they follow certain *regular* routines and habits. If you adhere to these principles and practices, you also may find them practical, useful, productive.

Work alone.

Economist John Kenneth Galbraith said that art is not something that can be decided by committee. Nor can the act of creation. You do not need to go off for days, weeks, or months to produce a lively, astute, 2-page essay or even a 20-page research paper. But you do need time alone to read, to collect your thoughts, to begin to organize them and set them down. You may require total silence. You may prefer a little music in the background. You may not mind the small murmur of voices and activities in your residence hall or campus library. You may or may not be able to tolerate the quiet presence of a roommate when you are writing. But you will need to work alone, perhaps to *be* alone, certainly to experiment with different levels of noise. And where do you go to be alone? A park bench may be better than a study hall or a library. Experiment. Try writing at home, in your residence hall room, in the car, in an empty church, in the reference room, in an empty classroom. One student did his writing in the poultry building on campus. The place smelled so bad that he knew he could be alone there. Choose a place that is comfortable, quiet, and convenient. But since you will likely need certain equipment and source materials, an "office" of sorts may be best. You do not want to be writing in the middle of a cow pasture and suddenly realize that you need a pencil sharpener or the *Encyclopedia of Banking and Finance* to finish your paper.

Work regularly.

Professional athletes and professional writers know that physical and creative muscles go soft when they are not used. Writing can be very intimidating, but it is never more so than when you have not written in many days, when you have procrastinated, postponed getting started until the task seems overwhelming. Tackle writing chores immediately (as soon as assigned), work at them *hard* for an hour or so, then put them aside until the next day. Always, before you quit, decide when you will start writing again. If you cannot make yourself write the entire paper, begin, at least, to compose the introduction. Try Hemingway's method of overcoming reluctance and fear: always stop writing at the place where you are certain to be able to pick up again in an hour or a day, even if that point is in midsentence. If the only writing you ever do is that assigned in freshman composition—and often no more than once every week or so—you will be frightened when you approach the typewriter, the yellow legal pad, the word processor, especially if you waited until the last minute. Just as you converse regularly, socialize regularly, and study regularly to achieve maximum performance and pleasure, you will need to write regularly, sometimes just for fun, in order to take the fear and mystery out of writing.

In between assignments, do some writing on your own. A little free writing, a nightly entry in a journal, a dashed-off poem or insight, even a love letter—all these writing activities will keep you loose, easy, a little more relaxed about writing. If all of your writing is based solely on necessity—because it was assigned, it is "due," and you will get a grade on it—then writing will seem to be a duty or a burden, not a pleasure. Let writing be a friend to your private thoughts, not just a grim and unwelcome usurper of your sack time.

Have a regular place to write.

When you select a regular place to write, you do yourself several favors. The setting gives off signals that it is time to get down to work, just as a bar signals revelry or a bedroom, rest. Then, too, when you leave the writing work place, wherever it is, you are clearly taking a break, letting yourself unwind. Finally, if you have a regular place to write, you will more than likely stock it with the materials and comforts you need.

You have often heard that it is unwise to mix business with pleasure, and there is some truth to the tired maxim. Newlywed couples would not want to contaminate the bridal suite with business memos and crisp calls back to the home office. And because you are trying to approach writing in a professional manner, you do not want to handicap your work by starting out in a place that is not conducive to thinking and writing. You are wise not to choose a spot that speaks too loudly of past pleasures, sleep, family tensions, unsettling experiences. Sitting cross-legged on the bed to write may give you other, better ideas. Beginning your writing assignment in the empty lab where you regularly study biology, which, perhaps, you dislike, will surely block your writing progress.

If you look for a regular writing place, you will find it. And going to that place and no other will transmit signals of getting down to your writing business. Do not assume that writing is never a pleasure. Sometimes it is. But writing is also hard work, and familiar, no-nonsense writing surroundings will leave you free to focus on the actual task at hand. It is important that you choose a place where you *enjoy* going and that you wear comfortable clothes that make you feel good. Do not let your "place" be something as casual and awkward as the surface of your lap. Writing proceeds more smoothly when you have a table or a desk on which to work, a chair that is the proper height, good lighting, perhaps a pleasing poster or a flower in view. Having found your "place," be patient until you can get to it before you begin working. Energy builds while you wait. The moment of sitting down to begin gains importance. It is official. You are writing.

Have adequate equipment and resources.

You get a good idea. You jot down some notes, a rough plan. You set down your thesis. You get midway through the writing assignment, and one of several disasters occurs: your pen runs out of ink; your typewriter keys get stuck; you cannot find the dictionary; your white-out is gummy; you run out of paper (except for some wrinkled sheets that the cat walked on with muddy paws). Whatever writing success and ease you were enjoying instantly stops, and you begin the frantic search for the writing paraphernalia and resources you need. By the time you return to your desk, you have forgotten what you planned to say. And you may have lost your writing momentum as well. Often, these pesky delays put a quick and unexpected end to what might have been a finished work. Procrastination and negative reinforcement set in. You simply cannot force yourself to return to the work. It is important, therefore, to stock up *before* you begin writing. Let all your breaks from writing be intentional, not accidental.

A well-equipped writing place can save you time and effort and can conserve and harness your energy and enthusiasm for the writing itself. Have your equipment, even if your equipment is only a ballpoint pen or an old manual typewriter, in good working condition. Your work space or desk or portable writing briefcase should be supplied with white-out, correction tape, spare typewriter ribbons, sharpened pencils, paperclips, rubber bands, clean folders, envelopes, plenty of pens, notebook paper, index cards, manuals, and an extra ribbon cassette for your printer if you use a word processor.

Your reference library must also be within arm's reach or telephone's reach. You may want your dictionary to be open beside you when you write. Depending on your needs, you may also find handy grammar handbooks; literary anthologies; atlases; almanacs; encyclopedias; a thesaurus; collections of quotations; shelves of novels, poems, essays, plays, art works; recent issues

of magazines; biographies; journals; works of history or science
or mythology. Here is a basic writer's library, certainly not complete unto itself, but one that you should consider *owning:*

1. Dictionary
2. Thesaurus
3. Desk encyclopedia
4. Almanac
5. Grammar handbook
6. Style book

You never know what reference work you will need next, and
you learn to be prepared.

If you worry that you will not be able to afford an extensive
library, you may be pleasantly surprised; you may already have
one. The textbooks you purchase for various courses will serve
as excellent sources. You can also build a serviceable, extensive
library of paperbacks, not fancy, leatherbound editions. You can
pick up old reference books at flea markets or garage sales,
sometimes for only a quarter or two for best-selling novels or
anthologies. You can dust off unread books on your parents'
shelves and borrow them for your own library, where they will
have good and regular use.

Then, too, you can depend on your local public or campus library to give you information, statistics, and facts you need in a
hurry. One writer I know regularly calls the university library
reference department to ask everything from how to spell "ligustrum" to what a family of four earned on the average in the
United States in 1987. Reference librarians do not know everything, of course, and some are too busy to take calls, but they all
know how to look things up and are usually delighted to supply
you with free answers to tough questions.

Know your audience.

Writing does not exist in isolation. As you have seen, writing
grows out of experience, connects to the past and future, deals
with the present. Whether you write for personal, professional,
practical, or creative reasons, your written words will usually be
read by teachers, friends, relatives, employers, colleagues, and,

perhaps, your grandchildren and great-grandchildren. These readers are your audience, and they will bring to their reading of your work experiences, interpretations, biases, knowledge, and insights different from your own. You do not have the last word. They do. And your awareness of their presence, whether ominous or friendly, may block your writing progress.

You may think that if you give due consideration to the audience you will be selling out or compromising your principles. Remember that in everyday conversation, you regularly tailor your remarks to fit the occasion, sometimes just a little, sometimes a lot. You adopt a breezy, slangy style with friends, an intimate style with a loved one, an informal style with acquaintances. You are more formal when you converse with employers or your grandparents. You use simple, clear language when you talk to children, sophisticated language when you address experts in your field. And writing is like conversation in that respect. Though you do not want to deny your experience, compromise your integrity, or play a role, you will nonetheless need to keep in mind what sort of people for whom you are writing and why.

Various audiences come to mind and the myriad contexts in which you find them: kindergarten students, college administrators, senior citizens, feminists, Republicans, family members, strangers, newspaper readers, *Popular Mechanics* readers, *National Enquirer* readers, Bible readers, fraternity or sorority members, professors, ministers, Indians, Asians, Africans, Jews, Protestants, Eskimos, politicians, businesspeople, lawmakers, doctors, actors, dancers, musicians, mountaineers, beach bums, farmers. Imagine writing one essay that would appeal to every one of them. You probably cannot. But you can write in a tone, language, and style adjusted to the values and tastes of many of them.

And "audience" is not simply a matter of people. Those people exist in a context: the temper of the times, the customs of the region, the stateliness or informality of the writing occasion. What writers could get away with in the late 1960s may not be socially or morally acceptable in the 1980s. What you write for your diary may not be appropriate for your résumé. What you explain in a research paper may not belong in an essay or poem.

The way to define the audience is through questions. The questions may seem simple, even obvious, but they will keep you attuned to your reader, who, after all, will supply you with a concrete, immediate measure of your writing success or failure.

1. Who is the audience? Adults? Children? Both? Mostly women? Mostly men? Minority or majority? Conservative or liberal? Raucous or sedate? Lay people or experts? Educated or uneducated? Homogeneous or diverse? Familiar or strange? Savvy or stodgy? Deadly dull or witty? Rural or urban?

2. What is the writing occasion? A feasibility study? A letter home? An in-class essay? A research project? A news story? A journal entry? A letter of application? A reminiscence? A critical review? An obituary? A sports column? An introduction for a speaker? A parody?

3. When is the writing deadline? Tomorrow? Last week? In two months? In a year? In 50 minutes?

4. Where will your writing go public? In the classroom? In the professor's office? In the family den? In the pulpit? In the school auditorium? In a seminar or conference room? In the back room of a bar?

5. Why is the audience reading your essay? Because they get paid to read it? Because they love you and do not want to hurt your feelings? Because they think you have something to say? Because they want to be entertained? Because they seek confirmation of their own opinions? Because they want to change their minds? Because they are a captive audience? Because they are a captivated audience?

The questions go on and on. Will the audience catch your references, allusions? If you mention, say, Walker Percy, can you assume that the members of the audience have read some of his novels? Will they understand Lazarus, lasers, leitmotifs, lithium, lust? Do they know that *Hamlet* is not something you make with eggs? Do you, in short, speak the audience's language? If not, can you think of special ways to make them catch your meaning without offending, alienating, or boring them?

Certainly, in a typical freshman composition course, your audience is your teacher. And this writing setting may seem somewhat artificial. The audience is one, not dozens or hundreds or thousands of readers, as in a newspaper or magazine. Nevertheless, whether the audience is one or many, show the utmost care and respect for the reader. Even though the instructor may not be an expert on, say, ornithology or skeet shooting, he or she must be helped to understand the language and point of your essay. And, often, even though the teacher serves as the final arbiter of the quality of your writing in a composition course, you may present the essay to your classmates for critical comment and suggestions.

In the end, it is always your responsibility, as writer, to make yourself intelligible to the reader, not the other way around. You cannot slough off this responsibility, blaming your failure to communicate on the apathy, ignorance, or hostility of the audience. If the audience does not *get* it, you probably did not *give* it to them.

◆

Activities

1. Write a short essay describing the "typical" audience, in your view, of a popular magazine. What are the readers of *Cosmopolitan* like? What sort of person reads *Time? People? Esquire? Playboy? Atlantic Monthly? TV Guide?* the *Socialist Worker? Rolling Stone? Seventeen? National Geographic? Mad Magazine? Sports Illustrated? Oui? Soldiers of Fortune? Low Rider? Reader's Digest? Bon Appetit? Architectural Digest? Mother Earth News? Vogue?* If you were the editor of any one of these magazines, what composite picture of a subscriber would you carry in your mind's eye?

2. Write a paragraph or two to your best friend, explaining your feelings about a touchy subject: a scrape you have gotten yourself into, a moral dilemma, a bad habit, a poor academic performance, or a social blunder. Now write again about the same problem, but this time address your words to an "authority" figure, someone around whom you must be on your best behavior.

3. Write a short speech to students about a controversial campus policy, whether academic or social. Now, write a speech on the same campus policy, but this time address your remarks to the president, dean, or chancellor of your university or college.

4. Select a fairly complex literary, scientific, historical, or philosophical concept you are currently studying in one of your academic courses. Then write your explanation of it to a first grader.

2
Getting Started

Begin with the essay.

You have probably studied various literary *genres:* letters, poems, stories, plays, novels, autobiographies, biographies, journals. The essay—often called the "familiar" essay—is also a distinct genre. The essay is usually short, often 500 to 1,000 words, and it deals with one subject. The essay form is enormously flexible, offering you the freedom to be expressive, argumentative, digressive, factual, witty, and serious in turn or even all at once. It is, for all these reasons, the staple of freshman composition. The essay is a good place to begin to define yourself, order your thoughts, make sense of the world and your place in it.

The essay will seem like an old friend if you happen to have grown up in a family with strong opinions and critical attitudes. Do you come from a family of talkers, people who speak their minds on a variety of issues? Growing up in an argumentative, opinionated family helps the essayist. The essay form does not take well to timidity or shyness, though once an allegedly shy person gets hold of a pencil and paper, he or she can sometimes astonish the world with a rush of feeling and conviction. Many famous writers were apparently shy and quiet in school. What they were doing was watching—and paying attention to what they saw. Eudora Welty describes herself in *One Writer's Beginnings* as having been a quiet observer when she was a young girl. She was storing up impressions that would later find their way into her stories, novels, essays, speeches.

Trust the essay. Even though you think you may prefer writing computer programs or lab reports to essays or stories, you will be surprised to discover that the essay will let anybody in, even a person who hates to write. The essay will allow you to draw from many different sources—science or history, modern or ancient, public or private, strange or familiar—and to approach your material in many different ways—with clinical detachment or passionate intensity, with thoughtful introspection or chatty informality. It is a place for information, persuasion, entertainment, controversy, agreement, wisdom. The essay teaches you to think, and in the words of Daniel Defoe's famous heroine Moll Flanders, "to think, indeed, is one real advance from hell to heaven."

◆

Activities

1. The essay sometimes reveals as much about an author as it does about the subject under consideration. Write a lifestyle profile of a particular syndicated columnist (such as Ann Landers, Art Buchwald, George Will, William F. Buckley, Ellen Goodman, Erma Bombeck, or William Raspberry), basing your views on the positions the columnist regularly takes on public and private issues. The columnist may give advice; analyze political events; inform about health, good manners, sex, gardening. But what do you think he or she is *really like*, at home, with shoes kicked off and feet propped up on the coffee table?

2. Find a cartoon you think is especially funny, and write a paragraph explaining why you think it is amusing. What causes some people to guffaw and other people to grimace at the same thing?

3. Write a short essay detailing your reading history and present-day reading habits. Include specific titles of publications, indicate whether the reading was required, describe at what age and in what situation you did the reading, and summarize the impact of favorite books and magazines.

Claim your point of view.

Much of what you believe to be real or true depends on your particular angle of seeing. Where are you standing in relation to events? Are you in the middle of the street fight or well across the street, hiding behind the lamppost? Your position in each scene affects your perceptions, as well as your degree of fear or understanding. And crisscrossing your angle of vision are the differing perceptions of a few, hundreds, or millions of other people.

Point of view—the writer's angle of vision—is, therefore, a fundamental consideration. When you write, you need to accept responsibility for your own authoritative *voice*, for choosing the angle from which you can relate what happens and why. This "voice" may speak from first-, second-, or thirdhand experience. It may be center stage or hiding in the wings, so to speak. Depending on whom you talk to, it may be "right" or "wrong." But the first important lesson a writer must learn is to ground each piece of writing in a point of view, using the memories, feelings, impressions, and intuitions only he or she can draw from.

The *personal essay* invites you to begin with *yourself* and what you know firsthand. The first-person point of view, the unabashed "I," is the central voice in a personal essay. You may have been advised in other, more formal, writing situations to avoid using the first person. The advice is usually sound. Nobody at a medical conference wants to hear how much you have suffered from lumbago. A gathering of doctors is more interested in diagnosis, treatment, and research on the problem than in your own case history. But the personal essay offers opportunities for discovery and reflection that cannot be had in an academic conference or in a business letter. In the personal essay, the first-person report is legitimate, even welcome.

You may distrust the "I" for several reasons. Perhaps you have been taught to disregard your own thoughts and feelings in favor of the "experts." Certainly, you want to be able to identify with and empathize with other views and other events. But you cannot stand on an equal footing with others until you can first claim your own experiences as legitimate, at least as a starting place.

Claiming the first-person point of view as a worthy angle of vision is the first step in learning to write lively, authentic, original essays. Starting with "I" as a subject will lead you to a thesis that no one else can possibly write. Instead of a general platitude, the bland opinions of other people, you will be expressing the concrete, supportable position of one. Philosopher Søren Kierkegaard believed that the minority, not the majority, is right—even though the majority may be more powerful. Why? Because by the time everybody thinks it, feels it, or does it— whatever "it" is—*it* has become wrong.

And so the predictability and bland sameness of mediocre essays is most often the result of beginning with the *general*, not the particular, point of view. The insecure writer, uncertain of herself and uncomfortable with what she knows, falls back on what she reads in the newspapers, hears from her parents, studies in books. Her prose thus becomes a watered-down version of what she has heard and read.

The first person, however, demands much more of you than recycled or secondhand opinions. There is a big difference between stating what "they" think and what "I" think. The former is vague, dispersed, imprecise, lacking in risk or responsibility. *How do you know* what "they" think or believe? Who is "they," anyway? "They" say it's going to rain. "They" say that Harvard is "good," that apartheid and Three Mile Island are "bad." "They" say the world is going to be blown up in four years. "They" say young people do not have any idealism anymore. These assertions are vacuous unless you have felt them on an inner level. What do *you* have to say?

Of course, a mature writer learns gradually to take in—if not consciously, then at least subconsciously—the lives, times, tragedies, and perspectives of others. As you write more and more and for different occasions and reasons, you will shift from the "I/we" stance to the "he/she/they" position. Good. Maturity in writing and life increases when you can consider the feelings of the group, as well as your own. But even then, you will find yourself returning again and again to the well-focused "I" for freshness, authority, and authenticity in writing. All the almanac statistics in the world cannot compare to a single credible testimony, eloquently expressed. Talk to the parents of an AIDS victim or to the parents of a young man whose name is carved on the monument to veterans of the war in Vietnam. You will hear a story that makes absurd the generalities and statistics that you may have read in an encyclopedia somewhere.

◆

Questions for discussion

1. Do you gravitate, in your reading, more often to the writer who is "objective" or "subjective"? Why or why not? Do you think of "objectivity" as cold, factual, truthful? Do you think

of "subjectivity" as messy, inaccurate, or emotional? Are you more likely to tune in to a presidential press conference or to the reporter's roundtable discussion following the press conference? Are you more likely to read an autobiography or a biography, a collection of letters or a history book? Why?

2. Is the television camera "objective"? Why or why not? How does the camera angle affect our perception of news events?

3. What literary work has influenced or pleased you most? Was it written in the first or third person, or did the author use the omniscient point of view? (See the glossary in Chapter 11). Would the impact of that literary work be more or less profound if the author shifted points of view? What, for example, might be the effect on Daniel Defoe's *Robinson Crusoe* if Defoe had taken a step back from Crusoe, telling Crusoe's story in the third person rather than permitting the character to recount his own experience?

Activities

1. Find a short, factual news report about a person and rewrite the story, including all the same information, in the first person. How does the mood change? Is the impact greater or less when you use the first person?

2. Describe, in a couple of paragraphs, a recent family argument, presenting first one angle of vision, then another. You may change your position of seeing, or you may try looking through the eyes of another family member, letting his or her perception be your own. How do the scenes differ, depending on whether you are in the next room or, in a sense, momentarily "becoming" another person? Which scene conveys what "really" happened?

3. Explain, in a few sentences, your experiences with teachers who have discouraged you from using the first-person point of view. What was their reasoning? Did you agree or disagree? Why?

Pick a subject close to home.

One of the most frequently asked questions is "What shall I write about?" It is not just composition students who want to know. *What to write about* is a problem for Nobel prize-winning novelists as much as it is for engineers who write reports and proposals, business people who write advertising and letters and memos, ministers who send condolences, and anyone who has ever been required to write an essay when applying for a job or for admission into a program or school.

In answer to the question, instructors usually say to their students: "Write about what you know." The instructor may assign a developmental scheme (comparison, contrast, argument), a list of categories (pets, war, politics), or a specific mood and tone (reminiscence, prophecy, story with a "message"). But they frequently ask you to come up with your own basic subject. What do you do with so much freedom?

First, remember that writing is very much tied to *feeling* as well as *thought*. If you do not care about your subject, then you will not know it intimately, and any writing you do on that subject will seem dull, superficial, contrived. But if you see writing as a further exploration and elaboration of what is happening in *your* world, then you will be pleased and amazed by what you discover. Just as you may find your lost car keys in your backpack—right where you left them, but after much searching, the very last place you thought to look—so too will you find your best writing subjects in a most unusual place: *right in front of you.*

You may think, in between writing assignments, that there is no need to prepare, no need to think about writing. However, *the writer's business is to pay attention to writing by paying attention to life.* As a writer, instead of spending nights worrying about your topic, try to live as fully as you can. Go to different kinds of restaurants and order things you have never tried before. Try hang gliding and tap dancing. Tune in to boxing and go-cart racing on television instead of the "soaps." Buy one or more shares of IBM stock and watch its price go up or down. Read everything in sight, especially things you do not have to read but want to. Spend more time in bookstores off campus. When you go to a big party, make sure you talk, *really talk*, to at least one person. When you need to sit in airports or on buses, study the different ways people say hello and good-bye. Study the faces and shuffle of street people. What do you see, hear, feel? Let everything that happens to you be grist for your writing.

You may not yet be convinced that topics are all around you and that all of them, freshly and ingeniously written, are fit for the essay. Look at the following list, and notice the scope and variety of essays created by some famous writers:

Richard Steele—a walk through London

Joseph Addison—tulips

Jonathan Swift—the art of lying

Sir Francis Bacon—revenge

G. K. Chesterton—nonsense and its charms

Robert Benchley—his face in the mirror

Virginia Woolf—how to read a book

Flannery O'Connor—suitable reading for eighth graders

Nora Ephron—on getting her first bra

E. B. White—on a hurricane that never arrived

Elizabeth Hardwick—books about poverty

Since the listed writers span the history of the English essay over the last 400 years, you can see that no subject has ever been considered too small for a great essay. The essence of a good subject is that it is one you know thoroughly and feel some inner attachment to. You can increase your sphere of knowledge and your sensitivity by *listening carefully* and *writing things down* when they occur to you. Day by day, you will gain confidence and authority as the *whole world* becomes your "home."

Make an assigned topic your own.

Assigned topics may often seem arbitrary, intimidating, and foreign to you and your experience. But even when the topic comes from the outside, you can make it your own by deciding how you will handle it, by putting the stamp of your own personality on it. Few teachers would, without a very good reason, force you to take a certain position with regard to a topic, though teachers may steer you away from unsupportable or unnecessarily dogmatic approaches to the subject. But within the bounds of logic, legality, and factuality, you are free to move around in a body of information or a sea of controversy. What are your freedoms with regard to an assigned subject? For illustration, let's say the assigned topic is "Backpacking."

1. Adjust the topic according to the assignment.

   Purpose: write a passing essay for composition

   Length: 500 words

   Time: overnight

2. Decide which aspect of the topic is most interesting to you.

   Slant: backpacking in serene, natural settings for recreational purposes

3. Determine how you will treat the topic. You can write about the topic in a *subjective* voice—out of your own experience and using the first person—or in an *objective* voice—reporting what you have observed or discovered by researching the topic.

   Subjective: your first backpacking trip along the Appalachian Trail

   Objective: environmental hazards, equipment, procedures and tips

4. Create a tone that is natural to you. Your tone can be perhaps formal, perhaps informal, maybe hilarious, maybe merely funny, maybe very serious, maybe introspective and philosophical.

   a. Ridicule backpacking bumblers in Keds and nylon socks.

   b. Lament the loss of privacy and peace in nature due to the popularity of this pastime.

   c. Dispassionately inform novices about how to outfit themselves for the journey.

   d. Take an ironic tone toward the sissies riding up and down the Blue Ridge Parkway in Lincoln Continentals with the windows rolled up and the cameras clicking at nature.

   e. Exhort the government to greater protection of the environment and of citizens in public recreational parks, using your tangle with a bear or despair over the effects of acid rain or smog as examples.

   f. Eloquently and entertainingly record the sights, sounds, and characters you meet along the trail.

As you find a way to make the assigned topic your own, you will be developing an overall scheme for completing the essay. Thinking precedes writing. Finding your particular angle on the topic will lead you to an outline. You will then proceed more easily through the various stages of writing: first draft, editing, second draft, proofreading. But until you decide how you want to approach the assigned topic and where you want to go with it, nothing much will happen. The topic will be nothing more than a vague impulse, as when you sit around talking about backpacking on the Appalachian Trail and never quite get around to doing it.

◆

Activities

1. Make a list of three things you know how to do well and of three things you would like to learn how to do.

2. Write an advertisement for the personals section of a newspaper, describing yourself for a prospective date.

3. Starting from this exact moment, go backward in time, recording details, conversations, and incidents of the last hour.

4. If you could be anywhere else right this minute, where would it be and why? Write down what the place looks like, who would be with you, what you would be doing. Careful!

5. Write a brief summary of a current major news event that particularly interests, infuriates, or pleases you. Include the people or countries involved, the reason for the newsworthiness, and an explanation of why the event is important to you.

6. Write a short letter to the editor about a controversial local subject, indicating your position on the issue. Be assured that the letter will be published and that millions of people will read it.

7. What is your favorite joke? Write it out in its entirety, being careful to write it exactly as you would tell it.

8. Write a few paragraphs on the effect that being the oldest, youngest, or middle child has had on your personality. What if you are an only child? An only daughter? Only son? A twin? How has the number of siblings and their genders affected your treatment in the family?

PART
II
Creating the Essay

CHAPTER
3
Writing with a Thesis

Define the thesis.

A good writer needs a clear thesis for the same reason that a traveler needs a map and a committee chairperson, an agenda. The thesis is not merely your purpose for writing. In the first place, you are probably picking up the pen or sitting down to the typewriter because an essay or a research paper has been *assigned*. But though you may have a topic, either of your own choice or assigned, you do not have a thesis until you have formed an opinion or taken a position on that topic. A thesis is the vehicle you need to carry you through the topic.

Like any complete sentence, a thesis requires both a subject (or topic) and a predicate (a point or position about that topic). A thesis expresses a complete idea about and attitude toward that subject.

Writers sometimes confuse statements of *fact* with thesis statements, especially when the fact is not a number or a date or a small piece of information. For example, if you state that your resting pulse rate is 50, you are stating a fact, not a thesis. If you state, instead, that jogging dramatically reduces a person's pulse rate and supplies that person with greater energy, endurance, aerobic capacity, and peace of mind, then you are expressing a position or thesis. This statement makes a claim, one that requires support and that might be disputed by a sedentary reader who claims he's in great shape. An essay without a thesis is like a painting without a focal point or a politician without a platform. A thesis offers a slant, an energy, a personal commitment normally not available in charts, statistics, almanacs, and lab reports.

Here are some examples of subjects being transformed into possible thesis statements:

Subject: The study of Latin

Point or Position: Provides an excellent grammar review for using the English language

Point or Position: Is a waste of time, and its study is actually detrimental to English education in this century

Subject: The Society for the Prevention of Cruelty to Animals

Point or Position: Views pet population control through spaying or neutering as a serious responsibility for pet owners

Point or Position: Has been unnecessarily intrusive in interrupting animal research in laboratories

Subject: Abstinence

Point or Position: Makes the heart grow fonder

Point or Position: Makes Jack a desperate boy

Subject: Some television evangelists

Point or Position: Seem more interested in taking in dollars and achieving fame than in saving souls

Point or Position: Are giving much hope and solace to lonely, depressed shut-ins

Subject: Chemistry

Point or Position: Is as much at home in the kitchen as in the science lab

Point or Position: Has brought about chemical warfare, air pollution, and drug abuse

Subject: Political platforms

Point or Position: Have a way of crumbling under the weight of public opinion and the practical realities of high office

Point or Position: Have the effect of building consensus in a fragmented society

Subject: Some college athletes after graduation

Point or Position: May resent or regret their lack of solid academic credentials and skills

Point or Position: Are grateful for the upward mobility created through social contacts and financial support in college

Subject: Home

Point or Position: Is where the hate is

Point or Position: Is only a state of mind, not a place

The position may be intellectual or intuitive, based on a gut feeling or derived from careful observation and research. The thesis may be based on what you think or what somebody else thinks. It may come from personal experience, hearsay, or reliable sources. But whatever its origins, it will carry you through the essay and bring you safely to your destination, the concluding paragraph.

◆

Activities

Just for fun and practice, add a predicate to the following subjects, being sure to make the predicate express a point or position about the subject. Even if, at first glance, the subject seems completely alien to you and your experience, find a way to express that alienation honestly.

Example:

Subject: Garbage collecting

Possible thesis (with predicate expressing point or position with regard to the subject):

Some days, garbage collecting seems to be a higher calling than motherhood.

Now you try it.

Boise	Heartburn
Airport layovers	Jukeboxes
Pigeons	Babies
Slow death	Seasickness

Overhead pro- jectors	Mass transit
Monopoly	Archaeological digs
Touch football	Moon Pies and R.C.
Lane Bryant	Wine coolers
S'mores	"Lite" anything
Penny candy	Very Important People
Submarines	Foggy mornings
Good manners	Golden oldies
Heaven	John McEnroe
Hell	

Place the thesis.

Much debate rages about the proper place to put your thesis. Some say somewhere in the introductory paragraph. Others say that it *must* be the last sentence of the introductory paragraph. In a longer research paper, the thesis might not appear until somewhere in the second or third paragraph. But the important point, both for you and for the reader, is that the thesis appear *soon*. The thesis, appearing early in the writing, will keep you on course and tip off your reader about the direction and intent of your essay. The thesis serves both as a guide through the argument and as a hint of what will follow. The tired, disgruntled reader should not have to wait, tapping her foot and impatiently rustling the paper, while you meander into the thesis somewhere in the middle of the essay.

Create a lively, supportable thesis.

Discussing a thesis in isolation from the essay in which it appears is like describing a face you have not seen. The context is missing. The outline and essay do not yet exist. All you have is a topic and a general premise—a hunch, really—that may or may not lead you through a maze of possible meanings and interpretations. You have settled on a topic. You have a vague idea of what you want to do with that topic. But essays seldom spring, full-blown and breathtaking, to the blank page. How do you transform that free-floating image or theory into a lively, supportable thesis? How do you use that thesis to guide you through the entire writing task? Well, writing is like planning a perfect evening: it proceeds nicely and is a great success only if you do the necessary background work, go through the essential steps that carry you from the first hello to the last fond farewell.

First, you mull.

"Mulling" may seem an odd writing task, but if you do not do your share of it, you may jump into the subject too soon and find yourself paddling around in pools of meaning too deep, too shallow, or just plain muddy. Mulling always follows the selection of the subject. You spend an hour, a day, or a week just turning the subject in your mind, noticing striking characteristics, thinking about how the subject relates to you, considering what aspect of the subject interests you, recalling books or magazines or newspaper articles you have recently read that deal with the subject. You may do a little reading on the subject, not to steal ideas or thesis statements, but rather, to place your thoughts in context. But be careful of doing too much research at this early stage. Many so-called writers never get a word down on paper. They are too busy doing background reading and eventually are paralyzed and weighted down by "expert" opinion. You want to discover what *you* think about, for instance, the decision to place a nuclear waste dump in your state or town.

Mulling is an informal pastime, not a research project. You can mull while you are shaving, driving, eating, or chatting. You sort of put your brain on automatic and let it snoop around freely for a while.

Then, you jot.

The backs of envelopes, the yellow legal pad, the index cards, the paper you ripped from the spiral notebook—all these surfaces cry out for random scribbles and notes. Your jottings may be single words, phrases, complete sentences, and even—if you "think" in images, not words—little drawings. Do not concern yourself with order, neatness, or propriety. These jottings are for you, and they have one thing in common: they all relate, somehow, to your chosen topic. At this stage, you have advanced from mere mulling to serious thinking. The jotting stage has variously been called brainstorming or free writing, but whatever you call it, jotting begins to reveal, on the written page, what you have consciously or unconsciously been feeling, seeing, doing, and believing in the context of your subject.

How do you give yourself permission to jot after years of indoctrination (well-intentioned but damaging to the creative process) about following rules, being organized, dotting *is*, crossing *ts*? Understand that writing is creative and spontaneous *before* it is logical, precise, and ready for public view. When you jot, nothing is "wrong" or "right"; every foolish idea or thought is acceptable, even welcome. If you censor yourself too soon in the writing process, you may tarnish the bright concept you never knew you knew.

You can learn to jot even if no paper is assigned or no essay is due. Practice free writing on a variety of random topics. Teach yourself to relax at this early but crucial stage of creation. Pick a big, broad topic and start mulling and jotting: money, in-laws, discipline, homework, politics, government corruption, fleas, "ladies"' mags, classics, Big Wheels, extroverts, wisdom, rage, Food and Drug Administration, vacations.

Let's try "discipline":

Spare rod/spoil child

Orderliness—what too much, what too little?

Changes over generations—children to be seen not heard—children are people, too

Only children? What about adult disciplinaries? employers, company policy, punching clock, locked-in roles around house?

What good? what bad? worst—tyranny, power, victim of unhealthy control—best—self-discipline—how get? inner-directed—act responsibly with or without switch from mulberry bush or slap on rump

Gradual movement from external to internal discipline— conscience—over-active? just "right"?

How did I learn self-control? who taught? what method? Grandmother? quiet example—balance, moderation between work and fun—passion and rage pushed into healthy activities with friends, family—spirit of doing, not fuming, fretting, giving up—learned what to do with "unacceptable," out-of-control feelings, energy— Isn't that the secret of self-discipline? find way to make heart and mouth and hands behave without taking the "Life" out of life?

Use the rod/kill the child—Grandmother knew.

If you practice the technique of jotting, you will surprise yourself with how quickly you can transform an abstract word into a concrete reality. Writing is not simply a matter of putting words on the page in a way that, on the surface, makes "sense." Writing is also thinking, remembering, arguing, resolving, dramatizing, discovering. Don't deny yourself the pleasure (or pain) of finding out how your mind works and why.

Next, you see connections.

The writer's task is also to create order from seemingly random and unrelated events, people, attitudes, insights. Why does a certain song invariably conjure a memory of Joy perfume or Beacon Street or foghorns over a rolling ocean? Why does charity begin, more often, in foreign mission fields or Third World countries when your first cousin goes begging? Why does a parent scream, at the top of her lungs, "Stop yelling"? Why is sitting in the classroom not "real life," whereas punching a clock at a textile factory and sitting at a desk at Century 21 are? The writer learns to appreciate apparent contradictions and inconsistencies in human behavior and thought, notices similarities in unlike circumstances, and has empathy for alien settings and people.

After you jot, you will notice recurring themes and connections that tip you off to your real interest in a subject. You began at one place and ended up in quite another. You thought you were interested in investments and banking, but your jottings repeatedly mentioned an uncle who kept his money in a Maxwell House coffee can under the kitchen sink or an aunt who sewed hundred dollar bills into her bra. You imagined you wanted to define "shyness" but ended up praising pride. The brainstorming stage led you to what you *really* believed.

So you look at your jottings. Maybe a possible thesis is already on the page: fresh, supportable, imaginative, lively. Maybe certain jottings need to be scratched out. You were writing platitudes, letting yourself. be the spokesperson for your mother's or James Kilpatrick's opinion, repeating what you heard on the six o'clock news. Certain jottings will seem obvious, simple, too broad, too narrow, disjointed, or boring. Eliminate them. What is left? Related themes, ideas, and examples? One or two fresh insights into an old subject?

Say your jottings concern money. You scribbled the following:

Believe in sound banking and investment practices

Believe that credit cards are the backbone of American economy

UnAmerican not to charge it

Money burns hole in pocket

Who says so? Why?

What does a person need to survive?

Chair, table, food, roof over head—simple things, really

Are we too sophisticated about handling money?

Relatives always had "enough." Didn't worry so much about interest rates, taxes, clever real-estate investments

Kept their money like their loved ones—close to home! No brokerage fees, no 18 percent interest on credit cards, no danger of national depression, no stressful speculation, no outside interference

Primitive economics "better"? Weird economic practices may make for greater financial security. To heck with inflation and stock market. Long for bygone day when people had just enough money and knew how to hold on to it. Funny—pay cash, don't spend money you haven't got, don't let slick investment counsellor get hold of it, don't pay service charges—old-fashioned "banks" may be best in an uncertain world—hole in ground, behind brick in fireplace, in the big cookie jar on kitchen counter, "buy" a pound of sugar with a chicken, barter a

service (barn raising, quilt making, field planting) for a
product (plow, mule, shotgun)—trust, convenience, no
debt or deficit

These jottings began with the conventional wisdom and led
the writer to a place he had not expected to go. Maybe our ancestors had a better banking idea. The conventional wisdom in
the initial notes gives way to an amusing reminiscence about
how our ancestors managed their money and why their practices might be "sounder," in some ways, than the fancy wheeling
and dealing going on at Merrill Lynch or Lloyd's of London.

Finally, you create a thesis.

By the time you have thought about the topic and made some
random notes, you may have arrived at a clear thesis. Perhaps
you have already written, by accident, the central idea you wish
to prove in your essay. Perhaps some tinkering and clarification
will yet be necessary. But how will you know that the thesis is a
statement you can live with, use as a guide through your argument? How can you be certain that a prospective audience will
respond enthusiastically to your initial assertion?

Thesis statements are as varied as the people who create
them, but a "good" thesis will have several or all of the following
characteristics.

The thesis has bite.   You have expressed an opinion or idea
that a reader could sink her teeth into, thoughtfully chew on for
a while. A very simple, superficial thesis statement is too soon
and too easily digested. Why proceed with writing the essay—or
reading it—if your assertion is as bland and obvious as the
moral to a conservative parent's lecture? The following thesis
statements show the crucial difference between stating what everybody knows and agrees with and stating what has never
crossed the reader's mind—or yours either, for that matter.

Children need a strict moral upbringing to become responsible ethical adults.

Nothing can drive a child to a life of filth and degradation faster than growing up in a houseful of righteous indignation.

The first example expresses yawningly conventional thinking. The second example questions and challenges the traditional opinion.

The thesis is ingenious, surprising. This point is related to the first, but it goes a step further: even conventional ideas can be expressed bitingly, and the reader may momentarily think he is learning something new. But if the thesis is also novel, fresh, the bite will be more flavorful, crunchier, more exotic.

How do you achieve freshness? One writer suggested that you make 10 statements with which you would agree about a subject, and then write on the eleventh. In other words, you force yourself to toss aside opinions or ideas you have heard or read and look for a new way to approach the subject. This extra effort illustrates the complexity and variety of life. Every event, idea, scene, person, animal, job, or philosophy has room for a fresh, novel approach. Your task is to find it.

On Achieving Freshness

Sometimes I have difficulty finding a fresh, surprising thesis in the growing pile of recycled or secondhand opinions. But here are some of the ways I strive for freshness. Sometimes I take the generally accepted, predictable argument and search for holes in it. Then, having found the holes in the conventional wisdom, I wiggle into one and find a new passage, a hidden corridor of meaning. I have argued, for example, that the trouble with self-improvement is the notion that one needs improving. I have noticed that once your tummy is flat, your shoulders are muscled, your teeth are capped, your disposition is pleasant, your manners are exquisite, nobody likes you anymore. I have called slobs perfectionists at heart, reasoning that they never get anything accomplished because they won't start until they can be perfect.

You can also achieve freshness by writing about what has not yet become newsworthy. Sometimes, when I have felt my columns becoming too timely (another tirade for or against abortion, prayer in the schools, jogging, evil lyrics in rock music), I have written about something so small, so close to home, so out of the mainstream that it is not yet a trend, fad, craze. I wrote about the dangers of being born again way before born-againism became a national fad. I just told the simple story of going down the aisle of the First Baptist Church during a revival, largely so I could sit next to Jimmy Honeycutt, not so I could meet my Maker. In the middle of the craft craze, I wrote about why I don't tat, macramé, crochet, needlepoint, or make plant holders out of popsicle sticks: I need to keep my hands free for smoking.

One quality of a good writer, then, is his or her ability to stay one jump or thought ahead of the general view. You try it. Test the winds of public opinion. Is a new movement, philosophy, fad about to blow? Then see in your thesis statements whether you can stand in the front of the brewing storm and report your impressions back to the gathering, soggy crowd-followers. You don't want to be left behind, like the teachers who called me after my essay on education was published and said, "You wrote the essay I kept intending to write." But they never did.

I used to tell my students—and I believe it still—that with a good thesis in hand they could write about an orange, a gnat, a comedian, Queen Elizabeth, nuclear war, or garbage.

The thesis makes sense, either literally or figuratively. A thesis is, at bottom, plausible. Even very original, somewhat exotic assertions must nevertheless bear up under the weight of nononsense logic common among humorless or grumpy readers. The "best" fairy tales, jokes, nursery rhymes, riddles, and science fiction tales have an underlying logic that holds the fantasy together and makes the tale endure. You cannot write just any old thing and expect to get away with it. Your thesis can be as clever, original, and bizarre as you want it to be, but it must have a kernel of truth in it—though the kernel may be as small as the sleep-disturbing pea under the princess's mattress. If your thesis sounds like an outrageous old wives' tale, then reconsider before you try to defend it. A thesis statement is no place for the absurd, though it may be a place for the imaginative and inventive approach.

What is a ridiculous thesis? How will you know when you have gone too far? Experience will correct your judgment. If you can find no facts, information, or statistics to support your thesis, then change it. If the thesis is so outrageous that its meaning frequently eludes even you, then forget it. If you sense that you are simply using your thesis to show off or to get attention, then abandon it.

You may assume that you cannot be "wrong" when you express an opinion about a political event, a scientific discovery, a literary work. But you can. And if you begin your essay with the highly questionable assertion that the phases of the moon caused World War II or your grandmother likes rocky road ice cream because she grew up in Kansas or that *Anna Karenina* has a happy ending, then you are just being silly, not witty.

The thesis is concrete.   You may be confused about the difference between being factual and being concrete. The thesis is certainly a concept, not a fact, but it is nevertheless as specific and tangible as you can make it. Vagueness and abstraction are as unwelcome in lively, supportable thesis statements as are factual dead-ends. Evoke a concrete image in the reader's mind if you can. Try to appeal to as many of the five senses as possible. Express your opinion in a specific context, with a specific tone and attitude. The following examples illustrate the difference between being too factual and too abstract or vague.

Factual assertion:

In 1855, *Huckleberry Finn* was banned in Concord, Massachusetts, largely because of Louisa May Alcott's objections to the novel.

The fact is a dead end and could not serve as a thesis. Where is the writer's opinion? What is the angle? How can the fact be used to support a larger concept or idea?

Vague, abstract assertion:

The banning of *Huckleberry Finn* in 1855 proves that censorship is an age-old American problem.

This thesis is weak because, though it contains specific information, the slant is vague, the expression of it, bland. Notice the general words: age-old, problem, censorship. Where is Mark Twain in the thesis? Where is the reader's strong reaction? Where is the unusual or fresh slant?

Thesis:

> Mark Twain had Louisa May Alcott to thank for the banning of *Huckleberry Finn* in 1855, an act of censorship that made him the happiest author in Christendom and thoroughly routed the pietists and bible thumpers.

In this thesis, you can see Mark Twain grinning, can discover the necessary context and information, and can detect the fresh direction in which the writer is heading. What is the best thing about book banning? It puts otherwise unread books on the best-seller list.

The following suggestions may lead you to an original thesis.

Take a position running directly counter to public opinion. It is popular to be self-righteously opposed to discrimination. However, a professor saw his essay published in a respected national magazine because he took the opposite position. The subject? Discrimination. The slant? He was in favor of it. And the magazine paid him $1000 to defend this unpopular thesis.

Begin with a seemingly small incident, perhaps close to home, and make it have large implications. Wise writers do not start big and get small. Rather, they start small and get big. They notice in passing faces, fleeting moments, and private lives the broad, even universal, significance. For example, instead of creating a thesis about troubled relationships in American families, you might, instead, begin with a thesis that focuses on a chilling and specific scene. You are walking down Park Avenue, a Mercedes rounds the corner, and you see in the car the enraged face of an irate husband and the crumpled visage of a frightened wife. You hear shouts, obscenities, through the open windows. A child cowers in the back seat, sobbing. What does it all mean? How does this family quarrel relate to you, to society? Your thesis is not Out There—somewhere in the pages of *Psychology Today* or *Reader's Digest*. It is in this passing car, in the middle of this domestic battle.

Create a new twist on an old truism. Much that passes for great wisdom and eternal truth is simply unexamined notions and opinions. You can sometimes find a fresh thesis by arguing with the staid pronouncements of saints, sages, and self-styled experts. Is the best defense a good offense? Is necessity the mother of invention? Does power corrupt and absolute power corrupt absolutely? If so, then why do the idealists shout, "Power to the people"? Old saws get rusty, but you can always sharpen them, or give them a new edge, by challenging their wisdom in all places and all times.

Hypothesize, fantasize.   The imagination is a rich place to go for inventive, fresh thesis statements. Ask "what if" questions, and see where they lead you. What if television was banned as a hazard to national mental health? What if adults grew down as children grew up? What if a poetry reading was held in the Houston Astrodome? What if people were not permitted to attend college until they were over 30 years old? What if adolescents were legally bound to pay room and board to their parents? What if the work week was two days long and the weekend was five? You might assume that this wild and crazy thinking would lead nowhere, but in fact, these fanciful questions might lead you to an original thesis, the kind that makes the reader thump himself on the side of the head and say, "Now why didn't *I* think of that?"

You can break a stereotype by spoofing a stereotype.   One writer, a wife, wrote an essay called "I Want a Wife." Another wrote about her ideal male secretary, the one with the great telephone voice and sexy figure. Woody Allen wrote about a prostitute with a genius-level IQ who sold intelligent conversations about literature and philosophy rather than sex. You might call this the bait-and-switch technique. Whatever gender, race, career, or regional stereotype the reader expects, you substitute the opposite. The thesis will then be both fresh and instructive—and often very funny.

You can see connections between apparently unrelated events, people, ideas, things.   An essayist—indeed, any writer, scientist, administrator, entrepreneur, or thinker—is a synthesizer. Can you draw an analogy, see parallels, between your relationship with your pick-up truck or Trans Am and your rela-

tionship with your significant other? Does a family reunion remind you of a Bacchanalian feast in ancient Rome? Is a prism a
poem? Is a workshop on procrastination just another way to
postpone doing what needs doing? Could the techniques of
coaching athletics be successfully applied in history class?

These suggestions and questions are intended only to get you
started in the search for new ways to look at old subjects and
overworked theses. Be assured that there is always a bright,
clever slant if you will only take the necessary time to dust off or
polish old notions and opinions—or better yet, invent new ones.

◆

Activities

1. *Step 1:* Some people collect rocks, butterflies, stamps, and
   baseball cards. Try collecting thesis statements. Go to a
   weekly newsmagazine *(Time, Newsweek, U.S. News & World
   Report)* or to your morning newspaper, turn to the columns
   or the editorial page, and write down the thesis statements
   you find there. If the columnist does not have a clear thesis,
   analyze what his or her overall purpose might be. Then compare thesis statements. What does Jack Kilpatrick have to
   say? What is Meg Greenfield's main point? What is William
   Raspberry asserting? Here are some writers you will probably encounter in your local newspaper or in national publications: Ellen Goodman, Mary McGrory, Russell Baker, Art
   Buchwald, Anthony Lewis, George Will. These people write
   opinion pieces. They have strong opinions, and you will
   want to study how they express those opinions.

   Step 2: Collect three columns on the same subject, and compare or contrast the thesis statements.

2. Think of some fads and trends in recent years: jogging, owning a BMW or Mercedes, building channels of communication, weight lifting, drinking white wine, dressing for success, taking vitamins and calcium tablets, avoiding stress,
   eliminating guilt, increasing aerobic capacity, attending
   workshops and seminars, taking cruises, dieting, network-
   ing. Now, develop a thesis about one of those fads or trends
   that is different from the conventional wisdom.

3. *Step 1:* Write down the opinion that polls show most people
   in your community have on a controversial issue. Some possible controversies are:

Building a civic center

Expanding the city limits

Permitting the licensing of a nearby nuclear power plant

Using chemical weapons in warfare

Rezoning a particular residential area into a commercial district

Requiring that public school teachers pass competency tests

Banning smoking in public places

Prohibiting public marches by militant groups such as the Nazi party or the Ku Klux Klan

Building a new cross-town freeway

Enforcing leash laws for cats

Raising the drinking age from 18 to 21

Requiring year-round public school attendance

Eliminating abortion clinics

Charging owners of satellite dishes for cable television programming

Requiring journalists to reveal their confidential news sources

Monitoring television news for evidence of political bias

Imposing heavy penalties on college graduates who fail to repay student loans

Making all college campuses coeducational

Requiring that ingredients and nutritional information be listed on take-out food

Ending tax subsidies of public transportation

Step 2: Now write a thesis that argues for the opposite position, even if you disagree with what you are asserting. (After all, you may agree with the majority, but you should train yourself to "see" the minority view.)

4. Summarize in one sentence a strong parental objection to something you desperately wanted to do but were forbidden to do.

5. Write a one-sentence statement of your purpose for being in college.

6. Study the lyrics of your favorite song and find its central thesis. Is it the title? The song may not directly state a thesis. Can you guess what the main idea of the song might be, basing your statement on the mood, overall feeling, and repetition of certain words or phrases?

7. Create the thesis you would like to have carved on your tombstone as an epitaph. (Poet John Keats's epitaph, for example, reads, "Here lies one whose name was writ in water.")

8. Choose a subject from the following list, and develop a thesis for a 500-word essay. For each subject, I have supplied the audience for whom you will be writing and the setting or context of the essay.

> Homemade soup (for a teenager who does not know how to boil water)
>
> Academic achievement (to be read to parents, faculty, and students at commencement exercises)
>
> Sexuality (informing your younger sibling or cousin about the subject)
>
> Pets (for an animal hater)
>
> Friendship (for a shy person or a loner)
>
> Contemporary moral standards (to be read at a press conference for a rock group)
>
> Tennis or any other individual sport (an amateur's view to be presented to a group of professional players)
>
> Reagan's presidency (to be presented at a Young Democrats' meeting)
>
> Censorship (to the executives who have masterminded Home Box Office, MTV, and the Playboy channel)

Narrow the thesis.

A good thesis says something specific about the topic under consideration. The essay is short. The thesis must, therefore, be tidy, neat, manageable, pinned down. And though the thesis can sometimes be too broad, it can seldom be too narrow. You cannot write about cars or even Toyotas, but you can write about the feeling of power you get when you are out cruising around, the funny noise under the hood, the first car you ever owned and what you did in it, or the competition between the makers of foreign cars and American car manufacturers.

A sufficiently narrowed thesis helps you because it forces you to look at and describe what is going on behind the broad surfaces of life. Unfortunately, however, most people—perhaps including you—are big, bold generalizers. They certainly do not need to be encouraged in what they already do, but rather, in what they do not do. And what some writers do not do is get down to specifics. Though you live very much in the particular—setting the table for dinner, listening to the radio, flossing your teeth, taking a nap, shopping for clothes—you may seem, perpetually, to write in the general, uttering sweeping generalizations, high-flown theories, unsubstantiated claims on big topics. Perhaps you believe that the concrete (for example, a family fight) is not as interesting as Western civilization, the solar system, or the Vietnam War. Perhaps you fear that if you get down to specifics, you will not know as much about the subject as you thought—or, perhaps, as you feel you should. You can make many bold statements about the need for tax reform, but your ignorance may become apparent when you try to formulate one specific statement that might lead to massive tax reform.

The fact is, you will seldom create a thesis you cannot safely narrow. But the narrowing seems riskier than the expanding. Your brain says you cannot write about the kings and queens of England, the whole of *War and Peace,* or the latest cancer treatment, but your heart says, "Give it a shot. What have I got to lose?" What you have to lose, of course, is a good essay.

As you grow more skilled at creating thesis statements, you may be able to risk broadness. But initially at least, you will wedge your argumentative or persuasive intention into the smallest space possible, thereby pushing yourself to look carefully and understand fully every facet of your subject. For now, theorize about the kitchen junk drawer, not the whole messy house; the causes for an end to your romantic involvement, not the way love does or does not make the world go round; the central character's loss of innocence in the novel, not the whole cast of characters; the side effects of one antidepressant, not the entire, drug-abuse scene.

Unfortunately, you will sometimes be unable to determine whether a thesis is narrow enough until you have begun to support or defend it. But there are certain decisions you can make in narrowing the thesis even before you begin to write.

Is the thesis narrow enough to generate only 3 or 4 supporting ideas, facts, examples, images—not 18 or 22? And under those 3 or 4 major supporting points, can you think of an equal number of arguments or facts for each? If, having formulated a thesis, you cannot "see" anything in your mind's eye or think of any concrete supports or proofs, the thesis is likely too broad or vague. If the thesis is to serve as a controlling device or guide, it should instantly catapult you into the concrete, visible world, not daydreams and fantasy. Compare the following examples:

Broad and vague:

Cats are indifferent to their owners.

Narrowed and specific:

My cat, Nipper, arrogantly believes that if she could open a can of Puss 'n' Boots tuna, she wouldn't need me at all.

Now, rather than writing generally about the aloof, disdainful behavior of cats, the writer can analyze and illustrate the particular behavior of his own cat, thereby using one specific example to "prove" the truth of the general and bring the specific to the level of the universal. The second thesis evokes a concrete image and setting and yet leaves the writer free to explore the larger significance of cat arrogance.

Does the thesis provide good control over your content, perhaps even showing the shape and organization of the essay that will follow?

No control:

Student housing is increasingly becoming a problem.

Revision:

> Overcrowding in student dorms often forces students to move into tiny, shabby apartments far from campus; to advertise for roommates with whom to share exorbitant rent and utility bills; and to depend on unreliable public transportation.

This thesis arrangement may seem awkward, but if you are just beginning to learn how to organize and support a thesis, it can save you from feeling at loose ends. The infinitive phrases provide the overall organization for the essay. All that remains is to set up three supporting paragraphs with the separate points (isolation from campus, high cost, and transportation) serving as the main ideas of supporting paragraphs.

Do you feel overwhelmed by examples, proofs, facts, and details? If your thesis creates a helpless, I-don't-know-where-to-begin feeling, then it is likely too broad. You can get a grip on your thesis simply by narrowing the boundaries of your subject. Instead of setting up a thesis that obligates you to a discussion of three scenes in a novel, choose only two. Instead of exploring the advantages and disadvantages of two kinds of home computers, analyze the merits of only one. Compare the folowing thesis statements:

Broad boundaries:

> The nuclear disasters at Three Mile Island and at Chernobyl destroyed in a moment the public-relations image utility companies had polished for decades.

Narrowed boundaries:

> The nuclear disaster at Three Mile Island destroyed in a moment the public-relations image utility companies had polished for decades.

Note: If you were planning to write a long, well-researched paper on the public-relations image promoted by utility companies in America and Russia, you might choose the first thesis.

But if you were planning to write an essay of two or three pages, you might choose the second thesis, concentrating solely on the public-relations image of the American plant at Three Mile Island.

Of course, it is possible to create a thesis so narrow that there is no room for discussion, comment, or argument. How? By stating a fact, not expressing a concept. If you tend to confuse facts and concepts, you may remedy the problem by taking a position on a fact or placing a fact in context.

Fact (too narrow):

Washington Square, at the foot of Fifth Avenue in New York City, is in the center of Greenwich Village.

Broadened with slant:

Washington Square, at the foot of Fifth Avenue in New York City, is a landmark in Greenwich Village, a colorful Bohemian community, and a major tourist attraction.

For the thesis, zoom in from a wide-angle view to a close-up: from sports, to baseball, to favorite pitchers, to Dwight Gooden's fast ball and how he throws it; from hobbies, to hiking, to hiking on the Appalachian Trail, to your hike down the Appalachian Trail, to why you'll never do a dumb thing like that again; from how times change, to social customs, to courtship, to why living together may not be such a great idea, after all; from inflation, to the high cost of living, to the high cost of housing, to the cost of housing in Poughkeepsie, to why you're still stuck in Poughkeepsie, living with your parents (itself a starting point).

Use methods to narrow the thesis.

You narrow the thesis by first narrowing the subject. Here are some examples of broad areas of consideration reduced to manageable topics.

economics > high cost of education > high cost of higher education > economic programs to help the student handle the high cost of higher education > student loan programs > student loan programs at your university > qualifications and procedures for loan applicants at your university

favorite foods > sweets > ice cream > ice cream with chocolate in it > the taste sensations of rocky road ice cream

entertainers > singers > country-western singers > country-western singers who can't sing > how country-western singers who can't sing get to be rich and famous > why Johnny Cash got to be rich and famous as a country-western singer, even though he can't sing

careers in television > behind-the-scenes careers in television > operating television cameras > job requirements and education necessary for career as television cameraperson

life > daily life > ruts > job ruts > career burnout > ways to avoid career burnout

playing > playing as a kid > outdoor play > climbing trees > how it feels to be a kid dangling from a tree limb

One you have narrowed the subject, you can continue with the question technique. Good thesis questions begin with the questions that elicit all good writing: Who? What? When? Where? How? Why? So what? The "who" is your perception or attitude about the subject, your slant; the "what" is the subject; the "when" and "where" are the context or setting; the "how" and "why" are the reasons for pursuing the subject, the reasons the subject matters to you. The "so what" is the reason the subject will matter to the audience.

The subjects suggested above might elicit the following thesis statements.

1. Students who apply for loans at my university feel as if they are being investigated by the CIA.

The thesis leads to research, a gathering of information from campus administrators, admissions offices, perhaps the Office of Student Affairs. If you yourself had applied for a student loan, you might make the thesis more personal, explaining what you had to do to qualify for a student loan.

2. My tongue goes on a fascinating journey when it travels through a two-dip cone of rocky road.

Only a chocolate ice cream lover could handle this thesis with enthusiasm and originality. The writer could carry the idea of the journey throughout the essay. Rocky road ice cream, for example, has plenty of bumpy, interesting detours through flecks of chocolate and nuts; the tongue travels sensuously through creamy chocolate and marshmallow. This thesis would require careful, meticulous description of a small and satisfying event.

3. Johnny Cash's remarkable career in Country-Western music proves that charisma and staging may bring more success than talent.

This strong opinion about Johnny Cash is clearly personal, but it is supportable. You may think Johnny Cash has a great voice. Fine. That position is also supportable.

4. A television camera person may not need a college degree, but he or she must have the hand-eye coordination of an air-traffic controller and the steady nerves of a great poker player.

The comparisons set up in this thesis would provide control and organization for the assertion about television camera technicians. You might need to know or have been a television camera-person to write convincingly about this thesis.

5. Teachers could avoid career burnout by having smaller classes, participating more fully in decision making, and receiving more respect as professionals.

With this thesis, you would, of course, be supporting the teacher's point of view. Notice how the three ways to avoid career burnout appear in the thesis. The supporting paragraphs are already in order, the overall organizational scheme intact. Of course, you might want to develop a more personal thesis, one that explains how you, a student, avoid career burnout. After all, although you do not get paid for going to college, earning a degree is certainly a full-time job.

♦

Activities

Narrow the following thesis statements, making them as specific as possible. Be sure you include specific names of people, places, and things; specific details; a specific slant or attitude; and, if possible, a specific image or mental picture.

Example:

> Sometimes my relatives come to visit. (no slant)
>
> I don't like visits from my relatives. (slant, but too general, broad)
>
> I don't like visits from my mother's relatives. (slant, getting more specific but not specific enough)
>
> Preparing for a visit from my mother's Aunt Gertrude is worse than getting ready for an inspection at a military dress parade. (slant, specific names, specific details, concrete image)

Now you try the same narrowing techniques for the following examples, remembering to use the who, what, when, where, how, and why questions.

1. Dating is a meat market.
2. I like sheet music.
3. I am unhappy about living in the nuclear age.
4. Everybody in my family is an anarchist.
5. Winning is everything.
6. Astronauts must have an interesting life.
7. The law requiring me to wear a seat belt is an invasion of my privacy and a violation of my freedom.
8. Nonsmokers are invading my lifespace.
9. There is no life after graduation.
10. There is no life before graduation.

Most of these thesis statements are adequate, but they are vague, broad, and boring. Although the thesis is a general assertion that demands proof or support, it can nonetheless be lively, specific, narrow, and tight. The reader will respond more favorably to a snappy thesis. And you will write with greater energy and confidence.

Tone the thesis.

Just as musicians tune their instruments before they begin to play, essayists "tone" their thesis statements before they begin to write: the writer strikes the right note with the audience, not jarring, not irritating. The thesis should also be in tune with you, your voice, and your personality.

In fact, the word "tone" really means "tone of voice." When your elders or betters say, "Don't take that tone of voice with me, young man (or young lady)," they are resonating to something you *sound* like, not something you are saying. By changing your tone of voice, you can give shades of meaning, nuances, to a word or a sentence. For example, if your friend is a procrastinator and says, blithely, "I can get that paper in on time," you say, "Sure." But you drag out the word, letting your voice dip and rise dramatically. The "sure" is sarcastic. But if your friend has never missed a deadline and makes the same bold claim, you answer, "Sure!" as if to say, "Natch! No problem." Or if your friend asks you for a favor and you do not want to do it but you owe him one, you say, "Sure," tentatively or with deep resignation about the inevitable and dreaded duty.

But the spoken word differs from the written word in that there are no auditory or visual signals on the page, no gestures, no physical expressions of disgust or delight. And these missed signals of body language or tone of voice can cause a reader to miss your point or tonality. Even though you intend a tongue-in-cheek stance in your thesis, the reader may take you seriously and be offended. Even if you are dead serious, the reader may think you are just kidding and may laugh in all the wrong places.

But how do you make your words, without sound, *sound right?* First, you remember the purpose of your thesis, which is to invite the reader's participation in the exploration of your idea. The atmosphere must be at least moderately cordial and inviting, or the reader will not stay to read how you defended that thesis.

You must, therefore, avoid "fighting" words, words that have unsavory connotations or that have picked up a huge load of emotional baggage. You avoid cuss words, sexist words, racist words, stereotypical words, judgment words, bigoted words. You might slip in a few of the words later in the essay, after the reader has come to realize that you are either kidding or not kidding. But a strident, abrasive tone in the thesis might remove any chance to prove your point to an alienated reader. You take out the words "old maid" and replace them with "single woman." You soften or change words like "slut," "creep," "idiot," "fool," "dumb jock." You'd surely be taking the wrong tone with the audience and spoiling your chance to make a good point if you wrote in your thesis, "The president of the United States is an imbecile about economic matters." You would lose your audience before you had even begun to support your assertion. Your thesis can be strong in meaning, yet amiable in tone. You want your idea or opinion to carry force and power, not your blustering, fanatical expression of it. Leave the careless, dangerous tone to zealots, idiots, and bigots, of which you are surely not one.

Flippancy is risky, except perhaps with an audience for *Saturday Night Live*. You do not glibly assert that the only place a person cannot get a good education is in college. You are not a stand-up comedian. You are a rational person trying to make a rational point. A flippant and careless tone is as damaging to the writer's credibility as it is alienating to the reader. You expect savvy, street-smart wisecrackers to be glib—even vulgar. The audience has been primed, in recent years, to expect such behavior. But the writer whose audience does not yet know him or her has no such luxury of expression. If you err, err on the side of caution, not excess. When in doubt, take it out, whether the "it" be a word or a phrase. Let your thesis be original in content, even radical, but let the way you express that idea be kindly, friendly, and welcoming.

Though you will resolutely avoid flippancy, vulgarity, and smart-aleckiness in your thesis, you still have a wide range of tones available to you: serious, superserious, light, funny, mildly sarcastic, rollicking, whimsical, pensive, weighty, relaxed, patient, urgent, measured, sad, compassionate, benevolent. The following thesis statements evoke different moods and convey different tones of voice. The views expressed do not contain stereotypes, vulgarities, or "fighting" words, though the thesis statements might be startling or at least fresh.

> *My cat taught me about lust, full-blooded and howling.* (The tone is risqué, funny. But what would happen if you substituted the word "slut" or "stud" for "cat"? You'd get hostile letters from incensed feminists, both male and female, from all over the country.)

> *Life is like bad art: the proportions are all wrong.* (The tone is disgruntled, but most readers might be nodding at this

point, having had a bad day. But what if you wrote, "Life is ugly and grotesque as Picasso's creepy abstract paintings of freakish broads"? *You'd* be acting ugly if you wrote such a thesis, and nice people would write off both you and your assertion.)

When I'm not being a secular humanist, a rabble-rousing Democrat, or a Bible-totin' Christian, I have fascist tendencies. (The tone is tongue-in-cheek and certainly strident, but you can risk more because you are writing about you. What if you made this same brash assertion about someone else? A lawsuit, perhaps?)

Maintain the tone.

Of course, toning the thesis is only the beginning. The entire essay should have the same tone, or the reader may become confused. If the central voice in the essay shifts from arrogant to humble, from reckless to cautious, from hilarious to sedate, the reader may become frustrated. An uneven tone removes one of the key signals in an essay: what goes on between the lines, so to speak, where nothing is stated but much is hinted. A teacher, for example, who writes sarcastically about his or her "stupid" students is revealing more about himself or herself than about the students, even though certain students may not be as bright as others. A student who writes scathingly and disparagingly about every phase of education is going to lose credibility with the reader.

The overall tone of the essay, therefore, must be appropriate to the occasion, considerate of differences in taste and mores among the readers, and consistent, thereby providing valuable clues, not mixed signals, to enhance understanding. You cannot relate very well to a person who "hits" you wrong, even if what he or she is saying may be true. Neither can readers respond favorably to a writer who offends, disgusts, or teases them.

On Tone

My experiences as a writer have taught me the crucial importance of taking the right tone with the reader. My tone, a strong one, has often overwhelmed my point; the reader could not see through the strident, abrasive me to look more closely at my views. I tell you this sad story not to gain sympathy but to issue a warning: I am convinced that you can make any outrageous statement if you say it nicely. I am equally convinced that a reader will not stay with you for long if you write like a know-it-all—or worse, a wimp. "Noodle" tones can be, after all, more irritating than strident tones. If you don't believe me, consider how distasteful limp handshakes, indecisiveness, effusive apologies, or fawning can be.

◆

Activities

Find a way to soften the jarring tone of the following theses, even as you retain the essential idea or opinion. Strive for a tone that will keep the reader from telling you to wipe that expression off your face.

1. There's no question about it: abortion is vicious, premeditated, cold-blooded murder.

2. The best way to become a politician is to be a crook first.

3. My mother was a saint, the sweetest, dearest woman who ever lived.

4. People who don't pay cash for everything are nuts.

5. Capital punishment is too good for these crazy lunatics running loose in the streets.

6. This business about keeping prayer in the schools is absolute and total nonsense.

7. Nobody could pay me enough to live in dirty, smelly, dangerous New York.

8. These damned sicko artist types are a menace to right-thinking people everywhere.

9. Poetry is nothing but a silly bunch of mumbo jumbo to me.

10. My father's advice wasn't worth a penny, much less two whole cents.

Revise the thesis.

If a crack appeared in your ceiling, would you (a) tear down the house, (b) sell it and move to Palm Beach, (c) plug up the crack, or (d) paint over it and pray? If you answered (a) or (b), you are either very rich or very crazy. If you answered (c) or (d), you are short of funds, canny, and practical—not a bad combination for a regular human being.

The multiple-choice test applies similarly to the thesis. Some reckless folks, full of bravado and rich in ideas, prefer to tear down the whole essay when it does not support what they originally asserted in the thesis. They have figurative houses in New York, Florida, and the Bahamas. They have servants to wait on them, plenty of time to take second or fifty-second chances. But having seen how hard it is to write an essay that supports a thesis you thought you agreed with, you will become more realistic.

If you discover, in writing the rest of the essay, that your examples, illustrations, facts, and anecdotes are not supporting your original assertion, you are wise to change the thesis rather than tossing out the entire writing project. *The sturdiest and, paradoxically, the most flexible sentence in the essay is your thesis.*

If you have written an essay that seems, somehow, not to prove what you had originally intended, you can return to the thesis to modify or correct your overall purpose. You may discover your real intention as you go along. You may change your mind. You may simply want to shift the emphasis a bit. Here is a thesis undergoing transitions, revisions, and adjustments of tone and attitude.

1. I am convinced that all forms of censorship are violations of the American citizen's right to see, hear, read, or say whatever he or she pleases.

The writer takes a very strong position against censorship. In supporting this thesis, she uses a personal example, the influence of Home Box Office on her teenaged children. She begins very energetically, her mind seemingly made up, to assert that her children have the right to watch whatever they please on Home Box Office and that they are responsible for making wise viewing choices. But midway through the essay, the writer begins to be a bit uncomfortable. What happens when these teenagers do not make wise choices, when they become indifferent or even callous about extreme violence, pornography, the portrayal of men and women alike in manipulative, cruel, or stereotypical roles? After all, what is fine in theory is not fine in the particular. The teenaged children even seem to *like* trashy movies and trashy values. And these children are the writer's own. What is the parent's responsibility? The writer decides to tone down the thesis a bit and to shift the emphasis from freedom to responsibility.

2. Because Americans are guaranteed the right to freedom of speech and freedom of the press, individuals have a grave responsibility to censor themselves.

This thesis argues for personal responsibility in the context of public freedom. But again, the writer is facing the knotty problem of what to do when her adolescent offspring refuse to accept their responsibilities as television consumers. The writer mulls over the difficulty still further. She passionately believes in the First Amendment of the Bill of Rights, but she must face the consequences of that freedom. Certainly she does not believe that government censorship can be condoned or encouraged. But what about private censorship? Can she, as a parent, feel justified in censoring her children's television viewing? Reluctantly, she sacrifices the sweeping generalization to the rigid demands of the particular situation. She cancels HBO until her teenaged children are able to make responsible viewing choices. The teenagers scream that their rights are being violated. She responds that their mental and emotional health is more important in this very specific context. And she again revises the thesis to accommodate the issue of private censorship.

3. Though the Bill of Rights asserts that government censorship is a violation of our rights as citizens, parents must nonetheless accept responsibility for censoring what their children read, see, and hear.

The thesis now incorporates the writer's true feelings about censorship—where it is appropriate and necessary and where it is harmful. The example about her experience with Home Box Office and its influence on her adolescent children now "works." The tension between public and private censorship can be faced and examined. The practical solution—canceling HBO because of its harmful effects on her children—can find some justification. The importance of parental responsibility for curbing certain personal freedoms for a greater good—that is, the mental and emotional well-being of minors—can be supported. The solution is not ideal. But, then, neither is the original idealistic and adamant assertion often cited by disgruntled youngsters deprived of watching their "favorite" shows—namely, that they have a "right" to watch any program they choose. And so the writer gives up her first thesis, the one she thought she agreed with, because it conflicts with the hard reality of a personal censorship dilemma.

But revision of the thesis is not always necessary because of a tough philosophical or ethical problem. Sometimes you will change your thesis several times simply to tone it down, sharpen it, and narrow it a bit. Here is another thesis in transition.

> *Sometimes I think I know more than I do at other times.* (The original thesis is vague, broad, conventional in expression, neutral in tone. Know *what?* Why? Is the sense of knowing a good or a bad thing?)

> *Some days I am right on target in my thinking.* (You have days like that, don't you?—days when your mind is sharp, your aim sure. Yet the writer uses a cliché, a tired expression ("right on target") to express the idea. And the expression of the idea is again vague and dull. But at least the slant is clear. The knowing seems to be positive. But what kind of knowing is involved here? Is the knowing just the ability to remember where the writer put the scissors, or is it the deep knowing that leads to insight, understanding, change?)

> *Sometimes I feel like the wise old oracular owl of the world, moaning "who" across the morning and knowing what, when, where, why, and how as well.* (So this knowing is big, deep, profound. The simile—a short comparison using "like" or "as"—is fresh, providing a clear mental image for the reader. The thesis creates mystery. The reader will be curious to read on, to discover what the writer means by this special kind of knowing. All that remains for the writer is to support the thesis with examples of special, sudden understanding—the kind that comes to everybody from time to time. The word "oracular" carries a feeling of prophecy, suggesting that the insights will be miraculous, such as suddenly realizing God is

God, or in midmigraine, how to get the cap off the aspirin bottle.)

Several tinkerings are possible with the thesis, whether you have not yet begun to write the essay, are halfway through the essay, or have finished the essay.

1. You can make the expression of the idea livelier, fresher, and more original simply by creating a mental picture.

2. You can tone down the thesis or make it more forceful by changing the slant words: from "enraged" to "irritated," from "maybe" to "absolutely," from "gorgeous" to "appealing," from "brilliant" to "smart." (Grandmother's tirades against the federal government enraged/irritated me.)

3. You can broaden the scope of the essay by writing about two contrasting ideas or exploring categories of people, places, or things rather than writing about a single person, place, or thing.

4. You can focus on a single idea or event, thereby narrowing the thesis.

5. Having found that you disagree with what you have written, you can change your mind by changing your thesis.

♦

Activities

1. Select one of the following topics, and experiment with several possible thesis statements. For example, first state the position with which you would agree, then state the opposite position. Change the tone of each thesis by softening or sharpening slant words and images. Expand or narrow the thesis by introducing comparisons or by focusing on a single point. You should be able to write at least four thesis statements for the topic you choose.

Example: Capital punishment

a. Capital punishment is absolutely necessary because it is a major deterrent to crime.

b. Capital punishment uses murder to avenge murder and is, therefore, an absurd solution to the problem of crime. (Opposite argument)

c. Capital punishment might function as a deterrent to crime and could, therefore, be a necessary evil. (Softening the tone of the first thesis, making it more tentative)

d. Using murder to deter the murderer is as absurd as giving salt water to a person dying of thirst. (Using mental picture to enliven thesis, same position as second thesis)

Now you try the same exercise, using one of the following topics:

Paying college athletes versus salaried "amateurs"

The good life versus the fast life

Farming versus source of water pollution

Walking or riding

Having brothers or sisters

Family reunions

Writing letters home

Registering to vote

2. Revise each of the following thesis statements, following the instructions given within the parentheses.

a. Many adults spend half their lives citing the injustices of sexism and the other half being sexist. (Create a mental picture.)

b. I crave a good sentence the way a fat person craves Twinkies. (Change the mental picture, and state the opposite position.)

c. Administrators and educators created school holidays to destroy parent–child relationships. (State the opposite position, or soften the tone of the thesis as it is already stated.)

d. I was in my 30s before I noticed that most people did not follow the rules, and that when they didn't, nothing bad happened to them. (Restate the same idea more concisely, using a mental image.)

e. Sleep first began to look very good to me when I was 13. (Make the tone more forceful.)

f. Despite what Ben Franklin said, a penny saved is a penny devalued. (State the same thesis in other words, using your factual knowledge of present economic realities.)

Have a plan.

Now that you have created a thesis, expanded or narrowed the scope of it, adjusted the tone of it, and made it agree with your personal perception or with the observable facts, you may think you are ready to begin writing the essay. But additional planning is necessary. Your early jottings on scratch paper will not serve adequately as a final guide through an essay of several paragraphs. You need a careful blueprint for an architectural design of great beauty, usefulness, and durability. Similarly, you need a careful outline for an essay of creditable or even spectacular design.

An outline is a guide through the intricacies of your argument. Like the thesis, it is sturdy and serviceable. Also like the thesis, it is flexible. Your attitude toward making an outline may be negative. Perhaps you believe you do not need a careful plan for a short essay. Perhaps the outline seems tyrannical, cramping your style, keeping you to a plodding obedience, not a high-stepping liberation. But, when viewed rightly, the outline is, in fact, liberating even as it offers control and order. The outline is a freeing mechanism, releasing your mind from hesitancy about where to go next, leaving your mind free to be creative as you write. After all, if you have to stop every few sentences to think about what comes next, you might lose the train of thought and find yourself derailed in midessay, thoughts spinning, pen smoking, engine roaring, but getting nowhere.

Choose an outline format.

Outlines may be very formal or very informal, but they will have two characteristics in common. They will

1. Indicate the major ideas of the supporting paragraphs;
2. Place those ideas in the most effective, logical, and compelling order.

The formal outline.   An outline is formal when it has a definite and unvarying structure. The pattern of organization alternates between Roman and Arabic numbers and capitalized and uncapitalized letters, and each section of the outline has no fewer than two parts. In addition, those parts must be parallel, meaning that the parts have the same grammatical structure: nouns with nouns, phrases with phrases, gerunds with gerunds, complete sentences with complete sentences.

Why must each section of the outline have at least two parts? Because if a topic of consideration is important enough to warrant its own section, it is important enough to warrant two points for consideration. If the point to be taken up deserves only one entry, then that entry can easily be integrated into a larger section.

Original:

I. Disadvantage of competency testing
   A. Discriminates against cultural variations
II. Advantage of competency testing
   A. Provides uniform standards

Revision:

I. Discrimination as a disadvantage of competency testing
II. Uniform standards as an advantage of competency testing

Here follows an example of a formal outline, illustrating the differing parallel structures available to you.

Thesis:

Christmas may be the unmerriest time of the year.
I. Christmas myths
   A. High expectations
      1. In religion
      2. In story
      3. In song
   B. Commercial hype
   C. Romantic images of the family
II. Christmas realities
   A. Preparing the festive celebration
   B. Shopping
      1. Expenses
      2. Cost of procrastination
   C. Growing tension within the family
III. Remedies for Christmas blues
   A. Lowering expectations

B. Simplifying preparations
C. Finding time away from the family
D. Holding on to the reality, not the fantasy

Conclusion:

If you develop a realistic attitude toward Christmas, putting it in its proper place, so to speak, you can find pleasure and peace in this hectic holiday.

Depending on the assigned length requirements for this essay on Christmas depression, you might develop fewer categories for consideration under the subheadings. But with this essay outline, you have at least developed three broad categories that might serve as the major points within the body of your essay: myths, realities, remedies. You might adjust the outline, including only a discussion of family tensions or of commercial financial pressures. Or you might simply write of the problems of whipping up a feast for a family dinner serving 20 or 30 people. And, of course, if your major holiday is not Christmas but some other holy or high day, you could nonetheless make substitutions without sacrificing the point. All red-letter days—weddings, graduations, bar mitzvahs, Thanksgiving, the New Year—are fraught with similar lofty expectations and heart-shattering disappointments. In other words, the outline is flexible. You are in control. The outline is only a trusty guide. It goes where you want it to go.

The topic sentence outline. If you find all the fuss and bother about Roman numerals and parallel parts frustrating, the topic sentence outline can perhaps better serve your purposes—or the purposes of your thesis. Once you have originated a thesis, you develop a topic sentence outline by writing down the five or six opinions or observations you have to make about that thesis. And because the topic sentence expresses the central idea of each supporting paragraph, you will then have painlessly arranged your paragraphs. All that remains for each topic sentence is the support, which may take the form of examples, illustrations, details, anecdotes, facts, and quoted authorities.

When you write a topic sentence outline, you simply write down the thesis, study it, then write down five or six additional sentences about that thesis. You then order those sentences, moving from the weakest point to the strongest. And there you have it: a dependable, sturdy structure that will provide logic and order for your ideas. Here's how the topic sentence outline works.

Thesis:

Summer is the time to get down to some serious reading.

1. *Every June, when the temperature starts to climb, literary aspirations decline.* (You begin by citing specific examples of the preponderance of articles in newspapers and magazines about suggested light summer reading. You might draw an analogy between light menus [salads, coolers, gazpacho] and light books [mysteries, romances, westerns, spy thrillers].)

2. *Book editors and reviewers seem to think Americans put their brains on hold in the good old summertime.* (Examine why and where they got the notion that summer is the time to revel in trashy, frothy, light-weight reading. Why do we think we cannot read anything heavy when we are lolling in a hammock, sitting in a rocking chair, sipping lemonade or beer in the shade of a maple tree?)

3. *Summer is a season of leisure and rest and, therefore, the ideal time to give the mind an energizing workout.* (Discuss how the mind can function better when the body has hours or weeks of freedom from the drudgery of schools or offices. When Americans are not tied to routines, carpooling, alarm clocks, committee meetings, and other dreary winter obligations, explain how at last they can have the mental sharpness and the physical endurance to tackle some of the important books they have always wanted to read but never got a chance to.)

4. *Americans unfortunately have a do-nothing attitude in summer, an attitude that extends even to pleasurable mental stimulation.* (Explore ways to relieve Americans of this deeply ingrained prejudice against heavy reading. Show how, when the pressure is off and the pleasure is on, Shakespeare or Dostoevsky might be a better reading choice than Barbara Cartland or Robert Ludlum.)

5. *Summer is the ideal time to dust off the great books of the world and lug them to the hammock or poolside.* (Conclude by chastising habitual attitudes toward reading and study—

attitudes promoted, ironically, by the men and women who are supposed to love books. Suggest a course of study for summer: the complete works of Shakespeare, *War and Peace*, Proust, the eighteenth-century Romantic poets, Plato, twentieth-century poets, histories of world wars or British royalty—anything, just as long as it is heavy.)

The topic sentences could stand, then, as the bare bones of the essay, awaiting only the fleshing out of details, examples, and proofs that would make for a humorous essay about heavy reading in the light atmosphere of summer. You might cite articles on book-review pages urging readers to drop history or biography in favor of romance. You might describe the kind of reading you do (or do not do) in summer. You might imagine amusing scenes: Kierkegaard in the wading pool, the Blessed Juliana of Norwich at the Holiday Inn, Homer between the dunes, James Joyce at the volleyball game, Darwin at the zoo, Doris Lessing in the cow pasture. But whatever you include, the topic sentences and their arrangement will provide the structure and organization you need to proceed with ease and pleasure—rather like floating through June, not dragging through January.

◆

Activities

Using the following essay, construct both a formal outline and a topic sentence outline. Remember to locate the thesis of the essay and to place it at the top of both outlines.

MORE THAN JUST A HOUSE

Time was when a house was not just a house. It was a treasure chest, a storage chest, a hope chest, the museum of history, the public library, the corner store, a work of art, a garden of delights. Not long ago, I peeked through the windows of such a house and had a vision of a world within a world, self-contained and lush as a tropical island, practical as a factory assembly line.

The dying world I gazed at was a huge Victorian mansion, set in the flat farm country of North Carolina. A porch wrapped the house in shady comfort. Tall turrets hinted of secret hideaways for diary keeping, romance, or tears. The dining room could seat 20. The paneled library could satisfy the literary passions of any inquisitive scholar. A small playhouse in the back yard and a rubber tire dangling from a tree could entertain a village full of rambunctious children. A shed and two barns could amply supply whatever the main house lacked.

The fourth-generation offspring of the original owners were off in Baltimore and Boston, leaving this Southern world to decay. Burs gathered in the once-green lawn. The outlying buildings were rotting. Cardboard boxes on the back porch spilled old letters, postcards, yellowed documents. Mildew worked its relentless way over whole histories of worlds and lives.

The grown-up offspring would very likely say the house was obsolete, impractical. The house was surely expensive to maintain, hard to heat, too large to clean. And it lacked all the modern conveniences: garbage disposal, central heat and air, stainless steel sinks, formica countertops, tile bathrooms. Then, too, the house was miles from a movie theater, quick-stop grocery, filling station. You could not leave this house and walk anywhere except up the road, across the fields, into the woods.

I thought of my efficient condo life, and I didn't like what I was thinking. Convenience to shopping and schools, easy maintenance, simplicity of chores were conventional attractions. But what price did I pay by thinking always of short-term advantages?

My modern residence was in some ways more costly and impractical than I realized. Everything I wanted to buy, for example, I had to purchase in amounts small enough to store. I couldn't keep a wardrobe in the attic until its style came around again. I couldn't hang a rack of cured hams in a shed I didn't have. I couldn't save old jars, used bicycle parts, yesterday's newspaper. I had no space for workshops, sewing machines, lawn mowers, huge soup pots and roasting pans. My library was a few paperbacks vying for space with a portable TV and a couple of sofas. My plants I threw out at the end of the season, going back to the costly nursery each spring for freshly potted geraniums.

The more I thought about drafty, creaking country houses such as this one, the more I realized that a lifetime of real economy lay in them. In my friend's country place, for example, a piece of wire is as near as the shed; the exact tool she needs is ten steps from the kitchen door. Preserves and pickles are there, too, along with old boards for new fences, paint, varnish, sand paper, steel wool. Large walk-in closets and ample back porches keep clothes, shoes, medicine, blankets, brooms, mops, and good-sized buckets. In short, if what you need is in your home already, then home is where you can safely stay.

My grandmother had a home that was much more than a house. Her attic held old lamps, odd pieces of furniture, suitcases, back issues of *National Geographic* and *Life*—good reading for a bored kid on a rainy day. Off her bedroom was a sun roof where teenaged granddaughters tanned in beachless splendor all summer long. The basement held an extra bedroom, a bathroom. Her yard had a large garage, big enough for an Oldsmobile and a boat, with room left over for several rowdy grandchildren to build a fort. Books and plants filled the sun porch. The bedrooms were large enough for two people to avoid each other in. The closet was as big as a modern bedroom, with space for vaporizers, heating pads, hot-water bottles, quilts, used wrapping paper, and ribbons.

Grandmother didn't go out much, not because she didn't want to but because she didn't need to. She kept her money in a safe at the top of the stairs. She had no need of expensive entertainments since her garden and her steady stream of visitors, some of whom stayed for weeks or months, kept her busy. She never lacked privacy since it was as close as the basement, the attic, the walk-in closet, the greenhouse. She had no need of rediscovering the past by visiting museums or snooping around in public archives. Her family history was as close as the letters, poems, and photos spilling from the huge mahogany secretary in the living room.

Sometimes, standing in my closet looking for one box to mail a present in or one corner to be alone in, I wish I had a many-turreted, self-sustaining, peaceful world within a world. Then perhaps I could feel the knot in my stomach loosen. And I could skip the endless trips to the drug store, bank, grocery store, department store. And I could, in my happy mansion, find a way to put the heating bill in perspective, across the long, sloping meadow of a lifetime, not a day.

Create a title.

I am always surprised by the frequent question, "Does this paper have to have a title?" Yes. Articles, books, poems, plays, business reports, and very important people have titles. So do compositions, and for several very good reasons. A title

1. Gives a sense of completion to an essay,
2. Catches the attention of the reader,
3. Serves as a clue to the reader about what is coming,

4. Enables people to refer easily to the essay, and

5. Often makes the essay memorable.

Those reasons for titling may seem obvious, but defining a "good" title is more difficult. Titles are often a matter of personal taste. Some people like them short, sweet, catchy. Others are distracted by such breeziness and prefer a title that says, straightforwardly, what the written piece contains. Still others might prefer a title that is lofty, erudite, elegant. But writers know the importance of titles and spend hours or months thinking about them. A good title can have as much to do with the making of a best-seller as the literary work itself. What if *For Whom the Bell Tolls* had been called *For Whom the Bell Rings?* You might think the Avon lady had come to call.

Creativity in Titling

A newspaper staffer dreamed up a title for one of my columns that was a decided threat to my ego. The title was better than the essay. I wrote about having taken my teenaged son to the Metropolitan Museum of Art and being rewarded for my troubles by his glassy-eyed indifference to one of the finest art collections in the world. I then generalized from the experience with my son to the doomed attempt to force people to love art of all kinds, as if culture were a pill a person could pop. The headline read, "You Can Lead 'Em to Watteau, But You Can't Make 'Em Think." Pretty catchy, huh?

And when one of my essays appeared in *Newsweek*, the editors came up with a very good title. I had begun the essay by writing, "Caesar was right. Thin people need watching." The editors called my piece "That Lean and Hungry Look," an allusion to a line from William Shakespeare's play *Julius Caesar*. The title immensely improved the essay, enraging skinny people and causing fat people to slap their chubby thighs and roar with laughter.

Some people insist that, as with human beings, every good title should have a colon. The portion of the title preceding the colon is inventive. The portion of the title following the colon explains the first part. For example, poet Robert Penn Warren entitled a critical essay "Uncorrupted Consciousness: The Stories of Katherine Anne Porter." And poet Wallace Stevens called one of his books *The Necessary Angel: Essays on Reality and the Imagination.*

How do you find a title for your essay? It is usually derived from the thesis and is, in effect, a short summary of the central idea of the essay. Sometimes the title may simply be a recurring word or phrase in the essay. Occasionally the title is not specifically derived from the thesis or from the essay but is, rather, lifted from another source—perhaps being a famous quotation, the context and meaning of which would be clear to most readers. For example, *For Whom the Bell Tolls* is a reference to John Donne's "Meditation XVII": "and therefore never send to know for whom the bell tolls; it tolls for thee."

Favorite Titles

Tastes vary in titling. I prefer titles that are short or very short, that evoke images, that use everyday language, and that are alliterative (repetition of initial consonant sounds). Such titles are hard to forget, like the line or beat of a song that keeps running through your head. Here are some of my favorites:

Rabbit, Run—a novel by John Updike
Art and Ardor—a collection of essays by Cynthia Ozick
Leaves of Grass—poems by Walt Whitman
Sad Heart at the Supermarket—a collection of essays by Randall Jarrell
"Dream Children; a Reverie"—an essay by Charles Lamb
"Goodbye to All That"—an essay by Robert Graves
Mystery and Manners—a collection of essays by Flannery O'Connor
"Farewell, My Lovely!"—an essay by E. B. White
"My Face"—an essay by Robert Benchley

Of course I also like the following title, which contradicts every previous assertion about "good" titles: "A Modest Proposal for Preventing the Children of Ireland from being a Burden to their Parents or Country and for making them beneficial to the Publick," an essay by Jonathan Swift. The title is funny and mock pompous, leading to a bitterly satirical essay proposing that poor children be fricasseed for dinner.

Be thoughtful when titling your essay.

Essay titles are often somewhat less interesting than are titles of novels or plays. Some titles of famous essays are, for example,

"On Friendship," "On the Art of Conversing," "Of Adversity," "Of Bashfulness." Perhaps essays sometimes fail to inspire clever titles because essays usually deal with one fairly clear-cut subject, theme, or concept. Nevertheless, you would surely enhance the impact and quality of your essay by finding a title that entertains and also instructs the reader as to the probable content of the essay.

Use the correct form for titles.

You may be confused about when to underline the title, when to set it off with quotation marks, and when to capitalize the first letters of words. You underline titles of long works, using an unbroken line. Such "long" works include books, magazines, long poems, plays, newspapers, record albums, television series, long musical compositions. You put quotation marks around titles of short works: essays, poems, short stories, chapter headings, magazine and newspaper articles, songs, episodes of a television series. But when you place a title on the title page or at the top of the first page of your essay, do *not* use quotation marks or italics (unless the title contains a title). The placement indicates that it is a title. Also, the underlining applies only to handwritten or typewritten works, not to published works in which the use of italics indicates titles.

You also capitalize the first and last words of titles and all intervening words except articles, conjunctions, and prepositions of four or fewer letters. Even if the title is a complete sentence, you nonetheless capitalize the first and last words and all important words.

Examples:

"Here Is New York"—E. B. White

"What Is a Classic?"—C. A. Sainte-Beuve

"How Should One Read a Book?"—Virginia Woolf

◆

Activities

1. Using five headlines in your local newspaper, create five suitable titles for essays on the same subjects.

2. Correctly punctuate and capitalize the following titles:

what did orwell think about the english language—an essay by A. M. Tibbetts

george eliot the emergent self—a biography by Ruby V. Redinger

college composition and communication—a journal

assessing english and language arts teachers' attitudes toward writers and writing—an article by Robert W. Blake

i know why the caged bird sings—an autobiography by Maya Angelou

3. Create a title for each of the following thesis statements:

Most yards, even those that seem to have hopeless problems, can be improved with a little commonsense landscaping.—from *Better Homes and Gardens*

Fashion designers and fashion directors give as much thought and time to accessorizing clothes as they do to the clothes themselves.—from *Working Wardrobe* by Janet Wallach

Books about writing often make dismal reading, partly because they attempt to cover all rules for all writers.—from Introduction to *A Writer's Guide* by Harold H. Kolb, Jr.

Einstein strongly believed in nature's inherent harmony, and his deepest concern throughout his life was to find a unified foundation of physics.—from "The Tao of Physics" by Fritjof Capra

4

Structuring the Essay

Introduce the subject.

Good introductions may vary in tone, technique, or content, but they all share one essential quality: they make the reader want to stay and finish the essay. Generally, the introduction places the subject in context, creates a cordial or simulating atmosphere, and provides some indication of the writer's intention or focus. Good introductions invite the reader to sit a spell on the front porch, so to speak, of your particular experience or opinion.

What makes an introduction enticing to a prospective reader? Your methods will vary according to your audience and purposes. But the balance between the particular and the general is delicate. A fact-filled introduction is top heavy, weighing the reader down before he or she can catch the drift of your intentions. A one-sentence introduction, on the other hand, is breezy, even flippant, asking too much of the reader's power to accept, unquestioningly, the grounds of your assertion. And an introduction with no clear thesis, no focus, is disorienting to the reader, making him or her feel as though the effort of discovering your secret motive is too much trouble.

On Introductions

Being on the lecture circuit has convinced me of the importance of introductions. Invariably, a couple of weeks before the scheduled speech, the program chairperson calls me up and requests some biographical information to be used for an introduction. I oblige by mailing him or her my *vita*, a one-page summary of my personal and professional history. Then I put the matter in the chairperson's hands, hoping the hands will be capable.

But the introductions that result from that résumé are as different as Reagan and Carter, corned-beef hash and prime rib. After the banqueters have eaten the last canned garden pea, the chairperson steps up to the podium, raps on the microphone, and begins the introduction. I am praying all the while. If I am well set up, the audience will be more receptive.

I am always shocked at the impact the introduction has on my performance. Sometimes, mispronouncing my name, the introducer dolefully reads out the entire résumé. I am groaning by now, wishing I had taken the time to send him a *real* introduction. The audience yawns, hearing more than they ever wanted to know about the speaker. By the time I step up to the podium, the audience is exhausted, and so am I.

Other introducers are better about culling irrelevant facts. They reel off a couple of educational degrees, maybe a book or a magazine article. But the introduction contains nothing compelling, nothing provocative, humorous. This introduction sounds no different from the introduction of a utility company executive, come to talk to Kiwanians about kilowatt conservation.

Occasionally, the introducer decides to abdicate his or her responsibility. "Our speaker needs no introduction," says the introducer, and I walk up to the podium, feeling as weightless and disoriented as an astronaut on the moon. The audience feels the same. "Who is this woman, anyway?" they mumble. So then I give my speech in a vacuum of sorts, lacking credentials, identity, familiarity.

But some introducers know what an introduction is for. These introducers give the audience just enough information to pique their interest, to make them sit up straight, to create a happy feeling of expectancy. The introduction contains a light sprinkling of facts, perhaps an anecdote that reveals something of the speaker's personality, some hint about the upcoming subject, maybe a line or two from an essay. By the time the introduction is over, the audience is chuckling, primed, respectful, ready to receive whatever I have to offer.

Here are three versions of the same introduction, illustrating the importance of balance and intention:

First version of introduction:

At 9:32 a.m., Eastern Daylight Time, on July 16, 1969, three astronauts—Neil Armstrong, Michael Collins, and Edwin Aldrin—lifted off in Apollo 11, which was powered by a 364-foot-tall Saturn V rocket. Pausing 115 miles above the earth to check their instruments, the astronauts then began the trip to the moon, traveling at a speed of 24,300 mph. Five million people were watching the broadcast being presented live and in color. At 1:22 p.m., Eastern Daylight Time, July 19, the astronauts went into an elliptical orbit around the moon. After orbiting, the Eagle—the Lunar Module—undocked from the Columbia—the Command Module; Armstrong and Aldrin crawled through the pressurized tunnel between the two modules and entered the Eagle, which would eventually carry them to the surface of the moon. When Armstrong said, "The Eagle has landed," his heart was beating at twice its usual rate. Several hours later, Armstrong climbed down the nine-rung ladder and uttered the words that brought chills and smiles to the faces of the 5 million people sitting in their dens: "That's one small step for a man, one giant leap for mankind." And the moon, that place of dreams and wishes, of green cheese and romance, of fairy tale and song, suddenly became a place of dust and stone, gray and barren as the modern imagination.

Of course, this introductory paragraph is absurdly overloaded with irrelevant and tedious facts, none of which foretell the essayist's real intention. The scientific readers might be enchanted, but they will face dismal disappointment by the time the thesis appears. The poetic types will have drifted off to sleep and will discover only upon awakening that the essayist intends to write about the moon as creative and romantic symbol, about the death of dreams and fantasy in modern culture, about the moon humankind thought it knew and the moon that actually existed.

Second version of introduction:

The moon, that place of dreams and wishes, of green cheese and romance, of fairy tale and song, suddenly became a place of dust and stone, gray and barren as the modern imagination.

Whoa. Hold on. What is going on here? This one-sentence thesis has no context, no foundation on which to rest its whimsical, nostalgic assertion. When did the moon "die" in the modern imagination? Where is the contrast between past and present assumptions about the faraway places of the universe? How can the writer introduce the subject, place it in context, supply just enough information to steady the reader, clue in the reader about the tone of the upcoming essay, declare the real intention or purpose, and at the same time, get on with the essay?

Third version of introduction:

When Neil Armstrong, the first person ever to walk on the surface of the moon, uttered the thrilling words, "That's one small step for a man, one giant leap for mankind," I felt a shudder of apprehension as well. The scientific achievement was unparalleled. The benefits of pushing past human frontiers into the secrets of the universe were obvious to all the 5 million viewers of that historic moment. But surely there was a twinge of regret as well, a feeling akin to the passing of childhood, the discovery of Santa Claus's true identity, the death of grandparents, the cold stab of reality. Where was the man in the moon? What would the cow jump over? The moon, that place of dreams and wishes, of green cheese and romance, had suddenly become a place of dust and stone, gray and barren as the modern imagination.

This introductory paragraph works for several reasons. The initial facts and the direct quotation supply a specific context and indicate the knowledgeability of the writer about this event. The introduction flows gradually into the thesis, speculating, creating a nostalgic mood, priming the reader about what to expect. The thesis will lead the writer into an essay about the price dreams pay in the service of scientific advancement and discovery. The writer will seek to prove that the modern imagination may have become barren, stony, and gray as the moon's surface. Balance and intention are appropriate and clear.

Know your audience.

Nowhere is the advice "Know your audience" more important than in the introductory paragraph of your essay. Here, first impressions are crucial. It is helpful, therefore, to analyze the kinds of audiences that might be meeting you for the first time in that opening paragraph. Very likely, you already know these people, but perhaps you have not systematically categorized them.

Some people, for example, do not like to meet an argument head on. They would be scared to death, for fear the writer might actually be intending to *say* something, and something profound at that. An anecdote that carries the seeds of your argument works nicely with these folks, folks who hate controversy worse than they hate strange neighborhoods and exotic cuisine.

Other people are brisk, to-the-point, up-front types, who like for the writer to get on with it. They hate a poetic introduction. They hate to watch the writer sidle up, slow-pokey and ambling, to the thesis. They do not want to savor the anticipation of the first delicious moment of contact between thesis and proof. They want to get down to business. Tell a long anecdote, give too much background material, and these efficient types will declare that reading your essay is a waste of their time and will turn to something else.

Other people are not willing to put much effort into reading. They will need more information, if only to alert them to the fact that a utilitarian is not someone who operates a can opener.

Still others are swift, canny, and receptive, but they have high literary standards as well. They seek information and instruction, but they demand entertainment and wit as well. For them, the introduction must be a model of symmetry, of balance between creating an inviting atmosphere and establishing the credentials and, therefore, the credibility of the writer. They want to know how come you think you're so smart. They will need to feel, in the introduction, that you are a person who knows what you're talking about. These people love satire, paradox, irony, wit, inventiveness, originality. They like to laugh, always knowingly, as if the club you are inviting them to join is not one just anybody can get into. With groups such as these, often in the humanities, the arts, the culture racket, you flatter their intelligence, knowing that if you can get them on your side you will be rewarded with the best audience of all—though possibly also the meanest—the kind that gets the poetry and point all at once.

Grab the Reader's Attention

If I could stand on my head in an introduction, I would. But since words are all I have, I will do anything necessary to get the reader's attention. I try to use humor to make my point, so I will tell jokes, fairy tales, gossip. I will stick out my tongue at a sacred cow. I will let myself be the butt of the humor. I will ask questions to which there are no clear answers. I will elevate the ridiculous to the sublime or vice versa. I figure that my primary responsibility is to wake up the reader, to offer him or her reality, with the sun, moon, and stars thrown in as well.

Models of introductory paragraphs.

The following introductory paragraphs work, although they are all quite different. The location of the thesis varies, sometimes appearing as the first sentence and sometimes in the more traditional spot, as the last sentence of the introduction. Some paragraphs do not explicitly state the thesis, though the writer's subject and purpose are implied in the meaning of the whole paragraph. The introductions vary widely in tone: some serious, some funny, some sarcastic. A few contain many specific details, whereas others are rather general. Some use anecdote. Still others quote respected authorities. Some use the shock technqiue, overturning, in a moment, a popular, widely accepted view. Some are long; others, short. Some seek primarily to inform; others, to persuade, But all of these introductions have one purpose in common: they seek to woo the reader, to win the person over with an engaging proposal. The thesis is italicized in each introduction.

Example 1:

Despite what the health commercials say, I have never believed that if you've got your health you've got everything. I know people in perfect health who don't have anything.

I know physical wrecks who possess the moon and the stars. You make your choices, and you take your consequences.

The tone is fairly serious, the statements exaggerated. The thesis contradicts the absurd claims made in commercials that sell tonics and elixirs with 40 percent alcohol content. The paragraph is short, but there is some elaboration on the thesis. The writer then goes on, in the supporting paragraphs, to prove that health is not the be-all and end-all of existence, a philosophy directly counter to America's pervasive health obsession.

Example 2:

Everybody knows and fears the bogeyman. He was the fierce fellow of our childhood who would jump out from under the bed and eat us all up if we didn't do right. *Well, unfortunately the bogeyman follows us straight into adulthood, but he gets more dangerous as time goes on.*

The tone is serious, with a touch of playfulness elicited by the image of the bogeyman. The thesis appears in the traditional spot, coming from a general claim made in the first sentence and following a concrete description intended to remind the adult reader of childhood fears. An implicit contrast is set up. The writer will go on to discuss how adult fears differ from childhood fears. The slant is clear: the writer thinks adult fears are more dangerous. The reader has to go on to find out why.

Example 3:

Among my favorite Christmas gifts this year was a potholder on which appeared the words "Eat! Drink! And Be Quiet!" The letters were big, bold, and black. The tone was evocative, poignant, nostalgic. Where had I heard those words before, and what had happened to the world since they last pounded in my ear? The guy who gave me the potholder was a literary fellow, sensitive to tone, allert to allusion. *He grew up, as did I, in the Sit-Up-Straight Age, when Mom operated from her command module and all was emphatic with the world.*

The tone is half-serious, half-funny, evoking the memory of a time when Mom took on the aura of a drill sergeant. The paragraph begins with a specific description of the potholder and the exact quotation appearing on the potholder. Speculative questions follow, questions which will be answered in the essay itself. There is a concrete image of Mom barking orders. The writer's thesis echoes a famous line written by poet Robert Browning: "God's in His heaven, and all's right with the world." The slant is clear: maybe direct commands were a good thing, a clear thing, something to hold on to in an uncertain world. The essay then goes on to show how giving children too many choices might frustrate them and discombobulate their parents. All that remains is to arrange excellent examples of Mother yelling out orders and of the effect of such orders on an indecisive youngster.

Example 4:

On January 1, 1971, cigarette advertising on television ended, the result of a government edict about the hazards of smoking. Since that time, public attitudes toward smoking have changed. The image of the Marlboro man has become tarnished. The feisty, sophisticated woman who had "come a long way, baby," is now merely reckless and decidedly passé. The antismoking campaigns on television now picture puffing pregnant mothers, filthy ashtrays, hacking office workers. The huge campaign against smoking, with its subtle and bold portrayals of smokers as self-indulgent, spineless addicts, proves the power of advertising to sell ideas and images, not simply products. Television has become, for good or ill, an instrument for social, ethical, and psychological change. *Television advertising has come a long way, baby, sacrificing entertainment for stuffy pedantry.*

The banning of cigarette smoking and its impact on public attitudes is only the jumping-off place for the actual thesis of this introduction. The writer surprises by coming out against excessive moralizing and didacticism in television advertising, a medium, after all, that seeks to make major bucks on human weakness and neurosis. The implicit question—Can it be "bad" to be "good"?—can then be supported by examples of tearful celebrity pleas for good causes, of earnest and predictable sermons about physical health, of little moral lessons even about the care of pets and the flossing of teeth.

Example 5:

> Psychologist William James unwittingly rapped the knuckles of many experts and know-it-alls when he said, "Knowledge about a thing is not the thing itself." *The distinction is increasingly important in a society where expertise is perceived as the thing itself and direct experience is trivialized, patronized, or discounted.* We give jobs, raises, and honors for what people have studied, not for what they have done.

Again the writer begins with a quotation from a respected authority but applies a personal interpretation to the Jamesian assertion. The contrast between knowing and doing will be developed throughout the essay. And the bias against those who are merely expert in the theoretical sense is clear. The writer will sympathize with the capable, practical doer, who finishes last because he or she lacks the right credentials, even as the degree-laden expert gets promoted. The last sentence in the paragraph is only an elaboration on the thesis, which appears in the middle of the introduction.

Example 6:

> *I was raised in the Bible Belt and therefore feel quilty whether I've done anything wrong or not.* Perhaps you are one of my kind: we break into a cold sweat when we see a patrolperson conducting a license check on the road ahead; we think we're headed for the slammer when we're ten dollars behind on our Visa payment; we ask permission to walk on the grass, even when there's no sign telling us we can't; we won't let our children pass for twelve at the movie theater when they are really fourteen and short for their ages.

The tone of the thesis is part funny, part sad. The subject, irrational guilt over trivial matters, will be elaborated on in the essay that follows. The writer does not like this guilt over pesky issues and will likely explain why guilt has little to do with right and wrong, being the result of conditioning and environment, not rational cause and effect. Notice, too, that the introductory paragraph is packed with specific details that will set other guilt-ridden readers nodding. They will be relieved to know that a few people remain on the planet who refuse to run a stop sign, even at three o'clock in the morning.

Example 7:

> When was the last time you stood on your head? When you stand on your head, everything changes. Your cheeks sag in reverse, falling toward your forehead. Your eyes bulge. The blood rushes to your face. Your hair stands on end. The lint balls on the floor take on a menacing importance. The smell of the rug permeates your nose. You feel lengthened and reedy.

This introduction leads to an essay about the difficulty and importance of changing perspectives. The paragraph begins with a startling question, particularly since it is addressed to an adult audience. The writer then very specifically describes how odd it feels to stand on one's head. Implicit in the meaning are the awkwardness, the new insight, and the strange sensations that come from changing perspectives on oneself. The thesis does not appear until the second paragraph, but surely the reader stays to discover why a grown-up would be standing on his head.

◆

Activities

1. Go to the essays of Montaigne, Francis Bacon, Ralph Waldo Emerson, G. K. Chesterton, E. M. Forster, Max Beerbohm, James Baldwin, Elizabeth Hardwick, Nora Ephron, Annie Dillard, or others of your choice. Select several introductory paragraphs, and study the following aspects: tone, placement of thesis, use of rhetorical questions and direct quotations, number of details and facts. If these introductory paragraphs generate ideas of your own, make a few notes for future help in creating your own essays. Often, good ideas for essays come simply from reacting strongly to what someone else has written.

2. Now study several introductory paragraphs written by newspaper columnists, noting differences between these in-

troductions and those of the above essayists. Also, contrast the introductory paragraphs of columnists with article introductions written by news reporters.

3. Pretend that you are a talk-show host, about to introduce your favorite celebrity. Write a one-paragraph introduction about the person who is coming on stage, but try to avoid conventional television hype: "super," "fantastic," and "a lovely lady," "the hottest singer to hit Las Vegas since Wayne Newton,"—you know what I mean.

4. Write a one-paragraph anecdote with an inherent message, something that would suggest a thesis without your actually stating it. Can your friends deduce your major point and develop a thesis that corresponds to the implicit meaning in your introductory paragraph? Try the experiment.

5. You have a 10-year-old daughter, son, niece, or nephew—or perhaps know the child of a close friend. Imagine that you have been entrusted with the great responsibility of giving this youngster the facts about sex. Now, in one paragraph, gently introduce the subject.

Develop the middle.

Where the introduction entices, challenges, makes a claim, takes a position, and tries to make a good impression, the middle mediates and supports. No matter how flashy, clever, or impressive the introduction, no real change can occur and no new insight can be gained unless the middle is as solid and patient, calm and thorough, sensible and factual as a negotiator in the middle of a union strike. Slow and easy, specific and logical, win the point for the writer. The middle is, after all, that long stretch between birth and death, and only what you put into it gives the beginning and ending meaning.

The middle of the essay contains three or four miniature essays (paragraphs), with a minithesis (topic sentence) for each paragraph. Here, you support your general statements with the facts: one general, three or eight specifics; another general, four or five specifics. Every general needs a whole battalion of troops to keep a war going. What would the world be if one general did the fighting and fifty-thousand soldiers sat back giving orders? Politicians start wars. Generals plan wars. Thousands of foot soldiers fight them. Your facts, details, illustrations, anecdotes, footnotes, and quotations are the foot soldiers of your essay, marching your grand thesis (a five-star general) to its happy, victorious conclusion.

It is difficult, though not impossible, to make the middle as fascinating as the beginning and ending. Journalists, for example, when assigned such drab topics as rezoning, make liberal use of quotations. Or perhaps the editor gives the middle punch by making it short and unduly snappy. *Reader's Digest* enjoys huge popularity because the middle is scrunched up, packed down, tightened, making way for crisp beginnings and tidy endings.

The Dependable Middle

The middle tends to be, well, unmemorable. When I was studying one of those books about developing good study habits, I learned that I should study in 15-minute segments. I thought the frequently scheduled breaks were for trips to the refrigerator for a cold chicken leg. I was wrong. Experts reported that most people remember beginnings and endings better than they remember middles. The more breaks I took, the more beginnings and endings and, therefore, the greater my retention.

But over the writing years, I've developed greater respect for the middle. In an essay, the middle is often not flashy, not sassy, not glib. But in the middle, the quiet, steady work of proving the truth of our assertions goes on. We call the middle of the essay "the body," and the body is not especially lovely. But it holds up our hearts, souls, minds. It keeps on walking, carrying us where we need to go.

A two-page essay will not have a very fat middle, but it will surely be fatter than the introduction and conclusion. An inadequately developed, skinny middle is both boring and vague. If you have managed to keep your readers' attention throughout the introduction, it would be a shame to lose them in the body of the essay, after they have come to know you. *An inadequately developed middle fails to fulfill the promise of the thesis.*

Suppose, for example, that you create the following thesis:

> The feminist movement has left the American male confused, disoriented, and lacking in confidence. He does not know where to turn, how to act, what role to play.

Now suppose the body that supports that thesis is as follows:

> In social situations, for example, men don't know whether to open doors for women, let women go first, pick up the tab for women, or take the lead in the romance department.
>
> Then, too, men feel threatened by the possibility that women will enter traditionally male fields and take away the best jobs. Also, fathers are confused about how much of the child care responsibility they should assume. And in sexual matters, who should initiate? The world has changed too much and too fast for men, and they are depressed, anxious, and angry.
>
> So, in summary, men have become confused and disoriented because of the women's movement and its effect on male roles and identity.

The above example shows how wide the gap may be between the assertion and its proof. Whether or not readers agree with the thesis, the writer's job is to convince them that there may be at least some validity to the idea, even if total agreement is impossible. But the inadequately developed, poorly organized middle in this example is not convincing. Here are the difficulties:

1. Every sentence is general.

2. No concrete images, details, or facts appear.

3. No quotations are used, either from experts or from male friends and family members of the writer.

4. The paragraphs contain several possible areas for consideration rather than one central idea *per* paragraph.

5. No single area of consideration is thoroughly explored.

6. The reader, therefore, is as confused as the writer claims the American male to be.

What would improve the essay?

Each of the body paragraphs could discuss one central idea: possibly the American male's feelings in the work place, in social situations, in the family. Or perhaps the topic sentences could deal with these headings: males in the bedroom, males in the work place, males as fathers. Or maybe the writer could single out one aspect of the male identity crisis, writing the entire essay on confusion about etiquette or about sex roles or about professional conflicts.

Then, having settled on three or four central ideas or one central idea with three or four dimensions, the writer could get down to specifics. The writer must make the reader *see* the male in action; *feel* the male's pain; *discover* the male's perception. What gave the writer the idea of writing about this problem in the first place? Did he or she read an article on the subject? Why not cite it? Did he or she have a conversation about this subject? Why not quote from it? Did he or she personally experience the conflict and confusion? Why not recount the experience? Did he or she notice some revealing statistic about this subject? Why not include it?

Though inadequate development is certainly the major difficulty among student writers, problems may also result from excessive development. The optimal word is "adequate." But some students, having been exhorted time and again to be more specific, to include "lots" of details and facts, may make their paragraphs fat for no good purpose. The reader is stuffed, not merely satisfied. The irrational piling up of information solely to achieve the "required" paragraph length is as much a flaw as being too general. The good writer chooses only details that are relevant, only the portion of the quotation that is pertinent, only the fact that best supports the assertion. Otherwise, the middle scatters in all directions, and the reader feels bombarded with more than he or she ever wanted to know about male insecurity.

Inadequate development places too much responsibility on the audience to read between the lines, to supply logical connections, to imagine situations that might prove the thesis. On the other hand, excessive development is an insult to the reader. In such cases, the writer does not trust the reader to grasp the meaning with one or two good examples. Also, the reader is expected to sort out relevant examples without any clues to aid her. But whether the development of the middle is inadequate or far more than adequate, the writer's laziness comes through. The writer has abdicated all responsibility either for making his or her assertion believable or for selecting among several proofs the ones that best serve his or her purposes. What to include, what to omit, what to skim over, what to elaborate on—those are the writer's responsibilities, not the reader's.

Model for an adequately developed middle

The following essay on dread and anticipation contains a fat middle, eight paragraphs. The middle could be tightened or expanded by omitting weaker arguments and combining others under a broader topic sentence. Each paragraph in the middle contains a topic sentence that, like the thesis, indicates the main idea of the paragraph, the writer's angle or slant, and the topic of the paragraph. The general topic sentence is followed by several specific examples or elaborations.

Inadequate development in the middle of the essay nearly always results in malnourishment for the reader. He or she is starved for facts, proofs, illustrations—all the nutritious stuff that makes for a healthy, muscled reader's understanding of the essay.

So you can see how important the proportion of general to specific is, and how best to develop the middle, each paragraph is followed by a short commentary. But though the essay is broken up, it is printed in its entirety, with thesis and topic sentences in italics.

DREAD AND ANTICIPATION

Of all the emotional states available to me, I have the lowest opinion of dread and anticipation. Sadness, anger, boredom, happiness, even depression, I can handle. Just let me be free of dread and anticipation.

> *The introductory paragraph leaves no doubt about the writer's attitude. The second and third sentences provide background and emphasis for the opening thesis. The reader might nod that dread is bad, but he or she would likely read on to discover what is wrong with happy anticipation and what connection it could possibly have to dread.*

First Paragraph of the Body:

Some people think these two are opposites, but I'm not fooled. Though one looks forward with joy to magical moments and one shudders, in advance, over all the awful disasters that could befall us, they are really kin. They may not look alike, but they are the offspring of unreality. And the damage they do is much worse than anything life has to offer. I know people who have been full of dread all their lives to whom nothing bad has happened. I know people fraught with happy anticipation to whom nothing good has happened.

> *This middle paragraph defines dread and anticipation and establishes their close relationship, calling them "the offspring of unreality." The writer heightens their awfulness by contrasting them to reality. Two examples follow which, though referring to some people in general, nevertheless mention them in a very specific context.*

Second paragraph of the body:

Dread and anticipation wear us out for no good reason. We have to live through what actually happens to us and what doesn't happen as well. And, echoing the fearful Hamlet, the times are "out of joint": dread and anticipation always last much longer than the events that inspire them. I spent six months anticipating a wedding that was over in seven minutes. I've been known to spend a year dreading a speech that was over in twenty minutes.

> *The writer makes a general assertion followed by two good reasons why dread and anticipation wear us out. The writer then gives two very specific examples to support the assertion. Also, the direct quotation from Shakespeare's* Hamlet *gives concreteness, vitality. The reader can picture Hamlet, the prince of Dread.*

Third paragraph of the body:

Then, too, all the time we are dreading and anticipating, we are not living. People may be able to prune the azaleas and yell at the neighborhood children at the same time, but they can't do two really hard things at once. Living in reality and living in the imagination are both hard. Living in the past, present, and future simultaneously is impossible. The effort will either give us a crick in the neck or kill us.

> *The "then, too" is a signal to the reader that another reason is about to appear. And that reason, "not living," recalls the idea in the introduction—that dread and anticipation are the offspring of unreality. Proofs follow, with concrete images and details— pruning azaleas, yelling at neighborhood children, crick in the*

neck. The writer elaborates on the topic sentence, making clear
what is meant by "not living."

Fourth paragraph of the body:

   I used to lie awake for three nights in a row, alternately dreading
and anticipating having company for dinner. Now I try to live out
whatever's happening right up to the second something else
starts happening. For example, as the dinner guests are ringing
the doorbell, I am filling the ice bucket and tossing the boned
chicken breasts into the microwave oven.

> *The writer is getting more specific, even introducing details into*
> *the topic sentence. But the topic sentence is nonetheless a*
> *concept, an assertion, and requires proof. The writer uses herself*
> *as an example, describing a social evening and using details the*
> *reader can visualize—not just guests coming in, but guests*
> *ringing the doorbell; not just fixing drinks, but filling the ice*
> *bucket; not just food, but boned chicken breasts; not just oven,*
> *but microwave oven. These details make the picture clear to the*
> *reader.*

Fifth paragraph of the body:

   Some people are especially plagued by dread. I have already
passed the habit of dread to my daughter. She dreads everything
way in advance. I have never known her to settle comfortably
into the present moment. She has already asked me to write a
note for her to be excused from physical education classes for
the next school year. I told her I was sorry, but I wouldn't make
a single move to find a sharpened pencil and a scrap of paper
until one minute before next year. And that's that.

> *Here the writer moves away from her own habit of dread to other*
> *people's: specifically, her daughter's. The paragraph recounts a*
> *very specific incident, filled with concrete details, that proves how*
> *full of dread the daughter has become. The indirect quotation at*
> *the end of the paragraph evokes the tone and image of firm*
> *parents.*

Sixth paragraph of the body:

   Perhaps more dangerous than the habit of dread is the habit of
anticipation children pick up from their parents. Adults are bad

about looking forward to the weekend, to a raise, to retirement, to when their ship will come in. Parents set a very bad example in thinking so much about the future. Children would be better off learning contemplation, which is a healthy habit and goes well with the present. Anticipation is the enemy of the present moment, stirring the stomach and raising the sights to a far, often inaccessible horizon.

> *Mentioning the daughter and the school physical education program has provided a transition to the next assertion, the effect of parents on childish anticipation. The paragraph centers on parents and children and includes typical adult anticipation, plus specific details about the effect of living too much in the future.*

Seventh paragraph of the body:

In the spring, most of the nation's children are full of happy anticipation for summer vacation. They are strongly encouraged in this bad habit by school administrators and teachers, all of whom are playing a game called "Counting the Days Until School Is Out." It is death to the present moment. By the time vacation arrives, everyone is exhausted from anticipating it, and the vacation isn't half as much fun as the children expected. One week into summer vacation, many children start whining about how bored they are. This emphasis on summer is very bad, lasting even into adulthood. I was thirty before I recovered my happy perspective on fall, winter, and spring. I managed only recently to teach myself to appreciate Monday, which, to the naked eye, is indistinguishable from Friday: same sun, same sky, same twittering birds.

> *The writer continues with the idea of children and the bad habit of anticipation, using summer vacation as an example. Educators (parents in absentia) get the blame here. The writer then returns to the effect of her childhood school indoctrination on attitudes toward Monday and Friday, seasons. Again, there are several concrete images.*

Eighth paragraph of the body:

Dread and anticipation always distort reality, yanking us out of the solid present and binding us to old fears of a dead past or tossing us, willy-nilly, into an uncertain future. Unfortunately, the concepts of heaven and hell have taught us to neglect the present. We've been so busy anticipating heaven and dreading hell that we haven't noticed how abundantly the present moment supplies both. I once watched an old man spend his last earthly hours berating himself for having been a sinner and dreading his punishment in hell. He couldn't see the sun out his window or the circle of loving relatives gathered around his bed.

> *The essay is beginning to wind down, with reiterations of ideas expressed in several paragraphs. Yet the concrete details and specific examples continue.*

Conclusion:

Only reality can annihilate feelings of dread and anticipation. The present is truly remarkable, offering a sturdy system of checks and balances, an instant reference point, for the wilder flights of the imagination. The present has choices, whereas dread and anticipation, largely compulsive, drive you to terrible places you'd rather not go while you sit helplessly in the back seat, fearing your sad fate or awaiting your miraculous rescue. The minute that is right in front of you is the one to live in. And you can drive there any time you want to, not once getting lost.

> *The writer returns to the original mention of unreality, only this time the emphasis is on reality and its charms. Even in the conclusion, the writer creates a concrete image, evoking the earlier discussions of how children and adults spoil the present moment.*

◆

Activities

1. *Newsweek* runs a regular feature, "My Turn," in which famous and unfamous folks express their views in essays of about 1,000 words. Select one of these essays on a subject that interests you. Locate the thesis statement. Now, look at all the supporting paragraphs, and write down the topic sentence of each one. Then, under each topic sentence, jot down the author's proofs, examples, facts, and figures. Note the proportion of general to specific, and the different types of proofs. Does the author convince you of the truth or validity of his or her position? Why or why not? If not, how could you improve the essay? What examples, facts, personal

experiences could you provide that would be more convincing than the author's own?

2. Here is a topic sentence outline. Regardless of whether you agree with the thesis, seek proofs and examples, facts and statistics, anecdotes and personal experiences to support it. Place your proofs under each topic sentence of the three body paragraphs (a–c). Be certain to include more than one proof, preferably three or four.

    Thesis: A straight-A average in high school is no longer any guarantee that a student will gain admission to the college of his or her choice.

    a. Grade inflation has made the A student as common as garden-variety daisies.

    b. The definition of "education" has subtly changed and expanded, and book learning is no longer the sole criterion for judging a student's success in college.

    c. College admissions people look these days for qualities other than excellent academic records in prospective students, ranging from leadership ability to special talents in sports, music, and art.

    Using the topic sentence outline, document these assertions with personal experiences; library sources, and interviews with faculty and administrators, with students who have been admitted to colleges with low academic averages, and with students who have not been admitted to college despite impeccable academic credentials. Arrange your findings under the appropriate topic sentences.

3. Topic sentences provide better paragraph control when they are concepts or theories, not facts. It is difficult to elaborate on a fact. There is a tremendous difference between saying "Economic inflation is an increase in currency and credit beyond the available goods, thereby resulting in a sharp increase in prices" and saying "Economic inflation is causing a steady decline in the American standard of living." The first statement sounds pretty fancy, but it is not disputable. It is a definition. It is factual at all times and in all situations. The latter assertion is arguable. Even though inflation is on the rise, some Americans are enjoying a rise in their standard of living. In other words, the second statement starts up a conversation with the reader, whereas the first is a dead end. Learning to recognize the differences between

facts and concepts will help you to develop better thesis statements and topic sentences. Would the following sentences serve better as topic sentences or as proofs and supports? Why?

a. Every fall, I have a yard sale.

b. A perfect résumé does not provide automatic entry into the job of your choice.

c. In *Aspects of the Novel*, E. M. Forster says that "the fundamental aspect of the novel is its story-telling aspect."

d. The Nile is the longest river in the world.

e. People who fear heights are suffering from acrophobia.

f. Abraham Lincoln's mother, Nancy Hanks Lincoln, was an illegitimate child.

g. Dramatist George Bernard Shaw believed that the perfect love affair is "one conducted entirely by post."

h. Margaret Mead's reputation as an anthropologist has declined in recent years.

i. The thirty-second commercial is a high art form, worthy of respect and attention.

4. Select one of the following quotations to serve as your thesis. Then develop three middle paragraphs to support it, each with a topic sentence as the first sentence of the paragraph.

Where ignorance is bliss, / 'Tis folly to be wise.

—Thomas Gray

Accordingly we conclude that the appropriate age for marriage is about the eighteenth year for girls and for men the thirty-seventh plus or minus.

—Aristotle

The creative process must be explored not as the product of sickness, but as representing the highest degree of emotional health, as the expression of normal people in the act of actualizing themselves.

—Rollo May

An individual who has lived close to nature, on a farm, for instance, knows that "natural" man was never in nature; he had to fight nature, at the cost of his own spontaneity and, indeed, his own humanity.

—Joyce Carol Oates

Everything you are and do from fifteen to eighteen is what you are and will do through life.

—F. Scott Fitzgerald

Summarize and conclude.

If you have ever been in an argument, you know the great satisfaction that derives from having the last word—and of making it a snappy, clever one. You imagine yourself making a dramatic exit from a formerly fine romance. You stride toward the door. You turn. You sling your trenchcoat over your shoulder; you flick the ash from your cigarette; and you say. . . . Well, the curtain falls on your great line, because crisp conclusions are nothing when they are out of context. But if the glamorous movie stars can deliver the perfect clincher, the apt summation, so can you. Just as you do not want to flub your final retort in the scenes played out in your imagination, so you do not want to fall flat on your face at the end of a fine essay. You want to have the last word with the reader, and you want him or her to remember it.

Good conclusions are crucial to the impact of an essay. They are also cunning, canny, candid, and concise. Writers have great respect for the artful and appropriate conclusion, primarily because the last word is what the reader takes away, stores up, and recalls. Comedians depend on punch lines to leave the audience laughing. Lawyers depend on the summation of the case to sway the jurors in the client's favor. Even children, engaged in harmless bickering, will declare the victor to be the one who gets in the last word: Did not! Did too! Did not! Did too! The one who speaks last wins.

You have been studying how to introduce a subject and how to develop the body of the essay, the convincing middle. Now you must learn how to conclude and summarize, if only to guarantee that the point you tried so hard to support and defend will stick in the reader's mind, will bring lasting change, real insight.

Some people believe that a good essay comes full circle. They glibly assert, "Tell 'em what you're going to say. Then tell 'em. Then tell 'em what you've said." I disagree. The pattern is too simple, too pat. In following it, the writer underestimates his or her own powers of interpretation and understanding, and the reader's as well. To say, simply, that a "good" conclusion consists only of a restatement of thesis is to carry the reader back to where he or she started. It suggests that nothing has happened, nothing has been learned.

The final paragraph of your essay, of course, will summarize and reiterate. But it will also carry you to a new place in your thinking. The most effective conclusions are bigger, more profound, more dramatic than what you originally stated in your thesis.

So how do you gracefully exit from an essay? What goes into the last word that will make it memorable?

First, the reader will need signals that the essay is winding down. Some obvious signals—and less sophisticated ones—are transitional words or phrases: "and finally," "in conclusion," "to sum up." But these devices are artificial. The sense of winding down must come, rather, in the content and tone of the final paragraphs, not in arbitrary words of farewell. The business of concluding begins *before* the final paragraph: perhaps in the transitional sentence leading to the last paragraph; perhaps in a widening of focus; perhaps in a decrease in the number of facts, details, and examples that packed your solid middle. The meaning broadens as the specific decreases. Introductions and conclusions are more general than middles. But they are not vague. In the conclusion, therefore, you begin to address the implications and applications of what you have been proving in the middle. And the astute reader feels the change in technique and tone.

Second, the reader will also want to have his or her memory refreshed, but only slightly. After all, an essay is usually short. The reader will not have forgotten, over six or eight paragraphs, the thesis and major ideas in the supporting paragraphs. But you will want, nonetheless, to show the reader the courtesy of brushing up the thesis by offering a variation on your earlier assertion. Sometimes students wrongly assume that the restatement of thesis means precisely repeating the earlier assertion.

But much has happened in between. What began as an unsup-ported assertion has now become, if the middle has done its work, a reality or at least a possibility to the reader. The restate-ment of thesis, taken too literally, can, in effect, insult the read-er. For example, if you began by writing

Statistics refute the notion that women are bad drivers,

you might be tempted to conclude,

In conclusion, it is clear that statistics refute the notion that women are bad drivers.

Of course, the above restatement of thesis is so bland that the reader will leave the essay yawning. A more sophisticated reiter-ation will restate the point even as it expands and broadens the original premise. So instead you might conclude,

Reports of women's ineptness behind the wheel are greatly exaggerated.

Or you might write,

Women, then, have shown themselves to be among Ameri-ca's safest drivers.

Or,

The remarkable safety record of women drivers shatters stereotypes and might even be the beginning of the end of other myths about women and machines.

This last reiteration recalls the original premise and broadens the implications of the assertion as well.

Third, the reader will seek a psychological feeling of comple-tion, of wholeness. A good writer does not simply stop writing; he or she concludes, tying up loose ends, presenting the reader with the gift of a tidily wrapped package in which rests the the-sis, the support of the thesis, the impact of the thesis. Nobody likes messy, untidy endings, whether in writing or life. Is there a nagging question remaining? Is there a tiny gap in the argument or defense? A single phrase might serve, in the conclusion, to close that gap. The artful concluder might admit, even as he or she reiterates the major point, for example, that all the facts are not in. The case is not necessarily closed. And the reader will appreciate the writer's honesty. After an essay in which you have supported the current notion among doctors that a bland diet has little effect on curing ulcers, you might, in the conclusion, interject a word of caution, without sacrificing credibility with the reader. For example, you might write,

> Though most doctors have lately abandoned bland diets in their treatment of ulcers, choosing, instead, to recommend drugs such as Tagamet and small, frequent feedings of *any* food, the public might be wise to proceed with caution. Common sense, not slavish obedience to expert medical opinion, might be the wiser course for ulcer patients. After all, if you wouldn't fill a baby's tender stomach with three-alarm chili, would you dare heap that spicy abuse on your bleeding ulcer? Even if a warm bowl of oatmeal doesn't effect a physical cure, the food of childhood can perhaps go a long way toward soothing your tender psyche—and maybe your stomach as well.

Fourth, though the conclusion may expand the meaning and implications of your original assertion, it does not introduce brand-new material, information. *The conclusion is solely a place for reiteration and summation.* The reader would be disconcerted and confused to read, in the concluding paragraphs of an essay about the safety record of women drivers, an assertion regarding the driving habits of adolescents. That is another essay. Nor would a reader, having been carried through a persuasive essay about the need for more nutritious school lunches, know what to do with a sudden and inexplicable reference to better toilet facilities in schools, better fitness programs in schools, or better courses in nutrition in schools. In the conclusion, you are climbing down from the soapbox. Your reader would be very surprised, just as he or she is politely applauding your performance, to see you climb back on the soapbox and deliver another treatise on a related subject, throw in one more fact, tackle a new issue.

Fifth, the last sentence of the conclusion, the very final word, should be as dramatic, snappy, clever, crisp, and memorable as you can make it. Can you elicit one final guffaw? Can you manage to give the reader a goosebump or two? Can you leave him or her nodding vigorously? Or, at the very least, can you make the reader say, a little impressed, "Not bad. Not bad at all"? How do you achieve these heightened effects in the final sentence? You might try an anecdote. You might end with a provocative question. You might use an apt quotation from some famous or unfamous person. You might use an effective metaphor or simile. You might end with a very short, crisp sentence, perhaps of only three or four words. Or you might stumble over the perfect final word or phrase in the regions of your own mind. But the time you spend on your final sentence will be worth the effort. Try various approaches. Tinker with the phrasing. Revise the last sentences until, like Archimedes, upon his discovery of the principle of gravity, you can say, "Eureka!"

The following excerpts demonstrate the subtle differences between introducing a subject and concluding it. Though the middles are missing, you may deduce from the opening thesis and its summation the direction and emphasis the writer takes through the convincing middle.

Introducing an essay about heat:

> Like everyone else, I am very much a prisoner of whatever is bearing down on me at the exact moment I'm in: meetings, partings, tantrums, unfinished tasks, social blunders, bills. And what is bearing down on me at this exact moment is heat. I promise that you're not about to hear another whew-ain't-it-hot lament. There's enough of that kind of empty talk going around. I think, rather, that heat is a fascinating subject, with waves and motions, illusions and allusions, all its own.

The last sentence is the thesis. The essay goes on to analyze heat, to give examples of heat, to discuss the effects of heat on the imagination, to contrast heat with the cold indifference of winter. The essay leads to an odd conclusion. The writer parodies a famous poem by Robert Frost. Though the thesis is not restated exactly, the writer nonetheless is in favor of heat.

Concluding an essay about heat:

I have a summer poem for Robert Frost.

> Some say the world will end in fire,
> Some say in ice.
> From what I've tasted of desire
> I hold with those who love July.
> But if I had to perish twice,
> I think I know enough of hate
> To say that for destruction
> Winter's nice
> And would suffice.

This conclusion is certainly unusual, but the element of surprise is an excellent way to leave the reader both convinced and entertained. The conclusion certainly affirms heat. It does not introduce new material. And it sums up. But it also strives for originality and freshness in concluding.

Introducing an essay about fun:

Fun, a rare jewel, is hard to have. But somewhere along the line, people got the modern idea that fun was there for the asking, that people *deserved* fun. "Was it fun?" became the question that overshadowed all other questions—good questions, like was it moral, was it kind, was it honest, was it beneficial, was it generous, was it necessary, was it selfless.

The introduction puts the issue of fun in context, after first asserting the thesis in the opening sentence. The writer will then go on to prove that Americans have tried to grab fun, to have more fun than life actually offers, to cheapen fun by making it a daily necessity, not an occasional luxury. The writer asserts, in the essay, that fun feelings are not products that big bucks can purchase, not emotions that are linked to big occasions, holidays, vacation trips.

Concluding an essay about fun:

It occurred to me, while I was sitting around waiting for the fun to begin, that not much is and that I should tell you just in case you're worried about your fun capacity. Fun cannot be caught like a virus, trapped like an animal. It is a mystery. When fun comes in on little dancing feet, you probably won't be expecting it. It may even come on a Tuesday.

I remember one day, long ago, on which I had an especially good time. Pammy Lou and I walked to the drug store on Saturday morning. We were twelve (fun ages). She got her Bit-O'-Honey. I got my M & Ms. We started back to her house. I was going to spend the night. We had the whole Saturday in front of us. We had plenty of candy. It was a long way to Pammy Lou's house, but every time we got weary, Pammy Lou would put her hand over her eyes, scan the horizon like a sailor, and say, "Oughta reach home by nightfall," at which point the two of us would laugh until we couldn't stand it another minute. Then, after we got calm, she'd say it again. You should have been there. It was the kind of day and friendship that made me deeply regret having to grow up. It was fun.

The writer concludes with an anecdote that carries within it a definition of kid fun, the kind that adults are always trying to grab but have lost the capacity for. The conclusion reiterates the major points of the essay: the simplicity, rarity, pricelessness of genuine fun; the fun that comes when it chooses and always naturally, not when it is manufactured, bought, forced.

Introducing an essay about being specific:

When English teachers get down on their knees at night, they pray for freshman composition students who will be specific. They are smart to pray: any sensible person knows that heaven is concrete and hell is abstract.

After introducing the subject—the importance of being specific—and putting the importance into a context, the writer then goes on to contrast the general and the specific, to explain why people more often tend to generalize and need to be encouraged to be specific. The essay deals primarily with the importance of being specific in good writing and refers to Dr. Samuel Johnson's view of the role of the poet as it contrasts with William Blake's view. Dr. Johnson says that a good poet "examines

the species" as a whole. Blake says, in contrast, that "to generalize is to be an idiot." The writer, of course, agrees with Blake.

Concluding an essay about being specific:

The specific is, after all, the only source of the original.
That's why no two geniuses, works of art, conversations,
people, events, and streaks of the tulip are alike. But plenty
of bad poems, bad speeches, bad novels, bad theories, and
bad people are.

The conclusion alludes to a line from Dr. Johnson, namely
that poets should not "number the streaks of a tulip." The reiteration comes in the first sentence, with an expansion of meaning.
The writer has sought to prove that being specific is more than
heavenly. It is the only source of the original. And the last sentence, if the reader has followed the argument, clinches the matter. What is "bad" about books, people, events is their dreary
predictability, their sameness. And that, of course, is what is
"bad" about many conclusions.

◆

Questions for discussion

1. Think of several of your favorite jokes, remembering the
   punch lines. What do the punch lines have in common?
   What would happen to the quality or hilarity of the joke if
   you changed even one word, altered the order of the words?
   In what ways is a good conclusion like a good punch line?

2. The television commercial is remarkable for containing, in
   30 seconds or 2 minutes, a beginning, middle, and ending.
   Since the advertiser wants to have the last word with the
   viewer, analyze the various methods of concluding commercials. How does the commercial give the viewer a sense of
   wholeness, completion? Is the thesis restated? What about
   the snappy final word? Can you remember four or five of the
   last sentences in your favorite commercials? Why do you remember them?

3. How might the conclusion of a novel or story differ from the
   conclusion of an essay? Study several endings you have
   found memorable, both in fiction and nonfiction. What do
   these endings have in common? Why do they continue to
   haunt you?

Activities

1. Choose one of your earlier essays and revise the concluding paragraph or paragraphs several times. First, experiment with an anecdote that might round off your essay. Then, experiment with enlarging on the meaning, implications, and applications of your thesis even as you restate it. Finally, try writing a conclusion that uses a direct quotation, employs figurative language, or contains speculative questions that leave the reader thinking.

2. Write a one- or two-paragraph summary of a short story, poem, article, or movie of your choice. Recap the main points, restate the central thesis, address the wider implications of that thesis, and exit with a snappy final sentence. You will, of course, need to study and thoroughly understand the work under consideration before you begin attempting such a summary. If you cannot find the point, you will not be able to relay it to the reader. If you cannot imagine summing up a book or movie in a few sentences, check the *New Yorker, Time,* or *Newsweek* for proof that it can be done.

CHAPTER

5

Developing the Essay

As you sift through the wealth of information you have gathered to support or defend your thesis, you may notice certain organizational patterns emerging. Your thesis may appear to be contrasting or comparing two related items, events, or people. You may, upon examining your notes, see that certain areas of facts or memories fall into categories or groups. Perhaps you have a sense that the material lends itself well to a step-by-step approach. Maybe you are trying to define your terms, establish a causal relationship between one event and a set of prior circumstances, or isolate parts of a whole. You already know that your essay will have an introduction, body, and conclusion. But its interior life will need a structure as well. And these patterns or inner structures will provide additional strength and order for your burgeoning ideas.

Your decisions about the organizational pattern of your essay will begin in the planning stage and proceed throughout the writing. In a sense, you do not choose a pattern. Rather, a pattern chooses you. The process is flowing and organic, not static and artificial. Indeed, you may use more than one pattern in a single essay. But you will develop your essay with greater confidence once you have studied each developmental mode individually.

Choose among essay types.

All the essays you write will fall broadly into four categories or types: description, narration, information (or exposition), and persuasion or argumentation. Though you will seldom write an essay that is purely one type or another, you will find the categories useful for determining your overall approach in relation to your purpose, your thesis. Description and narration will best serve your writing purposes when you are trying to show, not tell; to represent the world as it exists, not to interpret, alter, theorize, philosophize, or convert. However, when your primary purpose is to inform, convince, or interpret, you will be operating in the latter two modes: exposition and persuasion. Description and narration record life as it goes by. Information and persuasion clarify and comment on the life passing by.

Here is a topic finding its voice and purpose within the four essay types.

Description.   You describe a typical commercial street, the "strip," on a typical Saturday night in your hometown, where teenagers gather to cruise, gossip, make connections.

Narration.   You recount the events on the night you cruised the strip, feeling very lusty and adventuresome, and found yourself beside the girl (or boy) of your fantasy in the front seat of a Porsche.

Information.   You explain the rituals and rites of dating and mating on the strip—what is acceptable, what is unacceptable; how you succeed or fail to make promising contacts; why this Saturday-night routine is so important to the adolescent culture.

Persuasion.   You convince adult citizens to accept this adolescent ritual as a normal rite of passage to adulthood, to freedom, to personal responsibility; you make a plea for greater compassion toward teenagers from the police, the city council, the business people who seek to prohibit such cruising and carousing in these gathering places; perhaps you make a case for a taxpayer-subsidized "youth club" that would give teenagers a safe, attractive setting in which to meet and greet each other, thereby getting young people off the streets and out of the parking lots without depriving them of their right to socialize.

Choose among methods of development.

When you write essays of description or narration, you are primarily conveying your version of reality to a reader. You are helping the reader to see, hear, taste, touch, and smell your world, or you are offering the reader "true" accounts, in chronological order, of what happens in your world. Description and narration are reports rendered as accurately as you can deliver them. But with informing and persuading, you are moving away from the role of reporter and chronicler and into the role of explainer, interpreter, convincer, analyzer. And within these two types of essays, you will need to develop strategies for informing and/or persuading, such as *classifying, defining, giving examples, explaining processes, considering causes and effects,* and *analyzing.* These methods of development lend credibility to your information, carry your point, win your argument, and produce insight or change in the reader. They can help you organize your material, give you ways to write about complex topics and controversial issues, and steady the motions of your thought on the page.

When you develop the middle of your essay, you will surely employ one, several, or all of the following methods:

1. When you *classify,* you will be grouping and typing related people, events, ideas, customs, animals, or things on the basis of one consideration. Under the category of "students," for example, you will be grouping the students perhaps on the basis of academic achievement, perhaps on the basis of socioeconomic levels, perhaps on the basis of dating and mating habits.

2. When you *define,* you will be explaining how a term or idea differs from other terms or ideas within a similar category. When you begin, for example, to define "confidence," you must first explain how it differs from "arrogance," "pride," and "egotism." You will then further refine the definition of "confidence" by placing it in certain contexts, by explaining its denotative (literal and objective) meanings and its connotative (figurative and subjective) meanings. You have succeeded in your task of defining when the reader has an unmistakable understanding of and appreciation for what *you* mean when you use this particular term.

3. When you *give examples,* you will be illustrating, providing proof or support by giving telling instances of what you mean by what you are asserting. The outrageous and feisty assertion that the only people who seem to know how to raise children are those who do not have any or who have

failed with the ones they have might be supported by a bar-
rage of examples fired from your own life and experience:
the judgmental and advice-giving aunt or uncle whose expertise on children is inversely proportional to their willing-
ness to tell you how to raise yours; the celibate priest or nun
who piously intones remedies for family crises; the barely
pubescent social worker who has never diapered a squalling
baby but presumes to advise you on safety pin techniques
and day-care decisions; the parents who have produced a
hell-raiser, an addict, and a psychotic but nonetheless offer
"tips" on raising civic-minded, ethical, responsible children.

4. When you *explain a process*, you carry a reader through a
   procedure—whether step by step or by general stages—explaining where to begin, how to advance, and where to stop.
   Though the arrangement may be sequential or chronological, it differs from narration: narration recounts only a non-
   recurring incident, whereas process explains the steps to follow or stages to advance through time and time again.

5. When you *compare and contrast*, you say how two related
   things, people, ideas, or places are alike and how they are
   different. Generally, though not always, you first stress the
   similarities so you have a basis for noting the differences.
   The purpose, of course, is understanding and insight. Comparing and contrasting give reality to the unknown by setting it against what is known. If the reader has never flown
   on a discount commercial airline, you first compare the services offered by major airlines versus discount carriers, and
   you then discuss the differences in quality of service, prices,
   schedules, and safety. Or you may compare and contrast on
   only one or two bases, not several, perhaps keeping a discussion of the similarities and differences in tent camping and
   trailer camping only to comfort or convenience, or only to
   cost and safety.

6. When you *consider causes and effects*, you ponder the consequences (effects) of various actions or explore the reasons for
   various actions (causes). Usually, you proceed from known
   effects back to causes; however, you may also predict the future effects of present actions. Most actions, therefore, can
   go both ways, being either causes or effects, depending on
   your perspective. If you smoke, for example, you might analyze why you began—making the habit an effect of certain
   traits in your personality, of tactics in advertising, of local
   custom. Or you might predict (though the predictions have,

of late, become certainties) the probable consequences of smoking with respect to your physical health, making smoking the cause of future health problems.

7. When you *analyze*, you are dividing the whole into parts for insight into how the whole functions. This method of development is also sometimes called division or partition. Just as you take apart an engine to see how it works, so you may take apart a novel, a human body, a theory, a personality to see how it works. After the dissection, judgment may enter in, but not until you have first done the work of looking at those parts and seeing how they fit, what they do separately and as part of the whole.

Classify a group of related items.

Americans love to classify. We put people, animals, political parties, personalities, flaws, levels of intelligence, literary works, movies, and television shows into categories. Why are we not happy until we have everybody and everything safely slotted, pigeonholed, labeled, typed? Because we hope, in the categorizing, to make sense of a complex world.

Classifying is a kind of shorthand, useful in conveying information, handy for quick reference, dependable and efficient for sorting out and arranging a hodgepodge of facts, figures, experiences, events. Suppose we had to look at each minuscule aspect of a subject. We would be lost, wandering forever in a maze of meanings, each one leading to dead ends and despair. And so we resort to classification, knowing that the categories into which we place subjects will expand our understanding of the individual members.

When you put people, places, things, or ideas into groups of three or more, you are classifying on the basis of certain characteristics. You get to know the animal kingdom, for example, by putting diverse creatures into a family, genus, and then species. You begin to see, then, how humankind relates to the hairy ape. What you seek is a way to understand similarities and differences, a way to take in large bodies of information in a moment, a way to establish connections between those areas of information.

Think of the classifications you already know about: blood types; the four food groups; full, associate, and assistant professors; neurotics, psychotics, depressives, obsessives, compulsives;

genius, above average intelligence, average intelligence, retarded, profoundly retarded; generals, colonels, majors, captains, lieutenants, sergeants, corporals, privates; business, residential, and industrial districts. You get the idea and, no doubt, comprehend the risk. Classification can lead to stereotyping. You may be labeled the dumb one or the class clown and spend a lifetime trying to break out of that category or, wondrous hope, to defy classification altogether. But, more important, astute classification can lead to greater understanding and can provide a way to deal with seemingly unmanageable masses of information.

How do you use classification to provide structure and development for your essay? Formal classification is a systematic analysis of groups.

1. You first identify a group of related items: trees or cab drivers or gossips or candy bars or skin cancers.

2. You then determine on what basis you intend to classify these related items. The choices are endless, but you will settle on one basis of comparison and stay with that throughout the essay. You might classify trees on the basis of leaf formations; cab drivers on the basis of driving skills; gossips on the basis of gossiping techniques; candy bars on the basis of flavor; skin cancers on the basis of ease of treatment. The basis of the classification will be logical. You would not, for example, classify gossips on the basis of how they dress, because clothes are not a unifying and relevant factor among gossips. Nor would you attempt to classify taxicab riders, because some riders would be passengers and others would be drivers.

3. Finally, you divide the class on that basis. Often, your thesis will set up your organizational plan, indicating the class, the basis of classification, and the division into subgroups. Classification provides a basic organizational plan. Outlining is, after all, a classification method. In each division of the outline, you group subjects on a single basis. Your thesis also will reflect this basic organization, giving you a clear path through your essay.

Here are some thesis statements that use classification as the organizing principle. Notice that the divisions of the classification are grammatically parallel.

Go to a funeral, and you will encounter among the mourners the dry-eyed stoics, the handwringers, and the sobbers, each grieving in his or her own way.

I question the motives of people who write letters to the editor: most of them simply want to nitpick, to show off, or, worst of all, to preach.

Suburbia these days is a fascinating patchwork of architectural styles: the streets are lined with colonials, English Tudors, and Mediterraneans.

The features section, the sports page, and the comics provide newspaper readers with happy diversion from bad news.

Some classification is just for fun, though it will provide both development and support for your thesis. If your primary purpose is entertainment, with only a pinch of instruction and information thrown in, you might classify types of guests: moochers, dropper-inners, permanent live-ins, eat-and-runners, reciprocators. Or you could get into junk foods: crunchy, salty, sweet, squishy, seminutritious, lethal. Or blind dates: the ones in safari suits from L. L. Bean, the ones in pinstripes, the ones in polyester, the ones in iridescent T-shirts and chains.

You may think that if you classify for frivolous reasons you will be disrespectful of the high calling of the communicator: to instruct, inform, persuade. But sometimes silly classification can produce spectacular results, giving the reader insight even as he or she chuckles. That you even *thought* to classify people, habits, or customs on a certain basis indicates that the classification has some merit, some truth. Here is a quick classification with just enough truth in it to send a slight chill up the bony spine of a skinny person.

Caesar was right. Thin people need watching. I've been watching them for most of my adult life, and I don't like what I see. When these narrow fellows spring at me, I'm zero at the bone. Thin people come in all personalities, most of them menacing. You've got your "together" thin person, your mechanical thin person, your condescending thin person, your tsk-tsk thin person, and your efficiency-expert thin person. All of them are dangerous.

Classification and definition are closely related. What is definition, after all, but a word neatly placed in all its categories, origins, and uses? The following essay demonstrates how describing, narrating, informing, defining, and classifying can produce a well-developed essay that supports a clear-cut thesis. "Junk" is a big subject, and the classifications provide a way to write about what is, at first glance, too messy to handle.

JUNK

No one ever sings the praises of junk. Junk falls into several categories: the junk you read, the junk you eat, the junk you see, and the junk you create. I like all kinds. Junk keeps us humble. Junk reminds us to plant our high-stepping feet on the dirty old ground.

I have never trusted the junkless condition: it is too perfect, too empty, too all-American, too evil. Into the junkless category I must put all theme parks, most chain motels and restaurants, several airports, the Osmond family, some fundamentalist television preachers, *National Geographic,* exclusive residential subdivisions, Tupperware, the four food groups, and Mr. Rogers' whole neighborhood.

Being a connoisseur of junk has wonderfully mucked up my entire life. You know those junkless songs about raindrops on roses and whiskers on kittens. Well, I've got my own list of favorite things, and none of them has anything to do with Helen Steiner Rice greeting cards, Barry Manilow, Rotarians, or the Mormon Tabernacle Choir. I like unsavory characters, the kitchen drawer beside the phone, the Sunday clutter around the house, the sweaty odor of a person I love, the smoke-filled room in which I got to inhale the equivalent of eleven cigarettes without breaking my promise to quit, the grease under the fingernails of a gas-station attendant (if you can still find one), the rusty Brillo on the sink, the bathroom glass placidly growing bacteria for the whole family, *People Magazine,* a dog-eared paperback, a really great emotional tirade.

Clean is mean. The shoddier the values, the spicker-and-spanner the surface. Why would you want to know anyone whose floors are clean enough to eat off of? Americans, who will do almost anything for a buck or a kick, are the most pious, anti-germ, disinfected, deodorized, health-obsessed, shocked and dismayed, wholesome-loving, A-rated people in the world. They will evade their taxes, but they will not take a slug of milk right out of the carton. They will divorce their spouses, but they will not miss a single day of bran and jogging. They will mooch off their relatives, but they will not come to the table in their undershirts.

Americans want to be encapsulated in clean. They will spray it, unfray it. They will purify, sterilize, homogenize, sanitize, and standardize it. They will zone it, condemn it, remodel it, and ban it. No jacked-up car will ever cross their field of vision. No crabgrass will disturb their fairways. No mention of death, disease, pestilence, and plague will spoil their Sunday outing to Disneyland.

Every time a person, place, or thing begins to get pleasantly junky, Americans will fire it, retire it, or decry it. If you have enough money, you can live and die in America without once coming into contact with junk. You might never have a swing made out of a rubber tire, a washing machine on the back porch, and a pair of jeans that aren't designer.

The closest Americans come to junk is synthetic, controlled junk. This kind of junk is no fair. Junk has to have integrity, honesty, dignity. Americans will, instead, make some fake junk. They will batter a brand new piece of furniture to make it look distressed, stain shingles to look weatherbeaten, scatter sawdust on the tavern floor, put down tiles that resemble brick, and hang around flea markets, trying to fill the junkless gaps in their existences.

Not long ago I spent the night in the kingdom of junkdom. It was a motel-restaurant on the outer fringes of eastern North Carolina, so remote that only the mosquitoes could find it. Big business and high-level management had never laid a manicured hand on this establishment. The pattern of the curtains in my room had nothing whatsoever to do with the pattern of the bedspread. The walls were dark and unpaneled. The Bible on the bedside table was family, not Gideon. The pipes in the shower stall were exposed. The water dripping on the floor made a rust spot, the color of North Carolina clay. The place had no color TV, no air conditioning, no phone, no plastic, and no A-rating. The food in the restaurant was served by a woman in green eyeshadow and tennis shoes. Hunting trophies and family photos lined the walls. I ate a greasy sausage sandwich on white bread and drank a cup of thick, black coffee from a chipped mug. When I went to bed, I slept like a tired farmer. When I awoke, the first thing I saw was geese flying in perfect formation across the dingy curtains at the windows. I knew instantly I was somewhere, not nowhere. Junk is helpful that way.

It puts nondescript, homogeneous, environmentally controlled, tightly zoned America on the map.

Questions for discussion

1. The essay has elements of classification. Where are they?
2. What is the implicit, not explicit, classification of different types of Americans?
3. What are the different categories of "clean"?
4. How does the writer classify the various methods of eliminating junk from the surface of the planet?

In the following passage from *How We Think*, one of philosopher John Dewey's major works on education, Dewey uses classification—as well as elements of contrast and definition—to analyze the process of thought. Before he can properly define thought, he must first categorize types of nonthought. Classification as a rhetorical mode aids Dewey in sorting out and organizing the seemingly unmanageable world of the brain, where randomness and daydreaming often pass for rational, logical thinking. To explain what thinking is, Dewey must first classify what thinking is *not*.

THE PROCESS OF THOUGHT

John Dewey

No one can tell another person in any definite way how he *should* think, any more than how he ought to breathe or to have his blood circulate. But the various ways in which men *do* think can be told and can be described in their general features. Some of these ways are better than others; the reasons why they are better can be set forth. The person who understands what the better ways of thinking are and why they are better can, if he will, change his own personal ways until they become more effective; until, that is to say, they do better the work that thinking can do and that other mental operations cannot do so well. The better way of thinking that is to be considered in this book

---

From John Dewey, *How We Think: A Restatement of the Relation of Reflective Thinking to the Educative Process.* Lexington, Mass.: D. C. Heath, 1933, pp. 1–9.

is called reflective thinking: the kind of thinking that consists in turning a subject over in the mind and giving it serious and consecutive consideration. Before we take up this main theme, we shall, however, first take note briefly of some other mental processes to which the name *thought* is sometimes given.

The "Stream of Consciousness." All the time we are awake and sometimes when we are asleep, something is, as we say, going through our heads. When we are asleep we call that kind of sequence "dreaming." We also have daydreams, reveries, castles built in the air, and mental streams that are even more idle and chaotic. To this uncontrolled coursing of ideas through our heads the name of "thinking" is sometimes given. It is automatic and unregulated. Many a child has attempted to see whether he could not "stop thinking"—that is, stop this procession of mental states through his mind—and in vain. More of our waking life than most of us would care to admit is whiled away in this inconsequential trifling with mental pictures, random recollections, pleasant but unfounded hopes, flitting, half-developed impressions. Hence it is that he who offers "a penny for your thoughts" does not expect to drive any great bargain if his offer is taken; he will only find out what happens to be "going through the mind" and what "goes" in this fashion rarely leaves much that is worth while behind.

Reflective Thought Is a Chain. In this sense, silly folk and dullards *think*. The story is told of a man in slight repute for intelligence, who, desiring to be chosen selectman in his New England town, addressed a knot of neighbors in this wise: "I hear you don't believe I know enough to hold office. I wish you to understand that I am thinking about something or other most of the time." Now, reflective thought is like this random coursing of things through the mind in that it consists of a succession of things thought of, but it is unlike in that the mere chance occurrence of any chance "something or other" in an irregular sequence does not suffice. Reflection involves not simply a sequence of ideas, but a *con*-sequence—a consecutive ordering in such a way that each determines the next as its proper outcome, while each outcome in turn leans back on, or refers to, its predecessors. The successive portions of a reflective thought grow out of one another and support one another; they do not come and go in a medley. Each phase is a step from something to something—technically speaking, it is a *term* of thought. Each term leaves a deposit that is utilized in the next term. The stream or flow becomes a train or chain. There are in any reflective thought definite units that are linked together so that there is a sustained movement to a common end.

Thinking Usually Restricted to Things Not Directly Perceived.
The second meaning of thinking limits it to things not sensed or directly perceived, to things *not* seen, heard, touched, smelled, or tasted. We ask the man telling a story if he saw a certain incident happen, and his reply may be, "No, I only thought of it." A note of invention, as distinct from faithful record of observation, is present. Most important in this class are successions of imaginative incidents and episodes that have a certain coherence, hang together on a continuous thread, and thus lie between kaleidoscopic flights of fancy and considerations deliberately employed to establish a conclusion. The imaginative stories poured forth by children possess all degrees of internal congruity; some are disjointed, some are articulated. When connected, they simulate reflective thought; indeed, they usually occur in minds of logical capacity. These imaginative enterprises often precede thinking of the close-knit type and prepare the way for it. In this sense, a thought or idea is a mental picture of something not actually present, and thinking is the succession of such pictures.

Reflective Thinking Aims at a Conclusion. In contrast, reflective thinking has a purpose beyond the entertainment afforded by the train of agreeable mental inventions and pictures. The train must lead somewhere; it must tend to a conclusion that can be substantiated outside the course of the images. A story of a giant may satisfy merely because of the story itself; a reflective conclusion that a giant lived at a certain date and place on the earth would have to have some justification outside of the chain of ideas in order to be a valid or sound conclusion. This contrasting element is probably best conveyed in the ordinary saying: "Think it *out.*" The phrase suggests an entanglement to be straightened out, something obscure to be cleared up through the application of thought. There is a goal to be reached, and this end sets a task that controls the sequence of ideas.

Thinking as Practically Synonymous with Believing. A third meaning of thought is practically synonymous with *belief.* "I think it is going to be colder tomorrow" or "I think Hungary is larger than Yugoslavia" is equivalent to "I believe so-and-so." When we say, "Men used to think the world was flat," we obviously refer to a belief that was held by our ancestors. This meaning of thought is narrower than those previously mentioned. A belief refers to something beyond itself by which its value is tested; it makes an assertion about some matter of fact or some principle or law. It means that a specified state of fact or law is accepted or rejected, that it is something proper to be affirmed or at least acquiesced in. It is hardly necessary to lay stress upon the importance of belief. It covers all the matters of which we have no sure knowledge and yet which we are sufficiently confident of to act upon and also the matters that we now accept as certainly true, as knowledge, but which nevertheless may be questioned in the future—just as much that passed as knowledge in the past has now passed into the limbo of mere opinion or of error.

There is nothing in the mere fact of thought as identical with belief that reveals whether the belief is well founded or not. Two different men say, "I believe the world is spherical." One man, if challenged, could produce little or no evidence for thinking as he does. It is an idea that he has picked up from others and that he accepts because the idea is generally current, not because he has examined into the matter and not because his own mind has taken any active part in reaching and framing the belief.

Such "thoughts" grow up unconsciously. They are picked up— we know not how. From obscure sources and by unnoticed channels they insinuate themselves into the mind and become unconsciously a part of our mental furniture. Tradition, instruction, imitation—all of which depend upon authority in some form, or appeal to our own advantage, or fall in with a strong passion— are responsible for them. Such thoughts are prejudices; that is, prejudgments, not conclusions reached as the result of personal mental activity, such as observing, collecting, and examining evidence. Even when they happen to be correct, their correctness is a matter of accident as far as the person who entertains them is concerned.

Reflective Thinking Impels to Inquiry. Thus we are brought again, by way of contrast, to the particular kind of thinking that we are to study in this volume, *reflective thinking.* Thought, in the two first senses mentioned, may be harmful to the mind because it distracts attention from the real world, and because it may be a waste of time. On the other hand, if indulged in judiciously these thoughts may afford genuine enjoyment and also be a source of needed recreation. But in either case they can make no claim to truth; they cannot hold themselves up as something that the mind should accept, assert, and be willing to act upon. They may involve a kind of emotional commitment, but not intellectual and practical commitment. Beliefs, on the other hand, do involve precisely this commitment and consequently sooner or later they demand our investigation to find out upon what grounds they rest. To think of a cloud as a whale or a camel—in the sense of to "fancy"—does not commit one to the conclusion that the person having the idea would ride the camel or extract oil from the whale. But when Columbus "thought" the world was round, in the sense of "believed it to be so," he and his followers were thereby committed to a series of other beliefs and actions: to beliefs about routes to India, about what would happen if ships traveled far westward on the Atlantic, etc., precisely as thinking that the world was flat had committed those who held it to belief in the impossibility of circumnavigation, and in the limitation of the earth to regions in the small civilized part of it Europeans were already acquainted with, etc.

The earlier thought, belief in the flatness of the earth, had some foundation in evidence; it rested upon what men could see easily within the limits of their vision. But this evidence was not further looked into; it was not checked by considering other evidence; there was no search for new evidence. Ultimately the belief rested on laziness, inertia, custom, absence of courage and energy in investigation. The later belief rests upon careful and extensive study, upon purposeful widening of the area of observation, upon reasoning out the conclusions of alternative conceptions to see what would follow in case one or the other were adopted for belief. As distinct from the first kind of thinking there was an orderly chain of ideas; as distinct from the second, there was a controlling purpose and end; as distinct from the third, there was personal examination, scrutiny, inquiry.

Because Columbus did not accept unhesitatingly the current traditional theory, because he doubted and inquired, he arrived at his thought. Skeptical of what, from long habit, seemed most certain, and credulous of what seemed impossible, he went on thinking until he could produce evidence for both his confidence and his disbelief. Even if his conclusion had finally turned out wrong, it would have been a different sort of belief from those it antagonized, because it was reached by a different method. *Active, persistent, and careful consideration of any belief or supposed form of knowledge in the light of the grounds that support it and the further conclusions to which it tends* constitutes reflective thought. Any one of the first three kinds of thought may elicit this type; but once begun, it includes a conscious and voluntary effort to establish belief upon a firm basis of evidence and rationality.

Questions for discussion

1. How does Dewey classify "some other mental processes to which the name *thought* is sometimes given"?

2. On what basis does Dewey classify nonthought? What do the three types of nonthought have in common? How do these types of nonthinking contrast with thinking?

3. Dewey begins with classification, but at what points in the passage does he depend on definition or contrast to support his original assertion? What *is* his thesis?

4. How could you relate these types of nonthought to your own mental processes? Give examples, and explain the connection. What about the dim region between waking and sleeping? What about your mental processes when you are gazing out the window during a class lecture or sitting on a park bench and watching the pigeons? Could you classify your dream states, your moments of feeling empty in the head but alive in all your senses? How would you classify your moments of attention, your moments of inattention, your moments of fancy or imagination?

◆

Activities

Write an essay in which you classify one of the following on a single basis. Your thesis will indicate the organizational plan. Remember that the basis of the classification will be logical and the categories will not overlap.

Types of spirituality or religious experiences

Types of street people

Types of bad teachers

Types of *A* students

Types of drop-outs

Types of commercials for pain relievers

Types of bargains in commercial air travel

Types of kiddie shows

Types of bars, restaurants, motels, or bowling alleys

Types of health nuts

Types of deadbeats

Types of suburban lawns

Types of mortgages

Types of lemons, duds

Types of cleanliness

Types of dirt

Define your terms.

Language has always been fluid, as ready to change with the times as are people, customs, and scientific and technological methods. After all, people use words, and people are always changing. Therefore, the denotative (or literal) meanings of words pick up the baggage of connotative (or figurative and emotional) meanings. So, just as we must update data and buy the latest equipment, we must constantly be re-examining words. Yesterday's "bad" is today's compliment. Yesterday's gay gathering (a party) is today's homosexual demonstration. Yesterday's conversation is today's channel of communication. Words reflect the prejudices, style, fears, and thinking of the culture. Going to a dictionary will tell you what a word means. Peeking in a thesaurus will give you synonyms for that word. But using a word in context will add new dimensions and sometimes will subtly alter the word's meaning. Put your hand up to a passing stranger, say "Hi," and you will get a "Hi" in return. Put your thumbs up, wiggle your hips, shrug your shoulders, say "Hey-y-y," and much more than a simple greeting will emerge. This sassy exchange could be the start of who knows what.

Definition is closely linked to both description and exposition. When you explore the world of words, you are putting words in a context of sight, sound, and use. You are giving the reader a taste and eye for the connotative, the figurative, the emotion-packed verbal implication. But you are also informing. No one can ask the right questions about a word processor unless he or she first knows the language of word processing: control, load, save, store, print, program, initialize, and so forth. And no understanding or knowledge is gained when the language you use is unintelligible to your reader.

Dictionary definitions simply offer synonyms for a word or place the word in a class and then show how that word differs from others of its class. However, when you use defining as a method of development and support, you will be writing an extended definition. And in this more ambitious effort to make meanings clear, you will find yourself using one or several of the developmental methods in this chapter, including comparing and contrasting, giving examples, or analyzing. You may also find yourself explaining what a word means by explaining what it does *not* mean, a useful device for expressing the inexpressible. For example, if you are struggling to define "wisdom," you might begin by asserting that it is not simply intelligence or common sense or reason. Or you may list the characteristics of the term—defining "endogenous depression," for example, by listing the symptoms of the disease.

You will find yourself relying on definition as a way to support and develop your ideas. You will find yourself pausing to define your terms, place them in context, dust off the emotions and fears that have begun to cling to certain words. All of us are constantly adding new words to the language, bandying about slang expressions, coining new words, humming buzz words, allowing words to slide out of their safe slots and into the wide berth of connotation. Sometimes words reach such a fever pitch of danger that they lose their usefulness: liberal, conservative, chauvinist, fundamentalist, pinko commie. Sometimes a person's abstract definition of, say, marriage changes dramatically over 50 years to become, as one friend dolefully called it, "wedded weddedness."

A good writer respects language, chooses his or her words carefully, relies on definition to explain or transmit information, and struggles to communicate in a world where messages are garbled, meanings muddled.

You may not think you can write even one paragraph about what a word means. But you can, in fact, write an entire essay using this method of support and development. The following essay explores the meanings, both connotative and denotative, of the word *fine*—a simple word, an apparently clear word. The writer, however, discovers hidden meanings, places the term in several contexts, analyzes the psychological impact of the word, describes the settings in which it appears, and informs the reader about the dangers in the overuse of the word.

I AM ALWAYS FINE

Recently, my eye fell on a short quotation with long implications. The quotation was as follows:

> Whenever I met Lili
> and asked her
> How are you Lili
> she said
> Fine
> I am always fine.

I had no choice but to find a piece of notebook paper and a pencil to write down the words. Knowledgeable friends found the source of the quotation for me. It's in the dead center of a play called *The Investigation,* by Peter Weiss. Lili Toffler turned out to be a young woman who escaped being sent to the gas ovens at Auschwitz by being shot twice in the heart. Lucky Lili.

Lili Toffler's words ring in my head like an old echo. I have heard her words dropping like dead husks on the cold ground of many a human life. The words are especially evocative in the South, among Southern women. On a cold morning, I saw a stream of well-dressed women pouring from the doors of a Baptist church. I'll bet if I asked them how they were, they would each answer, "Fine. I am always fine." A friend from Pennsylvania noticed that the standard Southern exchange goes this way: "Hey, how you?" "Fine, how you?" He's right. Every time I put the Pennsylvanian's formula to the Southern test, the equation balances.

Then one night at supper I got another unexpected commentary on the word "fine." A relative, who never met Lili, told me that when he asks how I am and I say fine, he knows that I am lying, hiding, resisting, or—that worst of all hedges against life—numbing up.

Being finely tuned to the state of fineness, I tested the question on a Southern friend. I called her up and said, "How you doing?" With a voice that trembled and turned cold by turns, she said she was "fine, really fine." Double alarms went off in my head. What if Lili had said she was "always fine" two or ten times over? I suspected the degree of fineness was geometrically, not arithmetically, related. One fine: hell. Four fines (as in "fine, fine, fine, thank you"): sixteen hells and sinking fast.

Of course, Lili was "always fine," so we cannot calculate the depth of her misery. I'll bet prisoners say they're fine all the way to the electric chair. I'll bet children who have been daily beaten or starved would say, down at the social worker's office, that they're fine, just fine.

The word "fine" is amusingly defined in the *American Heritage Dictionary*, on the terribly safe ground of the printed page. In greetings, fine means "quite well" or "in good health." In gold, fine is "pure." In instruments or methods, fine is "precise." In manners, fine is "elegant." So Lili was a bitter ironist or an out-and-out liar. She was about as well, healthy, pure, precise, and elegant as the Holocaust.

The trouble with dictionaries is that they leave out the finer shades of meaning, the way we really use words. You've got to watch those words: the Nazis said the "one way to freedom" was through "obedience, diligence, cleanliness, honesty, truthfulness, and love of country." I've always suspected freedom might lie in the opposite direction. You've got to watch those Nazis.

Of course, we learn, like Lili, in the prisons of our own lives, to be fine, always fine. The word is our strong defense, relieving both the speaker and the listener of any obligation or pain. Pouters will, after three days of silence, tell us they're fine every time. Children who have grown too big to cry but not big enough to run away will answer "fine." Perhaps the only people who are not fine are children under two who haven't been shaped by the world and psychotics who can't live in it.

Ever-fine Lili didn't die in vain. She has executed that word in my mouth and life. I am not fine anymore, not always and maybe not ever. I am stretching my vocabulary to include, upon your inquiry after my health, "sick," "sad," "ecstatic," "content," "bewildered," "lonely," "calm," "despairing," "hopeful," "indifferent," "happy," or "lost." Those words are as short and easy to say as "fine." They shouldn't delay unduly the swift progress of passing friends or strangers down a city sidewalk.

Questions for discussion

1. The essay employs description, definition, and even some narration, but it seeks primarily to inform. What is the information the writer wishes the reader to comprehend?

2. The essay is specifically about the word "fine," but could it be saying something also about all the ways in which we use words? What are the risks of saying what's on your mind? What are the advantages of circumlocution?

3. Can you think of certain standard greetings, farewells, conversational gambits common to your region, family, friends, social group? What is the purpose of ritualized patterns of speech?

4. Find in the essay the denotative meanings of the word "fine." Now state, if you can, the connotative meanings of the word "fine," according to the author of this essay.

5. Think of examples in public or private life when saying what you mean and meaning what you say could get you fired, demoted, or ostracized from the group. Which groups in our culture seem to thrive on saying what they don't mean and saying it in two thousand words or more? Be specific in your answers. Do you think success depends on the slippery use of words? What do we mean by the word "success"?

In the following excerpt from E. M. Forster's *Aspects of the Novel*, Forster is defining what is meant by the word "story" and explaining its importance in the novel. As you read the passage, notice the various rhetorical devices he uses to make his amusing and surprisingly simple point.

ASPECTS OF THE NOVEL

E. M. Forster

We shall all agree that the fundamental aspect of the novel is its story-telling aspect, but we shall voice our assent in different tones, and it is on the precise tone of voice we employ now that our subsequent conclusions will depend.

Let us listen to three voices. If you ask one type of man, "What does a novel do?" he will reply placidly: "Well—I don't know— it seems a funny sort of question to ask—a novel's a novel— well, I don't know—I suppose it kind of tells a story, so to speak." He is quite good-tempered and vague, and probably driving a motor-bus at the same time and paying no more attention to literature than it merits. Another man, whom I visualize as on a golf-course, will be aggressive and brisk. He will reply: "What does a novel do? Why, tell a story of course, and I've no use for it if it didn't. I like a story. Very bad taste on my part, no doubt, but I like a story. You can take your art, you can take your literature, you can take your music, but give me a good story. And I like a story to be a story, mind, and my wife's the same." And a third man he says in a sort of drooping regretful voice, "Yes—oh, dear, yes—the novel tells a story." I respect and admire the first speaker. I detest and fear the second. And the third is myself. Yes—oh, dear, yes—the novel tells a story. That is the fundamental aspect without which it could not exist. That is the highest factor common to all novels, and I wish that it was not so, that it could be something different—melody, or perception of the truth, not this low atavistic form.

For the more we look at the story (the story that is a story, mind), the more we disentangle it from the finer growths that it supports, the less shall we find to admire. It runs like a backbone—or may I say a tapeworm, for its beginning and end are arbitrary. It is immensely old—goes back to neolithic times, perhaps to paleolithic. Neanderthal man listened to stories, if

From E. M. Forster, *Aspects of the Novel.* New York: Harcourt, Brace, 1954, pp. 25–29.

one may judge by the shape of his skull. The primitive audience was an audience of shock-heads, gaping round the campfire, fatigued with contending against the mammoth or the woolly rhinoceros, and only kept awake by suspense. What would happen next? The novelist droned on, and as soon as the audience guessed what happened next, they either fell asleep or killed him. We can estimate the dangers incurred when we think of the career of Scheherazade in somewhat later times. Scheherazade avoided her fate because she knew how to wield the weapon of suspense—the only literary tool that has any effect upon tyrants and savages. Great novelist though she was—exquisite in her descriptions, tolerant in her judgments, ingenious in her incidents, advanced in her morality, vivid in her delineations of character, expert in her knowledge of three Oriental capitals—it was yet on none of these gifts that she relied when trying to save her life from her intolerable husband. They were but incidental. She only survived because she managed to keep the king wondering what would happen next. Each time she saw the sun rising she stopped in the middle of a sentence, and left him gaping. "At this moment Scheherazade saw the morning appearing and, discreet, was silent." This uninteresting little phrase is the backbone of the *One Thousand and One Nights*, the tapeworm by which they are tied together and the life of a most accomplished princess was preserved.

We are all like Scheherazade's husband, in that we want to know what happens next. That is universal and that is why the backbone of a novel has to be a story. Some of us want to know nothing else—there is nothing in us but primeval curiosity, and consequently our other literary judgments are ludicrous. And now the story can be defined. It is a narrative of events arranged in their time sequence—dinner coming after breakfast, Tuesday after Monday, decay after death, and so on. *Qua* story, it can only have one merit: that of making the audience want to know what happens next. And conversely it can only have one fault: that of making the audience not want to know what happens next. These are the only two criticisms that can be made on the story that is a story. It is the lowest and simplest of literary organisms. Yet it is the highest factor common to all the very complicated organisms known as novels.

When we isolate the story like this from the nobler aspects through which it moves, and hold it out on the forceps—wriggling and interminable, the naked worm of time—it presents an appearance that is both unlovely and dull. But we have much to learn from it. Let us begin by considering it in connection with daily life.

Daily life is also full of the time-sense. We think one event occurs after or before another, the thought is often in our minds, and much of our talk and action proceeds on the assumption. Much of our talk and action, but not all; there seems something else in life besides time, something which may conveniently be called "value," something which is measured not by minutes or hours, but by intensity, so that when we look at our past it does not stretch back evenly but piles up into a few notable pinnacles, and when we look at the future it seems sometimes a wall, sometimes a cloud, sometimes a sun, but never a chronological chart. Neither memory nor anticipation is much interested in Father Time, and all dreamers, artists and lovers are partially delivered from his tyranny; he can kill them, but he cannot secure their attention, and at the very moment of doom, when the clock collected in the tower its strength and struck, they may be looking the other way. So daily life, whatever it may be really, is practically composed of two lives—the life in time and the life by values—and our conduct reveals a double allegiance. "I only saw her for five minutes, but it was worth it." There you have both allegiances in a single sentence. And what the story does is to narrate the life in time. And what the entire novel does—if it is a good novel—is to include the life by values as well; using devices hereafter to be examined. It, also, pays a double allegiance. But in it, in the novel, the allegiance to time is imperative: no novel could be written without it. Whereas in daily life the allegiance may not be necessary: we do not know, and the experience of certain mystics suggests, indeed, that it is not necessary, and that we are quite mistaken in supposing that Monday is followed by Tuesday, or death by decay. It is always possible for you or me in daily life to deny that time exists and act accordingly even if we become unintelligible and are sent by our fellow citizens to what they choose to call a lunatic asylum. But it is never possible for a novelist to deny time inside the fabric of his novel: he must cling however lightly to the thread of his story, he must touch the interminable tapeworm, otherwise he becomes unintelligible, which, in his case, is a blunder.

I am trying not to be philosophic about time, for it is (experts assure us) a most dangerous hobby for an outsider, far more fatal than place; and quite eminent metaphysicians have been dethroned through referring to it improperly. I am only trying to explain that as I lecture now I hear that clock ticking or do not hear it ticking, I retain or lose the time sense; whereas in a novel there is always a clock. The author may dislike his clock. Emily Brontë in *Wuthering Heights* tried to hide hers. Sterne, in *Tristram Shandy*, turned his upside down. Marcel Proust, still more ingenious, kept altering the hands, so that his hero was at the same period entertaining a mistress to supper and playing ball with his nurse in the park. All these devices are legitimate, but none of them contravene our thesis: the basis of a novel is a story, and a story is a narrative of events arranged in time sequence.

Questions for discussion

1. Find in the passage Forster's definition of the story, and quote it exactly. Now note the parenthetical distinction Forster makes between "story" and "plot." Though no explanation is provided at this point in the book, can you guess how a story might differ from a plot? What is the definition of "plot"?

2. Forster uses figurative language to help him define the story. To what does he compare the story?

3. It is important in defining words to place them in context. Forster meets this requirement by providing a historical perspective on the origins of story. He calls the story a "low atavistic form." What does he mean by that definition?

4. What, in Forster's view, is the aspect of the story most essential to the novel? Why must a novelist also be a skilled storyteller? To what does Forster attribute the storytelling power of Scheherazade (the fictional narrator in *One Thousand and One Nights)?*

5. Forster uses several rhetorical devices to support his definition: classification, comparison and contrast, example. Identify these devices.

6. Why is the narrative line in a novel unlike the melody in a song?

7. Forster implicitly supplies several different meanings for the word "time." How can time be deceptive, show itself in different ways in the novel, have—as Forster calls it—"value"? What is the difference between "the life in time" and "the life by values"?

◆

Activities

1. Develop a thesis in which you express an opinion about success. Then, in three supporting paragraphs, offer three

possible definitions of the word "success," using concrete details, scenes, conversations, examples. Your supporting paragraphs should, of course, give credibility and validity to your broad assertion. Your feelings about "success" may be positive or negative. You may want to enlarge on your personal definition by including parental, religious, or professional definitions of success.

2.   Dr. Samuel Johnson, an essayist and lexicographer in eighteenth-century England, wrote a dictionary that makes entertaining reading for moderns. He let his prejudices creep into this allegedly factual reference book. For example, he defines a "stateswoman" as "a woman who meddles with publick affairs." "To trape," says Dr. Johnson, is "to run idly and sluttishly about" and is used "only of women." Men, apparently, did not trape. A husband is defined as "the male of animals." A wife is a "woman of low employment." And finally, says Dr. Johnson, "Whist is a game at cards, requiring close attention and silence." You will find Dr. Johnson's dictionary in your library. Examine some of his definitions, and write three paragraphs taking him to task for one of his definitions.

3.   Select a highly specialized field with a language all its own—for example, meteorology, auto mechanics, computers, economics, nursing, psychology, medicine, sociology, statistics, some aspect of zoology or biology—and write three paragraphs explaining the definitions of one or two technical terms to a lay reader. What, for example, is a "neutron star"? What are "nucleotides"? What is a heat sink effect? A mutual fund? A basal cell carcinoma? Remember that your audience is composed of lay people, not experts.

4.   Select one of the following words, and write three paragraphs about its denotative and connotative meanings.

Spinster	Trash	Learning
Hag	Bookworm	Hard rock
Tyrant	Wisdom	Chaos
Hick	Loser	Gossip
Science	Bachelor	Quality
Education	Nag	Scholar
Muzak	Boss	Intelligence
Order	Redneck	Classics
Chitchat	Art	

Explain a process.

When you classify, you group people or things according to similar traits: you neatly categorize the world. But process goes further. With process, you explain how the world and the myriad things in it progress through steps and stages. And what you are describing or explaining refuses to stand still. Categories, after all, are one-dimensional, static. Furthermore, the classifying occurs after the fact, with keen and orderly hindsight. But with process you take your reader through the procedures, techniques, and methods, using a step-by-step approach. It is hard to explain a procedure you yourself have not followed. And certain procedures are difficult to explain because you have been doing them so long that you have forgotten the sequential nature of the task. Could you explain, at this late date, how to ride a bicycle, drive a car with a five-speed stick shift, or do the box step you learned in eighth-grade dance class? Recapturing the exact sequence would be as hard as remembering how to breathe.

Explaining a process helps to develop skills of describing, narrating, and informing. You see the procedure as it flows from one step to the next. You often place the steps in chronological order, as anyone who ever took the lens cover off a camera *after* he snapped the picture can tell you. And, in the end, you have accurately informed the reader of how to move from the recipe to the finished cake, the click of the camera to the finished photo, the unsterile surgeon to the squeaky clean, white-robed person about to remove your appendix. The more machines and inventions and gadgets and gimmicks there are in the world, the more someone needs to explain how to start them, stop them, repair them, make a million dollars on them.

Book publishers cater endlessly to America's process mania. Books proliferate on how to grow tomatoes, how to have a better sex life, how to stay married, how to get divorced, how to dress for success, how to be assertive, how to lose weight, how to communicate, how to prioritize, publicize, decriminalize, verbalize, merchandise, therapize. Nouns are in the process of becoming verbs, perhaps because psychologized processing is ongoing. The dinner may get "done," but the human personality resists completion. Things in process, then, will move from a fixed point to a definite conclusion. People, ideas, and philosophies will not.

The more specific and practical the process, the more grateful the reader will be that you presented it to him or her. People, after all, thrive on the feeling of accomplishment that comes from knowing how to cook, build a patio, fix a car, select a reliable real-estate agent, get a healthy body, throw a pot, paint a picture, write a paragraph, give a manicure, repair a fence, unstop the toilet, apply for college, send off for a birth certificate, or travel from New York to Paris for the lowest possible price. Competence is at the bottom of the process passion, and the more people can *do*, the better they feel.

Process is of two types. The first is the practical business of explaining how to do something, of giving directions, of instructing (how to clean a fish or how to study for exams). The second focuses on information, on how something was done. With the second type of process, you are not concerned with telling your reader how to do something, but rather how you or somebody else once accomplished a task, met a goal (how you decided on a college major or how the polio vaccine was developed).

Much of process is chronological, as is narration, but process carries the reader through to a specific result. Often, too, the exact chronology of steps is of crucial importance. If one step in refinishing a pine table is overlooked, the result will be disappointing. You cannot, for example, apply the stain and then remove the layers of old paint. However, some processes cannot be broken into individual steps because the parts of the process are going on simultaneously. If you try to explain what happens when you puff on a cigarette and nicotine enters the body, you will need to group the processes into general stages, not chronological steps: the impact of nicotine on the heart, then on the blood vessels, then on the brain, then on the adrenal gland.

Explaining a process requires that the writer be able to establish a logical connection between the first step and the last, the beginning and the end. When you consider how many instructions, manuals, and diagrams leave the obedient assembler screaming with frustration, you will appreciate more fully the demands of this particular method of development. The kit for assembling the charcoal grill leaves out the step about putting Screw A into Hole B. The highway patrol officer tells you everything about getting a driver's license, but when you show up, you learn that you must have your birth certificate with you. All these breakdowns in process can cause mental breakdowns in the victims. The charcoal grill teeters on its shaky tripod; the prospective driver goes back home to call the Department of Vital Statistics and learn the procedure for getting a birth certificate. When you explain a process, you do not want to leave your reader in doubt about how to begin, where to go next, what will be the probable result of the procedure.

Process Cut Short

I remember a classic example of the way in which process does not always live up to its lofty reputation. A guy I once knew, very into process and how-to, was busily showing me how to operate an electric hedge pruner. "Here is how you turn it on," he said. "Here is how you adjust the speed," he said. "Here is how you run it over the ligustrum," he said. "Now you try it," he said, turning to hand the machine to me. But just as he turned, the blade accidentally sliced the cord into two very neat, very well-organized pieces. I like to died laughing, as they say in the South. The culmination of the process popped into my head. "So *that's* how you turn off the machine," I said. "Just cut the cord in two."

In the following essay, the writer explains a very small process with major regional consequences. The essay is humorous, but the writer's attitude toward the process is dead serious.

ALREADY SWEETENED ICED TEA

Among Southerners, big debates rage about how best to prepare barbecue. But barbecue has never interested me much. I am not so blasé, however, about my already sweetened iced tea. Some people don't care much what kind of iced tea they get. They'd just as soon have a Mountain Dew or sweet milk. But these people have never suffered long-term iced-tea deprivation. This deprivation is an experience which, once you've been through it, you never forget.

Real Southerners have always had a nice gallon pickle jar full of iced tea waiting in the refrigerator. Tea is part of their daily lives. All their Tupperware has tea stains on it. And they've never left home and gone to a place where nobody ever heard of iced tea for lunch and supper all year round.

Well, I do not take my already sweetened iced tea lightly. I once spent three years in the wilds of Connecticut, and those folks don't even know how to make already sweetened iced tea.

On a January day, go in a Howard Johnson's off the Merritt Parkway, ask for iced tea with your fried clams, and the waitress will call the manager out of the back office. The waitress and manager will do one of two things: either they will ask you to leave; or they will bring you a small glass with ice, a little pot of very hot tea, a wedge of lemon, and two packets of Sweet 'n' Low. After they walk away, shaking their heads, you pour the hot tea over the tiny chips of ice, and the ice instantly melts. What you have now is neither here nor there: lukewarm tea, the color of ginger ale.

And you have to remember to say *iced* tea, not just tea. If you say you want tea in any months other than July or August, you will get hot tea, like folks do in England. Only you are not from England, so why should people in Connecticut, who aren't from England either, treat you like you are?

Well, I stayed up there in Connecticut, without any good iced tea, for a long time. I will never again take my tea for granted.

My friend Nancy taught me how to make good tea. Good tea does not cloud up or taste bitter. Good tea is not made with powder. And you don't fix good tea with lemon. Good tea is dark brown, maybe three shades darker than bourbon.

You do not make good tea by following the directions on the box. You make good tea by doing just what I tell you to do. First, you fill a gallon pickle jar half full of cold water and one cup of sugar and let the jar sit there on the kitchen counter beside the sink. Then you get out a medium-sized pot and fill it with cold water and set it on a cold burner on the stove. Then you put three family-sized tea bags (Tetley or Lipton) in the pot, being careful to drop the labels in as well so the labels won't hit the hot burner and go up in flames. The taste of the labels won't hurt the tea. Then you turn the burner on high. The minute, the very minute, the water with the tea bags in it comes to a boil, you pour it into the big pickle jar, being sure to take out the tea bags and any floating labels. Then you stir and set the jar in the refrigerator. Serve in big jelly glasses over six ice cubes twice a day every day for the rest of your life.

Some final advice: the first thing you do every morning if you live in the South is get up and make your tea. Also remember that Southern restaurants that don't serve a meat, three vegetables, and banana pudding for dessert generally do not serve good tea. Here is the kind of restaurant you want: if, in the restaurant, the sink for washing your hands is in plain view and a picture of the owner's grandbabies is taped to the cash register, the tea there will very likely be the best you ever tasted.

Questions for discussion

1. One paragraph in the essay explains the process. What function do the other paragraphs serve?

2. What methods of development and support can you find in the essay? Name them, and give examples.

3. Are there regional foods, family culinary specialties, favorite and local beverages that you wish you could eat or drink right now? Do you know how to make them? Could you put the importance of those taste sensations in context, convincing the other members of the class, the ones who come from other places, of the reason that certain foods and drinks fill you with longing, remind you of home? Try it. Convince suspicious classmates that they haven't really lived until they've tasted grits, vichyssoise, boiled beef tongue, gazpacho, borscht, Peking duck, paella, pasties, trifle, springerles, white lightnin', fish-house punch, clabbered milk, or mint juleps. If you know how to make these foods, concoct these drinks, then hold the thought or, rather, the process.

The following short essay explains a very important process: how to drive defensively.

DRIVING DEFENSIVELY

Car-safety campaigns repeatedly warn the driver that there are two major hazards on the nation's highways: the driver himself and all the other drivers. Even if you yourself have a safe driving record, even if you earned an A on your driving test, you must nonetheless learn to handle the mistakes and miscalculations of other drivers who may be drunk, reckless, or simply unskilled. But learning how to drive defensively may be difficult, especially since the *other* driver is an unknown quantity. You must, then, assume that accidents in which you are not at fault are as much your responsibility as accidents you cause.

The most obvious and basic safety tips apply to all drivers in all driving situations. First, fasten your seat belt, thereby reducing the chance of injury or death should you be involved in an accident. Second, sit up straight because erect posture will help to keep your mind sharp, your reflexes quick. Third, adjust the steering angle and seat so you can assume a comfortable, bent-arm position, placing your hands on the wheel at three o'clock and nine o'clock to provide good control. Fourth, start the engine and carefully enter the appropriate driving lane.

Because most accidents occur as the result of following too closely, you must avoid bumper-hugging. Watch the car in front of you pass a given point, and then see how long it takes you to reach that same point. Allow three to four seconds of reaction time when you are following a car. Then, when the car in front makes a sudden stop, you will not find your bumper permanently hugging his bumper, instead of merely flirting with it.

The wise defensive driver also pays attention to the road far ahead, not simply to the car directly in front. Learn to scan the horizon for pile-ups down the road, construction warnings, stoplights. If you are alert to the twenty or twenty-five cars ahead and see their brake lights coming on, automatically take your foot off the accelerator and begin to slow down.

Many accidents also occur when drivers are changing lanes. You must learn to check your rear-view mirror constantly before you pull out in the other lane to pass. Your car may have a blind spot, a point at which you cannot see the car coming around you in the next lane. Turn your head slightly so that you can glimpse the movement of the passing car with your peripheral vision. Do not, however, turn your head too far, or you may find yourself plowing into the rear of the car ahead.

Car safety also depends on good car maintenance. Proper air pressure in the tires, for example, can give you a better feel for what your car is doing. When you turn a corner, the sidewall of the tire flexes. Firm air pressure causes less flexing and gives your car better control. The recommended air pressure for most tires is between 32 and 35 pounds, though the higher pressure is preferred by some people who like a firmer ride.

Questions for discussion

1. In the first example of explaining a process, "Already Sweetened Iced Tea," the sequence was a primary consideration. This essay about driving defensively is also explaining how to do something, but chronology is less important. What if the writer explained another "car" process—say, changing the oil in the car? Does chronology, sequence, matter in this procedure? Why or why not?

2. How does the writer develop a thesis and a topic sentence for each phase of the process? Do the topic sentences provide control for explaining the process? How?

In the following essay, novelist Virginia Woolf explains a process that you may think you have already mastered or that, at first glance, seems obvious. After all, you may say, the way to read a book is to open it at page one and keep reading until the last page. Woolf, however, goes beyond the obvious to explore the process of meaningful reading, of how to approach an author or a certain literary genre, of how to appreciate the need for various types or classifications of reading. Perhaps if you "hate" to read, you have simply failed to consider these general preconditions and stages of reading.

HOW SHOULD ONE READ A BOOK?

Virginia Woolf

In the first place, I want to emphasize the note of interrogation at the end of my title. Even if I could answer the question for myself, the answer would apply only to me and not to you. The only advice, indeed, that one person can give another about reading is to take no advice, to follow your own instincts, to use your own reason, to come to your own conclusions. If this is agreed between us, then I feel at liberty to put forward a few ideas and suggestions because you will not allow them to fetter that independence which is the most important quality that a reader can possess. After all, what laws can be laid down about books? The battle of Waterloo was certainly fought on a certain day; but is *Hamlet* a better play than *Lear?* Nobody can say. Each must decide that question for himself. To admit authorities, however heavily furred and gowned, into our libraries and let them tell us how to read, what to read, what value to place upon what we read, is to destroy the spirit of freedom which is the breath of those sanctuaries. Everywhere else we may be bound by laws and conventions—there we have none.

But to enjoy freedom, if the platitude is pardonable, we have of course to control ourselves. We must not squander our powers, helplessly and ignorantly, squirting half the house in order to water a single rosebush; we must train them, exactly and powerfully, here on the very spot. This, it may be, is one of the first difficulties that faces us in a library. What is "the very spot"? There may well seem to be nothing but a conglomeration and huddle of confusion. Poems and novels, histories and

From Virginia Woolf, *Collected Essays*, Vol. 2. New York: Harcourt, Brace, 1966, pp. 5–14.

memoirs, dictionaries and bluebooks; books written in all languages by men and women of all tempers, races, and ages jostle each other on the shelf. And outside the donkey brays, the women gossip at the pump, the colts gallop across the fields. Where are we to begin? How are we to bring order into this multitudinous chaos and get the deepest and widest pleasure from what we read?

It is simple enough to say that since books have classes—fiction, biography, poetry—we should separate them and take from each what it is right that each should give us. Yet few people ask from books what books can give us. Most commonly we come to books with blurred and divided minds, asking of fiction that it shall be true, of poetry that it shall be false, of biography that it shall be flattering, of history that it shall enforce our own prejudices. If we could banish all such preconceptions when we read, that would be an admirable beginning. Do not dictate to your author; try to become him. Be his fellow-worker and accomplice. If you hang back, and reserve and criticize at first, you are preventing yourself from getting the fullest possible value from what you read. But if you open your mind as widely as possible, then signs and hints of almost imperceptible fineness, from the twist and turn of the first sentences, will bring you into the presence of a human being unlike any other. Steep yourself in this, acquaint yourself with this, and soon you will find that your author is giving you, or attempting to give you, something far more definite. The thirty-two chapters of a novel—if we consider how to read a novel first—are an attempt to make something as formed and controlled as a building: but words are more impalpable than bricks; reading is a longer and more complicated process than seeing. Perhaps the quickest way to understand the elements of what a novelist is doing is not to read, but to write; to make your own experiment with the dangers and difficulties of words. Recall, then, some event that has left a distinct impression on you—how at the corner of the street, perhaps, you passed two people talking. A tree shook; an electric light danced; the tone of the talk was comic, but also tragic; a whole vision, an entire conception, seemed contained in that moment.

But when you attempt to reconstruct it in words, you will find that it breaks into a thousand conflicting impressions. Some must be subdued; others emphasized; in the process you will lose, probably, all grasp upon the emotion itself. Then turn from your blurred and littered pages to the opening pages of some great novelist—Defoe, Jane Austen, Hardy. Now you will be better able to appreciate their mastery. It is not merely that we are in the presence of a different person—Defoe, Jane Austen, or Thomas Hardy—but that we are living in a different world. Here, in *Robinson Crusoe*, we are trudging a plain high road; one thing happens after another; the fact and the order of the fact is enough. But if the open air and adventure mean everything to Defoe they mean nothing to Jane Austen. Hers is the drawing-room, and people talking, and by the many mirrors of their talk revealing their characters. And if, when we have accustomed ourselves to the drawing-room and its reflections, we turn to Hardy, we are once more spun around. The moors are round us and the stars are above our heads. The other side of the mind is now exposed—the dark side that comes uppermost in solitude, not the light side that shows in company. Our relations are not towards people, but towards Nature and destiny. Yet different as these worlds are, each is consistent with itself. The maker of each is careful to observe the laws of his own perspective, and however great a strain they may put upon us they will never confuse us, as lesser writers so frequently do, by introducing two different kinds of reality into the same book. Thus to go from one great novelist to another—from Jane Austen to Hardy, from Peacock to Trollope, from Scott to Meredith—is to be wrenched and uprooted; to be thrown this way and then that. To read a novel is a difficult and complex art. You must be capable not only of great finesse of perception, but of great boldness of imagination if you are going to make use of all that the novelist—the great artist—gives you.

But a glance at the heterogeneous company on the shelf will show you that writers are very seldom "great artists"; far more often a book makes no claim to be a work of art at all. These biographies and autobiographies, for example, lives of great men, of men long dead and forgotten, that stand cheek by jowl with the novels and poems, are we to refuse to read them because they are not "art"? Or shall we read them, but read them in a different way, with a different aim? Shall we read them in the first place to satisfy that curiosity which possesses us sometimes when in the evening we linger in front of a house where the lights are lit and the blinds not yet drawn, and each floor of the house shows us a different section of human life in being? Then we are consumed with curiosity about the lives of these people—the servants gossiping, the gentlemen dining, the girl dressing for a party, the old woman at the window with her knitting. Who are they, what are they, what are their names, their occupations, their thoughts, and adventures?

Biographies and memoirs answer such questions, light up innumerable such houses; they show us people going about their daily affairs, toiling, failing, succeeding, eating, hating, loving, until they die. And sometimes as we watch, the house fades and the iron railings vanish and we are out at sea; we are hunting, sailing, fighting; we are among savages and soldiers; we are taking part in great campaigns. Or if we like to stay here in England, in London, still the scene changes; the street narrows; the house becomes small, cramped, diamond-paned, and malodorous. We see a poet, Donne, driven from such a house because the walls were so thin that when the children cried their voices cut through them. We can follow him, through the paths that lie in the pages of books, to Twickenham; to Lady Bedford's Park, a famous meeting-ground for nobles and poets; and then turn our steps to Wilton, the great house under the downs, and hear Sidney read the *Arcadia* to his sister; and ramble among the very marshes and see the very herons that figure in that famous romance; and then again travel north with that other Lady Pembroke, Anne Clifford, to her wild moors, or plunge into the city and control our merriment at the sight of Gabriel Harvey in his black velvet suit arguing about poetry with Spenser. Nothing is more fascinating than to grope and stumble in the alternate darkness and splendour of Elizabethan London. But there is no staying there. The Temples and the Swifts, the Harleys and the St. Johns beckon us on; hour upon hour can be spent disentangling their quarrels and deciphering their characters; and when we tire of them we can stroll on, past a lady in black wearing diamonds, to Samuel Johnson and Goldsmith and Garrick; or cross the channel, if we like, and meet Voltaire and Diderot, Madame du Deffand; and so back to England and Twickenham—how certain places repeat themselves and certain names!—where Lady Bedford had her Park once and Pope lived later, to Walpole's home at Strawberry Hill. But Walpole introduces us to such a swarm of new acquaintances, there are so many houses to visit and bells to ring that we may well hesitate for a moment, on the Miss Berrys' doorstep, for example, when behold, up comes Thackeray; he is the friend of the woman whom Walpole loved; so that merely by going from friend to friend, from garden to garden, from house to house, we have passed from one end of English literature to another and wake to find ourselves here again in the present, if we can so differentiate this moment from all that have gone before. This, then, is one of the ways in which we can read these lives and letters; we can make them light up the many windows of the past; we can

watch the famous dead in their familiar habits and fancy sometimes that we are very close and can surprise their secrets, and
sometimes we may pull out a play or a poem that they have
written and see whether it reads differently in the presence of
the author. But this again rouses other questions. How far, we
must ask ourselves, is a book influenced by its writer's life—how
far is it safe to let the man interpret the writer? How far shall
we resist or give way to the sympathies and antipathies that the
man himself rouses in us—so sensitive are words, so receptive
of the character of the author? These are questions that press
upon us when we read lives and letters, and we must answer
them for ourselves, for nothing can be more fatal than to be
guided by the preferences of others in a matter so personal.

But also we can read such books with another aim, not to
throw light on literature, not to become familiar with famous
people, but to refresh and exercise our own creative powers. Is
there not an open window on the right hand of the bookcase?
How delightful to stop reading and look out! How stimulating the
scene is, in its unconsciousness, its irrelevance, its perpetual
movement—the colts galloping round the field, the woman filling
her pail at the well, the donkey throwing back his head and
emitting his long, acrid moan. The greater part of any library is
nothing but the record of such fleeting moments in the lives of
men, women, and donkeys. Every literature, as it grows old, has
its rubbish-heap, its records of vanished moments and forgotten
lives told in faltering and feeble accents that have perished. But
if you give yourself up to the delight of rubbish-reading you will
be surprised, indeed you will be overcome, by the relics of human life that have been cast out to moulder. It may be one letter—but what a vision it gives! It may be a few sentences—but
what vistas they suggest! Sometimes a whole story will come together with such beautiful humour and pathos and completeness that it seems as if a great novelist had been at work, yet it
is only an old actor, Tate Wilkinson, remembering the strange
story of Captain Jones; it is only a young subaltern serving under Arthur Wellesley and falling in love with a pretty girl at Lis-
bon; it is only Maria Allen letting fall her sewing in the empty
drawing-room and sighing how she wishes she had taken Dr.
Burney's good advice and had never eloped with her Rishy.
None of this has any value; it is negligible in the extreme; yet
how absorbing it is now and again to go through the rubbish-
heaps and find rings and scissors and broken noses buried in the
huge past and try to piece them together while the colt gallops
round the field, the woman fills her pail at the well, and the donkey brays.

But we tire of rubbish-reading in the long run. We tire of searching for what is needed to complete the half-truth which is all that the Wilkinsons, the Bunburys, and the Maria Allens are able to offer us. They had not the artist's power of mastering and eliminating; they could not tell the whole truth even about their own lives; they have disfigured the story that might have been so shapely. Facts are all that they can offer us, and facts are a very inferior form of fiction. Thus the desire grows upon us to have done with half-statements and approximations; to cease from searching out the minute shades of human character, to enjoy the greater abstractness, the purer truth of fiction. Thus we create the mood, intense and generalized, unaware of detail, but stressed by some regular, recurrent beat, whose natural expression is poetry; and that is the time to read poetry when we are almost able to write it.

> Western wind, when wilt thou blow?
> The small rain down can rain.
> Christ, if my love were in my arms,
> And I in my bed again!

The impact of poetry is so hard and direct that for the moment there is no other sensation except that of the poem itself. What profound depths we visit then—how sudden and complete is our immersion! There is nothing here to catch hold of; nothing to stay us in our flight. The illusion of fiction is gradual; its effects are prepared; but who when they read these four lines stops to ask who wrote them, or conjures up the thought of Donne's house or Sidney's secretary; or enmeshes them in the intricacy of the past and the succession of generations? The poet is always our contemporary. Our being for the moment is centred and constricted, as in any violent shock of personal emotion. Afterwards, it is true, the sensation begins to spread in wider rings through our minds; remoter senses are reached; these begin to sound and to comment and we are aware of echoes and relflections. The intensity of poetry covers an immense range of emotion. We have only to compare the force and directness of

> I shall fall like a tree, and find my grave
> Only remembering that I grieve,

with the wavering modulation of

> Minutes are numbered by the fall of sands,
> As by an hour glass; the span of time
> Doth waste us to our graves, and we look on it;

> An age of pleasure, revelled out, comes home
> At last and ends in sorrow; but the life,
> Weary of riot, numbers every sand,
> Wailing in sighs, until the last drop down,
> So to conclude calamity in rest,

or place the meditative calm of

> whether we be young or old,
> Our destiny, our being's heart and home,
> Is with infinitude, and only there;
> With hope it is, hope that can never die,
> Effort, and expectation, and desire,
> And something evermore about to be,

beside the complete and inexhaustible loveliness of

> The moving Moon went up the sky,
> And no where did abide:
> Softly she was going up,
> And a star or two beside—

or the splendid fantasy of

> And the woodland haunter
> Shall not cease to saunter
>   When, far down some glade,
> Of the great world's burning,
> One soft flame upturning
> Seems, to his discerning,
> Crocus in the shade.

to bethink us of the varied art of the poet; his power to make us at once actors and spectators; his power to run his hand into character as if it were a glove, and be Falstaff or Lear; his power to condense, to widen, to state, once and for ever.

"We have only to compare"—with those words the cat is out of the bag, and the true complexity of reading is admitted. The first process, to receive impressions with the utmost understanding, is only half the process of reading; it must be completed, if we are to get the whole pleasure from a book, by another. We must pass judgment upon these multitudinous impressions; we must make of these fleeting shapes one that is hard and lasting. But not directly. Wait for the dust of reading to settle; for the conflict and the questioning to die down; walk, talk, pull the dead petals from a rose, or fall asleep. Then suddenly without our willing it, for it is thus that Nature undertakes these transitions, the book will return, but differently. It will float to the top of the mind as a whole. And the book as a whole is different from the book received currently in separate phrases. Details now fit themselves into their places. We see the shape from start to finish; it is a barn, a pigsty, or a cathedral. Now then we can compare book with book as we compare building with building. But this act of comparison means that our attitude has changed; we are no longer the friends of the writer, but his judges; and just as we cannot be too sympathetic as friends, so as judges we cannot be too severe. Are they not criminals, books that have wasted our time and sympathy; are they not the most insidious enemies of society, corrupters, defilers, the writers of false books, faked books, books that fill the air with decay and disease? Let us then be severe in our judgments; let us compare each book with the greatest of its kind. There they hang in the mind the shapes of the books we have read solidified by the judgments we have passed on them—*Robinson Crusoe, Emma, The Return of the Native.* Compare the novels with these—even the latest and least of novels has a right to be judged with the best. And so with poetry—when the intoxication of rhythm has died down and the splendour of words has faded a visionary shape will return to us and this must be compared with *Lear,* with *Phèdre,* with *The Prelude;* or if not with these, with whatever is the best or seems to us to be the best in its own kind. And we may be sure that the newness of new poetry and fiction is its most superficial quality and that we have only to alter slightly, not to recast, the standards by which we have judged the old.

It would be foolish, then, to pretend that the second part of reading, to judge, to compare, is as simple as the first—to open the mind wide to the fast flocking of innumerable impressions. To continue reading without the book before you, to hold one shadow-shape against another, to have read widely enough and with enough understanding to make such comparisons alive and illuminating—that is difficult; it is still more difficult to press further and to say, "Not only is the book of this sort, but it is of this value; here it fails; here it succeeds; this is bad; that is good." To carry out this part of a reader's duty needs such imagination, insight, and learning that it is hard to conceive any one mind sufficiently endowed; impossible for the most self-confident to find more than the seeds of such powers in himself. Would it not be wiser, then, to remit this part of reading and to allow the critics, the gowned and furred authorities of the library, to decide the question of the book's absolute value for us? Yet how impossible! We may stress the value of sympathy; we may try to sink our own identity as we read. But we know that we cannot sympathize wholly or immerse ourselves wholly; there is always a demon in us who whispers, "I hate, I love," and we cannot silence him. Indeed, it is precisely because we hate and we love that our relation with the poets and novelists is so intimate that we find the presence of another person intolerable. And even if the results are abhorrent and our judgments are wrong, still our taste, the nerve of sensation that sends shocks through us, is our chief illuminant; we learn through feeling; we cannot suppress our own idiosyncrasy without impoverishing it. But as time goes on perhaps we can train our taste; perhaps we can make it submit to some control. When it has fed greedily and lavishly upon books of all sorts—poetry, fiction, history, biography—and has stopped reading and looked for long spaces upon the variety, the incongruity of the living world, we shall find that it is changing a little; it is not so greedy, it is more reflective. It will begin to bring us not merely judgments on particular books, but it will tell us that there is a quality common to certain books. Listen, it will say, what shall we call *this?* And it will read us perhaps *Lear* and then perhaps *Agamemnon* in order to bring out that common quality. Thus, with our taste to guide us, we shall venture beyond the particular book in search of qualities that group books together; we shall give them names and thus frame a rule that brings order into our perceptions. We shall gain a further and a rarer pleasure from that discrimination. But as a rule only lives when it is perpetually broken by contact with the books themselves—nothing is easier and more stultifying than to make rules which exist out of touch with facts, in a vacuum—now at least, in order to steady ourselves in this difficult attempt, it may be well to turn to the very rare writers who are able to enlighten us upon literature as an art. Coleridge and Dryden and Johnson, in their considered criticism, the poets and novelists themselves in their unconsidered sayings, are often surprisingly relevant; they light up and solidify the vague ideas that have been tumbling in the misty depths of our minds. But they are only able to help us if we come to them laden with questions and suggestions won honestly in the course of our own reading. They can do nothing for us if we herd ourselves under their authority and lie down like sheep in the shade of a hedge. We can only understand their ruling when it comes in conflict with our own and vanquishes it.

If this is so, if to read a book as it should be read calls for the rarest qualities of imagination, insight, and judgment, you may perhaps conclude that literature is a very complex art and that it is unlikely that we shall be able, even after a lifetime of reading, to make any valuable contribution to its criticism. We must remain readers; we shall not put on the further glory that belongs to those rare beings who are also critics. But still we have our responsibilities as readers and even our importance. The standards we raise and the judgments we pass steal into the air and become part of the atmosphere which writers breathe as they work. An influence is created which tells upon them even if it never finds its way into print. And that influence, if it were well instructed, vigorous and individual and sincere, might be of great value now when criticism is necessarily in abeyance; when books pass in review like the procession of animals in a shooting gallery, and the critic has only one second in which to load and aim and shoot and may well be pardoned if he mistakes rabbits for tigers, eagles for barn-door fowls, or misses altogether and wastes his shot upon some peaceful sow grazing in a further field. If behind the erratic gunfire of the press the author felt that there was another kind of criticism, the opinion of people reading for the love of reading, slowly and unprofessionally, and judging with great sympathy and yet with great severity, might this not improve the quality of his work? And if by our means books were to become stronger, richer, and more varied, that would be an end worth reaching.

Yet who reads to bring about an end however desirable? Are there not some pursuits that we practise because they are good in themselves, and some pleasures that are final? And is not this among them? I have sometimes dreamt, at least, that when the Day of Judgment dawns and the great conquerors and lawyers and statesmen come to receive their rewards—their crowns, their laurels, their names carved indelibly upon imperishable marble—the Almighty will turn to Peter and will say, not without a certain envy when He sees us coming with our books under our arms, "Look, these need no reward. We have nothing to give them here. They have loved reading."

Questions for discussion

1. What, in Woolf's view, is the very first "step" in learning how to read a book?

2. Very broadly, what are the stages of reading Woolf describes? Are they sequential? If you skipped a step, would you sacrifice the overall usefulness and sense of the process?

3. Woolf's initial premise is that no one can tell anyone else how to read. Why, then, does she proceed to do just that?

What is the precondition to the reading process she insists on at the outset of the essay? What, in her view, is the "law" of the library?

4. Woolf suggests that attempts to write can aid you in learning how to read better. Do you agree or disagree? Why?

5. Why does Woolf direct her attention to "rubbish-reading"? How does "rubbish-reading" differ from what one might call—for lack of a better word—"quality" reading?

6. In her concluding paragraphs, Woolf groups the stages of reading into two broad categories. What are those stages? What is the importance of pushing our reading selves into the latter stage?

7. Having followed Woolf's advice, will you then discover a definite conclusion to the process—a point at which you have "arrived" as a sophisticated, astute critic? Where does Woolf think you should end up? What is your reading destination, your reading responsibility, your reading influence?

◆

Activities

1. Write an essay in which you explain how to make a regional specialty or a favorite family recipe. First place the recipe in context, explaining to the reader in the introductory paragraph what happy associations the recipe holds for you, why you crave it, why you wish other people could have this taste experience. Your thesis will convey your enthusiasm. Your topic sentences will group the stages of preparation.

2. Explain two procedures, choosing from the following list. Select one procedure that does not necessarily require a chronological or sequential presentation and one that does. Be sure to develop a thesis or statement of purpose, and write at least three paragraphs in which the steps or techniques are grouped under topic sentences.

   How to study

   How to deal with a bore

   How to get rid of a boy (girl) you can't stand who keeps asking you out

   How to lose two pounds per week

How to dissect a frog

How to tell a bad joke

How to fight unfairly

How to flunk out of school

How to apply for U.S. citizenship

How to give blood at the blood bank

How to administer artificial resuscitation

How to apply make-up

How to tell a friend his fly is open, he has spinach in his teeth, and he has halitosis

How to apply for a credit card

How to make new friends

How to keep old ones

How to rent an apartment

How to place a long-distance call to Moscow

How to outfit yourself for hiking, skiing, spelunking, whitewater rafting, mountain climbing, or sky diving

How to put the friendship back into a romance

Compare or contrast two related items.

Classifying or categorizing calls forth your powers of observation and requires you to see relationships among, between, and within groups. Comparing and contrasting demand from you a similar way of looking at and understanding the world. When you compare, you stress the similarities between two related objects, people, or ideas. When you contrast, you stress the differences, but the things or people or ideas being contrasted must have some basis of comparison as well. After all, what gain in insight or information could possibly be made if you compared or contrasted your grandmother and Afghanistan, popcorn and Porsches?

But if the basis for comparison or contrast is logical, then this method of development and support can lead to remarkable, dramatic comprehension in the reader. Sometimes—as with

God, Truth, the size of Texas, the distance to the moon, the theory of relativity, the power in a boxer's punch, the flavor of a food, the aroma of a perfume, the intelligence of a member of Mensa—we cannot explain or define or describe those quantities and qualities except by discussing them in terms of something else.

Comparison and contrast, therefore, always occur in context and always, if the similarities and differences are clearly delineated, result in a better grasp of the unknown quantity, the quantity we are struggling to define or explain. At least one side of the comparison or contrast, therefore, is often familiar to the reader. What knowledge or information derives from asserting that your next-door neighbor looks like your mother, neither of whom the reader knows? How much clearer is the comparison when you assert that your next-door neighbor looks like Katherine Hepburn or Marilyn Monroe? By the same token, you cannot explain capitalism as it contrasts with socialism unless the reader has some familiarity with at least one of these economic systems. The most effective comparisons and contrasts, then, draw from a common pool of experience or information and form new creeks and rivers of previously unexplored waters.

Sometimes, however, both sides of the comparison or contrast may be unfamiliar, and you will need to look for ways to make these two unknowns familiar. For example, in the essay on General Grant and General Lee (see page 157), the two generals are, perhaps, unknown quantities. How does Bruce Catton make the comparisons and contrasts come alive for the reader? He grounds the men in regions, customs, and historical events that might be familiar to most readers. You may know little or nothing about these generals, but you surely know something of the characters of North and South, of the history of the Civil War, of the meaning of "aristocracy" and "frontier life." The comparison and contrast, therefore, are comprehensible in the context of other details, examples, and other comparisons and contrasts.

Developing skill with comparing and contrasting will enable you to assimilate and integrate information, to see relationships, recurring patterns, themes, motifs. You will surely have noticed that essay questions on exams often employ comparison or contrast as a method of organization and development. Using this method, the professor can, in effect, cover two subjects with one developmental mode, checking simultaneously your knowledge of Wordsworth and Coleridge as poets in the Romantic period, your understanding of presidential duties versus vice presidential duties, your comprehension of the advantages and disadvantages of one system of government and another.

Comparing and/or contrasting gives a voice to what is elusive, inexplicable, strange, exotic. When you cannot find words to say what you mean, you can rely on *simile*—a short comparison using "like" or "as." Or you can depend on *metaphor* to express the inexpressible, referring to a certain kind of affection as puppy love, because the love of which you speak is akin to the adoration that puppies show to their owners.

Looking at the surfaces of apparently unrelated objects, personalities, or philosophies and finding what makes them different or what makes them alike can sharpen your powers of perception. These two methods of development and support will help you see what you have never seen, hear what you have never heard, and think what you have never thought. With comparison and contrast, you can take your reader into outer space, plunk him down on top of the Andes, ride him down the Ganges, convince him of what a Martian, a UFO, or a rice paddy really look like, really *are* like.

> ### A Telling Comparison
>
> The theory of relativity meant nothing to me until I saw it compared, on a television show, to a person riding away from Big Ben on a bus. Presenting me directly with the formula $e = mc^2$ did me no good at all. The concept was meaningless except in the context of comparison. Buses, clocks, motions, Big Ben, I could understand. And that understanding led me, in a somewhat roundabout way, to an understanding of the theory.

Comparing and contrasting will call forth your finest organizational skills. It is hard enough to write about one thing. Writing about two, and always in terms of the other, requires an artful juggling of presentation and coordination. There are three methods of organization from which you may select.

1. By far, the simplest organizational pattern is to write, in the first half of the essay, about one side of the comparison or contrast, and then, in the second half of the essay, to write

about the other side of the comparison or contrast. But the resulting essay will feel like two essays. And the reader will have the uneasy sensation that you have not thought very deeply about how best to display the similarities and differences. This arrangement may be useful, however, when there are only one or two points of difference or similarity.

2. You might also use the alternating paragraph approach, setting forth one side of the comparison or contrast in one paragraph and following it in the next paragraph with the other side of the comparison or contrast. So, for example, if you are contrasting the health benefits of swimming and jogging, you write a paragraph about the aerobic benefits in jogging and follow it with another paragraph about the aerobic benefits in swimming. The effect is somewhat tighter, more organic than is the first method of organization. But the movement through the argument or information still seems somewhat sluggish, plodding, or even choppy. You might use this arrangement when you wish to compare or contrast on the basis of three or four points.

3. By far the superior organizational scheme is to incorporate discussion of both sides of the comparison or contrast within each paragraph. How do you discuss two aspects of a subject within a single paragraph? You create a topic sentence that sets up the comparison or contrast on the basis of one similarity or difference. You write, for example, "Swimming and jogging can dramatically increase one's aerobic capacity." Then, in the paragraph that follows, you can cite which of the two provides superior aerobic exercise, how the aerobic benefits occur, what are the pros and cons of both forms of exercise. The resulting essay holds together very tightly, so much so that the reader has no feeling of being dragged back and forth between one side and the other. Instead, ideas and assertions move as one, even though there are clearly two subjects under consideration.

The last organizational arrangement requires careful attention, balance, control. You cannot let one side of your comparison slide away while you are clutching too hard at the other. You cannot change the basis of comparison or contrast within the paragraph. You have to look at both sides of the road, even though you are walking straight through a subject. This final arrangement works best when you are comparing or contrasting on numerous points, meticulously, thoroughly.

The following essay is devoted entirely to contrasting thin people and fat people. The writer usually incorporates a discussion of the differences between thin people and fat people within paragraphs, using the third method of organization. However, one side of the contrast occasionally dominates the middle paragraphs. Italicized explanations follow each paragraph of the essay so you can understand better how the writer manages to keep both sides of the contrast constantly before the reader's eye. The two sides of the contrast appear in italics, offering you an easy way to see how the contrast is set up and alternates throughout the essay.

THAT LEAN AND HUNGRY LOOK

Caesar was right. *Thin people* need watching. I've been watching them for most of my adult life, and I don't like what I see. When these narrow fellows spring at me, I'm zero at the bone. Thin people come in all personalities, most of them menacing. You've got your "together" thin person, your mechanical thin person, your condescending thin person, your tsk-tsk thin person, and your efficiency-expert thin person. All of them are dangerous.

> *In the introductory paragraph, the focus is squarely and solely on thin people who are, after all, the group under attack: "All of them are dangerous."*

In the first place, *thin people* aren't fun. They don't know how to goof off, at least not in the best, fat sense of the word. They've always got to be a-doing. Give them a coffee break, and they'll jog around the block. Supply them with a quiet evening at home, and they'll fix the screen door or clip coupons. They say things like "there aren't enough hours in the day." *Fat people* never say that. Fat people think the day is too damn long already.

> *Here the writer introduces the other side of the contrast—fat people. The writer assumes that since skinniness is so much admired in our culture, an effective way to dispel the myth of skinny perfection is to find a good thing to say about fat people. Notice that the topic sentence about fun is supported by numerous examples of the thin person's not having any.*

Thin people make me tired. They've got speedy little metabolisms that cause them to bustle briskly. They're forever rubbing their bony hands together and looking for new problems to tackle. I like to surround myself with sluggish, inert, easygoing *fat people*, the kind who believe that if you clean it up today it'll just get dirty again tomorrow.

> *Thin people and fat people again are contrasted in the same paragraph, this time on the basis of bustling or not bustling. The writer saves the fat people for the punch line.*

Some people say the business about the jolly *fat person* is a myth, that all of us chubbies are neurotic, sick, sad people. I disagree. Fat people may not be chortling all the day long, but they're a hell of a lot *nicer* than the wizened and shriveled. *Thin people* turn surly, mean, and hard at a young age because they never learn the value of a hot-fudge sundae for easing tension. Thin people don't like gooey things because they themselves are neither gooey nor soft. They are crunchy and dull, like carrots. They go straight to the jugular of things while *fat people* let things stay all blurry, hazy, and vague, the way life actually is.

> *Here, the fat people begin the contrast, and the thin people take second place. An alternating contrast goes on throughout the paragraph, and the two are being contrasted on the basis of personality. Food preferences are used figuratively to illustrate gooey and crunchy attitudes.*

Thin people want to face the truth. *Fat people* know there is no truth. One of my *thin friends* is always staring at complex, unsolvable problems and saying, "The key thing is—." *Fat people* never say that. They know there isn't any such thing as the key thing. And even if they found the key, it would be for the wrong door.

> *Now the writer slides into thin/fat philosophies. The thin people begin the contrast, followed by an immediate mention of fat people; and an alternating contrast continues throughout the paragraph.*

Thin people believe in logic. *Fat people* see all sides. The sides fat people see are rounded blobs, usually gray, always nebulous, and truly not worth worrying about. But the *thin person* persists: "If you consume more calories than you burn, you will gain weight. It's that simple." *Fat people* always grin when they hear statements like that. They know better. Fat people realize that life is both illogical and unfair. They know very well that God is not in his heaven and all is not right with the world. If

God was up there, fat people could have two doughnuts and a big orange drink any time they wanted to.

> *The basis of contrast is logic, rationality. Again the writer moves back and forth throughout the paragraph from thin to fat to thin and back to fat, using quotations and description to support the assertions.*

Thin people have a long list of logical things they are always spouting off to me. They spout them all day long, largely because their mouths are never full of mashed potatoes or Sugar Daddies. Thin people hold up one finger at a time as they go through the list, so I won't lose track. They speak slowly, as if to a young child: cigarettes kill; get a grip on yourself; you ought to eat three squares a day; no snacks; get in touch with your body; shape up; use sound fiscal management. Statements like that.

> *This paragraph appears to be devoted entirely to the logical pronouncements of thin people, but the writer, a chubby, appears indirectly.*

Thin people think these 2,000-point plans lead to happiness. Fat people know happiness is elusive and fleeting at best, and even if fat people could get the kind *thin people* are talking about, they wouldn't want it. *Fat people* see that such programs are too dull, too hard, too off the mark. They are never better than a whole cheese cake.

> *Again, the alternating contrast appears, and again the fat people have the last joke. The basis of contrast is the search for happiness.*

Fat people know all about the mystery of life. They are the ones acquainted with the night, with fate, with playing it by ear. One *thin person* I know suggested that we arrange all the parts of a jigsaw puzzle into groups, according to size, shape, and color. He figured this method would cut the time needed to complete the puzzle by fifty percent. I said I wouldn't do it. One, the whole idea turned me off. Two, I like to muddle through. Three, what good would it do to finish the puzzle early? And four, the puzzle wasn't the key thing. The key thing was the fun of four people (one *thin person* included) sitting around a card table, working a jigsaw puzzle. My *thin friend* had no use for my list. He stalked outside to prune the hedge. The three remaining *fat people* finished the puzzle and celebrated with a pan of double-fudge brownies.

> *The alternating contrast comes out, this time, in a narrative,*
> *with the fat person and the thin person functioning as*
> *characters in the story. You then get to see fat people and thin*
> *people in action—or, in the fat people's case, in inaction.*

The main problem with *thin people* is that they oppress. Their good intentions, bony torsos, tight ships, neat corners, cerebral machinations, and pat solutions loom darkly over the loose, comfortable, spread-out world of *fat people*. Long after *fat people* have removed their coats and shoes and put up their feet on the coffee table, *thin people* are still perched on the edge of the sofa, neat as a pin, discussing rutabagas.

> *The paragraph centers on the oppressive presence of thin people*
> *and how they spoil the fun. Fat people and thin people again*
> *appear in a little vignette, so that you can see how both types act*
> *in social situations.*

Fat people are heavily into fits of laughter, slapping their thighs, and whooping it up, while *thin people* are still politely waiting for the punch line. Thin people are downers. They like math and morality and reasoned evaluations of the limitations of human beings. They have their skinny little acts together. They expound, prognose, probe, and prick.

> *The paragraph begins with fat people but ends up focusing*
> *primarily on broad considerations of the limitations of thin*
> *people. The broadening indicates that the end is near. The writer*
> *will not mention thin people again. Thin people are finished.*
> *Notice the alliteration—the repetition of initial consonant*
> *sounds—"prognose, probe, and prick." The device appears again*
> *in the glorious conclusion about goodly gluttons.*

Fat people are convivial. They will like you even if you're irregular and have acne. They will come up with a good reason why you never wrote the great American novel. They will cry in your beer with you. They will put your name in the pot. They will let you off the hook. Fat people will gab, giggle, guffaw, gallumph, gyrate, and gossip. They are generous, goodly, and great. What you want when you're down is soft and jiggly, not muscled and hard. Fat people have plenty of room. Fat people will take you in.

> *The conclusion is a hymn of praise to the grandeur of fat people.*
> *The thin people have been squeezed out almost entirely, though*

*they make one tiny appearance in the phrase "muscled and
hard." The last sentence of the conclusion, the clincher, so to
speak, carries a double meaning. Has the writer taken you in?*

Questions for discussion

1. In this essay, the reader is treated to a feast of confirmation
   and support, stuffing the reader with details, description, examples, scenes, quotations. Is the piling up of proof too
   much, or does the abundance of proof relate to the theme?

2. In almost every paragraph, the basis of contrast makes possible the discussion of both sides of the contrast. What is the
   effect on the unity and coherence of the essay? How would
   the essay fare if the writer had first discussed all the traits
   and habits of skinny people and followed that discussion
   with a treatment of fat habits and personalities? Explain.

3. Does this contrast (or contrasts, generally) lead to still more
   stereotyping? Why or why not?

4. The writer uses several allusions or references to famous literary works. The following sentences echo the great literary
   works:

   Caesar was right. Thin people need watching.

   When these narrow fellows spring at me, I'm zero at the
   bone.

   They know very well that God is not in his heaven and all
   is not right with the world.

   They are the ones acquainted with the night.

   Can you identify the sources of the quotations? You may
   have studied the literary works in class, or you may locate
   them in a collection of famous quotations. Why does the
   writer use these literary allusions?

5. Is this essay about body size, or is it about something else?
   Explain.

6. Is hyperbole—exaggeration, that is—related to the theme of
   the essay? Why or why not?

The following essay relies on contrasting as its primary
method of development and support. Hatred, after all, is hard to
explain except in the context of love. The reverse is also true.

The writer uses several techniques to make these abstract ideas real to the reader. Also, the writer alternates discussions of love and hate, pitting the two against each other so that the reader can have a clearer understanding of both.

LOVE AND HATE

I used to want everybody to like me. Now I'm satisfied if nobody hates me. Indifference works just as well as hate and isn't half as messy. Hate stirs the acids in the stomach and contorts the face.

A woman once told me she was sorry we had lost the knack for full-blown hating, in the best, feuding, Hatfield versus McCoy sense. She said she'd rather really hate one person than be condemned to a lifetime of insipid niceness. I see her point, but disagree. Having recently seen the face of hate, I can say, unequivocally, that I hate hate.

I have gone to the source of all wisdom, *John Bartlett's Familiar Quotations*, to find the answers to my questions about love and hate. I counted 833 listings under "love," not counting "loved," "lover," "loves," "loveth," "loving," and "loving-kindness." "Hate" scored only 75, not counting "hated," "hateful," "hater," "hates," "hating," and "hatred." Some people might cite the score as evidence of love's victory. I'm not cynical, but I don't. Direct experience shows that love is losing in the real world, the world not according to *Bartlett's*. We write about love, but we act out hate.

Few of our written words have to do with hate. We don't sing hate songs, write hate sonnets, send hate greetings, or create Harlequin hate novels. The poison-pen note and the assassin's wild missive represent isolated flare-ups of hate. These hate words are off the charts, the obvious work, we say, of society's misfits. Love, however, pours from the pen onto the page, not into life.

Many times we write effusive declarations of love, but then we won't lift a finger or risk a reputation for the beloved. In contrast, we daily see hate in action, and not only in child abuse, murder, and rape. Hate functions in our daily lives, without words, silent and deadly: the killing glances of spouses over the morning newspaper; the sworn social enemies who exit through the back door while the object of their hate enters through the front door; the adolescent fist pushed through the wall or door; the blood-curdling scream reverberating through the suburban neighborhood.

Hate is so much a part of life, we scarcely try to hide it. Mothers bark ferociously at little children nipping at their heels. Obscenities fly across the ball field. The switchblade gleams in the school corridor, between history and poetry class.

Hate is vigorous. It seems justified. The excellent reasons for hating line up like crisply attired soldiers in a dress parade: she's so bossy, I can't stand her; he thinks he's so smart, the idiot; when she gets that look on her face, I could smack her; she's not "our kind of people." Hate rattles the world: the plate sails through the kitchen; doors slam; feet stomp; the fist goes in the stomach; the blow falls well below the belt.

Love is another, secret matter. Love operates underground, in hidden acts of tenderness and sympathy: hands grasp under the table; eyes seek eyes; small generosities and charities go unheralded, unnoticed. Love is speechless, blushing.

Love does not make the world go round. It makes the world uncomfortable. If you have ever loved someone, you will note that forces join to combat or crush it. All is hateful sabotage. We chalk up altruism to a neurotic need for glory. When mothers love sons, we whisper of sexual disorientation. When fathers love daughters, we imagine hidden lust. When love binds people, we look for ways to break the connection, sternly advising the lovers to keep their feet on the ground, their heads out of the clouds.

Love has a hard time loving. Asked why we love someone, we can scarcely name the reasons. No one is more tongue-tied than a lover stating the attributes of the beloved. But all the reasons for hating come out in measured, logical, well-rehearsed speeches. The hater seems sensible. He has good cause, we say, for striking people from his list, as if people were groceries, charts, categories in books. If we want to be entirely justified in hating, all we have to do is come up with a suitable label, and the hated object flutters and dies on the impeccably scientific field of justification and classification.

We resist love's flowing motion. Hate holds off the changes and adjustments we so much fear. Hate fossilizes. If we can stay in our deep rut of hating, we won't be vulnerable. We can petrify the world. We can hold on to the person we hate the way a dog guards an old bone.

Let one person speak of love, however, and all the no-nonsense folks will gather, prepared to shoot down every case for loving with the small stones of their objections: be careful; you might get hurt; save your love for heaven; plant your feet in hell for now.

Put my arguments for hate to any earthly test, and you will find me painfully right. If you take the risk of loving, you will

not go far along the green mountaintop of bliss before you encounter the granite face of hate.

You begin to suspect that hate is more often based not on
something you *did* but on something the hater *is*. Nothing will
appease a full-fledged hater. His brooding calculations work
against the lover. The hater has stayed awake all through the
black night, marshalling his defenses, planning his meticulous
strategies. While love works its wonders in the lives of those
who choose it, the hater pursues his dark work, alone.

If I could have one wish, I would choose love big enough to
take in all kinds and degrees of loving. I would let words of love
be replaced by sunny, open acts of loving. I would rather, in the
end, *be* in love than *write* about it. So, no doubt, would all the
poets, saints, and sages.

Questions for discussion

1. How does the writer make concrete the abstract concepts of
   love and hate?

2. What is the pattern of contrast *within* paragraphs, *between*
   paragraphs?

3. What are the examples of figurative language? What do hate
   and love look like, feel like? How do they behave?

4. What is the initial premise that makes the contrast possible?

5. What methods of development and support, besides contrast, does the writer use?

The following essay shows how comparison and contrast can
be put to serious purposes, not only providing an effective way
to analyze and inform readers about the two men being contrasted but also giving valuable additional insights about history, about how or why the Civil War was fought.

GRANT AND LEE: A STUDY IN CONTRASTS

Bruce Catton

When Ulysses S. Grant and Robert E. Lee met in the parlor of
a modest house at Appomattox Court House, Virginia, on April 9,

From Bruce Catton, "Grant and Lee: A Study in Contrasts," in *The American
Story.* New York: Broadcast Music, Inc., 1956.

1865, to work out the terms for the surrender of Lee's Army of Northern Virginia, a great chapter in American life came to a close, and a great new chapter began.

These men were bringing the Civil War to its virtual finish. To be sure, other armies had yet to surrender, and for a few days the fugitive Confederate government would struggle desperately and vainly, trying to find some way to go on living now that its chief support was gone. But in effect it was all over when Grant and Lee signed the papers. And the little room where they wrote out the terms was the scene of one of the poignant, dramatic contrasts in American history.

They were two strong men, these oddly different generals, and they represented the strengths of two conflicting currents that, through them, had come into final collision.

Back of Robert E. Lee was the notion that the old aristocratic concept might somehow survive and be dominant in American life. Lee was tidewater Virginia, and in his background were family, culture, and tradition . . . the age of chivalry transplanted to a New World which was making its own legends and its own myths. He embodied a way of life that had come down through the age of knighthood and the English country squire. America was a land that was beginning all over again, dedicated to nothing much more complicated than the rather hazy belief that all men had equal rights and should have an equal chance in the world. In such a land Lee stood for the feeling that it was somehow of advantage to human society to have a pronounced inequality in the social structure. There should be a leisure class, backed by ownership of land; in turn, society itself should be keyed to the land as the chief source of wealth and influence. It would bring forth (according to this ideal) a class of men with a strong sense of obligation to the community; men who lived not to gain advantage for themselves, but to meet the solemn obligations which had been laid on them by the very fact that they were privileged. From them the country would get its leadership; to them it could look for the higher values— of thought, of conduct, of personal deportment—to give it strength and virtue.

Lee embodied the noblest elements of this aristocratic ideal. Through him, the landed nobility justified itself. For four years, the Southern states had fought a desperate war to uphold the ideals for which Lee stood. In the end, it almost seemed as if the Confederacy fought for Lee; as if he himself was the Confederacy . . . the best thing that the way of life for which the Confederacy stood could ever have to offer. He had passed into legend before Appomattox. Thousands of tired, underfed, poorly clothed Confederate soldiers, long since past the simple enthusiasm of the early days of the struggle, somehow considered Lee the symbol of everything for which they had been willing to die. But they could not quite put this feeling into words. If the Lost Cause, sanctified by so much heroism and so many deaths, had a living justification, its justification was General Lee.

Grant, the son of a tanner on the Western frontier, was everything Lee was not. He had come up the hard way and embodied nothing in particular except the eternal toughness and sinewy fiber of the men who grew up beyond the mountains. He was one of a body of men who owed reverence and obeisance to no one, who were self-reliant to a fault, who cared hardly anything for the past but who had a sharp eye for the future.

These frontier men were the precise opposites of the tidewater aristocrats. Back of them, in the great surge that had taken people over the Alleghenies and into the opening Western country, there was a deep, implicit dissatisfaction with a past that had settled into grooves. They stood for democracy, not from any reasoned conclusion about the proper ordering of human society, but simply because they had grown up in the middle of democracy and knew how it worked. Their society might have privileges, but they would be privileges each man had won for himself. Forms and patterns meant nothing. No man was born to anything, except perhaps to a chance to show how far he could rise. Life was competition.

Yet along with this feeling had come a deep sense of belonging to a national community. The Westerner who developed a farm, opened a shop, or set up in business as a trader, could hope to prosper only as his own community prospered—and his community ran from the Atlantic to the Pacific and from Canada down to Mexico. If the land was settled, with towns and highways and accessible markets, he could better himself. He saw his fate in terms of the nation's own destiny. As its horizons expanded, so did his. He had, in other words, an acute dollars-and-cents stake in the continued growth and development of his country.

And that, perhaps, is where the contrast between Grant and Lee becomes most striking. The Virginia aristocrat, inevitably, saw himself in relation to his own region. He lived in a static society which could endure almost anything except change. Instinctively, his first loyalty would go to the locality in which that society existed. He would fight to the limit of endurance to defend it, because in defending it he was defending everything that gave his own life its deepest meaning.

The Westerner, on the other hand, would fight with an equal tenacity for the broader concept of society. He fought so because everything he lived by was tied to growth, expansion, and a constantly widening horizon. What he lived by would survive or fall with the nation itself. He could not possibly stand by unmoved in the face of an attempt to destroy the Union. He would combat it with everything he had, because he could only see it as an effort to cut the ground out from under his feet.

So Grant and Lee were in complete contrast, representing two diametrically opposed elements in American life. Grant was the modern man emerging; beyond him, ready to come on the stage, was the great age of steel and machinery, of crowded cities and a restless burgeoning vitality. Lee might have ridden down from the old age of chivalry, lance in hand, silken banner fluttering over his head. Each man was the perfect champion of his cause, drawing both his strengths and his weaknesses from the people he led.

Yet it was not all contrast, after all. Different as they were—in background, in personality, in underlying aspiration—these two great soldiers had much in common. Under everything else, they were marvelous fighters. Furthermore, their fighting qualities were really very much alike.

Each man had, to begin with, the great virtue of utter tenacity and fidelity. Grant fought his way down the Mississippi Valley in spite of acute personal discouragement and profound military handicaps. Lee hung on in the trenches at Petersburg after hope itself had died. In each man there was an indomitable quality . . . the born fighter's refusal to give up as long as he can still remain on his feet and lift his two fists.

Daring and resourcefulness they had, too; the ability to think faster and move faster than the enemy. These were the qualities which gave Lee the dazzling campaigns of Second Manassas and Chancellorsville and won Vicksburg for Grant.

Lastly, and perhaps greatest of all, there was the ability, at the end, to turn quickly from war to peace once the fighting was over. Out of the way these two men behaved at Appomattox came the possibility of a peace of reconciliation. It was a possibility not wholly realized, in the years to come, but which did, in the end, help the two sections to become one nation again . . . after a war whose bitterness might have seemed to make such a reunion wholly impossible. No part of either man's life became him more than the part he played in their brief meeting in the McLean house at Appomattox. Their behavior there put all succeeding generations of Americans in their debt. Two great Americans, Grant and Lee—very different, yet under everything very much alike. Their encounter at Appomattox was one of the great moments of American history.

Questions for discussion

1. Catton both contrasts and compares General Lee and General Grant. What were their differences? What were their similarities?

2. What other ideas, events, regions, and philosophies are being compared and contrasted?

3. What is the pattern of contrast and comparison? Consider the arrangement of the paragraphs as they deal first with one man, then the other, then both, then both in relation to other comparisons and contrasts. Is the arrangement effective? Why or why not?

4. Notice that Catton is able to supply or hint at areas of concern far beyond the realm of these two individuals. What other great leaders could, in a sense, serve as symbols of larger events, regions, or philosophies? For example, what contrasts or comparisons between John F. Kennedy and Richard Nixon could lead you to a better understanding of the 1960s and 1970s? What two singers or singing groups could embody the direction and focus of popular or rock music in the last two decades? What two religious leaders could provide the starkest contrast between fundamental or orthodox religious beliefs and unorthodox or primarily humanistic beliefs?

In the following excerpt from writer Cynthia Ozick's essay "The Riddle of the Ordinary," Ozick uses contrast between the Extraordinary and the Ordinary to introduce a larger theme: the Jewish celebration of the Ordinary and its implications for the conduct of the whole of society. The rhetorical scheme shifts gradually toward persuasion. Notice how contrast gives way to exhortation on behalf of the simple, largely unnoticed aspects of daily life.

THE RIDDLE OF THE ORDINARY

Cynthia Ozick

Though we all claim to be monotheists, there is one rather ordinary way in which we are all also dualists: we all divide the

---

From Cynthia Ozick, "The Riddle of the Ordinary," in *Art and Ardor*. New York: Dutton, 1984, pp. 200–206.

world into the Ordinary and the Extraordinary. This is undoubtedly the most natural division the mind is subject to—plain and fancy, simple and recondite, commonplace and awesome, usual and unusual, credible and incredible, quotidian and intrusive, natural and unnatural, regular and irregular, boring and rhapsodic, secular and sacred, profane and holy: however the distinction is characterized, there is no human being who does not, in his own everydayness, feel the difference between the Ordinary and the Extraordinary.

The Extraordinary is easy. And the more extraordinary the Extraordinary is, the easier it is: "easy" in the sense that we can almost always recognize it. There is no one who does not know when something special is happening: the high, terrifying, tragic, and ecstatic moments are unmistakable in any life. Of course the Extraordinary can sometimes be a changeling, and can make its appearance in the cradle of the Ordinary; and then it is not until long afterward that we become aware of how the visitation was not, after all, an ordinary one. But by and large the difference between special times and ordinary moments is perfectly clear, and we are never in any doubt about which are the extraordinary ones.

How do we respond to the Extraordinary? This too is easy: by paying attention to it. The Extraordinary is so powerful that it commands from us a redundancy, a repetition of itself: it seizes us so undividedly, it declares itself so dazzlingly or killingly, it is so deafening with its LOOK! SEE! NOTICE! PAY ATTENTION!, that the only answer we can give is to look, see, notice, and pay attention. The Extraordinary sets its own terms for its reception, and its terms are inescapable. The Extraordinary does not let you shrug your shoulders and walk away.

But the Ordinary is a much harder case. In the first place, by making itself so noticeable—it is around us all the time—the Ordinary has got itself in a bad fix with us: we hardly ever notice it. The Ordinary, simply by *being* so ordinary, tends to make us ignorant or neglectful; when something does not insist on being noticed, when we aren't grabbed by the collar or struck on the skull by a presence or an event, we take for granted the very things that most deserve our gratitude.

And this is the chief vein and deepest point concerning the Ordinary: that it *does* deserve our gratitude. The Ordinary lets us live out our humanity; it doesn't scare us, it doesn't excite us, it doesn't distract us—it brings us the safe return of the school bus every day, it lets us eat one meal after another, put one foot in front of the other. In short, it is equal to the earth's provisions; it grants us life, continuity, the leisure to recognize who and what we are, and who and what our fellows are, these creatures who live out their everydayness side by side with us in their own unextraordinary ways. Ordinariness can be defined as a breathing-space: the breathing-space between getting born and dying, perhaps; or else the breathing-space between rapture and rapture; or, more usually, the breathing-space between one disaster and the next. Ordinariness is sometimes the *status quo*, sometimes the slow, unseen movement of a subtle but ineluctable cycle, like a ride on the hour hand of the clock; in any case the Ordinary is above all *what is expected*.

And what is expected is not often thought of as a gift.

The second thing that ought to be said about the Ordinary is that it is sometimes extraordinarily dangerous to notice it. And this is strange, because I have just spoken of the gratitude we owe to the unnoticed foundations of our lives, and how careless we always are about this gratitude, how unthinking we are to take for granted the humdrum dailiness that is all the luxury we are ever likely to know on this planet. There are ways to try to apprehend the nature of this luxury, but they are psychological tricks, and do no good. It is pointless to contemplate, only for the sake of feeling gratitude, the bitter, vicious, crippled, drugged, diseased, deformed, despoiled, or corrupted lives that burst against their own mortality in hospitals, madhouses, prisons, all those horrendous lives chained to poverty and its variegated spawn in the long, bleak wastes on the outer margins of Ordinariness, mired in the dread of a ferocious Extraordinariness that slouches in insatiably every morning and never departs even in sleep—contemplating this, who would deny gratitude to our own Ordinariness, though it does not come easily, and has its demeaning price? Still, comparison confers relief more often than gratitude, and the gratitude that rises out of reflection on the extraordinary misfortune of others is misbegotten. —You remember how in one of the Old English poets we are told how the rejoicing hosts of heaven look down at the tortures of the damned, feeling the special pleasure of their own exemption. The consciousness of Ordinariness *is* the consciousness of exemption.

That is one way it is dangerous to take special notice of the Ordinary.

The second danger, I think, is even more terrible. But before I am ready to speak of this new, nevertheless very ancient, danger,

I want to ask this question: if we are willing to see the Ordinary as a treasure and a gift, what are we to *do* about it? Or, to put it another way, what is to be gained from noticing the Ordinary? Morally and metaphysically, what are our obligations to the Ordinary? Here art and philosophy meet with a quizzical harmony unusual between contenders. "Be one of those upon whom nothing is lost," Henry James advised; and that is one answer, the answer of what would appear to be the supreme aesthetician. For the sake of the honing of consciousness, for the sake of becoming sensitive, at every moment, *to* every moment, for the sake of making life as superlatively polished as the most sublime work of art, we ought to notice the Ordinary.

No one since the Greek sculptors and artisans has expressed this sense more powerfully than Walter Pater, that eloquent Victorian whose obsession with attaining the intensest sensations possible casts a familiar light out toward the century that followed him. Pater, like Coleridge before him and James after him, like the metaphysicians of what has come to be known as the Counterculture, was after all the highs he could accumulate in a lifetime. "We are all under sentence of death," he writes, ". . . we have an interval, and then our place knows us no more. Some spend this interval in listlessness, some in high passions, the wisest . . . in art and song. For our only chance lies in expanding that interval, in getting as many pulsations as possible into the given time. Great passions may give us this quickened sense of life. . . . Only be sure it is passion—that it does yield you this fruit of a quickened, multiplied consciousness. . . . Of this wisdom, the poetic passion, the desire for beauty, the love of art for art's sake, has most; for art comes to you professing frankly to give nothing but the highest quality to your moments as they pass, and simply for those moments' sake." And like a Zen master who seizes on the data of life only to transcend them, he announces: "Not the fruit of experience, but experience itself, is the end."

What—in this view, which once more has the allegiance of the *Zeitgeist*—what is Art? It is first noticing, and then sanctifying, the Ordinary. It is making the Ordinary into the Extraordinary. It is the impairment of the distinction between the Ordinary and the Extraordinary.

The aestheticians—the great Experiencers—can be refuted. I bring you a Hebrew melody to refute them with. It is called "The Choice"; the poet is Yeats; and since the poem is only eight lines long I would like to give over the whole of it. It begins by discriminating between essence and possession: life interpreted as *doing* beautiful things or *having* beautiful things:

> The intellect of man is forced to choose
> Perfection of the life, or of the work,
> And if it take the second must refuse
> A heavenly mansion, raging in the dark.
> When all that story's finished, what's the news?
> In luck or out the toil has left its mark:
> That old perplexity an empty purse,
> Or the day's vanity, the night's remorse.

Our choice, according to Yeats, is the choice between pursuing the life of Deed, where acts have consequences, where the fruit of experience is more gratifying than the experience itself, and pursuing the life of Art, which signifies the celebration of shape and mood. Art, he tells us, turns away from the divine preference, and finishes out a life in empty remorse; in the end the sum of the life of Art is nothing. The ironies here are multitudinous, for no one ever belonged more to the mansion of Art than Yeats himself, and it might be said that in this handful of remarkable lines Yeats condemned his own passions and his own will.

But there is a way in which the Yeats poem, though it praises Deed over Image, though it sees the human being as a creature to be judged by his acts rather than by how well he has made something—there is a way in which this poem is after all *not* a Hebrew melody. The Jewish perception of how the world is constituted also tells us that we are to go in the way of Commandment rather than symbol, goodness rather than sensation: but it will never declare that the price of Art, Beauty, Experience, Pleasure, Exaltation is a "raging in the dark" or a loss of the "heavenly mansion."

The Jewish understanding of the Ordinary is in some ways very close to Pater, and again very far from Yeats, who would punish the "perfection of the work" with an empty destiny.

With David the King we say, "All that is in the heaven and the earth is thine," meaning that it is all there for our wonder and our praise. "Be one of those upon whom nothing is lost"— James's words, but the impulse that drives them is the same as the one enjoining the observant Jew (the word "observant" is exact) to bless the moments of this world at least one hundred times a day. One hundred times: but Ordinariness is more frequent than that, Ordinariness crowds the day, we swim in the sense of our dailiness; and yet there is a blessing for every separate experience of the Ordinary.

Jewish life is crammed with such blessings—blessings that take note of every sight, sound, and smell, every rising-up and lying-down, every morsel brought to the mouth, every act of cleansing. Before he sits down to his meal, the Jew will speak the following: "Blessed are You, O Lord our God, Ruler of the Universe, whose Commandments hallow us, and who commands us to wash our hands." When he breaks his bread, he will bless God for having " brought forth bread from the earth." Each kind of food is similarly praised in turn, and every fruit in its season is praised for having renewed itself in the cycle of the seasons. And when the meal is done, a thanksgiving is said for the whole of it, and table songs are sung with exultation.

The world and its provisions, in short, are *observed*—in the two meanings of "observe." Creation is both noticed and felt to be sanctified. Everything is minutely paid attention to, and then ceremoniously praised. Here is a Talmudic saying: "Whoever makes a profane use of God's gifts—which means partaking of any worldly joy without thanking God for it—commits a theft against God." And a Talmudic dispute is recorded concerning which is the more important Scriptural utterance: loving your neighbor as yourself, or the idea that we are all the children of Adam. The sage who has the final word chooses the children-of-Adam thesis, because, he explains, our common creatureliness includes the necessity of love. But these celebrations through noticing are not self-centered and do not stop at humanity, but encompass every form of life and non-life. So there are blessings to rejoice in on smelling sweet woods or barks, fragrant plants, fruits, spices, or oils. There is a blessing on witnessing lightning, falling stars, great mountains and deserts: "Blessed are You . . . who fashioned Creation." The sound of thunder has its praise, and the sight of the sea, and a rainbow; beautiful animals are praised, and trees in their first blossoming of the year or for their beauty alone, and the new moon, and new clothing, and sexual delight. The sight of a sage brings a blessing for the creation of human wisdom, the sight of a disfigured person praises a Creator who varies the form of his creatures. From the stone to the human being, creatureliness is extolled.

This huge and unending shower of blessings on our scenes and habitations, on all the life that occupies the planet, on every plant and animal, and on every natural manifestation, serves us doubly: in the first place, what you are taught to praise you will not maim or exploit or destroy. In the second place, the categories and impulses of Art become the property of the simplest soul: because it is all the handiwork of the Creator, everything Ordinary is seen to be Extraordinary. The world, and every moment in it, is seen to be sublime, and not merely "seen to be,"but brought home to the intensest part of consciousness.

Questions for discussion

1. This essay differs from other examples in this chapter in that the rhetorical device of contrast is not sustained throughout. In this example, you learn that comparison or contrast (indeed, any one of the patterns of development discussed in this chapter) may be briefly used and then discarded as the essay progresses. Here, the contrast between the Extraordinary and the Ordinary simply introduces an in-depth discussion only of the Ordinary and of how it relates to Jewish life and all human life. At what point in the essay do you notice the shift? Why has Ozick begun with an analysis of the Extraordinary when she intends, in fact, to focus on the Ordinary? Why, according to Ozick, is the Extraordinary "easy"?

2. The topic sentences in the opening paragraphs give Ozick control over the contrast. Find those topic sentences, and then observe whether she faithfully adheres to each "side" of the contrast in the supporting paragraph.

3. List the characteristics, as Ozick presents them, first of the Extraordinary and then of the Ordinary. What details and examples does Ozick use to make the Extraordinary and the Ordinary concrete for the reader?

4. Ozick often uses figurative language to convey difficult or inexpressible meanings. For example, she refers to the Extraordinary as a "changeling" that sometimes makes "its appearance in the cradle of the Ordinary." Find other examples of such language—language that is figuratively expressive though not literally true.

5. What connection does the Ordinary have to Art, at least in the view of Henry James? What is the connection between James's famous quotation and the Jewish experience of the Ordinary?

6. How does Ozick expand her meanings beyond the initial contrast, beyond the Jewish experience, and into the larger world? What benefits could we all enjoy by having a greater

appreciation of and reverence for "every sight, sound, and smell, every rising-up and lying-down," for "lightning, falling stars, great mountains and deserts"?

◆

Activities

1. Develop a topic sentence incorporating both sides of a comparison or contrast. Keep in mind that sometimes comparing or contrasting is more interesting when you discover differences between apparently similar things and similarities between apparently different things. After you have developed the topic sentence, write a paragraph in which you convince the reader of the truth of your assertion, using details, description, anecdote, facts. Remember that because you are writing only one paragraph, you will establish only one basis for the comparing or contrasting.

Example:

Topic Sentence: Both of my best friends are A students, but Joe is a grade grabber and Ernie is a grade earner.

Joe will do anything to "get" an A: cheat, flatter the teacher, memorize with no real comprehension, even bribe friends into giving him their notes. Ernie, on the other hand, knows that grades are only an artificial symbol. He seeks real learning, the kind that comes from truly understanding the material, from thinking creatively about its uses and applications. Whereas Joe constantly ridicules the teachers and is pleased for having pulled off an academic coup, Ernie is grateful for the expertise the teacher can offer him and quietly, modestly receives his high marks as a measure of his effort, not of academic highjinks and derring-do. Long after the course is over, Ernie still remembers the concepts, information, and techniques he mastered in the course. Joe's mind is a blank. Joe forgets everything he memorized the moment the semester grades are posted. Joe uses the classroom for career advancement, prestige, success. Ernie wants something more: knowledge that will last a lifetime, insight that will enhance the quality of his existence. Joe gets an A for Ambition. Ernie gets an A for Academe, that shining place where knowledge dwells.

2. Choose one of the following, and write a short essay using comparing and contrasting as the primary method of devel-

opment. Set up the contrasts or comparisons either within the paragraphs or in alternating paragraphs.

Poker players and bridge players

Episcopalians and Baptists

Baseball fans and football fans

Tightwads and spendthrifts

Social butterflies and wallflowers

Rule followers and rule breakers

Moderates and radicals

Jargon and slang

Hypochondriacs and stoics

Hard rock and rock 'n' roll

Culture and kultur

Arrogance and confidence

Cash and credit

Talkers and do-ers

Women and ladies

Men and gentlemen

Psychologists and psychiatrists

Van and pick-up truck

Campers and Holiday Inners

Backpackers and owners of Pace Arrow Airstreams

Situation comedy and soap opera

Engineering major and agriculture major

Give examples.

You are having an argument with your roommate. You have just told her she is a complete and total slob. Those are, of course, fighting words; and they cry out for confirmation. Your friend turns and says, "Just give me ONE example." You lose if you cannot think of any. You win if you can think of 15: "Well, for one thing, you leave the cap off the toothpaste tube. For another, you've been wearing the same jeans for an entire week. For another, your stockings have runs, your hair looks like a rat's nest, your fingernails are dirty, your research paper is three weeks late, you talk rudely to your mother, your desk needs bulldozing, your sweat pants are under *my* bed, your hamster's cage needs cleaning, you stole my lipstick, you owe me five bucks, you're never on time, you forgot my birthday, and you have ring around the collar." This is the end of a beautiful friendship, but it is a beautiful example of giving examples.

Whether you are writing about scientific, personal, literary, historical, musical, domestic, or professional subjects, examples will bring credibility and concreteness to your assertions. Choosing the right examples simply means finding those examples that set the reader nodding in agreement with whatever point you are trying to make. Unfortunately, in conversation, good examples often elude the speaker. Forced to offer up "just ONE, single example," the speaker's mind goes blank. The writer, however, has the luxury of careful selection, prepared in advance. If a better example comes to mind, the writer can always delete the old and insert the new.

There are two approaches to using examples, both of which can be effective in providing development and support. First, you can use only two or three very startling and dramatic examples upon which you elaborate at some length. If, for example, you assert that, contrary to popular opinion, most folks are not over the hill at age 40, and the reader doubts you, you could tell about how your grandmother, at age 72, climbed on a Sunfish and went sailing or about Robert Frost getting his first book published at age 40 or about Daniel Defoe writing *Robinson Crusoe* at age 60 or about a Russian peasant who thrived at age 104 on dancing, vodka, and tobacco. One skillfully chosen, well-developed example can sometimes do more work than 10 weak examples in proving your point.

But sometimes you might want to support a point by supplying the reader with example after example, especially if your assertion is likely to be dismissed. This burst of quick examples, delivered in short sentences or phrases, can, in a sense, batter the reader into agreeable submission.

Here are two examples of the different approaches you may take when you give examples to support your assertion, the first using only one example to support its topic sentence; the second using 12. The first topic sentence is not as outrageous as the second, and one example serves to support the assertion.

Example A

The major danger of a technologically sophisticated world is not so much that we will destroy each other in the end but that we wouldn't miss each other if we did. E. M. Forster, in a short novel called *The Machine Stops*, illustrates this problem. In this science-fiction novel, the people have constructed barriers between themselves and life. They get their information second- or third-hand. They rely on experts. They are holed up in steel beehives of comfort and ease, with buttons and gadgets in easy reach. But their hearts are cold, their bodies pasty and atrophied, their emotions detached. Everything is neat in these lives: no passions, no messy divorces, no human contact, no doing. These people are encapsulated in ideas, not direct experience.

This one example from the Forster novel serves as the only support for the topic sentence of the paragraph. The writer elaborates on the example but, because the example is clear, feels no need to bring in examples from other sources or from the writer's own experience.

Example B

I have tried every way I know to get sick. I have responded to the women in the Geritol commercial in an unseemly fashion. I have not taken care of myself. I have skipped my vitamins. I have eaten a cellophane-wrapped array of dangerous chemicals, additives, fats, and sugars. I have, since birth, suffered a poor environment in a fallen world. I have kissed my children on the lips, drunk from the bacteria-laden communal cup in the bathroom, dried my hands on the same unspeakably dirty towel I use to wipe the kitchen counter, and taken a bite of a brownie whose ownership and point of origin were in question. I have associated with motley crews. I have loitered in public places. I have conversed with winos. But I have not been sick.

The bombardment of examples in this paragraph brings the outrageous assertion made in the topic sentence to the level of the credible. The reader, a serious sort, might not believe that people can *want* to get sick. But after the long list of examples, he or she will begin to appreciate the writer's desperate longing for a really great bout of the flu, with its cozy invitation to ease, abdication of responsibility, peace.

Of course, the sophisticated handling of examples calls forth the same skills of narration, description, and information that are always at the center of quality writing. The examples must be specific, must use words and images expressed to their maximum exactness, must carry authority and weight.

Examples may be short, perhaps appearing in one sentence. Or they may comprise the entire essay, as when a writer makes an assertion about the drudgery and tedium in a medical internship and then, over several paragraphs, offers the example of one "typical" medical intern who represents the miserable lot of all the rest.

But whenever you see the words "for example," "to illustrate," "for instance," or "in one case," you are about to be treated to a certain kind of proof, and a very effective one at that. The writer is struggling to bring home the reality of the assertion to the reader through actual or fictional examples that, in the end, convince the reader far more effectively than a series of dogmatic or general statements, reiterations, or summations.

In the following excerpt from an essay about the artist's struggle, the writer, in these middle paragraphs, uses examples to prove the truth of the assertions. The examples provide mental images, concrete situations, which the reader can scarcely dispute.

THE STATE OF THE ARTS

Artists are judged by standards alien to them and their art. I'm told, for example, that poet A. R. Ammons had his manuscript turned down by a secretary in a publishing office, who bounced the manuscript in her hands a couple of times, saying only that it was "too heavy." Ammons survived the insult and went on to win the National Book Award for his *Collected Poems,* the Bollingen Prize for Poetry, and an award from the American Academy of Letters. And Flannery O'Connor was a nonentity in her hometown of Milledgeville, Georgia, despite the publication of several novels and stories. But the moment one of her novels was made into a movie and appeared on television, the townspeople pronounced her a genuine celebrity.

Then, too, art has no place. My aunt painted her pictures on a creaky card table at her bedroom window. My friends have read their poems in shopping malls, standing between plastic plants, their voices drowned out by Muzak. The dance studio's broken windows gape darkly above the bright lights and noise of the beer joint below. All the light, air, space, and comfort are to be found in banks, executive offices, indoor athletic stadiums, and airports. Can you imagine dancers, poets, painters, and musicians free to have their way with the Houston Astrodome, the towers of the World Trade Center, the carpeted sanctuary of the First Presbyterian Church, the plush lobby of the Plaza Hotel?

Yet against all odds the artistic impulse will out. Nations, parents, economics, religion, and hard knocks of living can almost, but not quite, kill it. Poems pour from brothels, prisons, suburban ranch houses, skyscrapers, mental institutions. Anne Frank goes on keeping her diary. William Blake goes on drawing angels while the wolf howls at the door. What we can't seem entirely to kill is the aesthetic, nonfunctional, unmarketable side of ourselves, the side that has no price because it is priceless.

When I think of artists, I think of European cathedrals. Beautiful are the sculptures around the front door or the altar. But far more beautiful are the adornments in dark corners, where none but pigeons, rats, and keen-eyed tourists go. Artists, you see, are perfectionists of both the seen and the unseen. Pragmatists decorate only what shows; artists decorate what is hidden as well.

Questions for discussion

1. The writer is making a case for the struggle and the victory in the world of art as it competes with (and loses to) commercialism, practicality, public popularity, efficiency. But the point is brought home exclusively by the use of repeated examples. Are the examples convincing? Why? If not, explain how the examples could be more effective.

2. Count in each paragraph the number of examples. Now, notice the proportion of rather general examples and the proportion of very specific ones. Which kinds of examples are more compelling, convincing?

3. What other methods of development and support can you identify, even within the examples themselves?

4. Each paragraph has a topic sentence. Do all the examples in the paragraphs relate to and provide support for the topic sentence? Can you think of other examples—perhaps artist friends, perhaps your own experiences with art—that could support those same topic sentences?

In the following essay, "Baking Off," writer Nora Ephron relies almost exclusively on a series of carefully selected examples to carry her meanings. As you read and analyze the essay, note the proportion of general editorial comment to specific proof by way of telling—that is, vivid, revealing, pertinent—examples.

BAKING OFF

Nora Ephron

Roxanne Frisbie brought her own pan to the twenty-fourth annual Pillsbury Bake-Off. "I feel like a nut," she said. "It's just a plain old dumb pan, but everything I do is in that crazy pan." As it happens, Mrs. Frisbie had no cause whatsoever to feel like a nut: it seemed that at least half the 100 finalists in the Bake-It-Easy Bake-Off had brought something with them—their own sausages, their own pie pans, their own apples. Edna Buckley, who was fresh from representing New York State at the National Chicken Cooking Contest, where her recipe for fried chicken in a batter of beer, cheese, and crushed pretzels had gone down to defeat, brought with her a lucky handkerchief, a lucky horseshoe, a lucky dime for her shoe, a potholder with the Pillsbury Poppin' Fresh Doughboy on it, an Our Blessed Lady pin, and all of her jewelry, including a silver charm also in the shape of the doughboy. Mrs. Frisbie and Mrs. Buckley and the other finalists came to the Bake-Off to bake off for $65,000 in cash prizes; in Mrs. Frisbie's case, this meant making something she created herself and named Butterscotch Crescent Rolls— and which Pillsbury promptly, and to Mrs. Frisbie's dismay, renamed Sweet 'N Creamy Crescent Crisps. Almost all the recipes in the finals were renamed by Pillsbury using a lot of crispy snicky snacky words. An exception to this was Sharon Schubert's Wiki Wiki Coffee Cake, a name which ought to have been snicky snacky enough; but Pillsbury, in a moment of restraint, renamed it One-Step Tropical Fruit Cake. As it turned out, Mrs. Schubert ended up winning $5,000 for her cake, which made everybody pretty mad, even the contestants who had been saying for days that they did not care who won, that winning meant nothing and was quite beside the point; the fact was that Sharon Schubert was a previous Bake-Off winner, having won $10,000 three years before for her Crescent Apple Snacks, and in addition had walked off with a trip to Puerto Vallarta in the

From Nora Ephron, "Baking Off," in *Crazy Salad: Some Things About Women.* New York: Knopf, Bantam Books, 1975, pp. 114–122.

course of this year's festivities. Most of the contestants felt she had won a little more than was really fair. But I'm getting ahead of the story.

The Pillsbury Company has been holding Bake-Offs since 1948, when Eleanor Roosevelt, for reasons that are not clear, came to give the first one her blessing. This year's took place from Saturday, February 24, through Tuesday, February 27, at the Beverly Hilton Hotel in Beverly Hills. One hundred contestants—97 of them women, 2 twelve-year-old boys, and 1 male graduate student—were winnowed down from a field of almost 100,000 entrants to compete for prizes in five categories: flour, frosting mix, crescent main dish, crescent dessert, and hot-roll mix. They were all brought, or flown, to Los Angeles for the Bake-off itself, which took place on Monday, and a round of activities that included a tour of Universal Studios, a mini-version of television's *Let's Make a Deal* with Monty Hall himself, and a trip to Disneyland. The event is also attended by some 100 food editors, who turn it from a mere contest into the incredible publicity stunt Pillsbury intends it to be, and spend much of their time talking to each other about sixty-five new ways to use tuna fish and listening to various speakers lecture on the consumer movement and food and the appliance business. General Electric is co-sponsor of the event and donates a stove to each finalist, as well as the stoves for the Bake-Off; this year, it promoted a little Bake-Off of its own for the microwave oven, an appliance we were repeatedly told was the biggest improvement in cooking since the invention of the Willoughby System. Every one of the food editors seemed to know what the Willoughby System was, just as everyone seemed to know what Bundt pans were. "You will all be happy to hear," we were told at one point, "that only one of the finalists this year used a Bundt pan." The food editors burst into laughter at that point; I am not sure why. One Miss Alex Allard of San Antonio, Texas, had already won the microwave contest and $5,000, and she spent most of the Bake-Off turning out one Honey Drizzle Cake after another in the microwave ovens that ringed the Grand Ballroom of the Beverly Hilton Hotel. I never did taste the Honey Drizzle Cake, largely because I suspected—and this was weeks before the *Consumers Union* article on the subject—that microwave ovens were dangerous and probably caused peculiar diseases. If God had wanted us to make bacon in four minutes, He would have made bacon that cooked in four minutes.

"The Bake-Off is America," a General Electric executive announced just minutes before it began. "It's family. It's real people doing real things." Yes. The Pillsbury Bake-Off is an America that exists less and less, but exists nonetheless. It is women who still live on farms, who have six and seven children, who enter county fairs and sponsor 4-H Clubs. It is Grace Ferguson of Palm Springs, Florida, who entered the Bake-Off seventeen years in a row before reaching the finals this year, and who cooks at night and prays at the same time. It is Carol Hamilton, who once won a trip on a Greyhound bus to Hollywood for being the most popular girl in Youngstown, Ohio. There was a lot of talk at the Bake-Off about how the Bake-It-Easy theme had attracted a new breed of contestants this year, younger contestants—housewives, yes, but housewives who used whole-wheat flour and Granola and sour cream and similar supposedly hip ingredients in their recipes and were therefore somewhat more sophisticated, or urban, or something-of-the-sort than your usual Bake-Off contestant. There were a few of these—two, to be exact: Barbara Goldstein of New York City and Bonnie Brooks of Salisbury, Maryland, who actually visited the Los Angeles County Art Museum during a free afternoon. But there was also Suzie Sisson of Palatine, Illinois, twenty-five years old and the only Bundt-pan person in the finals, and her sentiments about life were the same as those that Bake-Off finalists presumably have had for years. "These are the beautiful people," she said, looking around the ballroom as she waited for her Bundt cake to come out of the oven. "They're not the little tiny rich people. They're nice and happy and religious types and family-oriented. Everyone talks about women's lib, which is ridiculous. If you're nice to your husband, he'll be nice to you. Your family is your job. They come first."

I was seven years old when the Pillsbury Bake-Off began, and as I grew up reading the advertisements for it in the women's magazines that were lying around the house, it always seemed to me that going to a Bake-Off would be the closest thing to a childhood fantasy of mine, which was to be locked overnight in a bakery. In reality, going to a Bake-Off *is* like being locked overnight in a bakery—a very bad bakery. I almost became sick right there on Range 95 after my sixth carbohydrate-packed sample—which happened, by coincidence, to be a taste of the aforementioned Mrs. Frisbie's aforementioned Sweet 'N Creamy Crescent Crisps.

But what is interesting about the Bake-Off—what is even significant about the event—is that it is, for the American housewife, what the Miss America contest used to represent to teenagers. The pinnacle of a certain kind of achievement. The best in field. To win the Pillsbury Bake-Off, even to be merely a finalist in it, is to be a great housewife. And a creative housewife. "Cooking is very creative." I must have heard that line thirty times as I interviewed the finalists. I don't happen to think that cooking is very creative—what interests me about it is, on the contrary, its utter mindlessness and mathematical certainty. "Cooking is very relaxing"—that's my bromide. On the other hand, I have to admit that some of the recipes that were concocted for the Bake-Off, amazing combinations of frosting mix and marshmallows and peanut butter and brown sugar and chocolate, were practically awe-inspiring. And cooking, it is quite clear, is only a small part of the apparently frenzied creativity that flourishes in these women's homes. I spent quite a bit of time at the Bake-Off chatting with Laura Aspis of Shaker Heights, Ohio, a seven-time Bake-Off finalist and duplicate-bridge player, and after we had discussed her high-protein macaroons made with coconut-almond frosting mix and Granola, I noticed that Mrs. Aspis was wearing green nail polish. On the theory that no one who wears green nail polish wants it to go unremarked upon, I remarked upon it.

"That's not green nail polish," Mrs. Aspis said. "It's platinum nail polish that I mix with green food coloring."

"Oh," I said.

"And the thing of it is," she went on, "when it chips, it doesn't matter."

"Why is that?" I asked.

"Because it stains your nails permanently," Mrs. Aspis said.

"You mean your nails are permanently green?"

"Well, not exactly," said Mrs. Aspis. "You see, last week they were blue, and the week before I made purple, so now my nails are a combination of all three. It looks like I'm in the last throes of something."

On Sunday afternoon, most of the finalists chose to spend their free time sitting around the hotel and socializing. Two of them—Marjorie Johnson of Robbinsdale, Minnesota, and Mary Finnegan of Minneota, Minnesota—were seated at a little round table just off the Hilton ballroom talking about a number of things, including Tupperware. Both of them love Tupperware.

"When I built my new house," Mrs. Johnson said, "I had so much Tupperware I had to build a cupboard just for it." Mrs. Johnson is a very tiny, fortyish mother of three, and she and her dentist husband have just moved into a fifteen-room house she cannot seem to stop talking about. "We have this first-floor kitchen, harvest gold and blue, and it's almost finished. Now I have a second kitchen on my walk-out level and that's going to be harvest gold and blue, too. Do you know about the new wax Congoleum? I think that's what I put in—either that or Shinyl Vinyl. I haven't had to wash my floors in three months. The house isn't done yet because of the Bake-Off. My husband says if I'd spent as much time on it as I did on the Bake-Off, we'd be finished. I sent in sixteen recipes—it took me nearly a year to do it."

"That's nothing," said Mrs. Finnegan. "It took me twenty years before I cracked it. I'm a contest nut. I'm a thirty-times winner in the *Better Homes & Gardens* contest. I won a thousand dollars from Fleischmann's Yeast. I won Jell-O this year, I'm getting a hundred and twenty-five dollars' worth of Revere cookware for that. The Knox Gelatine contest. I've won seven blenders and a quintisserie. It does four things—fries, bakes, roasts, there's a griddle. I sold the darn thing before I even used it."

"Don't tell me," said Mrs. Johnson. "Did you enter the Crystal Sugar Name the Lake Home contest?"

"Did I enter?" said Mrs Finnegan. "Wait till you see this." She took a pen and wrote her submission on a napkin and held it up for Mrs. Johnson. The napkin read "Our Entry Hall." "I should have won that one," said Mrs. Finnegan. "I did win the Crystal Sugar Name the Dessert contest. I called it 'Signtation Squares.' I think I got a blender on that one."

"Okay," said Mrs. Johnson. "They've got a contest now, Crystal Sugar Name a Sauce. It has pineapple in it."

"I don't think I won that," said Mrs. Finnegan, "but I'll show you what I sent in." She held up the napkin and this time what she had written made sense. "Hawaiian More Chant," it said.

"Oh, you're clever," said Mrs. Johnson.

"They have three more contests so I haven't given up," said Mrs. Finnegan.

On Monday morning at exactly 9 a.m., the one hundred finalists marched four abreast into the Hilton ballroom, led by Philip Pillsbury, former chairman of the board of the company. The band played "Nothin' Says Lovin' Like Somethin' from the Oven," and when it finished, Pillsbury announced: "Now you one hundred winners can go to your ranges."

Chaos. Shrieking. Frenzy. Furious activity. Cracking eggs. Chopping onions. Melting butter. Mixing, beating, blending. The band perking along with such carefully selected tunes as "If I Knew You Were Coming I'd Have Baked a Cake." Contestants

running to the refrigerators for more supplies. Floor assistants
rushing dirty dishes off to unseen dishwashers. All two hundred
members of the working press, plus television's Bob Barker, in-
terviewing any finalist they could get to drop a spoon. At 9:34
a.m., Mrs. Lorraine Walmann submitted her Cheesy Crescent
Twist-Ups to the judges and became the first finalist to finish. At
10 a.m., all the stoves were on, the television lights were blast-
ing, the temperature in the ballroom was up to the mid-nineties,
and Mrs. Marjorie Johnson, in the course of giving an interview
about her house to the Minneapolis *Star*, had forgotten whether
she had put one cup of sugar or two into her Crispy Apple Bake.
"You know, we're building this new house," she was saying.
"When I go back, I have to buy living-room furniture." By 11
a.m., Mae Wilkinson had burned her skillet corn bread and was
at work on a second. Laura Aspis had lost her potholder. Barbara Bellhorn was distraught because she was not used to Cali-
fornia apples. Alex Allard was turning out yet another Honey
Drizzle Cake. Dough and flour were all over the floor. Mary Finnegan was fussing because the crumbs on her Lemon Cream
Bars were too coarse. Marjorie Johnson was in the midst of yet
another interview on her house. "Well, let me tell you," she was
saying, "the shelves in the kitchen are built low. . . ." One by
one, the contestants, who were each given seven hours and four
tries to produce two perfect samples of their recipes, began to
finish up and deliver one tray to the judges and one tray to the
photographer. There were samples everywhere, try this, try that,
but after six tries, climaxed by Mrs. Frisbie's creation, I stopped
sampling. The overkill was unbearable: none of the recipes
seemed to contain one cup of sugar when two would do, or a delicate cheese when Kraft American would do, or an actual
minced onion when instant minced onions would do. It was
snack time. It was convenience-food time. It was less-work-for-
Mother time. All I could think about was a steak.

By 3 p.m., there were only two contestants left—Mrs. Johnson, whose dessert took only five minutes to make but whose interviews took considerably longer, and Bonnie Brooks, whose
third sour-cream-and-banana cake was still in the oven. Mrs.
Brooks brought her cake in last, at 3:37 p.m., and as she did, the
packing began. The skillets went into brown cartons, the mea-
suring spoons into barrels, the stoves were dismantled. The
Bake-Off itself was over—and all that remained was the trip to
Disneyland, and the breakfast at the Brown Derby . . . and the
prizes.

And so it is Tuesday morning, and the judges have reached a decision, and any second now, Bob Barker is going to announce the five winners over national television. All the contestants are wearing their best dresses and smiling, trying to smile anyway, good sports all, and now Bob Barker is announcing the winners. Bonnie Brooks and her cake and Albina Flieller and her Quick Pecan Pie win $25,000 each. Sharon Schubert and two others win $5,000. And suddenly the show is over and it is time to go home, and the ninety-five people who did not win the twenty-fourth annual Pillsbury Bake-Off are plucking the orchids from the centerpieces, signing each other's programs, and grumbling. They are grumbling about Sharon Schubert. And for a moment, as I hear the grumbling everywhere—"It really isn't fair." . . . "After all, she won the trip to Mexico"—I think that perhaps I am wrong about these women: perhaps they are capable of anger after all, or jealousy, or competitiveness, or something I think of as a human trait I can relate to. But the grumbling stops after a few minutes, and I find myself listening to Marjorie Johnson. "I'm so glad I didn't win the grand prize," she is saying, "because if you win that, you don't get to come back to the next Bake-Off. I'm gonna start now on my recipes for next year. I'm gonna think of something really good." She stopped for a moment. "You know," she said, "it's going to be very difficult to get back to normal living."

Questions for discussion

1. Ephron, even in the introductory paragraph, packs her essay with examples, but the examples all relate to a central, implied thesis. What is Ephron's thesis, after all? Try, if you can, to summarize the purpose, slant, and theme of this essay in only one sentence.

2. Many examples, well-chosen, can often "say" more than a few generalized assertions. In what ways do the examples in the essay carry larger meanings? How does Ephron make the examples come alive? How does the use of direct quotations improve the examples? What would Roxanne Frisbie's story lose if Ephron omitted Roxanne's remark, "It's just a plain old dumb pan, but everything I do is in that pan"?

3. An effective example depends on a faithful, meticulous rendering of scene, setting, detail, description. Is it possible, however, to overload an essay with descriptive details, facts, quoted conversation? Why or why not? Do you find the

abundance of concrete details in this essay appropriate or excessive? Explain.

4. Find the sentences or paragraphs in which Ephron permits her own views to influence the reader's position. Where does she editorialize? Do Ephron's comments serve as unifying devices? Why? How?

5. Though the essay seldom relies on topic sentences, how does Ephron organize and control her subject?

6. In a sense, the Pillsbury Bake-Off as a whole is an example— but of what? What does this contest symbolize, not just in terms of women but also in terms of men, America, the world?

7. At what point in the essay does Ephron shift from the use of examples to pure narration? How do you know when the shift occurs?

8. In the paragraph that begins "The Bake-Off is America," Ephron provides the reader with a series of concrete examples to prove two different assertions. What are those assertions? How many examples does Ephron use to support them?

◆

Activities

1. Folks are always making sweeping statements that center on nostalgia for the past. Here are several such statements which, though they cannot necessarily be supported by facts and statistics, can nonetheless be supported by examples. In other words, if you choose your examples wisely, you can convince a reader of almost anything. Select one of the statements, all of which have a familiar ring, and write three paragraphs that offer either one example upon which you elaborate or numerous examples delivered with staccato precision.

Americans no longer display the Yankee ingenuity, the frontier spirit, they once had.

The days of opulence, taste, and style are over.

Nowadays, a man or woman's word is as flimsy and unreliable as the grandiose promises of a used-car salesperson.

Money, not honor, talks.

The five-and-ten-cent store is as obsolete as last year's computer.

The days of unlocked screen doors and oral agreements are over.

Quality leisure has become more important to Americans than quality workmanship.

The national attention span is 15 minutes; the national reading level is eighth grade: Americans are slipping intellectually.

The definition of the word "family" has changed dramatically in recent years.

Ours is a group-think, team-playing, all-things-considered society, in which the individual has no place, no power, no real identity.

Privacy and peace are available only to the very rich.

Ours is a disposable society, more ready to throw out what no longer works than to restore and revitalize outworn notions, structures, and people.

2. Now, reverse your thinking and overturn one of those gloomy assertions by writing three paragraphs about the quality of modern life, the promise of the future. Give examples of what you mean by "progress." Or give examples of why you are pleased to be alive in the waning decades of the twentieth century. Consider the American standard of living, choices of lifestyle, improved health, greater conveniences, quality of leisure, safety in the work place, increased longevity. Again, develop a thesis that conveys your optimism about the present and the future, and use numerous examples to support that general assertion.

3. Relying on the knowledge you have gained in your area of expertise, develop a thesis and give examples of the applications or uses to which this knowledge might be put. For example, if you are majoring in botany, give the reader several convincing examples of how botany might enhance your life, of botany's relevance and importance to you and others in society. In other words, think of your passionate interest and convince the reader of its validity, worth, and relevance. Is it art, nutrition, mental health, geometry, foreign languages, music, photography, medicine, diplomacy, economics, crafts, plumbing, mechanics, ballet?

Establish relationships between causes and effects.

When you explain a process, you describe the steps between the beginning and the end. In other words, process puts you into the middle of activities, techniques, events. But a discussion of cause-and-effect relationships draws the reader's attention to beginnings and ends, to why events occur (causes) and to what happens as a result of those events (effects). Process, then, is *how*. Cause is *why*. Effect is *what*. Learning *how* to discover relationships between causes and effects requires careful logic, close analysis, cool objectivity. Courtrooms across the land are filled with lawyers arguing causes and effects, motives and results. In medicine, too, perplexing debates arise as to why one person gets cancer and another, having similar genes, similar environment, similar diet, similar health habits, does not. The traffic cop strives to establish the same relationships between what happened in an accident and what caused it. So you see how important this kind of reasoning can be, both in writing and in life.

Skill in identifying cause-and-effect relationships and in presenting them convincingly in writing can heighten the effectiveness of description or narration. It is one thing simply to describe what exists, as though it were an isolated event, with no beginning, no source. A child can say "What Is." He points heavenward and observes that the sky is blue. He can even say, if his imagination is unusually keen, that the blue of the sky reminds him of the color of his favorite blanket. In other words, he can establish a comparison. But the "why" of the blue sky eludes him, and so he asks his parents. If the parents are well read or perhaps taking a course in meteorology, they can answer his questions, having studied the causes of blue skies, the effects of smog or weather on the color.

In the same way, the writer must reason very closely if he or she hopes to see isolated occurrences in context, to trace the origins of the events, to predict the outcomes. And the writer who effectively conveys cause-and-effect relationships must be astute, mature, rational.

How do you isolate causes and effects?

1. Remember first that any event has both immediate and conclusive causes and effects. The immediate effect of cheating might be a zero on the test, but the ultimate effect might be dismissal from school for repeated acts of cheating or,

moving farther along the chain of events, long-term difficulties with personal integrity and credibility among friends,
family, coworkers. Likewise, the immediate cause of cheating might be a desire to watch the NBA tournament the
night before the test, but the ultimate cause might be a tendency to procrastinate in all areas of life or, moving backward along the chain of causes, a flaw in ethical thinking
picked up from parents or society.

2. Before you isolate causes and effects, you must speculate on
   (and gradually eliminate) those that are irrelevant. A student who has a personality conflict with a teacher might
   blame the teacher. But the parent, seeking the real cause,
   might mull over other troubled relationships the student has
   had with several authority figures. Patterns, certain common denominators, might emerge. An analysis of the student's behavior with all authority figures might reveal that
   the student's present crisis is related to long-standing problems with the student's own insecurity, competition, discipline. The ultimate cause might even be diagnosed as para-
   noia—the student's feeling that any person in authority is
   out to get him. So an analysis of real causes and real effects
   may require careful reasoning, some detective-like digging
   for truth.

3. Once you have settled on what you believe to be relevant
   causes and effects, you can begin the work of supporting
   your assertions with carefully chosen examples, facts—with
   expert testimony. If you are going to assert that the primary
   causes of illiteracy among students are television viewing,
   the lowering of academic standards, and the easing of academic requirements, you will need to seek confirmation
   from experts in the fields of psychology, sociology, or education. Here, one example of a friend who watches television
   all the time, makes good grades, and yet cannot read would
   suffice.

4. You must accept the responsibility in analyzing causes and
   effects of being as objective and accurate as possible. Most
   events have not one but many causes and effects. Your reputation as a close reasoner will come under suspicion if you
   glibly assert that the women's movement occurred because
   women were tired of cooking and changing diapers or that
   the effect of censorship will be that pornography will be out-
   lawed. Even an apparently simple event—a flat tire, for example—will have multiple causes and multiple effects.

5. You should attempt, as far as possible, to place all the possible causes and effects in an orderly progression from the most immediate to the final or conclusive causes and effects. Leaving out one link in this chain of reasoning would be rather like finding a defendant guilty of arson without bothering to mention the gasoline and the match.

Perhaps the first indication of a dysfunction in human perception is the inability to see the relationship between causes and effects. Maladjusted or psychotic people see events in isolation, become laws unto themselves, as if every action did not have its impact on other people, other days, other events. The masochist has lost the capacity to connect pain, for example, to physical injury. The person undergoing therapy for depression may have no idea what the source of his or her emotional numbness might be. For people who have, to one degree or another, lost touch with reality (which is to say, with context), the cure begins when the connections between causes and effects are restored.

Though analyzing causes and effects can require strenuous mental effort on the part of the writer, the result will be worth the effort. You have learned that describing, informing, narrating, comparing and/or contrasting, and explaining procedures all strengthen the perceptions of good writers. But analyzing causes and effects can take the writer even farther down the road to understanding and writing maturity. "Why?" is a very human question, the source of discovery, the foundation of truth. "What will happen?" is another good question, one that only the careful logician can answer and always on the basis of the available evidence.

Exploring causes and effects can be complicated by the simple fact that one event seldom has only one obvious cause, and vice versa. Sometimes causes are remote or invisible. Sometimes effects are only educated guesses. We know, for example, that nuclear war carries serious consequences, but until the destruction rains down on us, we will not fully grasp the effects. Then too, an event may be either a cause or an effect, a beginning or an end.

And even on smaller matters, we argue about probable causes, possible effects. What are the long-term effects of competency testing? Some say there is no connection between competency testing and the probable survival capabilities of the students who pass the test. Others say the competency test will only encourage students to study for tests, not to acquire knowledge. Still others assert that the competency test is so simple that it elicits scorn among students rather than increased respect for education. Still others say the competency test is just busy work.

And ferreting out causes from known effects can be just as difficult. Why do you start sneezing and breaking out every time you enter a certain room in the house? Is the cause an allergy to dust, plants, cats, dogs, some chemical? Or is the problem all in your head, a psychosomatic symptom that has to do with some deeply repressed anxiety? The only way to discover the cause of the sneezing is to isolate the culprit. But the result of such careful analysis of cause may be, unfortunately, that the suffering patient is allergic to virtually *everything*.

You can go two ways with cause and effect. You can begin by citing effects or evidence and then work backward to causes. Or you can look forward from the observable phenomena to the probable or possible effects.

In the following paragraphs, the writer observes that Americans have lost the power to feel things deeply, that a crisis of numbness has occurred. The writer must first give the evidence, the effects that prove the truth of the assertion. Then follows an explanation of possible causes.

A CRISIS OF NUMBNESS

We Americans yearn to get in touch with our feelings, yet we've never felt so dead at the center. Novelist Walker Percy's characters wander around the existential landscape, trying to find something against which they can scrape and say, unequivocally, "Ouch!" *(effect)*. Christians leave cold mainline churches and pump themselves up with emotional bellows *(effect)*. Lovers look for a turn-on *(effect)*. Addicts seek an artificial "high" that reality doesn't supply *(effect)*. The television audience yawns over theft, clucks the tongue over corporate crime, tsk-tsks over murder, flicks the channel in response to a plea on behalf of starving children, grumbles over the weekend telethon for muscular dystrophy *(several effects)*. Teenaged children are impassive to violence, indifferent to sex, unhorrified by horror movies *(several effects)*. When a friend or relative dies, the mourners struggle hard to squeeze out one good tear *(effect)*.

My question is why *(seeking the cause)*: why, in other times and places, did a woman's ankle inspire poetry; a lynching bring out the whole, ogling town; a death produce a three-day wake, with sobs and moans reverberating throughout the night; a monster movie bring goosebumps to children; a sidewalk mugging elicit shock and outrage from bystanders, rescue for the victim? Why do we now need lessons on how to feel, expensive therapy to tell us where our hearts are?

There are several causes for our current psychic numbness. First, Americans apparently have put feelings on a pedestal, have made feeling a moral and social imperative *(cause)*. We have come to admire feeling for its own sake *(cause)*, separating it from its source, making an abstract god of it *(cause)*. The great American pastime is getting in touch with our feelings *(cause)*, having "good" feelings about ourselves even though we have done nothing to warrant those feelings *(cause)*. Feeling has, therefore, become just another thing to work at, an obsessive-compulsive exercise, rather like a daily jog *(effect)*.

Then, too, we are constantly bombarded with feeling-producing events *(cause)* and have therefore lost our powers of discernment and discretion about what is worthy of strong feelings and what is decidedly not *(effect)*. Advertising is the culprit in our crisis of numbness *(major cause)*. Hype has wrung us out and hung our emotions up to dry *(reiteration of major causes)*.

The remainder of this essay explores the feeling-oriented language of advertisements for bath powder, make-up, gloves, tourism, cleansers, soap powder, alcohol, cigarettes, cars. The writer exposes the emotionally strung out, effusive ads for what, in the end, they truly are: merely products, not tragedies and joys. The writer asserts that by the time the consumer has finished feeling ecstatic about getting the toilet bowl clean or sipping beer with the gang or racing a four-wheeler over the desert, he or she has no feelings left over for divorce, death, childbirth, or starvation in Africa.

Questions for discussion

1. Does the writer convince you both of the effects and of the causes for a loss of feeling, a crisis of numbness? Why or why not? Do you agree with the original assertion? How would you characterize the feeling state of our society? Could you think of possible future effects of the present preoccupation with having good feelings about yourself? Would the effects be positive or negative?

2. The writer begins by describing the "reality" as she sees it. Can you look around you and find a similar "reality" in the

world as you see it? What, for example, might be the larger implications of a current fad, psychological emphasis, trend, fashion? Can you discover the causes, for example, behind the popularity of music videos or Christian television or pierced ears or urban cowboys or soap operas or game shows or vans or foreign cars or home computers or trivia games or lotteries? Can you predict the long-term effects of these trends, fads?

The following essay explores both causes and effects, using this method as the primary means of development and support. The writer uses a single example, extending over several paragraphs, to make a point about actions and logical consequences. The central idea, namely that consequences are messier and more long-lived than present actions, emerges in the telling of the story.

PRESENT ACTIONS AND LOGICAL CONSEQUENCES

In the past, when I went to renew my driver's license, the procedure was simple: I just walked into the license bureau, handed over my old card, looked through a machine at a few road signs, posed for my latest incredibly awful picture, waited five minutes, and picked up my card, safe for another four years on this small issue of legality. But this year is different. This year I have to take the written test. Why? Because I have been charged with a safe-moving violation and caught for speeding.

Having to take the written test puts me in mind of the long and messy consequences of careless or irresponsible behavior. Sometimes the obvious escapes us, though it is always there, signalling like the red light at the intersection that we should stop, look, listen. One of the happy perks of being grown up is that we don't have to take tests anymore, not if we are careful. By the time I finished school, I was pretty well tested out and ready to embark on the education life offered me, the one that would test my mettle, not my brains. Adults were people who made up and administered tests, not people who took them. Frequent testing was a cruelty we reserved for children. Our burden was survival. Theirs was passing.

I don't know how I was lulled into false security about logical consequences. My two traffic citations had been handed out months before. I had cheerfully received my sentence, forked over the big bucks, and allowed the memory to recede into the category of Lessons Learned. But I forgot about the other Lesson, the one that we'd just as soon not memorize: it is, simply, that consequences are messier, longer lived, more damaging of credibility than present actions. On one occasion, it took seconds to let my foot fall on the clutch instead of the brake and watch the car I was driving slide inexorably into the brand-new Pontiac on the road ahead. On another, it took five minutes to thank the policeman for giving me a ticket for going 65 in a 55 mile zone. But it took weeks to get the two cars repaired, and the clean-up is not over.

When I drove carelessly, I lost my credibility as a competent driver. I will need months, maybe even years, to restore it. Until then, I am, and very properly so, classified as an unsafe driver, in need of careful scrutiny to reassure the highway patrol that I meet minimum safety standards for highway competency. When I received the notice of driver's license renewal, the two dates of my downfall appeared on the card. I had earned a "C."

The ominous words, "This mistake goes on your record," should be emblazoned not only across documents but also across brains and hearts. From the trivial to the significant, every mistake we make is a strike against us and requires further testing to restore us to a class-A rating. When we don't clean our houses for a month, the dust rises up to mock us and demands three days, not merely one hour, of our time and energies. When we cut class at school, we must locate the friend who takes reliable notes, stop by to get our assignments from the teacher, make up the pop quiz. For a free fifty minutes, during which we were down at the Rathskeller, gleefully munching pretzels, we must spend many hours making up the missed work.

As the actions rise from the inconsequential to the monumental, the consequences multiply, deepen. One tirade delivered in a weak, tired moment can require months of careful, modulated, tender tones. One cruel word, hurled in an unguarded moment, can speak volumes in the other person's mind, and the words are almost impossible to erase. One moment of drunkenness, indiscretion, irrationality can net us years of distrust, suspicion, disgust, bitterness.

No matter what we do, we learn the bitter lesson that we must start from scratch, trying to smudge out the dirty fingerprints, the trail of incriminating evidence that our hasty actions leave behind. Even if we have been for the most part "good"— in the responsible, functioning, cooperative, ethical sense—our mistake lives on in the hearts and minds of those around us, producing nagging doubts and requiring arduous climbs back up the hill of hope from the boggy bottom of failure.

If you doubt the intensity and duration of consequences dogging the heels of immediate, sudden, irresponsible action, consider the questions on job applications, driver's licenses, college admissions forms. Have you ever been arrested? Have you ever received psychiatric treatment? Have you ever been admitted to a program for drug or alcohol treatment? What were your SAT scores? What is your credit record? Have you had hepatitis, herpes, cirrhosis of the liver? Have you ever been a socialist, communist?

The questions never seek to uncover the good that is in you: Do you donate regularly to charity? Did you join the Peace Corps? Do you make a great bowl of chili? Have you ever been happy? Have you ever been tolerant? Do you help the lame, defend the weak? Are you a barrel of laughs? Did you make the Honor Roll? Do you have lots of friends? Have you ever shown mercy?

Worst of all, the questions never deal with the present moment, with how you are doing right now, sitting up straight in your chair, smiling, your face washed, your pants pressed, your head clear, your heart at peace, your reason sharp, your voice well modulated, your wit witty, your mind healthy, your spirit whole.

Questions for discussion

1. How does the writer expand the meaning of her particular experience to include other causes, other effects?

2. In this essay, the writer claims that effects are longer and more tenacious than causes. Can you think of examples or situations in which the causes would be more serious than the effects? For example, what about "murderous" thoughts, feelings of revenge, that are never acted on?

3. Several methods of development and support appear in this essay. Cite them.

4. The movement from causes to probable or possible effects requires some imagination. Some people do not recognize the consequences of their actions until long after the effects commence. Can you think of causes that might have shadowy or uncertain effects, deriving your examples from the worlds of science, technology, law, commerce? What do you judge to be the long-term effects of taking aspirin, investing in real estate, cheating on taxes, having a credit card, going bankrupt, waiting until your 30s to marry or have children,

living with your parents even though you are over 20, putting children in day-care centers? What might be the effect of a swelling population, a shrinking work force?

In the following essay, "Violence: TV's Crowd-Catcher," Robert Lewis Shayon is primarily concerned with the question of why violence is so necessary to the television industry, not with the effects of violence on viewers. Notice how this emphasis on the causes of violence rather than its effects enables the writer to avoid difficult moral issues and to treat this subject with detachment.

VIOLENCE: TV'S CROWD-CATCHER

Robert Lewis Shayon

The President's Commission on the Causes and Prevention of Violence continues to hold hearings and to conduct studies on the subject of violence in TV programs. The commission's activities have energized the press to make surveys of its own. The editors of *McCall's* recently urged its readers to write letters to television executives to protest against the outpouring of TV violence. *The Christian Science Monitor* has reported the results of a six-week survey that show that video violence "still rides high on the air-waves, in spite of assurances by network chiefs that they are doing all they can to minimize the incidence of shootings, stabbings, killings, and beatings."

Social scientists discuss for the commission members the subtleties of defining violence, calculating its effects in terms of aggression, catharsis, and impact on social norms. Some witnesses have urged regulation and control even though research has as yet established no clear, causal relationship between violence in the media and in real life. Nobody, however, seems willing to talk about the true options that are available to the public, as it tries to decide what ought to be done about the problem of violence on TV. The implicit assumptions are that networks could cut down violence if they really wanted to do it; that corporations and advertising agencies have the power to reform the networks if they wished.

From Robert L. Shayon, "Violence: TV's Crowd-Catcher," *Saturday Review,* 52 (Jan. 11, 1969): 103.

Thus, Dr. Leo Bogart, general manager of the Bureau of Advertising of the American Newspaper Publishers Association, told the Commission on Violence that "it must appeal to top managers of corporations . . . in order to induce change in TV programing, and other advertiser-supported media. There is still among them an overwhelming acceptance of the need to do what is right." Perhaps so, but the question is not one of regulation by the industry, government, or any other constituted authority of "them" (people in TV). The real question is whether we—all of us—wish to regulate the American way of life, which is inextricably interwoven with violence on TV.

To understand what the game is all about, one has to get rid of the notion that television is in the program business; nothing could be further from the truth. Television is in the crowd-catching business. The networks and stations are instant crowd-catchers who deliver their catch to the advertisers who inoculate them with consumer messages. Proof of this is at hand in any broadcasting or advertising trade journal, where broadcasters, addressing their real clients, boast of what great crowd-catchers they are at how cheap a cost.

The catching of instant crowds is necessary for the sale of instant tea, coffee, headache relief, spot remover, and other assorted goods and services—not for profit maximization, as John Kenneth Galbraith has argued, but for the instant managing of demand. Planned growth, in his theory, is the driving rod of our industrial state; growth depends on assured flow of capital for long-term projections. Corporations cannot depend on the whims of the old "free market"—where the consumer was sovereign—for steady, reliable demand. Therefore, demand has to be "managed." Advertising is the manager, and broadcasting is the crowd-catcher.

Now, the essence of the art of catching crowds is conflict—the most contagious of all human experiences, the universal language. Of conflict there are many varieties, ranging from parliamentary debates and elections to strikes, games, and fights. Television could, and occasionally does, present conflicts of ideas, but you can't run a crowd-catching business at this level. Instant crowds require simple phenomena, quickly grasped. Furthermore, ideas are controversial, dangerous; people have convictions, they take sides, are easily offended. Crowd-catchers want only happy consumers.

The type of conflict that will deliver instant crowds most efficiently is physical violence. Consider what would happen if a crowd had three viewing choices on a street: watching a clown, a nude woman, or a no-holds-barred fight—which do you think would attract the biggest crowd? Physical violence grows in mesmeric power, while sex and humor diminish relatively. Violence, internal and external, is the young generation's hang-up, not sex. This is the way our world is; TV tells us so—TV is the true curriculum of our society. We fear violence and enjoy it with guilt, because it calls to our own deeply latent potential for violence in response to a violent world. With such a sure-fire, instant crowd-catcher providing the essential energy which runs our industries, our networks, our advertising agencies—in short, our style of life—to call for the voluntary or involuntary regulation of violence on TV is to call for instant self-destruction of the system. By "system," I mean TV based on advertiser support. Television can run on a different system, of course; it does so in other countries. Public funds can support TV directly; license-fees on sets, along with marginal income from controlled advertising, can provide another basis. But to choose another system is to opt for another style of life, one where corporate and consumer acquisitions are not the dominant values.

If the American citizen is to be addressed maturely on the subject of violence in TV, he ought, at least, to be accorded the dignity of being told what his real choices are. Anything less—any talk of regulating and minimizing physical violence on TV, while retaining the present advertiser-supported crowd-catching system—is to contribute to instant self-delusion.

Questions for discussion

1. Shayon only briefly touches on the effects of violence on television viewers. What are those possible effects? Why does he bring an abrupt halt to any further discussion of the effects and proceed, instead, to explore the causes or reasons for violence on television?

2. What are, in Shayon's view, the two major reasons for the prevalence of violence in television programming? How are these causes related to each other? Could the second cause be an effect of the first?

3. Why, according to Shayon, is violence a more effective crowd-catcher than sex or humor? Do you agree or disagree? Why or why not? Why is physical violence, not "strikes, games, and fights" or "parliamentary debate," more useful in attracting television viewers?

4. If, as Shayon suggests, Americans chose another system for television programming and management, what aspects of the American style of life would have to change? If "corporate and consumer acquisitions are not the dominant values," what, then, *are* the values in countries where television violence is minimal or nonexistent?

5. Shayon does not offer a strong opinion on whether or not violence is "good" or "bad," nor does he offer advice on changing the system. What is his purpose in writing, his stance? What does he seek to change or improve? What is his conclusion?

◆

Activities

1. It is the *modus operandi* of a poor reasoner to attribute one effect to one cause. Write three paragraphs on one of the following situations, citing three major effects or causes that come to mind in each case. Understand that each situation can be an end or a beginning, an effect or a cause.

Gum disease	Having bad manners
Mental retardation	Sunbathing
A funny knocking in the car	Getting parolled
Switching majors in college	Finding yourself lost on a trip
Being a bigot	Having a temper tantrum
Anemia	Getting fired
Family fighting	Dropping out of school
Growing up as a latchkey child	Going on strike
Getting a job	Being a successful salesperson
Being drunk	Osteoporosis

2. Using the same topic on which you stressed either causes or effects, reverse the focus. If, for example, you wrote on the probable or possible effects of dropping out of school, write now on the causes that lead a student to drop out of school. Again, write three paragraphs, thereby requiring that you explore several causes or effects, not just one.

Analyze.

When you want to know how or why something works, you take it apart, study its various pieces, and if you have paid attention, reassemble the object or idea with skill and ease. It should come as no surprise, therefore, that the language of analysis is often related to machinery. The talk-show host leans earnestly into the celebrity's face and says, "What makes you tick?" The hypochondriac complains that his motor is not running properly. The mental patient is "broken," the upbeat optimist is "humming," the psyche is "out of sync," the marriage is not "working." When you are fine, "all systems are go." When you are not fine, there is a "breakdown in communication," "a knock in the engine." You are "getting static" from friends, relatives, authorities. How do you "fix" these faulty mechanisms in your life and personality? You go in for a "tune-up." We call the fix-it expert a psycho*analyst*.

Any time you attempt to discover why something does or does not work, you are analyzing, whether the thing under study be a frog, a lung, an industry, a joke, a novel, a relationship, a behavior, a personality, a mind, a heart, or a soul. Analysis lends itself well to all aspects of life because it is calm, rational, objective, logical, somewhat detached. There is no place for hasty judgment, anger, prejudice, or falsehood in good analysis. You do not find out why your radio does not work by hurling it against the wall. You tinker, using the right tools, observing the radio's innards, tracing the wires to their point of origin, checking and rechecking batteries, cords, dials.

Though the purpose of analysis is greater understanding and insight with regard to the whole, the analyst must temporarily break down the novel, radio, human personality, if only to see the inner workings. A great novel is temporarily reduced to a construct of plot, character, scene, setting. But the technique of analysis, even though it temporarily reduces the grand and glorious whole, is nonetheless useful, if only to make the whole more manageable. If friends analyze you, they always leave out the essential, breathtaking reality of your individuality. But they can help you to function better by pointing out separate behaviors or habits that are destructive.

In a sense, many of the developmental methods depend, in one way or another, on analysis. When you classify, you first group items and then divide the individual items from the rest of the group, establishing a definition that differentiates the item from all others of its class. When you explain a process, you break down the procedure into separate steps or stages, to understand the movement from the beginning of the process to the desired end. When you isolate causes and effects, you are also using techniques of division or partition, beginning with the event itself and going backward to the whys of the event or forward to the consequences of the event.

Analysis offers a way to gather and organize ideas. Once you have divided the whole into parts, you can then see new relationships, new possibilities. And simply naming the parts of the whole will clarify what is unique about each part and how each part relates to the whole. Dissection is analysis. Literary criticism is analysis. Lists of characteristics are, in reality, analyses. You are analyzing when you take apart an engine to see why it does not work; when you list the ingredients in a frankfurter; when you divide a book into preface, introduction, chapters; when you break down a disease into symptoms, possible diagnoses, treatments. And when you reassemble these individually studied parts, you then have a greater understanding of the whole. At this point—the postanalytical stage—you can draw conclusions, make judgments, and set forth theories about the whole.

But analysis is not an attitude for all seasons. Analysis carries risks and cruelties as well, especially in the realm of the personal. Analysis does not work well in the bedroom, at a party, or in the middle of a riproaring argument. Passion will subside, the guests will stomp out the door, and the person with whom you are arguing will punch you in the nose. The trouble with analyzing is that it is like eating peanuts: you cannot eat just one. By the time you have finished dissecting your best friend, your parents, and your neighbors, you yourself will likely be the sole audience for further heartless dissections. But analysis tempered with intuition, empathy, compassion, and insight can produce spectacular results, whether in art, science, life, or friendships.

Value-free analysis is probably impossible—as absolute objectivity is impossible. No matter how hard we try to purge ourselves of prejudices, judgments, preconceived notions, we cannot shake off our humanity as a dog shakes water off its back.

Friends, lovers, poems, psyches do not take well to looking without feeling. The danger in careful analysis is that even if the zoologist makes an objective analysis of the behavior of gorillas in captivity, she may, all purity of perception aside, come to *love* the gorillas. Such a response to gorillas would not be bad; it would just be inexact, inexplicable, disconcerting, "unscientific."

Analysis is at the bottom of many kinds of writing, though it seldom exists in pure form. News commentators, after the Republican or Democratic conventions, sit around in chrome and leather chairs, analyzing what "really" went on. Newspapers often run articles carefully labelled "analysis." Book and movie reviewers aspire to analysis, but they are seldom able to keep their judgments out of the objective appraisal. And who would want them to? After they have finished analyzing what did and did not work in the movie, the readers want to know whether the reviewers *liked* it. At that point, analysis slides inexorably into persuasion.

Some people do not want to bother with careful analysis because it is too much trouble. It is much easier to say of a fad, food, work of fiction, or foible, "I hate it." Poor analyzers or lazy thinkers do not want to get at the why behind the reaction or judgment. They want to skip the hard part. Good writers, however, need to develop the analytical side of themselves, the side that requires them to present the workings of people and things as they are in reality, not as the writers would want them to be. In fact, the definition of bad writing might be, simply, that it is not analytical, true to the actual workings of politics or people or philosophies. If a literary work, for example, is sentimental, then it has sacrificed close observation of separate parts of life and human behavior to a hazy, general, superficial judgment. The characters are flat, either all good or all bad. The setting is anywhere. The dialogue is stilted. The impact is zero.

In the following paragraphs, you will see analytical treatments of a variety of subjects. Notice how in each example a dissection occurs, a breaking down of each subject under consideration into its component parts, the better to see and understand how the whole functions. Notice, too, that this somewhat scientific approach enhances the reader's understanding of decidedly unscientific subjects.

Analyzing the human brain

The human brain consists of perhaps 10 to 20 billion individual nerve cells, called neurons. The network they form is all the more impressive and intricate because of the nature of each cell. The typical neuron has a long extension called an axon, through which it can send nerve impulses. In addition the cell body puts out hundreds of delicate branches called dendrites; through these it can receive input from more than a thousand other neurons. At the nerve ending, the axon subdivides into as many as 10,000 terminals, each of which can inlfluence a separate neuron. Thus a single one of the brain's billions of nerve cells could conceivably set up several million conversations.[1]

Analyzing the neurotic personality

The neurotic feels entitled to special attention, consideration, deference on the part of others. These claims for deference are understandable enough, and sometimes obvious enough. But they are merely part and parcel of a more comprehensive claim—that all his needs growing out of his inhibitions, his fears, his conflicts, and his solutions ought to be satisfied or duly respected. Moreover, whatever he feels, thinks, or does ought not to carry any adverse consequences. This means in fact a claim that the psychic laws do not apply to him. Therefore he does not need to recognize—or at any rate to change—his difficulties. It is then no longer up to him to do something about his problems; it is up to others to see that they do not disturb him.[2]

Analyzing the history of myth

Our first tangible evidences of mythological thinking are from the period of Neanderthal Man, which endured from ca. 250,000 to ca. 50,000 B.C.; and these comprise, first, burials with food supplies, grave gear, tools, sacrificed ani-

---

[1]Solomon H. Snyder, "Wonders of the Brain," in *On the Brink of Tomorrow: Frontiers of Science* (Washington, D.C.: National Geographic Society, 1982), p. 177.
[2]Karen Horney, *Neurosis and Human Growth: The Struggle Toward Self-Realization* (New York: Norton, 1950), p. 41.

mals, and the like; and second, a number of chapels in high-mountain caves, where cave-bear skulls, ceremonially disposed in symbolic settings, have been preserved. The burials suggest the idea, if not exactly of immortality, then at least of some kind of life to come; and the almost inaccessible high-mountain bear-skull sanctuaries surely represent a cult in honor of that great, upright, manlike, hairy personage, the bear.[3]

Analyzing a creative stagnation

You write that I have grown lazy. This doesn't mean I have become any lazier than I used to be. I do as much work now as I did three or five years ago. Working and looking like a working person at intervals from nine in the morning to dinner and from evening tea until retiring have become habits with me, and in this respect I am like a regular official. If two stories a month don't emerge out of my efforts, or $10,000 yearly income, it is not laziness that is to blame, but my basic psychological makeup; for medicine I am not fond enough of money, and for literature I don't have sufficient passion, and, consequently, talent. My creative fire burns at a slow, even pace, without flash and crackle, although sometimes I may write fifty or sixty pages at one swoop in one night or, absorbed in my work, I will keep myself from going to bed when I feel sleepy; for the same reason I am not remarkable either for stupidity or brilliance. . . . I don't have much passion; add to this fact the following symptom of a psychopathic condition: for the past two years and for no earthly reason I have become sick of seeing my works in print, have grown indifferent to reviews, talks on literature, slanders, successes, failures, and big fees—in short, I have become an utter fool. There is a sort of stagnation in my soul. I explain this by the stagnation in my personal life. I am not disillusioned, not weary, not dispirited, but everything has just become less interesting somehow. I must add some gunpowder to my makeup.[4]

---

[3]Joseph Campbell, *Myths to Live By* (New York: Viking Press, Bantam, 1972), p. 31.
[4]Letter to Alexei Suvorin in Lillian Hellman, ed., *The Selected Letters of Anton Chekhov*, trans. by S. K. Lederer (New York: Farrar, Straus, 1955), p. 81.

Questions for discussion

1. All of the above examples are analytical in approach, each attempting to dissect or break down a whole into smaller parts. In each example, identify the named parts that make up the whole.

2. Analysis differs from persuasion, both in purpose and tone. Analysis seeks primarily to inform. Looking at all the above examples, isolate the facts presented. Can you derive a larger meaning for the word "fact" by studying these examples? Does Chekhov's letter also contain facts? What are they?

3. What is the tone of each of these analyses? Where does the writer stand in relation to the content? Is there analytical detachment even in Chekhov's analysis of his creative stagnation? Can you find slant words in each paragraph that influence the reader, even subtly?

4. What are the advantages and disadvantages in developing a critical, analytical approach even to subjective realms of emotion, passion, personality? What is gained? What is lost? Explain.

In the following essay, "Some Remarks on Humor," E. B. White begins by disparaging other analysts' attempts to dissect humor—and then proceeds to analyze it. Funny. As you read, ask yourself how this analysis of humor and humorists differs from or goes beyond mere definition.

SOME REMARKS ON HUMOR

E. B. White

Analysts have had their go at humor, and I have read some of this interpretative literature, but without being greatly instructed. Humor can be dissected, as a frog can, but the thing dies in the process and the innards are discouraging to any but the pure scientific mind.

Adapted from E. B. White, Preface to *A Subtreasury of American Humor*, ed. by E. B. White and Katharine S. White (New York: Coward-McCann, 1941), pp. xvii–xxii.

A certain type of humor has come to be big business in the United States. The gag factories are as impressive as Allis Chalmers, and will probably soon be taken over for defense purposes. Radio comedians employ their own corps of geniuses, who sit and think and think of something funny to say. It is sometimes rather grim business, this production for the big markets. In a newsreel theater the other day I saw a picture of a man who had developed the soap bubble to a higher point than it had ever before reached. He had become the ace soap bubble blower of America, had perfected the business of blowing bubbles, refined it, doubled it, squared it, and had even worked himself up into a convenient lather. The effect was not pretty. Some of the bubbles were too big to be beautiful, and the blower was always jumping into them or out of them, or playing some sort of unattractive trick with them. It was, if anything, a rather repulsive sight. Humor is a little like that: it won't stand much blowing up, and it won't stand much poking. It has a certain fragility, an evasiveness, which one had best respect. Essentially, it is a complete mystery. A human frame convulsed with laughter, and the laughter becoming hysterical and uncontrollable, is as far out of balance as one shaken with the hiccoughs or in the throes of a sneezing fit.

One of the things commonly said about humorists is that they are really very sad people—clowns with a breaking heart. There is some truth in it, but it is badly stated. It would be more accurate, I think, to say that there is a deep vein of melancholy running through everyone's life and that a humorist, perhaps more sensible of it than some others, compensates for it actively and positively. Practically everyone is a manic depressive of sorts, with his up moments and his down moments, and you certainly don't have to be a humorist to taste the sadness of situation and mood. But, as everyone knows, there is often a rather fine line between laughing and crying, and if a humorous piece of writing brings a person to the point where his emotional responses are untrustworthy and seem likely to break over into the opposite realm, it is because humorous writing, like poetical writing, has an extra content. It plays, like an active child, close to the big hot fire which is Truth. And sometimes the reader feels the heat.

The world likes humor, but it treats it patronizingly. It decorates its serious artists with laurel, and its wags with Brussels sprouts. It feels that if a thing is funny it can be presumed to be something less than great, because if it were truly great it would be wholly serious. Writers know this, and those who take their literary selves with great seriousness are at considerable pains never to associate their name with anything funny or flippant or nonsensical or "light." They suspect it would hurt their reputation, and they are right. Many a poet writing today signs his real name to his serious verse and a pseudonym to his comical verse, being unwilling to have the public discover him in any but a pensive and heavy moment. It is a wise precaution. (It is often a bad poet, too.)

When I was reading over some of the parody diaries of Franklin P. Adams, I came across this entry, for April 28, 1926:

> Read H. Canby's book, *Better Writing*, very excellent. But when he says, "A sense of humour is worth gold to any writer," I disagree with him vehemently. For the writers who amass the greatest gold have, it seems to me, no sense of humour; and I think also that if they had, it would be a terrible thing for them, for it would paralyze them so that they would not write at all. For in writing, emotion is more to be treasured than a sense of humour, and the two are often in conflict.

That is a sound observation. The conflict is fundamental. There constantly exists, for a certain sort of person of high emotional content, at work creatively, the danger of coming to a point where something cracks within himself or within the paragraph under construction—cracks and turns into a snicker. Here, then, is the very nub of the conflict: the careful form of art, and the careless shape of life itself. What a man does with this uninvited snicker (which may closely resemble a sob, at that) decides his destiny. If he resists it, conceals it, destroys it, he may keep his architectural scheme intact and save his building, and the world will never know. If he gives in to it, he becomes a humorist, and the sharp brim of the fool's cap leaves a mark forever on his brow.

I'm sure there isn't a humorist alive but can recall the day, in the early stages of his career, when someone he loved and respected took him anxiously into a corner and asked him when he was "going to write something serious." That day is memorable, for it gives a man pause to realize that the bright star he is following is held to be not of the first magnitude.

I think the stature of humor must vary some with the times. The court fool in Shakespeare's day had no social standing and was no better than a lackey, but he did have some artistic standing and was listened to with considerable attention, there being a well-founded belief that he had the truth hidden somewhere about his person. Artistically he stood probably higher than the humorist of today, who has gained social position but not the ear of the mighty. (Think of the trouble the world would save itself if it would pay some attention to nonsense!) A narrative poet at court, singing of great deeds, enjoyed a higher standing than the fool and was allowed to wear fine clothes; yet I suspect that the ballad singer was more often than not a second-rate stooge, flattering his monarch lyrically, while the fool must often have been a first-rate character, giving his monarch good advice in bad puns.

In the British Empire of our time, satirical humor of the Gilbert and Sullivan sort enjoys a solid position in the realm, and *Punch*, which is as British as vegetable marrow, is socially acceptable everywhere an Englishman is to be found. The *Punch* editors not only write the jokes but they help make the laws of England. Here in America we have an immensely humorous people in a land of milk and honey and wit, who cherish the ideal of the "sense" of humor and at the same time are highly suspicious of anything which is nonserious. Whatever else an American believes or disbelieves about himself, he is absolutely sure he has a sense of humor.

Frank Moore Colby, one of the most intelligent humorists operating in this country in the early years of the century, in an essay called "The Pursuit of Humor" described how the American loves and guards his most precious treasure:

> . . . Now it is the commonest thing in the world to hear people call the absence of a sense of humor the one fatal defect. No matter how owlish a man is, he will tell you that. It is a miserable falsehood, and it does incalculable harm. A life without humor is like a life without legs. You are haunted by a sense of incompleteness, and you cannot go where your friends go. You are also somewhat of a burden. But the only really fatal thing is the shamming of humor when you have it not. There are people whom nature meant to be solemn from their cradle to their grave. They are under bonds to remain so. In so far as they are true to themselves they are safe company for any one; but outside their proper field they are terrible. Solemnity is relatively a blessing, and the man who was born with it should never be encouraged to wrench himself away.
>
> We have praised humor so much that we have started an insincere cult, and there are many who think they must glorify it when they hate it from the bottom of their hearts. False humor-worship is the deadliest of social sins, and one of the commonest. People without a grain of humor in their composition will eulogize it by the hour. Men will confess to treason, murder, arson, false teeth, or a wig. How many of them will own up to a lack of humor? The courage that could draw this confession from a man would atone for everything.

Relatively few American humorists have become really famous, so that their name is known to everyone in the land in the way that many novelists and other solemn literary characters have become famous. Mark Twain made it. He had, of course, an auspicious start, since he was essentially a story teller and his humor was an added attraction. (It was also very, very good.) In this century Ring Lardner is the idol of professional humorists and of plenty of other people, too; but I think I am correct in saying that at the height of his career he was not one of the most widely known literary figures in this country, and the name Lardner was not known to the millions but only to the thousands. Even today he has not reached Mr. and Mrs. America and all the clippers at sea, to the extent that Mark Twain reached them, and I doubt if he ever will. On the whole, the humorists who contribute pleasure to a wide audience are the ones who create characters and tell tales, the ones who are story tellers at heart. Lardner told stories and gave birth to some characters, but I think he was a realist and a parodist and a satirist first of all, not essentially a writer of fiction. The general public needs something to get a grip on—a Penrod, a Huck Finn, a Brer Rabbit, or a Father Day. The subtleties of satire and burlesque and nonsense and parody and criticism are no dish for the masses; they are only for the top (or, if you want, for the bottom) layer of intellect. Clarence Day, for example, was relatively inconspicuous when he was oozing his incomparable "Thoughts without Words," which are his best creations; he became generally known and generally loved only after he had brought Father to life. (Advice to young writers who want to get ahead without any annoying delays: don't write about Man, write about *a* man.)

I was interested, in reading DeVoto's *Mark Twain in Eruption,* to come across some caustic remarks of Mr. Clemens's about an anthology of humor which his copyright lawyer had sent him and which Mark described as "a great fat, coarse, offensive volume." He was not amused. "This book is a cemetery," he wrote.

In this mortuary volume I find Nasby, Artemus Ward, Yawcob Strauss, Derby, Burdette, Eli Perkins, the Danbury News Man, Orpheus C. Kerr, Smith O'Brien, Josh Billings, and a score of others, maybe two score, whose writings and sayings were once in everybody's mouth but are now heard of no more and are no longer mentioned. Seventy-eight seems an incredible crop of well-known humorists for one forty-year period to have produced, and yet this book has not harvested the entire crop—far from it. It has no mention of Ike Partington, once so welcome and so well known; it has no mention of Doesticks, nor of the Pfaff crowd, nor of Artemus Ward's numerous and perishable imitators, nor of three very popular Southern humorists whose names I am not able to recall, nor of a dozen other sparkling transients whose light shone for a time but has now, years ago, gone out.

Why have they perished? Because they were merely humorists. Humorists of the "mere" sort cannot survive. Humor is only a fragrance, a decoration. Often it is merely an odd trick of speech and of spelling, as in the case of Ward and Billings and Nasby and the "Disbanded Volunteer," and presently the fashion passes and the fame along with it. There are those who say a novel should be a work of art solely, and you must not preach in it, you must not teach in it. That may be true as regards novels but it is not true as regards humor. Humor must not professedly teach, and it must not professedly preach, but it must do both if it would live forever. By forever, I mean thirty years. With all its preaching it is not likely to outlive so long a term as that. The very things it preaches about, and which are novelties when it preaches about them, can cease to be novelties and become commonplaces in thirty years. Then that sermon can thenceforth interest no one.

I have always preached. That is the reason that I have lasted thirty years. If the humor came of its own accord and uninvited, I have allowed it a place in my sermon, but I was not writing the sermon for the sake of humor. I should have written the sermon just the same, whether any humor applied for admission or not. I am saying these vain things in this frank way because I am a dead person speaking from the grave. Even I would be too modest to say them in life. I think we never become really and genuinely our entire and honest selves until we are dead—and not then until we have been dead years and years. People ought to start dead, and then they would be honest so much earlier.

Well, I didn't intend to get off onto the broad subject of humor, or even to let Mark Twain get off onto it. I don't think I agree that humor must preach in order to live; it need only speak the truth—and I notice it always does.

Questions for discussion

1. White begins, in the second paragraph, to analyze humor even as he assures the reader that humor is not analyzable. What are the parts of humor that contribute to its great "mystery"?

2. White's essay also includes analyses of humorists and of their reputations. If you dissected a humorist, what, in White's view, would you find? What are the traits in a humorist that together comprise his reputation or lack of

reputation? Mark Twain also analyzes humor in this essay. What, in Twain's view, are humor's essential "parts"? Do Twain and White agree about the nature of humor?

3. Implicit in the essay is a kind of psychoanalysis of human responses to humor. What is the role of the humorless in the propagation of humor? How does an audience see itself in the context of humor?

4. White contrasts the present status of humor with that of the past. How has humor fared since Shakespeare's day? What is the difference between the British and American views of humor?

5. What is the conflict between emotion and a sense of humor?

Mix your methods.

The best cooks seldom follow a recipe to the letter. Granted, they have the recipe in front of them. Certainly, they observe the basic proprieties. They would not broil when the recipe says bake. They would not salt when the recipe says pepper. They would not be cavalier about the larger ingredients. What is a pot roast without the roast? What is a pie without the crust? What is a cake without the icing? They are inventive, but they are not culinary anarchists.

But good cooks do love to experiment. And sometimes the experimentation is the result of laziness or convenience. Sensible cooks do not drive to the A&P, in midrecipe, to pick up basil when marjoram might be just as good. They know margarine will do if they are out of butter. Yogurt can replace sour cream. The stew can survive very nicely without the carrots.

The mixed-method, whatever-works approach to cooking and life applies as well to writing. Nobody argues with success; and so, even if your writing methods are a bit unorthodox, the product will satisfy even finicky literary palates if you trust yourself to be a genius at the typewriter. You will have failures, of course. But you will also enjoy spectacular successes. Best of all, you will avoid the bland predictability of the canned essay.

In reality, you do not "choose" a pattern or developmental scheme. The fact is, a pattern emerges as you write, a pattern chooses *you*. The techniques you studied in isolation begin to blend, the flavors merge, the writing stew is your own, not somebody else's. It comes out naturally in the way you set up your thesis, in the reasoning and support that defend that thesis.

> ### Patterns in Context
>
> When I write, I do not tell myself to use a particular developmental scheme. Only after the essay is finished do I notice that comparison has best served my writing purposes here, a brief narration has best served my purposes there. In other words, I can go back and identify the particular combinations of techniques that produced an essay that is unique, suited to my personal tastes, pleasing to the reader.

But how do you begin mixing methods effectively?

1. Bring to the writing of a good essay all the techniques, devices, developmental schemes that you have first studied as separate entities. After all, classifying, defining, illustrating, comparing, contrasting, persuading, and explaining causes and effects or processes are simply structures on which to hang your ideas. They help you organize, control, unify your thinking. But they are not the thought itself, only the vehicle for its expression.

2. Let your thesis, your topic sentences, your supports suggest an appropriate developmental scheme. The following thesis statements lead the writer very naturally into certain primary methods of development.

    I don't know why I derive so much malicious satisfaction from procrastination. (The "why" is a clue. You might be leading yourself into exploring the causes of procrastination. Or you might be intending to analyze the pleasures of procrastination. Or you might even, at some point, persuade the reader that procrastination is a virtue, not a vice, since most of what we do does not need doing anyway.)

    People who don't know an oil stick from a gear shift are wise to sign up for a course in car maintenance. (It sounds as though a process might be emerging. Or the essay could lead to persuasion, focusing less on how to care for your car and more on why caring for your car is important.)

*Employers are increasingly eager to hire students in the lib-
eral arts field, having realized that such students are better
able to communicate and to bring creativity and insight to
their jobs.* (Persuasion will surely dominate this essay, but
the writer might also be led into contrasting the advantages of a liberal arts background versus a technical or scientific background.)

3. Remember that you are in control in the writing of the essay
    and that your first responsibility is to use methods that pro-
    duce good results: a closely reasoned, well-supported thesis;
    a convinced reader; an enchanted or delighted reader; a
    writer whose essay achieved whatever he or she intended.

4. Fall back on the rules and regulations, the structures, when
    you feel your essay slipping out of control. Often, when a
    paragraph seems disjointed or illogical, you look very care-
    fully at it and discover, to your amazement, that it has no
    topic sentence, no organizing principle. At such times you
    can willingly return to the basic composition modes and
    methods that, in the end, do produce better, tighter, more ef-
    fective essays.

As you develop in your writing life, you will notice a steady
increase in experimentation. Sometimes a narration is a persuasive essay, though the story, not the theoretical stance, makes
your case. Sometimes you will begin with contrast, slide into
definition, pause for explication, alight briefly on classification,
throw in reasonable causes and logical effects, and return, in
your conclusion, not to a restatement of the thesis but to another story—perhaps an anecdote that perfectly sums up the
purpose of the essay. You set the pace. You vary the approach.
You are in charge.

The following essay demonstrates a variety of essay types and
methods of development: comparing, contrasting, giving examples, defining, persuading, analyzing, narrating, describing, and
even, to a certain extent, informing. As you study the essay,
identify the mixed types and methods that make up the whole.

GERMS AND ART

A young, bearded friend loaned me *Zen and the Art of Motor-
cycle Maintenance,* the seventies bestseller. I couldn't read it
then, and I can't read it now. The same friend urged me to read

Hermann Hesse's *Siddhartha;* and because I am into spiritual quests, I read it, ignoring the hoots of self-styled literary sophisticates. The borrowing and lending of books is a big part of my life, but I find, to my dismay, that one person's blockbuster is another person's lackluster. A book is as personal as a toothbrush; and I would never, even at gunpoint, put just anybody's toothbrush in my mouth. I am finicky about germs and Art.

Still, I continue to swap books and, in desperate moments, toothbrushes, on the off chance that healing and growth, not contamination and decay, will result. This act of faith comes hard to me for being so out of character. Some people are not squeamish. While they are flicking bugs out of their iced tea and nibbling on a child's leftover chicken leg, they will read anything that's handy, giving rapt and equal attention to the directions on the back of the box, the Gideon Bible in the motel room, and Dostoevsky. Though I look with wonder upon such undiscriminating taste, I am suspicious of it as well. If any book, any toothbrush will do, then what is the sense of having free will, where are the questions of good vs. evil, what is the meaning of life? A person who can pour himself into anything, especially a book, is sand, not rock, and has a shaky foundation on which to build a life.

I like people who make conscious choices, boldly walking out in the middle of a $4 movie, tossing a lousy book on the junkpile of broken dreams, pouring out a summer's drink filled with creepy-crawlers. I don't know what makes an exquisite palate, whether in cleanliness or Art, but I want my true friends to have one. I even have a grudging admiration for people with resolutely bad taste in books, believing that bad taste is better than no taste at all. A bad book, truly savored, is a place to start.

Over the years I have observed the whimsical variations in literary taste among friends and relatives. My mother hated *Final Payments,* but my father loved it. A lawyer friend tried to hook me on Robert Ludlum, but I wouldn't be caught. My father and I were tickled with *A Confederacy of Dunces,* but Mother thought it was the silliest book she'd ever read. A neighbor passed on a Doris Lessing novel, but Lessing is like cucumbers to me. I keep thinking a taste of her would be good but find she does not agree with me. On the recommendation of a professor friend, I nibbled gingerly at novelist Robe-Grillet, but clenched teeth blocked the way.

Literary taste, besides being as indefinable as the nature of God, is maddening for being so changeable. Ripeness is all. You can destroy a person's literary life by handing him a book too early or too late. The book you slam shut today, in a fit of disgust, may be the book you'll need to open in ten years. By the time my daughter got to *Little Women*, it was rotten fruit to her. She was fourteen, and the book was past her prime. I read it when I was eleven, and it was a sweet, fat plum to me. My son is too worldly wise and sassy for *The Secret Garden*, too innocent and cheerful for *The Catcher in the Rye*. I have missed his literary mark over and over, and he is skittish about reading and especially suspicious of my literary prosyletizing. My father was more astute. He nudged me to the bookshelf when I was on the cusp of adolescence, before I developed the teenage diseases of arrogance and apathy. He pushed me, all doe-eyed and bushy-tailed, into the classics.

But the times were not right for me in college. In the long march toward an A, good books and poems went right by me, like so many telephone poles on the highway of learning. I was a literary machine, checking Chaucer's *Canterbury Tales* off the list of required reading, spitting out the symbolism of Byzantium, spewing couplets. Literary taste is determined, at least in part, by hunger; and all my hungers were of the satiable, not insatiable, kind. As an adult, I developed raging hunger, hard to satisfy, and so went back and swallowed half the books I had spit out in my youth.

Experts claim the best relationships are built on sexual, religious, and socioeconomic compatibility. I think the best relationships are built on Art. You don't like my best and truest books? You don't like me. It all comes down, in the end, to the toothbrush. Show me a person whose shelves contain the books that changed my life, whose toothbrush looks as pure and inviting as the one I forgot to pack, and I'll show you a person with whom I can cheerfully spend a lifetime.

Questions for discussion

1. In the essay, several people, things, and ideas are being contrasted. What are they?

2. What is the primary method of development? Defend your choice with examples.

3. What is the writer trying to define and classify?

4. How does the writer analyze the problem of youthful indifference to reading? Do you agree or disagree that "arrogance" and "apathy" are at the bottom of adolescent rejection of "good" reading? If you disagree, explain why. If you "hate" to read, explore the causes and the possible effects.

5. Do you agree with the writer that friendship depends on a mutual admiration of Art, on liking the same books, movies, plays, poems, music? If you agree or disagree, explain why.

6. What are some examples of description and figurative language that especially appeal to you? Why?

7. How does the writer explain the problem of earning good grades as it conflicts with reading enjoyment? Can you testify to a similar conflict? Explain.

8. What examples does the writer use to support and defend the assertions? Can you think of examples in your own life that influenced your reading preferences or dislikes? What were they?

9. The writer clearly believes that reading *matters*. Do you agree or disagree? Why or why not?

◆

Activities

1. Return to several of the essays you have written in this course, and analyze the types and developmental methods you used. Can you find examples of all the essay types discussed in this chapter? Do certain essays contain examples of all or most of the methods of development? Which of the essays and paragraphs that you have written are your favorites? Explain why you prefer them.

2. Write a short essay in which you explain how you write, what techniques work for you, why certain methods or approaches are not as successful. Give specific examples, contrast your writing early in the semester and your present writing capability, and analyze what you believe are the secrets of good writing for you.

3. Write a short essay about a book you read too early, too late, or at just the right time in your life.

6

Supporting the Essay

All essays have in common a very broad structure: an introduction, a body, and a conclusion. Within that framework, the shape and organization of the content will vary. A pattern will emerge as you write—a method and approach that will give inherent order and structure to your meanings. Depending on your thesis and intention, you will find yourself defining, comparing, contrasting, classifying, explaining a process—indeed, using one or several of the patterns explained in Chapter 5. But even within these patterns, you will find certain categories of technique and support operating from paragraph to paragraph. If you can learn to identify and analyze these methods of support, you will further strengthen your content.

Analyze a cagey conversation with a resistant parent or doubtful friend, and you will immediately see these methods of support at work. How do you defend your right to move into your own apartment? You probably use description artfully, cannily. You leave out the part about the expense and instead describe the stunning colors, convenient floor plan, Olympic-sized pool, nice neighbors. You tell a fool-proof story about your buddy who got his own apartment and immediately saw an improvement in his grades, his sense of responsibility, his attitude. You recite a litany of facts about the number of students who now own their own condos, about the tax advantages, about the great resale value. And through it all, you display all the charm and ingenuity of a used-car dealer unloading a clunker. Certainly, you do not distract your listener with petty, irrelevant, or long-winded ramblings. You are supporting your case, not destroying it. If you can talk your way into or out of a tight spot, surely you can use these same devices to convince a reader—or even to change his or her behavior.

Your instructor may comment, from time to time, that your paragraphs seem thin, repetitive, inadequately developed. And you may feel a natural impulse to pack your paragraphs with something, anything, to make them seem dense, solid, and impressive. You are wise, however, not to equate fuller development with longer length. If your instructor suggests, for example, that careful description would improve your essay, he or she does not simply mean *more* description. If your instructor begs for facts, you are not simply to include in your essay about, say, the advantages of a home computer the whole dull manual.

Learning to describe, narrate, inform, and persuade means learning to be selective about what to include and what to leave out. Developing and supporting your assertions more fully means stronger, not longer, essays. Every detail, every story, every statistic, and every persuasive tactic will be useful only as it serves your overall writing purpose, your thesis. Good support is essential in fine writing, just as it is essential in families, friendships, cultures, and even shoes. You do not want your ideas to seem shaky, vague, ready to topple or fade away for lack of powerful details, vivid examples, solid evidence, and impeccable arguments. You want to stride across the page, giving your thesis whatever it needs to gain credibility and strength, to win the point or the day.

Describe aptly.

If you agree that seeing is believing, then you will appreciate the importance of using description to bring credibility to your thesis. All good writing depends on accurate seeing—20/20 vision in the mind's eye. If you cannot describe your friend's face, the motions of a cat at play, the way the afternoon light slants across the floor, the noise of clanking water pipes, the gestures of a politician, then your essay will not nudge, or even touch, reality.

Description, then, is the ideal place to begin building support and development for your thesis. But merely piling up details is pointless. *You must describe with a purpose.*

How carefully do you look at the world and yourself in it? Perhaps you wish to describe your family around the breakfast table at the horrifying hour of 6:30 a.m. Perhaps your purpose is to show the contrast between the rosy picture in the television commercial—all smiles and flapjacks and sizzling sausage and Mom with a pink ribbon in her hair and Dad reeking of Aqua Velva and success—and the real picture of the American family at dawn. Here's how it might really look:

> I remember dreary mornings at my house. I see my father and brothers staggering down the steps, heavy-lidded and unshaven, wearing wrinkled pajamas with holes in the elbows. I see my mother, banging pots and pans in the kitchen, her lips tight with the injustice of having to cook breakfast for six and teach school as well. I see us all sitting silently and sullenly around the breakfast table, recoiling from the fried eggs grinning at us from the plate. I see my brother Mike, globbing butter on his toast, and the toast sagging in the middle with the burden of so much fat and cholesterol. I see Mike balancing the toast delicately on his fingers and slowly, irritatingly, eating all the way around the crusty edges, moving inexorably toward the soggy middle. We were depressed, getting ready to face another gray winter day of rain, ice, tests, office jobs. We couldn't look at each other, much less talk, so great was the effort simply of breathing, of survival. We scraped the dried eggs from our plates, loaded up the dishwasher, showered and dressed, gathered our books and briefcases, and trudged out the door, looking like waifs in the tragedy of life.

And how did your breakfast fare? Cold cereal, Pop Tarts, nothing but black coffee, sudden family spats, an uproar about the just distribution of matching socks, unmade beds, complaints of insomnia, the din of television reports on war and pestilence in the background? Tell the truth now.

The Art of Seeing

Everybody assumes that he or she can see. I did. When I was about fifteen or sixteen, I signed up for an art course. I liked everything about the art class except the art work. I liked the smell of the studio. I liked the art teacher, a shy man who hid behind a desk piled high with papers, cracked coffee mugs, hasty sketches, rusty cans filled with paint brushes, boxes of broken charcoal. But I was there to learn to be an artist, not to soak up the atmosphere.

The first day, the teacher strolled into the middle of the room, put a battered coffee pot on the table, and told me to draw it. I was shocked. I had supposed I would begin my art career by painting something lovelier, more dramatic—nudes, still lifes of oranges, maybe a landscape filled with trilling birds and rippling streams.

Instead, I was staring at a coffee pot, with a black wooden handle, a little glass dome on top, a scorched bottom, and so many dents it would surely have rattled on the stove burner. I didn't want to think about what the coffee pot looked like on the inside—probably placidly growing green mildew. I picked up my pencil, feeling insulted, and began my attempt to make the pot a reality on the sketch pad.

But the reality wouldn't come. My coffee pot, the one I drew, left out all the aged character of the pot: no dents, no scorched bottom, no chipped wooden handle, no lights reflecting in the glass dome. How did you draw light, anyway? How did you make a coffee pot look grounded, not floating improbably in space? My pot was abstract and general. It lacked shading, detail, the whatevers that made it something concrete and specific. It was the *idea* of a coffee pot, not a coffee pot.

Writing, not art, taught me finally to see, to pay attention, to transfer that "seeing" to the page. A writer, after all, delivers up the visible world through words, not paints and charcoal. And so the beginning writer must watch, remember how trees look, listen to the bit of dialogue that exactly reveals character, keep a running log of interior feelings, catch the signals and nuances of human behavior.

Descriptive writing is the basis of all good essays, for whatever purpose. The proportion of general to specific is as crucial as the balance of sugar intake for a diabetic. Your thesis is general. Your topic sentences are pretty general. *And, I am boldly asserting, every other sentence in the essay must be specific, appealing as often as possible to the five senses: taste, smell, sound, touch, sight.*

The way you achieve the specific is to bring down every word to its maximum exactness. Instead of ice cream, write chocolate

ripple. Instead of chocolate ripple, write Sealtest chocolate ripple. Instead of car, write sedan. Instead of sedan, write Olds Cutlass. Instead of run, write lope, jog, trot, or race. Your nouns and
verbs yield excellent concrete images for the reader when the
nouns and verbs are specific. There is a world of difference, after
all, between the kind of person who spins down the road in an
Olds Cutlass and the kind of person who rattles along in a battered pickup. Exactness of detail makes ideas, people, events,
and objects come alive. And one detail, artfully selected, can reveal a world, an atmosphere, a season, a place, a character. In
John Updike's story "A&P," the girl named Queenie, going
through the checkout line, buys "Kingfish Fancy Herring Snacks
in Pure Sour Cream: 49 cents." You can't get much more specific
than that. But Updike is specific for a reason. The purchase reveals Queenie's character. The bag boy, Sammy, says,

> All of a sudden I slid right down her voice into her living
> room. Her father and the other men were standing around
> in ice-cream coats and bow ties and the women were in
> sandals picking up herring snacks on toothpicks off a big
> glass plate and they were all holding drinks the color of
> water with olives and sprigs of mint in them. When my
> parents have somebody over they get lemonade and if it's a
> real racy affair Schlitz in tall glasses with "They'll Do It
> Every Time" cartoons stencilled on.[1]

See? Of course you do, because this writer knows the importance of small, careful details for creating major meanings. Your
readers must be able to see your world; to see, in the seeing,
what that world means to you and how that world relates to
theirs.

Being There

Every small town, for example, looks much like another. I
used to live in one called Clinton. It had a main square, a
courthouse, a First Baptist Church, a couple of movie theaters.

---

[1]John Updike, "A&P," in *Pigeon Feathers and Other Stories* (New York: Knopf,
1962).

So far, so what? The general description fits any small town, and no picture comes to mind—only a vague impression. To make you see *my* small town, I'd have to tell you about Percy Holland's coffee shop on the corner; about the way Percy made a noise like a siren every time we kids walked in for a five-cent vanilla Pepsi; about the way the farmers squatted by the door of the hardware store, spitting large wads of tobacco on the steaming sidewalk; about the blind woman who ran the newsstand in the courthouse, feeling for the values of change; about the Colonial grocery store across the street from my grandparents' house; about Bennie Weeks's Sunoco station. Every town has a filling station. But every town doesn't have a Sunoco station run by a guy named Bennie Weeks.

See what I mean? Particularize. Particularize. Don't write like a bad joke teller who, when nobody laughs at his joke, says, "You had to *be* there." Good description means you *are* there, listening to Percy Holland make a noise like a siren even as he flips another burger on the grill.

◆

Activities

1. The purpose of the following descriptive essay is implicit in the details. What is its central meaning? What happens in this scene? What is the narrator learning from the other character? Write an introduction with a thesis that leads naturally into this scene. Give your essay a title, deriving the title either from your thesis or from the essay itself. State the main idea in each supporting paragraph.

   The black clouds have parted for the first time all day, and the rain has suddenly slacked off. We are riding our bikes down a long flat road in eastern North Carolina. We pass between fields too wet for ploughing. Everything waits. The bluets spring on the grass. The grass is the color of Ireland, as I carry her in my mind. The green shouts at the heavy gray sky the way a beautiful young daughter turns on her mother, the spring of her life, the water of her being. The last jonquils sing in the shadow of the redbud. The jonquils are finished. They make way for what is to come, what passes, down the lonely country road.

I tremble on the tear of this moment. Summoning all my daring, I bend to the far horizon and wheel past you. I am laughing. I want to race. You press your will to the effort, but soon I am far ahead of you, hearing you call, "I quit." You settle to a slow pedal, and I turn to see your smile gleaming behind me at the bend in the road.

Suddenly the air changes from warm to cold, and I push into a black cloud bearing down on the road ahead. I can see rain in the high places of the pines. I can feel the gathering wind, the approaching squall, like reprimands on my young face. A bug slaps my cheek and falls away to the ditch. I push harder and harder, a little frightened now, for the dirt driveway, the white farm house. Turning into the driveway, I can just see the small light burning in the kitchen. I can already smell the oil stove, the musty cabinets. At the last minute, driven by the black cloud, you swing into the lead and carry me, like a blue ship tugging a small green boat, into the soggy yard and up to the back door. I think, looking at your back hunched over the bicycle, of a planet first. But home is in your back as well and laughter, games, sighs, death.

Just as you shut the door, the cloud opens to drop more rain on the tin roof. You whisper in my ear the new secrets of rain, how the raindrops are all different, how the slant of the wind and the force of the droplets make, each one, a separate music. Obedient to your ears, I hold very still and catch the special music of each drop falling. I am afraid to breathe, live, in the shimmering impact of a million falling tears. You ask if I am afraid in rain. I remember only the rain of my city childhood, muffled on shingles, thudding on low, dull rooftops. These strong waters on the tin roof demand attention.

The rain falls all afternoon in torrents, sheets. The rain is imperative. I sit at the kitchen table, restless as storms, and feel your words falling over me, one by one.

The scene is descriptive, of course. But how is the description achieved? Some things—the color green, for example—are compared to other things—Ireland in the narrator's mind. Colors—gray, green, yellow, red, white, blue—are in the piece. Touch is there, and sound—the bug slapping the face, the rain on the tin roof. The writer must also orient the characters in space—first on the road together, then one passing the other, then the other taking the lead to the back door. The writer also names things specifically: eastern North Carolina, not just the country; jonquils, redbuds, bluets, pines, not just trees and flowers. The writer also makes figurative, not literal, comparisons: the characters are boats, ships, planets, home. Why is the exact relationship of the characters not defined?

2. Did you ever sneak down to the corner drug store, hide behind the paperback books, and read the "good" parts of racy bestsellers? With whom did you go? How did you get the word about which pages were juicier than others? Did you get caught? Describe, in three or four paragraphs, what happened, using details that appeal to the five senses. Here follows an example of the kind of descriptive writing that might characterize such a scene. Your details will, of course, be different. Maybe you gathered your illicit reading material at the public library, in some dark corner. Maybe you peeked in your father's sock drawer. Maybe you smuggled the desired reading into your cabin at summer camp. But describe what happened, and let the details carry the meaning.

Example:

This hot summer day pushes me into the past. I remember almost nothing of winter. But every summer leaf stirs something: a smell, a taste, a song, a passion. Screen doors bang open and shut. Dianne, with hair blonde as a beam of light and skin the color of good dirt, hollers from the yard next door. She is wearing white shorts and a blue shirt the color of swimming pools and ice. She is barefooted. As always, I am struck by her bare brown legs, the perfection of them. Her legs look like molded posts of very fine bannisters, as if fashioned by a superior craftsman, loving to work with wood. I am, at twelve years old, only a very large piece of misshapen clay.

Dianne and I start down the steep, rutted hill beside my house. Some orphans from the Methodist Home are trudging up the hill, taking the short cut to Sears and the Winston Movie Theater. I envy the orphans, on the bumpy, uncertain road that seems to belong exclusively to them. They reek, in my mind, of tar, thick with possibility. They have no true home and, being homeless, can afford to be lost and loud, vulgar and brave.

Shouts of laughter come from the group, the result of something a gangly girl with at least twenty tinkling bracelets on her thin arms has whispered. The orphans cut their eyes over to Dianne and me passing barefooted and silent down the street. I feel awkward, my shorts riding up between my chubby legs. But Dianne ignores the laughter and the looks. She is happy. We have abandoned our mothers and embarked on the short journey to the limits of our narrow freedom. We are going down the hill to Summit Street Pharmacy to get a Fudgsicle. We are going to read the good parts of *Lady Chatterley's Lover.* Dianne will show me, she of the sturdy legs and well-traveled eyes.

Does the description in this passage point to an underlying theme? What is Dianne's role? What is the point of mentioning the orphans? How does the sharing of this racy book at the drug store make the narrator feel? Why is the season summer? Why is Dianne blonde and tanned and sturdy? Why is the narrator awkward?

3. Descriptive possibilities are everywhere. Write three or four descriptive paragraphs on one of the following. Choose one in which you would appear, somehow, in the picture. Do not state a thesis directly. Let the details you select convey the underlying theme or purpose.

Twilight

Bus station

Encounter with a wino

Kitchen junk drawer

Medicine cabinet

Restaurant with a C-rating

Sensation of flying

Audience at a rock concert, revival, freshman orientation session

First meeting between two roommates

An evening at a drive-in theater

Sorority or fraternity rush party

Motel room

Children's "forts"

Dissecting a frog in biology lab

Family conferences

Narrate engagingly.

When you describe, you are encouraged to show, not tell. When you narrate, you are advised to tell, but there is no contradiction here. Obviously, you tell a story, joke, or anecdote. But the telling will turn into pontificating, moralizing, or judging if your story does not contain descriptive details, if the reader cannot "see" your characters, your setting, your theme, your insides and outsides. So narration is a variation on the descriptive theme, growing out of the concrete—as does all good writing.

Narration as a method of support is a much-neglected way of getting your point across in an essay. Here is a story that proves the point. Recently, a magazine article told of a college student who was sick of writing essays. She had one of those fine, old-fashioned English teachers, the kind you love to hate, who required 16 five-paragraph essays each semester. The essays were required to contain a thesis as the last sentence of an introductory paragraph. Three paragraphs must follow, with topic sentences for each and two facts or details to support the topic sentence. The conclusion must contain a restatement of thesis. This formulaic, five-paragraph model was surely teaching the young woman how to write essays. She could write them awake, asleep, with one hand tied behind her back, in a football stadium, or on the bathroom wall. But she was not happy writing them. Her teacher left little room for invention, for yarn spinning with a design, a purpose.

An essay, in fact, has plenty of room for narration. A narration is a story. It has plot, dialogue, rising action, resolution of conflict. It has anticipation and motion. It may or may not have a moral, but it will carry some sort of inherent message.

A Story About Stories

When I grow weary of writing essays, I sometimes write something like a story, though not a story at all. Instead of citing studies of student apathy toward reading, I might, instead, tell the story of my walking in the woods near the junior high school and of finding, under piles of wet leaves, a soggy biology textbook. If I am trying to cover poverty, and feel the tragedy slipping away in abstract theories and sociological data, I might tell the story of one family living in a shack with only a bag of grits on the shelf and a bill collector knocking on the door. Of course, the story I use would not be the entire essay. But it would surely bring down the general facts to the specific reality, thereby enlivening the essay and stimulating interest. If a picture is worth a thousand words, then a story is worth a thousand precepts.

I am not suggesting that you transform freshman composition into a course in creative writing, though if you are an expert storyteller, your writing will surely improve. Remember, I am an essayist, not a fiction writer. The philosophical, theoretical, instructional dimension of the essay prohibits pure storytelling. Sooner or later, the essayist will have to establish the connection between the story and the thesis, the anecdote and the topic sentence, the dramatization and the purpose. After the pained-looking woman on the television commercial tells the story of her tension headache, the man in the pin-striped suit will still hold up the aspirin bottle, cite the impressive statistics, and make the pitch. But because Mrs. So-and-So has taken the viewer through the experience of the tension headache, the viewer is more willing to respond to the thesis: Buy this extra-strength painkiller and no other.

You have many skills in the art of narration. When you gossip, you are telling a story. What is a rumor, after all, but another episode in the soap opera of life? Anecdotes are also stories. With an anecdote, you create a little scene, put in a couple of lines of dialogue, sketch out a recognizable character. But you are using a narrative only to prove a philosophical point. Confucius, Lao Tzu, Jesus, Aesop, and Chaucer all used stories, created little scenes or vignettes, told parables. They knew that if the people hear a story—in the beginning, once upon a time, this traveling salesman was stopping at a flea-bag hotel—ears will prick up, interest will quicken, eyes will brighten, pulses will race.

You would not think a medical textbook would be a good place to go for a story, would you? But even doctors can tell a story, though they call it a "case study." Every case study is, after all, a true story, one that begins at the beginning and proceeds chronologically to some conclusion: Mrs. X entered St. John's Hospital on January 12, 1983, complaining of sleeplessness and weight loss. She expressed feelings of despondency and worthlessness, saying that life was "hopeless," that she wished she were dead. Mrs. X had recently given birth to a boy and expressed tremendous feelings of guilt about "not loving" the baby. Conflicts with husband ensued. "He won't come near me," she said. "I just sit around in my bathrobe all day, crying."

And so the story goes, telling the reader better than any scientific treatise what severe, postpartum depression looks like, feels like. It is from the narrative in the case study that the reader begins to feel, in his or her bones, the debilitating effects of depression on this young mother. She is the central, tragic heroine of an old, old story. And the heart responds to her story in a way that the head cannot.

The next time you find yourself ranting and raving in an essay, trying to whack the reader over the head with proverbs and opinions, take a step back. Think of the eloquent incident that would break the monotony of monologue and maxim. Rely on story as a stylistic device, an excellent method of organization and support.

The following narrative passage is an excerpt from an essay about prayer in the schools and the issue of separation of church and state. The introduction in which the writer states a thesis and generally addresses this controversial issue is omitted. The entire middle of this essay is devoted to one childhood memory. The telling of it runs through several paragraphs. What, in your opinion, is the writer's attitude toward prayer in the schools? How does the writer define "prayer"? Are there other meanings or purposes in the narrative? Why is this story an essay? How does a chronological telling affect the topic sentences? What about descriptive details? Can you see Mr. Hawkins, the classroom, the students? What is the proportion of general to specific? Find the most general sentences, and discuss how and why they do or do not control the telling of the story.

MR. HAWKINS'S FIRST PRAYER

I remember poor Mr. Hawkins, my seventh-grade English teacher, trying to pray. He was a terrible teacher, given to assigning busy work. He had slick black hair, dapper clothes, a taste for the finer things in life, denied him by being a public-school teacher. He had much to pray about, as did, I'm sure, his sullen charges. The public schools, in those days, required morning prayer; and Mr. Hawkins, being the only grown-up in the room, was condemned to deliver blessings on our undeserving heads.

One morning the bell rang, and we obediently bowed our little heads. So did Mr. Hawkins, though his bent head gave the impression of a man heading into a storm, not heaven. "Our Father," he hesitantly began, and we waited for the pat recitation to proceed. But Mr. Hawkins stopped. The clock ticked loudly. Heads lifted. Tightly shut eyes peeked open. We coughed, blushed, waited. Still, nothing happened.

Children are easily embarrassed by public displays of incompetence. Mr. Hawkins had already proved himself to be an incompetent teacher; and, with the unerring, cruel judgments of children, we had crucified him for this sin. Now he was proving to be spiritually incompetent as well, a total bust.

The atmosphere was thick as Bunyan's Slough of Despond in *Pilgrim's Progress*. The silence was loud as a resounding "Amen." Finally, Mr. Hawkins muttered, "I just can't do it," then turned on his heels and left the room. I was too young to realize that I had just heard my first *real* prayer, though I had spent what seemed like an eternity on the pews of the First Baptist Church.

The next example of narration serves as the method of support for an essay about the difference between public and private faces, public and private lives. The narrative begins in the paragraph following the introduction and continues, again, over several paragraphs. Notice that at several points in setting up and describing the scene, the writer breaks the flow of the narrative to make general statements about overall meanings. But the specific details abound, predominate. What are the topic sentences in this middle, and how do they control the narrative, the paragraphs?

BEHIND CLOSED DOORS

And then there were the Tidballs, who lived underneath my apartment. They spent the Sabbath arguing, and I spent the Sabbath in my living-room closet, listening to them argue. I was not really ashamed of this pastime. After all, the Tidballs' voices were audible to anyone within a three-mile radius of Hampton Terrace. But I like my eavesdropping like my radio audio: no static, no interference, a dependable stereo sound. The closet offered the best reception.

In conformity with my theory about what people show and what people hide, the Tidballs' public image was dull, even bordering on wimpishness. They both had concave chests; sweet, sad smiles; the slumped postures of people who have no strong passions, whether of rage or romance. Their passion was their secret, and mine as well, hunched in the closet, listening.

The Sunday quarrels covered some familiar and bumpy marital ground. Martin told Harriet she was "lazy, L-A-Z-Y, LAZY!" Harriet told Martin to "shaddup." I could hear little scuffles, fist banging, pot throwing. But then, in the glow of a pink sunset, after a day of violent battle, the two emerged from their apartment, clutching the chubby hands of their golden-haired son, Daniel, and walked slowly down the sidewalk—a Norman-Rockwell picture of family harmony, family contentment.

Sometimes the story is so small, so fleeting, that it seems more like an example. But these tiny vignettes can provide sturdy support, strong development, even within a single paragraph. In an essay about passive–aggressive and aggressive behavior, the writer comes out in favor of bold confrontation, not mincing manipulation. This paragraph appears near the end of the essay, when a dramatic finish might enhance earlier arguments in favor of arguing. The story is small but complete, one sentence, in fact.

I like better the bold, crisp confrontation, the one that lets everybody stay in the light and be illuminated by it. My favorite *Peanuts* cartoon is the one in which Lucy describes her confrontation with the neighborhood bully: "I didn't know what to say to him, so I hit him." Maybe that's why Lucy operates the five-cent psychiatry stand. She's fast. She's sharp. She's frank. She's cheap. Give her a nickel, and she'll give you the business.

The next passage provides development for an essay about the power of lust. The overriding contrast is between human lust and animal lust. The introductory paragraph contains a reference to President Jimmy Carter's famous remark in *Playboy*, namely that he had often lusted in his heart. The story of the cat puts this timid human lust in perspective.

LUST

One night, when I stepped out for a sedate, ladylike evening, I returned to find my cat whirling and spinning like a dervish on the sidewalk outside my front door. She was dancing all right, and grinning from ear to ear, her feet refusing to touch the ground, her eyes unwilling to meet mine.

"How did she get out?" I screamed, suspecting burglars had at last robbed me of my uninsured sterling silver. Then I saw the window of the second-floor bedroom, barely open from the top. The screen, bent and battered from some fierce impact, lay on the ligustrum bush beside the front door. "You don't suppose—" I said to my friend, not daring to complete the thought. "Looks like you've got a hot one here," said the friend, shaking her head in wonder.

And that's how I learned about lust, the power of, the boldness of, the primitive determination of. No amount of trifling human lust could make *me* sail from a second-story window to my lover below. I might get hurt. And pain, in my civilized opinion, is much worse than unfulfilled desire.

The final example of narration is used to provide support and development in an essay about the glamor and excitement surrounding Saturday night, the night of the week when Americans step out and cut up. The writer saves this story for last, because Helen, the character in the story, exactly conveys that Saturday-night mystique.

SATURDAY NIGHT

I remember one woman who seemed to get a real kick out of Saturday night. She was raised in the country, where the dogs howled mournfully at the Saturday moon and the silence of the back roads was thick as fear. She lucked up, marrying a city boy from a town of twelve thousand or so. She hit the big time. I used to run into her of a Saturday night, down at the Elks Club, eating fried flounder and getting her juices flowing for a night of jitterbugging. She was hot to trot.

One Saturday night, I saw her smoking a cigarette at the far end of the raucous banquet table. "Helen," I hollered, "I didn't know you smoked." "Honey," she answered, in a Southern drawl slow as a seductive shimmy, "I'll do *anything* on Sattidy night."

The following model essays achieve their development and support primarily through description and narration. Yet each contains a thesis and topic sentences that control the purpose and direction of the essay. The thesis and topic sentences are italicized. Study how the writer uses detail and story to make a point. Questions for discussion follow each essay.

Example A

THE FRONT PORCH

I miss my grandparents' front porch. By the time I came along, my parents had already made the move into a two-story, mock colonial, with a cement slab and three brick steps barely large enough for two to dream on. *But my grandparents had a porch worthy of the name: it was the essence of porches, not so much pretty or handsome as RIGHT.*

The entrance to the porch, the view I saw coming back from the dime store, created a feeling of solidity. Six fat steps, painted gray, marked the exact center of the porch. On either side of the steps were big, square pillars of white brick. At the base of these steps were two ledges, gray again, for perching on when I wanted intimacy with the street. From the ledges I could see or be seen, dangling my legs and popping my bubblegum, peeking up the street at the Austin Theater, shimmering in the heat at the bend of College Street. The cement ledges in summer felt cool and rough on the backs of my thighs. My dangling legs grew pleasantly heavy and limp, separate and free of the burden of me. The only touch of pretension about the porch was two decorative pots holding boxwoods. The boxwoods sent up pungent odors of possibility, as if nature were whispering messages through the cobwebs, the small, shiny leaves—something about summer and the bend in the street down which I looked.

We went to the porch because the porch was where life went. Inside the house, Grandmother went around closing windows and blinds against the noise and dirt of the street, challenging the effrontery of sunlight fading the brocaded backs of chairs and sofas. The dining room, barely used except for company, sat cold and heavy in the dead center of the house, filled with mahogany and tarnished silver. It was a room we children went around rather than through. Three clocks, resting on various mantels, tolled the passing of this summer vacation and the next, as surely as Grandmother's late-night snores stirred childhood fears of death. But when we stepped onto the porch and slammed the screen door behind us, we were free, part of the pulsing world of commerce and nature.

The porch changed mood and tone as often as the clock chimed the hours. In the mornings, after Granddaddy left for his insurance office, Grandmother, my brothers, and I would spend the morning sitting on the porch until the noon heat drove us in for lunch. Grandmother settled herself in the chair by the door and began to rock, her legs folded neatly at the ankle, one eye on the street. Sometimes she sat with a brown paper bag at her feet and a battered metal bowl in her lap, snapping beans for lunch. She let us help until we began tossing the stringy ends into the bowl, and then she shooed us into the swing. Sometimes Grandmother would descend into the yard, broom in hand, to sweep the dirt in swirls, to eradicate the footprints of our rough play. The yard, like many yards in eastern North Carolina, wouldn't keep a stand of grass. It was merely an expanse of grayish dirt with, here and there, especially around the base of the pecan tree, a thick, dazzling layer of green moss. In the early morning, the yard, the spindly nandina bushes, the ivy, and the tired box-woods gave off a fragrance of mulch, as leaves, dead creatures, and wet dirt offered up moisture to the sun.

In the middle of the day, the porch stood empty, as if anticipating the relief of twilight. Grandmother napped or put the heating pad to her bad back. We wandered uptown to the movie or went to Granddaddy's office to get a nickel for a cherry Coke at Butler's Drug Store.

The porch grew conspiratorial, intimate, toward evening. Full of pork chops and biscuits from supper, we children rocked ourselves gently in the swing and listened to the grown-up talk rising at the far end of the porch. Granddaddy railed at the young girls wearing short shorts uptown or cursed a teenager doing 55 in a 35-mile zone. Miss Thelma strolled over from next door, pressed us to her bosom in an obligatory hug, then slipped into the chair beside Grandmother. The two of them began whispering, in cahoots against the folks beyond the boundaries of the porch. The cardboard fans with Jesus on the front and Royal's Funeral Home on the back flew faster and faster as the women gathered steam, let fly the words. Granddaddy sat up near the railing, putting in his two-cents' worth, tipping his hat to passers-by, cussing at gnats.

We children, meanwhile, were swinging higher and higher, growing more and more exuberant as the wind stirred and the sun went lower and lower in the pink sky. We were carried away with the summer air and the huckleberries for supper and the delicious spitefulness of grown-up talk. Our hearts went crazy. We sang all the verses of "Sixteen Tons," sealing our doom with every chorus.

A time would come when Grandmother would begin to notice our rambunctiousness. Irritation set in. Miss Thelma, glaring at us, excused herself and went home. Joy faded. "It's high time we got these children to bed, Mangum," Grandmother would say to

Granddaddy, then she pushed herself from her chair with a groan and herded us, weak with wrongdoing, into giant beds surrounded by monstrous shadows of clocks and dreams.

Questions for discussion

1. In what sense can this essay be called a narrative? Or in what sense can this narrative be called an essay?

2. How does the writer set the scene, suggest the time period, sketch out the characters?

3. Are certain things in the story characters as well?

4. What descriptive details appeal to the senses of taste, touch, smell, sound, sight?

5. Where does the essay exhibit more of the descriptive mode than of the narrative?

6. Can you speculate on the character, personality, age of the narrator? What leads you to these conclusions?

7. How does the writer establish the contrast between the inside of the house and the porch? What does the porch represent? What recurring elements in the essay point to symbolic importance, having several levels of meaning?

Example B

THE ROAD TO ARCADY

When I left the big city for a weekend in the country, visions of tranquillity danced in my head. The fields were fat and green with soybeans and peanuts. The smoke and fumes on the beltline gave way to the elixir of fresh air. The only pollutant on the horizon was the frailty I carried within myself, and it, like the poor, would always be with me. *My cloud of cigarette smoke, my raucous laughter, my free-floating anxiety were along for the ride, but I was counting on Nature to drive them away.*

The first thing that happened on the road to idyllic Arcady was a serious car wreck. I drive all year round in the fast lane of the city, with two-ton trucks and joy riders all around me, and never have a wreck. This car accident, a smoking, screeching thing, occurred between two towns so small you probably never heard of them, on a two-lane road you wouldn't go down unless you lived there. Everybody was nice, even the man whose

Pontiac I smashed in the rear. After every perception was duly recorded and I had received my ticket for a safe-movement violation, the man went home for supper, saying only that accidents will happen.

But I had three broken bones in my foot. *At last in the country real and countrified, I watched my foot swell big as the myth about the simple pleasures of bucolic life.* The doctor's office was open on Saturday, though he would be headed at noon for the beach at Nag's Head, seeking his own idyllic setting. He had X-ray equipment, a sharp eye for the evidence. I knew, deep in my bones, that the bones were broken. But his diagnosis made my limping, hopping, and being waited on more credible. The first time he X-rayed he saw one broken bone. The second time, he saw three. I grabbed the crutches and the local sympathy, praising God all the while that I was not, to toy with Nixon's phrase, a crock.

The accident and injuries behind us, my friend and I returned to the peaceful fields and farm house for what remained of the shattered weekend. I parked my body on a lawn chair under the towering pecan tree, propped my gimpy foot on a fluffy pillow, opened my novel, *Precious Bane,* and let the breeze blow away city fears, city nightmares.

Precious Bane destroyed another myth. In the Shropshire countryside, the characters sowed and reaped, but what they sowed and reaped was nothing like the abundant harvests from the fat fields of our foolish dreams. Three suicides, one arson, two murders, and one flogging later, I came to the end of the novel of simple Shropshire life, exhausted with despair. Was no place in Nature exempt from human conflict, human misery? Could Nature, wrapped in concrete and bordered by multifamily housing, be somehow safer than the isolated cottage and lonely mere of which Mary Webb had written?

Every place has its dangers and its darkness, even in the brilliant, shining green of fertile fields. Saturday afternoon, when the only sounds were of the bees and the roll of the dice in our game of Trivial Pursuit, we suddenly entered a war zone. Eight or 10 fancy, rigged-out vans and trucks pulled up alongside the peanut field. Walkie-talkies ominously muttered up and down the road. Men and boys spilled from the tanker-sized vans and poured into the peanut fields, crushing the plump plants, mutilating the harvest. We heard shouts, then shots. Men and boys alike wore camouflage suits and sported shotguns. The trivial pursuits of city folks seemed silly in the midst of scattershot and manly strategies. It was the opening of dove season. The birds of peace, the bearers of olive branches, dropped from the sky like old notions, worn-out dreams.

All afternoon the shots whizzed and zinged around the brooding fields. Once a shot came so close I forgot my mangled foot and raced across the yard to cuss out the lawless renegade. But the soldiers hid in the field. I couldn't find a single face to shake a finger in. At suppertime, the men and boys recrossed the field, climbed into their souped-up, twenty-thousand-dollar trail blazers, and went home to roast a pig and rip it apart with their bare hands.

But on Sunday, all was quiet on the farm front, except, of course, for the roar of Oldsmobiles and Fords heading for the Baptist church. Again parked under the trees, I sipped a beer in defiance of local custom and watched the people go by in their Sunday best, costumed and corseted by ritual as much as any city person.

Pantheism is not a religion to lie down in. I did think about lying down in the grass, but an army of ants dissuaded me. I did stare up through the branches of the pecan trees and feel a certain something stirring in the air, something lost and essential, never to be recovered. James, the farm hand, sat a spell and said farming would never be the same again. The day before, I had watched huge red farm machines, looking odd and menacing as giant insects, moving over the corn and taking down in a moment what Nature had needed a season to grow.

So I came home on Monday, back to the city, back to the shimmering fields of pavement and the weedless paths of concrete, knowing we carry our frailty with us, in the smoking weapons of our beings. Yet I was hopeful, too, that the sky over one is the sky over all.

Questions for discussion

1. The narration is chronological, arranged sequentially in time. How, then, does the writer create topic sentences that will provide thematic unity for each paragraph?

2. Again, description and narration combine to prove an assertion. What is the writer contrasting? How does the writer evoke the city atmosphere, even in the country, and vice versa?

3. How does the writer connect various themes and images into one organic telling? The writer mentions city, country, the novel *Precious Bane*, the car accident, dove season, farming.

And yet all are somehow related to the theme. How are those incidents and details used to support the main idea?

4. The writer uses a story to expose myths about the simple country life. Who or what is the villain in the story?

5. Who is Mary Webb? What is Arcady? How much do you know about Shropshire? Find out, so that you will catch the allusions and understand more fully the reasons the writer uses these reference points.

◆

Activities

1. Tell a story, in three or four paragraphs, about going to a strange place that did not live up to your expectations, a place about which you had heard or read. Set up a contrast between what you expected and what was, in fact, the reality. Include descriptive details that will help the reader see this place and feel your disappointment in it. Was it a vacation spot, a theme park, a dream house, a glamorous city, the family home place, a summer camp, the college of your choice, a dormitory room, your first train or airplane journey?

2. Your life is an anthology of stories, and sometimes the more inconspicuous the moment, the greater the narrative possibilities. Find one of these meaningful moments, develop a thesis that conveys your feelings about it, and write three paragraphs of narration and description that prove the validity of those feelings. Here follow some suggestions:

Afternoons from three to five

A coffee break

Five minutes until lights out

The narrow country between sleeping and waking

Happy hour

In the car on the way to the beach

Bonfire time

Waiting in line

Three hours in the emergency room

Laundromat life

Blue Friday

Three people in the bathroom

Surprise party

After supper (winter)

After supper (summer)

First night away from home

Inform accurately.

Description offers up the visible world by details of seeing, hearing, tasting, smelling, touching. Narration supports assertions with story, anecdote, vignette, parable, joke. But in expository writing, in which the primary intention is to inform, support and development come from facts, statistics, respected authorities, polls, laboratory studies and numbers. The popularity of trivia games and television quiz shows proves the American enchantment with facts. How many whiskers does the average man have? How many dogs have played the role of Lassie? What percentage of the college population is female?

Put facts in context.

If Americans like facts out of context, they will surely find them even more fascinating in context. The information a writer gathers to support an assertion, theory, or opinion can provide sturdy support and development for the middles of essays. Facts in isolation are, well, trivia. Facts in context, however, can be staggering, arresting, shocking, mind bending. Well-chosen facts, in combination with effective description and narration, can win the point for the writer and change the minds of the readers.

Some people think facts are dry. And so facts are—that is, until they line themselves up as proofs of a provocative or controversial assertion. Suppose you read that Vermont has no ocean coastline. You might yawn. Suppose you then learn that it is the only New England state lacking an ocean coastline. You might begin to perk up a bit. Suppose you then read, "Because Vermont is the only New England state lacking an ocean coastline, its people have developed an independence, a rugged individualism, an insularity that has shaped their character." Then the fact, in context, becomes interesting. The reader proceeds to think about the connection between geography and its shaping of the culture and personality of the state's citizens. The reader might even begin to speculate on the connection between geography and international character. Can the physical define the psychological?

Here is another example. Suppose someone says that Wallace Stevens was an insurance lawyer. No context. No reaction. So what? Plenty of people are lawyers. But placing the fact in context, suppose the speaker adds that Wallace Stevens was a poet and an insurance lawyer. Interest quickens. Stereotypes about the personalities of businesspeople and poets are breaking up. Suppose you then develop a thesis asserting that artists, contrary to popular perceptions, are not impractical dreamers, unfit for gainful employment. Suppose you then support that assertion with facts such as these: Carl Sandburg was a newspaper man; poet William Carlos Williams was a practicing physician; poet Wallace Stevens was a lawyer; poet Robert Frost was a farmer; poet Marianne Moore worked on an ad campaign for the Ford Motor Company. The facts gain interest as they become pertinent to a theme or idea.

Juxtapose the facts.

Facts in Context

Facts heighten interest and credibility when they appear in arresting, dramatic combinations. Remember all the hoopla that surrounded a woman's first trip into outer space. I was impressed, too. But when I remarked delightedly that a woman was at last going into space, a friend wryly commented, "Yeah, *after* the monkey went." Oops. I had never looked at the facts *that* way, but suddenly my delight turned to outrage. The juxtaposition of these two bits of information put the issue in perspective, gave the alleged triumph of Sally Ride a context, albeit a depressing one.

Certain kinds of information can be very useful in certain kinds of essays. Essays that explain what something means, how something is done, how something is to be categorized, or what one thing means in terms of another will rely heavily on facts and information. Even in essays written primarily to persuade, a fact can be worth a million personal experiences, defenses, and suppositions. In an essay arguing that women are not, and never have been, treated equally, the fact that women still earn only about 70 cents for every dollar a man earns can be compelling. So is the fact that women got the vote in 1920, after slaves had been given the right to vote.

Because the human mind cannot always take in the implications of a fact, the writer's obligation is to make facts live

1. By using them to support assertions,
2. By placing them in arresting or startling combinations,
3. By checking their accuracy, and
4. By citing the sources of the information.

Responsible writers use facts reponsibly, even as they heighten the drama of facts by effective placement and logical support. Are you quoting from an authority? You must give the date, the speaker, and the occasion on which the fact was presented. A spokesman for the American Tobacco Institute, for example, is certainly not going to lay stress on the harmful effects of tobacco. A member of the American Medical Association is certainly not going to present, in unbiased fashion, the case for or against socialized medicine. A mother in MADD (Mothers Against Drunk Drivers) is not going to quote statistics that minimize the moment at which a 250-pound person is legally impaired. The president of an airline company, even after a year of frequent plane crashes and numerous resulting fatalities, is not going to blame faulty aircraft or pilot error. He or she will very likely fall back on the old saw, factually accurate but of no comfort to the relatives of a plane-crash fatality, that more people die in car accidents each year than in airplane crashes.

You see, then, how important it is to document facts correctly and fully. You see, also, how much depends on the writers' handling of facts. And you see how facts can be interpreted differently, depending on the philosophy or case or politics of the person wielding the fact. A fact is powerful, whether it is used for good or ill. Like the patient seeking a cure, you should check three or four sources before you seek to inform your reader about any subject. If the medical community cannot agree even about the importance of taking vitamins, then how can facts be taken solely at face value? Better make certain who is presenting the facts and for what motives. Then intellectual health, not weak or painful manipulation, may result.

The following passages use facts to support or develop assertions. Some of the information is secondary to the argument. Some facts simply document or verify rather placid, benign observations. Some facts are simply the stimulus for a thesis, the jumping-off place for discussion. But all facts, however they are used, have significance only in context and when directed toward a purpose.

Example A

The following passage is used to develop the middle of an essay about the Equal Rights Amendment. The writer chooses to go to the Constitution to find facts that would contradict widely held assumptions—namely, that the Constitution already says that women are equal and, in addition, that the Constitution is too sacred a document to be frivolously tampered with.

A CASE FOR ERA

Legislators have often had to eat their words, change their minds, or make the Constitution more legally explicit. Even though the Constitution promises to "establish justice, insure domestic tranquillity, provide for the common defense, promote the general welfare, and secure the blessings of liberty to ourselves and to our posterity," it doesn't. It doesn't unless it gets down to specifics; and specific is what the Constitution, in amendment after amendment, has had to get. The framers of the Constitution, after all, were not geniuses, saints, seers, gods. They also were not female or black.

Over the years, the Constitution has been changed to make explicit those high-flown and abstract sentiments expressed in the Preamble. In 1865, the Constitution was amended to abolish slavery. Then, in 1868, the Constitution was amended to turn freed slaves into citizens. Then in 1870, the Constitution was amended again to give blacks citizenship and the right to vote. Women, however, had to wait until 1920 for the Constitutionally guaranteed right to vote.

Interspersed among these important amendments have been other more foolish adjustments and tinkerings, proving that legislators can tamper with the Constitution any time they want and for whatever reason. In 1919, the Constitution was amended to prohibit the "manufacture, sale, or transportation of intoxicating liquors." Then in 1933, after the crime syndicates were safely established and the legislators were thirsty again, the Constitution was amended to restore alcohol to its rightful place in American society.

The writer, after this recitation of facts, ends the argument with this potent kicker—namely, that women's rights are certainly more important than a Constitutionally guaranteed slug of Jack Daniel's.

Example B

The following paragraph is based upon an essay about the sorry state of the arts. The writer quotes an author in the essay and is careful to give the name of the magazine as well, a magazine that has traditionally been sympathetic to the arts.

The question arises: can anybody poetic come out of New Jersey? Hugh Kenner, reviewing for *Harper's*, says somebody can, and the somebody is not Joyce Kilmer. Kenner touchingly reports on the life of William Carlos Williams, doctor/poet of Paterson, New Jersey. Kenner recalls that when Williams was in his mid-seventies, the poet was still opening rejection letters from the *Hudson Review*. Kenner goes on to describe a "pathetically" pleased Williams being invited one Christmas to read his poems in a Newark department store "with the Santa-bells jangling and the numbed throng ascending toward lawnjeray and p'fume." I am part of the numbed throng who blandly escalated past Williams's reciting voice. So, probably, are you. That is the response to art. We head for lawnjeray, where the profits are.

Example C

The following essay, intended primarily to inform, delivers up facts in an interesting context. The writer is discussing a scientific subject, holography, but the thesis focuses on how holography is used in everyday life. The information is directed toward a lay audience; and the subject, though certainly scientific, gains relevance by demonstrating how average folks might find this scientific technique operating in their own lives.

HOLOGRAPHY

Holography, the process of making a three-dimensional photograph by using mirrors and lasers, is finding wide use in the general population. Though still in its infancy, the process could eventually revolutionize entertainment and commerce. Furthermore, it could become as common in daily life as, well, credit cards and microwave cooking.

The layperson can best understand holography by comparing it to the working of the human eye. The eyes see at two different angles, and the brain takes the two different pictures and produces a three-dimensional image. The objects that humans see are actually reflecting light. A wave of light bouncing off an object is called a "wavefront." The wavefront carries all the information humans see—size, shape, color. The brain then takes the information supplied by the wavefront and processes the image, thereby creating a three-dimensional image.

The hologram operates similarly. The hologram is achieved by means of a laser, defined as "light amplification by simulated emission of radiation." Ordinary light is not coherent, but laser light waves are identical in length. A beam splitter divides the laser into two parts; the two resulting beams then go through a beam spreader, a process that widens the beams. One of the newly formed beams, the reference beam, then reflects on one of two mirrors as it falls on the photographic plate. The other of the two beams, the object beam, is then reflected by a mirror to the object that will be photographed. Some of the light scattered from the object will illuminate the photographic plate, thereby interfering with the reference beam. The inference pattern recorded on the plate codes information about the object being photographed. But the pattern does not look like an object until it is developed and a laser has passed through the photographic plate.

Though there are many types of holograms, the multiplex hologram is more commonly used in movies. In this rainbow hologram, a series of holographic strips are put together, just as though a movie were assembled from still photographs. There can be up to one thousand strips for a movie. These strips are put together on one flat piece of film. The film is then taped together at the ends to form a cylinder. An ordinary lightbulb placed inside the cylinder makes the movie-viewing possible. The image appears inside the cylinder and seems to move as one walks around it.

If you saw the movies *Logan's Run* or *The Kiss*, you witnessed the use of multiplex holography. In *The Kiss*, for example, a woman appears to be blowing a kiss to the viewer. But only a moment of holography can now be achieved. Since the capacity of multiplex holography is only one thousand frames, the movie can record for less than a minute.

But holography has made its way into other unexpected places. Holograms are used in various arcade games, such as "Space Invaders." Some types of jewelry incorporate the use of holography. Holography has been used, as well, for gunsights and aviation aid. In gunsights, a hologram is used to point directly at the target, thus increasing the chance of the shooter's hitting the mark exactly. And holograms can help pilots in bad weather. A holographic combiner, mounted in front of the pilot, can enable him or her to read information that would normally appear on the dashboard. The pilot can then focus attention more directly on the runway.

Holograms have also made their way into the routine activities of average citizens. Visa International credit cards carry doves that cover four digits of account numbers, thereby safeguarding the credit card against illegal tampering. And at the grocery counter, a laser linked to a computer can scan the Universal Price Code on various grocery items at supermarkets. Often the object for purchase is strangely shaped or held at an improper angle. IBM has, therefore, invented a wraparound reader, using holographic lenses. The laser can now see the bottom and sides of any items passed over the scanner window at almost any angle. Finally, holograms can be used to spot flaws in pipes or in structures of cars and boats. When unleashed, the holographic beam spreads out over the entire object, and a high concentration of light focuses on a flaw in the structure. Manufacturers can then screen for hidden flaws in advance and save the consumer from buying a clunker.

Holography promises to revolutionize the entertainment industry, to protect the consumer, to make its way into daily life with ever-increasing versatility. Even if you have never heard of holography, you are already experiencing many of its benefits.

Questions for discussion

1. How does the scope of the topic sentence affect the development of each paragraph?

2. An in-depth explanation of holography might require volumes of explanation and detail. How does the writer narrow the subject to a manageable length?

3. Would such an essay provide sufficient information for a paper to be read at a scientific conference? Why or why not?

4. The tone of the essay is mostly neutral, though the writer comes out, rather blandly, in favor of holography. Is the neutral tone sleep-inducing or stimulating? Why or why not? The essay is rather general, though it does give some specific definitions, examples, and details. How could the writer

make the reader feel a measure of awe about this scientific development?

5. The writer gets the information across in various ways, by defining, by giving examples, and by comparing. Find the places in the essay that demonstrate these different ways of supplying information.

◆

Activities

1. Are you fascinated by a new development in science, one that is just beginning to find its uses in society? Have you ever developed an invention, or are you haunted by an innovative commercial idea, something that is not yet on the market but that you think is unusually clever or necessary? First, develop a thesis that conveys your feelings or excitement about a product, theory, invention, or discovery. No brainstorm is too outrageous here. Think of lightbulbs, hula hoops, can openers, paperclips, that little plastic thing you hang on your car door and put your coffee cup in. Gadgetry, gimmickry, and frivolity are welcome. Then, write a short, informative essay, either selling your idea to a skeptical financial backer or explaining your passion for a recent scientific advancement.

2. Write an essay using exposition as the primary method of support and development. Some possible topics follow, but you may think of others. Choose a topic about which you know nothing and would like to learn something. Or choose a topic about which you are already knowledgeable but to which you seek converts in interest. For example, if you are an expert on the topic of hang gliding, and your significant other thinks hang gliding is a foolish and risky way to spend a pretty Sunday afternoon, let your presentation of the facts and fun in the hobby be convincing to the skeptic.

Reproduction of fleas	Applying for college entrance
Japanese flower arranging	Beginning ski instruction
Being a vegetarian	Health hazards in jogging or other recreation
Buying a 10-speed bicycle	
Cutting the electric bill in half	Free mental-health care available in your community
Form and content in sonnets	
	Flea-market finds

Uses of food processors or word processors	Campus entertainment
Building an at-home reference library	Working in the Peace Corps
Establishing good credit	Politics and the 18-year-old college student
Equipment necessary for spelunking	Foreign affairs on college campuses

Persuade forcefully.

Persuasion and argumentation represent the fourth type of essay, and they are sometimes used interchangeably. However, the two differ somewhat both in tone and in intention. How are these terms related?

1. Both persuasion and argument require that the writer take a position with regard to a topic. Of course, all writing carries some measure of advocacy, even so-called pure description, if only because the writer controls the selection and arrangement of the descriptive details. However, description and narration might carry only an implied thesis, an underlying message, whereas persuasion and argumentation state very clearly the writer's conviction, opinion, side of an issue.

2. Both persuasion and argument attempt to lead the reader away from a neutral position, either to embrace the writer's own conviction or at least to push the reader to take a stand for or against an issue, to make up his or her mind about an important matter, whether temporarily or once and for all.

3. Both persuasion and argument seek to make a reasonable defense of an opinion on a controversial topic.

And how are these terms different?

1. Persuasion and argument have slightly different aims. The aim of persuasion is to effect a change in human behavior, in policy; to produce action. With argument, however, the writer's primary goal is, very simply, to win the argument, to set the reader nodding in agreement, to change the reader's mind. The persuasive writer, for example, wants to get the reader to sign up for the Peace Corps. The writer who is engaged in argumentation simply wants the reader to become convinced of the validity and usefulness of the Peace Corps.

2. Persuasion and argument also differ in tone and stance. Whether persuasion is friendly, cajoling, wheedling, or aggressive, it is often subjective—appealing as often to emotions as to reason. Argument, on the other hand, is usually detached, intellectual, requiring that the debater rationally consider and weigh all the pros and cons of the issue. Some of you may be thinking that "argument" is a misnomer, connoting noisy, combative, hostile, quarrelsome exchanges. But in its pure form, the word "argument" simply means "a discussion involving conflicting points of view," "a course of reasoning," "a debate." Hence, a strange paradox: when you are persuading a reader, your tone is likely to be feisty; your approach less straightforward, clear-cut. You may, with effective persuasion, be even a bit devious—as anyone who has ever created a television commercial could tell you. But with argument, you will be keeping subjective emotions, irrational biases, out of the discussion. Cool reason will win the argument.

Some composition experts place persuasion under the category of argument, but a case can be made for the opposite position—namely, that persuasion subsumes argument. Though every argument does not ultimately persuade (spur readers to action), every persuasive essay will have first won the point (argued effectively) and then produced a change (persuasion). And whereas effective argument is detached, rational, eschewing appeals to the heart and directing ideas to the mind, effective persuasion will occur only when the writer connects with both the hearts and the minds of the readers. Emotional appeals without logic are often doomed to failure, and so persuasion must be grounded in the possible, the reasonable, the probable. But intellectualizing without taking into account the gut feelings, the intuitive sides of human beings, will produce paralysis among readers. If the logic on both sides of the argument is impeccable, *nothing* will happen. And so the effective persuader, in the end, stirs the souls and hearts of readers, not simply their brains.

At the bottom of many essays is the gentle art of persuasion. But perhaps "gentle" is too bland a word. Persuasion can be aggressive, as in the hard-sell ads delivered up by the fast-talking fellow on the car lot, urging you to come on down *right now* and get the best deals of the century on Ford pickups. Or persuasion may be subtle, as in the very indirect, very coy ads pushing baby powder or expensive perfumes, ads that evoke tenderness, glamor, sexiness, ads that focus on a feeling, not a product. Or persuasion may be implicit in the choice of details and examples, the decisions that go on behind the scenes regarding selectivity: what to leave in, what to take out, what to tone down, what to spice up.

Opinions and theories, philosophies and fads are only as vigorous, long-lived, credible, or popular as the persuader's skill. An invention, a chocolate-chip cookie, or a system of government is only as effecting of change, as useful, as the persuader's ability to bring the cookie or idea to the audience's attention. What good is the scientific assertion that the earth is round if the public persists in affirming its flatness? Most scientific discoveries have elicited debate and controversy, have demanded a persuasive selling job: Dr. Jonas Salk develops a vaccine for polio, but the public must be persuaded to swallow it.

By the same token, what good is an essay nobody stays to read? Of course, the possibility exists that a product or idea or scientific discovery will sell itself. But the salesperson or scientist knows that a gentle or insistent nudge will alert the public to the quality of the vacuum cleaner, the spread of AIDS, the benefits of good nutrition. Between the pure fact and its acceptance lies the persuasive realm of argument, debate, awareness, integration, assimilation. Acceptance and understanding often lag behind knowledge. Persuasion closes the gap.

Good persuasion is not shifty, but it had best be subtle or the people will stalk away, furious at being told what to do, how to think or feel. The persuader's tone is of crucial importance. Humans do not react well to control, power plays, direct commands. They want to feel, even if the feeling is false, that they are free to make up their own minds. And so astute persuaders are careful to respect this human need, to create an atmosphere of cordiality and choice, not intimidation and tyranny. The persuader's task, then, is to motivate, not manipulate.

But how do you use persuasion effectively and responsibly in your writing?

1. You first develop a critical eye for private and public uses of argument and persuasion. For a while, some people went around wearing T-shirts on which were written the words "Question authority." The advice is good, healthy. If you have never stopped to question how persuasion operates in the press, the marketplace, the family, you will not discover

which techniques are sane, which sinister. What is dangerous propaganda, after all, but persuasion carried to an extreme, where all is blind obedience and single-minded fanat-
icism? Good persuaders are both open-minded and mildly
suspicious. They come by their opinions honestly, having examined what they themselves think and feel in the context
of society. They are unwilling to accept, without question,
any philosophy or product without first exploring the presentation of the philosophy or product.

2. Effective persuaders have firm opinions, but ideally they
base those opinions on evidence, not hearsay; on direct experience, not abstract theory.

3. Logic, rationality, caution, and facts are behind effective
persuasion. A personal opinion, a prediction, a fear, a doubt
begins to form in the mind or heart of the writer. Does the
writer immediately begin to write? No. He or she mulls over
the truth of the opinion, the source of the frustration. Jottings begin. A thesis takes shape. Examples and facts come
to mind. The selection process begins, what to take out,
what to leave in. Slowly, having consulted his or her own experience and the experiences of others, the writer assumes
an arguable stance, a rational position, something that can
find support in reality, which is to say, in context.

4. The effective persuader then imagines the audience and purpose. Is the crowd friendly or hostile? Is the need for change
urgent, or can it wait? Will the available evidence suffice, or
will the writer need to nudge the reader toward a new
awareness? Will the "sell" be soft or hard, direct or indirect?
Can humor do the work of persuading, or is the tone to be
more dignified, more in keeping with the seriousness of the
purpose? The dumping of chemical wastes is not funny, no
matter where you live on the river. But a little levity can
keep humans from drowning in an ocean of self-pity, a flood
of petulance and pride.

5. Finally, the effective persuader tries to anticipate audience
objections, to foresee possibly negative reactions, probable
challenges to his or her argument.

A writer must be unusually skilled in persuasive techniques
because he or she has only the written word to make the point.
And on the page, all words look alike: same black type, same
white bond paper, same paragraphs. The writer has no luxury of
make-up, gesture, staging, lighting, voice, or scene on which to

play out his or her opinions and perceptions. Seen from afar, a page from Shakespeare's *Hamlet* and a page from *Gentlemen's Quarterly* look alike. Words, then, must leap from the page with all the vigor and truth, the wit and style, the reason and courtesy of powerful oration. And effective persuasion—considerate of audience, clear of purpose, effective of presentation—will carry the reader over doubts and into a reasonable conviction.

In the following paragraph, the writer is trying to calm the fears of parents who would seek to censor their children's reading. The persuasion depends on humor, even a touch of sarcasm. And concrete examples provide convincing proof that the parental fears are without foundation. The persuasive approach is indirect. Rather than piously ranting about the dangers of censorship, the writer focuses on the absurdity of assuming that children can be hurt or helped by a book they have not read. The writer also adds to the persuasive power by citing the opinions of experts—teachers.

> Then, too, the parental fear that children are reading at all seems fundamentally whacko. Most children don't read anything at all or read just enough to get by. They are in far greater danger of being unduly influenced by music video or Saturday-morning cartoons, and I never met a parent who would give up Saturday-morning sleep in favor of banning Sylvester's cruelty to Tweetie bird. My feeling about reading is one of indiscriminate urgency: if my children show signs of reading *anything*, I don't stand in the way, blocking their light. I know teachers who feel as I do. They wish the kids would read classic comic books, crossword puzzles, the ingredients on a box of cornflakes—something, anything. I even heard a teacher wistfully say that she'd be glad if her students would just get out a coloring book and color. So the dangers of reading dirty books are, I think, greatly exaggerated.

In the next example, the writer uses persuasion to combat persuasion. A critical appraisal of a commercial product exposes the fallacy in the premise. Several concrete details give credibility to the argument. And the reader begins to see how persuasion in the marketplace can momentarily blind consumers to a very simple truth, an obvious point. The focus is small, but the implications are large.

The New Yorker recently carried an essay on, of all things, Country Time lemonade. Actually, the article wasn't so much about Country Time as it was about the propaganda implicit in advertising. Country Time, you'll recall, "tastes like that good old-fashioned lemonade." In the commercial, a big happy family is gathered on the front porch. White-haired Grandma shows up, laden with a big pitcherful of that good old, instant, powdered lemonade, which tastes, say the advertisers, exactly like that real lemonade Grandma used to make before she got her hands on a can of powdered Country Time. The writer was simply pointing out—and high time, too—that the advertisers were misleading us. They were making us believe that we couldn't get real lemonade anymore, that real lemonade was *unavailable*. The *New Yorker* writer concluded by stating, in vigorous terms, that real lemonade was still "entirely within our capacities." With a few lemons, a little sugar and water, we can squeeze up a big pitcherful of lemonade any time we want it. Real lemonade is not obsolete. I was thrilled to be reminded. You see, I almost forgot.

The most effective persuasion pushes the reader to a new way of looking at an old issue, product, person. For example, when England's Prince Charles was questioned about his alleged vegetarianism, he bristled with irritation. Apparently, eating vegetables almost exclusively is perceived by the public as being bizarre, unnatural. Traditional stereotypes of the male's diet show him eating meat and potatoes, wolfing down steaks and hash browns. Prince Charles persuaded the audience of the absurdity of public reaction to eating vegetables by pointing out the obvious: nobody, said he, is the least bit shocked and appalled when a person *does not* eat his or her vegetables. He asserted that eating meat almost exclusively is considered, for some illogical reason, to be "perfectly" normal. The persuasion technique was effective, a good lesson for writers. Find the lie in the conventional thinking, come at the propaganda from an unusual angle, and the reader will more likely be convinced.

The next two essays are written primarily to persuade, to change human behavior. Both are about parent–child relationships, but the essays have different purposes, different audiences. The questions for discussion, therefore, involve considerations of the persuasive techniques in both.

PARENTS OR FRIENDS?

My parents are coming to visit. Mulling over the prospect, I find it pleasing. What sends a chill through many grown-up off-spring, what used to freeze me as well, has thawed through spring after spring of growing up. The family weather is often frosty in adolescence, but if you wait and watch, you finally see the sun break over the icy, treacherous terrain of childhood. The floes of anger and regret disperse. A warm sense of family well-being emerges.

You who are still a bit chilly may wonder how the change occurs. Advancing age produces the first thaw. How can an adult daughter not learn, at long last, that she is the mistress of her destiny? How can a parent not respect, at long last, the grown-up child's right to equal status in the relationship? I realized a while back, and with happy results, that my parents were free of the responsibility of me. And I was likewise free of the responsibility always to please them.

I used to visit them and be met with the usual parental nagging. Why aren't you wearing lipstick? Don't you wear anything except jeans? How are you doing financially? Why don't you change jobs, keep your job, make your children behave, buy a new car, lose some weight, stop driving at night? The questions were well-intentioned but inappropriate for a woman over twenty-one. But, and I know I'm right, a woman in her twenties is not grown up. She does, in her thirties and without much support, what men do in their twenties to drumrolls and thunderous applause: break the bonds.

I like the pistol-packing age of thirty-eight. I like the way every parental objection is shot down by my obvious ability to support myself, raise my children, keep my house in order and my wits about me. A mother whose daughter was forty-nine once asked me, half-facetiously, half-seriously, to take care of her "little girl." "I will not!" I hollered. "Can you think of a single thing a forty-nine-year-old woman can't do if she wants to?" "Not a thing," answered the mother, grinning.

Geographical location speeds the thawing process. My theory is that parents and children should live exactly two hours from each other. This proximity is perfect. Two hours each way is too far to travel comfortably in a day, so neither parents nor children drop in unannounced. But two hours is so close that regular visits are short. When I go home, I stay one night—two at the most. My parents keep the same snappy timetable. Unfortunately, some offspring foolishly believe that the wider the distance between their parents and them, the greater the harmony.

I know otherwise. When I lived in Connecticut, a trip home was such a long haul and so costly I felt compelled to stay a week or ten days, on the absurd theory that as long as I was home I might as well make the visit count.

The pattern of long visits home is unalterable. The first day, you fall on each other's necks and dive into the big dinner prepared in your honor. The second day, you catch up on the news and eat leftovers. The third day, you sink beneath the polite surfaces, dragging up old griefs and conflicts. The fourth day, you get into an argument about politics and find, to your dismay, that you have gone through the developing process and come out with a negative imprint. What they think is black, you call white. What they deem white, you are convinced is black. The fifth day, advice starts: you tell your parents they've gained weight; they say you've failed to teach your children good manners. The sixth day, to get out of the house, you run tiresome errands for your mother, just as you did in the old days. The seventh day, you and your parents lapse into glum silence over the breakfast cereal, just as you did every morning of your teenaged life.

The two-day visit is a must for good child-parent relationships. My father begged me not to move back to my hometown. I was surprised, thinking all good fathers wanted their children to settle next door. Then I remembered: he lives in a town packed with my mother's relatives. He warned of bad consequences: you know their business, and they know yours. "And besides," he said, "if you move to another town, your mother and I'll have some place to visit on weekends." A good point, not lost on me.

But other changes must occur. At some point, parents and adult children must realize they can't settle old scores. When we settle scores, we are not living. Parents must ultimately resign their parental role, and children must resign their childlike role. What is left? Friendship, of course, the kind everyone is capable of having. It's so obvious. Why can't a parent be more like a friend?

Friendship carries obligations. When my parents come to my house, they are my guests. I pay for their meals, change their sheets, pour their drinks, arrange for their entertainment. Parents who swoop in on adult children and take over the cooking or pick up the restaurant tab are denying their children adult status. When I go to my parents' house, I am their guest. My dad charcoals the steaks. My mother sets the table. I sit on the patio and await my dinner.

The rules are so simple, anyone can play. Let age carry its due weight, removing the burden of having to prove yourself over and over. Keep the visits short, sweet. Let parents and children take turns being guests. As far as possible, within the bounds of love and care, mind your own business.

CHILDREN EFFECTIVENESS TRAINING

I'm tired of books and workshops on parenting. I want to read a book about childrening. Experts say that parenting is the most important job in the world, and we have no training in it. Well, many totally unqualified daughters and sons are entering the world every minute, and yet we offer them no courses in daughtering and sonning. Daughtering and sonning are too important to leave to amateurs. I want a course in C.E.T., Children Effectiveness Training.

I would first break down cruel parental stereotypes, erected by unskilled, careless offspring. Lesson one would be entitled "The Parent as Human Being." I would demolish the images of parent as frump, dolt, walking encyclopedia, tyrant, sexual incompetent, scale of justice, physical wreck, blithering idiot, bore. Lesson one would conclude with the tidy maxim: "Parents are people, too."

After children accepted the radical notion that parents are capable of the full range of passions, talents, brains, and experience, I would teach the logical consequences of adulthood and expose childish ambivalence toward it. Children think they can put on adulthood like a new dress or a pin-striped suit and then, when they grow tired of the outfit, drop the mantle of adulthood and climb back into training pants and little T-shirts with ducks appliqued all over. When my children want to date, sniff glue, stay up until three a.m., pick their own friends, listen to hard rock, skip church, and neglect their schoolwork, they think they are forty-seven. When they have to put some frozen French fries on a cookie sheet and bake at 400 degrees for thirty minutes, they are suddenly two. One day they think they can spend the summer knocking around Europe. The next day, they can't match their socks.

I, the parent, do not have similar choices. When I want to skip school, spend all my money on new clothes, lie, gripe, loll, or burp, I can't. I have spells of gross immaturity, when I would like to climb back in the stroller and be pushed around; but I can't, any more than I can, with impunity, fail to report for work. If I claim my right to fail and pout and whine, in fine childish style, my children roll their eyes and mutter, "No fair."

"No fair" is the most childish remark a human being can make, but I am too caring to tell them.

Children Effectiveness Training would stress the high cost of adulthood. Children might then look with appropriate dismay and hesitancy on the alleged grandeur of being all grown up. They would know that being grown up means staying up until three a.m. and being comatose at six a.m., when the alarm goes off. They would know that talking back to employers means getting fired. They would notice that dinner at the best restaurant in town costs at least fifteen dollars, no matter how they slice their marinated chicken.

In my Child Effectiveness Training course, I would encourage attentiveness toward parents. My children display no interest whatsoever in my work, my pleasure, my little triumphs and failures. They never analyze me, marvel at me, really look at me. I am as boring to them as Muzak's rendition of last year's hit tune. They think I dry up and die when I am not flourishing in the rich soil of their little lives. I am supposed to brag on their report cards, drop everything to take them to karate, display a minute interest in conflicts with teachers or the child with whom my child is "going." But my children largely ignore me and my big life of the mind and soul. I say, "The electric bill was $152.00 this month." They say, "Pick me up from school at 3:30." I say, "I'm depressed." They say, "Have you done the wash yet? We don't have any clean underwear." If I were to say, "I've been convicted on a cocaine charge," my children would say, "I hate Mrs. Battle-ax. She gave me a 57 on my math test."

Children and experts on children use immaturity as an excuse for everything. But when I see my children playing the violin like Jascha Heifetz, building financial empires like John D. Rockefeller, handling a basketball like Spud Webb, dressing like Ralph Lauren, gourmandising like Julia Child, avoiding responsible action like Hamlet, cracking jokes like Eddie Murphy, preaching like St. Paul, agonizing like Woody Allen, dancing like John Travolta, and lying like a rug, I think immaturity is no excuse. In fact, were I dead and gone, I'll bet my children could make the house payments on the condo and eat one of the four food groups every day, entirely without my supervision.

My great respect for the ingenuity and intelligence of children forces me to demand from them respect and compassion as well. If I didn't think children were capable, as am I, of the full range of vices and virtues, I would not call for children-effectiveness-training programs. Children can do better than they are presently doing, better by parents and better by society. I wonder, sometimes, why they don't do better, and then I remember that parents have assumed a disproportionate share of blame and responsibility in the family. The generation gap is a small impasse, made passable by bridges, not still more one-way, dead-end streets.

Experts love to tell children how to get along with their peers. But my children are with their peers only 180 days a year, and then only on weekdays. I am with them 365 days a year, including nights and weekends. It's time children learned what parents are for and how, properly, to nurture and care for us.

Questions for discussion

1. Both of the essays dealing with parent-child relationships are attempting to persuade the audience to adopt a new point of view, a new way of thinking and acting. The writer uses several techniques of development and support to make the case, prove the point. Which ones are most convincing to you? Give examples from each essay of the persuasive devices that most strongly influence you. Which examples are most amusing? Which details remind you of home?

2. How do the essays differ in tone? Does the tone in either essay offend you, please you, make you laugh, cry, yawn? Why? Explain.

3. Are there examples and conclusions from both essays about relationships between parents and children that are similar, even though the essays come at the relationship from different perspectives? Cite the similarities.

4. What would be, according to the writer, the ideal relationship between parents and children? What would be your definition of an ideal relationship with your parents? Do you already have one? Why?

◆

Activities

1. Effective persuasion is often the result of taking a position that differs from the conventional side. In the following exercise, you are being given a side to take on the issues. Absurdity may result. But then, too, you may achieve originality, freshness, new insight. Select a position that seems unsupportable or that runs counter to your usual thinking. Then convince yourself and your reader of the validity of the

position. Write at least three persuasive paragraphs, supporting a thesis on one of the following:

In favor of worldly failure	In favor of poetry
Against saintly mothers	Against volunteerism
Against jockdom	In favor of eloping
Against fitness programs	In favor of solitude
In favor of soap operas	Against air conditioners
In favor of tactlessness	In favor of "mean" teachers
In favor of majoring in English	Against nice neighbors
Against majoring in business	In favor of procrastination
	Against doing your duty
In favor of cramming	
Against regular church attendance	

2. It is common practice to attack television as the culprit in a host of social ills. Commercials are awful. The media coverage is poor, vague, glib, manipulative. Sex and violence abound. Television keeps children from learning how to read, separates the family, encourages passive behavior. Sift through the rubble of conventional attitudes toward television and find a pearl of great value. Develop a thesis in support of some aspect of television, and convince the reader of the validity of your position. For example, you might boldly assert that television commercials are a high art form, perhaps the highest. Or you might assert that the family that watches television together does not bicker. In other words, find a good and original thing to say about television and persuasively support the assertion.

PART
III
Refining the Essay

7

Making Transitions

Supply coherent connections.

If audiences could read a writer's mind, they might be surprised and relieved to see a map there, a logical and orderly progression of ideas, a point or purpose growing out of a previous point or purpose, an overall direction, a coherence. But unfortunately, audiences are not mind readers; and the writer who asks too much of the reader in the way of comprehension and coherence often fails to supply the logical connections, the twists and turns of his or her thinking. The connections are loose, disjointed. The writer seems to jump abruptly from point to point, and the reader grows weary and anxious. You know how uneasy a moth can make you feel, don't you? You do not know where the thing is going next, and so you sit on the sofa, a little nervous, waiting to see where it will land. In the same way, the points of transitionless thinking are jumpy as moths, lurching here and there, crazily landing in odd spots, flapping scarily from the folds of the drapes, catching the reader off guard.

If you wish to convince, entertain, or inform the audience, you must provide transitions between one point abandoned and another taken up. You put a leash on the moth, so to speak, training it to obey your motions. And, of course, if you have a trained moth, you can go on a late-night talk show and get famous.

How do you train your thoughts to behave predictably, logically, coherently on the written page?

1. You first establish connections in your thinking, even before you begin writing. In the planning stages, you use an

outline, a map, to check and recheck the logical progression of your ideas. Then, as you write, you make certain those connections in your thinking travel from your mind to the written page.

2. You give clear signals about shifts in subject matter, about the relationship between one paragraph and another, about variations in tone, about distinctions, qualifications, similarities between ideas, examples, and facts.

3. You never assume that the reader can see into your mind. All the reader has, after all, is the essay at which he or she is staring. If your reader is scratching his head, having to go back and reread a sentence or a paragraph several times, looking befuddled, then you have assumed too much. Often, when the reader complains that your essay does not "make sense," he or she is simply frustrated at being asked to supply your connections. It is enough to demand of the reader attentiveness, courtesy, comprehension. You cannot ask the reader to discover your rationale, your structure, your mental map as well.

Achieve unity.

Transitions come in all sizes, tones, and structures. They are unifying devices. You can use them in several ways to unify your points, to make your ideas behave, as it were.

1. You may use certain transitional words or phrases to supply connections and make distinctions: *and, but, on the one hand, on the other hand, nevertheless, furthermore, moreover, besides, in addition, for example, at least, yet, so, what is more, similarly, in contrast, then, thus.* And you will want to use these words or phrases precisely, or you may find that your clear signal has pointed the reader in the wrong direction. For example, if you are supplying connecting words between several related points or examples, you do not write "nevertheless," "in contrast," or "yet." Those words and phrases suggest a shift in thinking. Rather, you write "furthermore," "moreover," "in addition," or "similarly"—words and phrases that signal a continuation of similar and related points. And if you wish to signal a broader meaning, you might write "then," a word that suggests summing up:

Public-school teachers are frustrated in their efforts to supply quality classroom instruction. They must, *for example*, compete with extracurricular activities that seem to inspire more enthusiasm among students and administrators than does academic excellence. *Moreover*, teachers see their low salaries as a measure of public attitudes toward the profession of teaching. *Furthermore*, teachers are often asked to take on burdensome and unprofessional responsibilities: lunchroom and bus duty, monitoring the halls, collecting locker fees. It follows, *then*, that major changes in priorities, higher salaries, and professional respect might ease teacher frustration.

2. You can achieve unity and coherence by repeating certain key words and phrases or by repeating patterns and structures of sentences:

Suddenly the air changes from warm to cold, and *I push* into a black cloud bearing down on the road ahead. *I can see* rain in the high places of the pines. *I can feel the gathering wind, the approaching squall*, in my open face. *I can smell* already *the stove, the blankets, the old kitchen, the place* of shelter and safety.

In the above example, the writer repeats the words "I can," signaling a series of descriptive details that are related. The writer also repeats certain phrases with structural similarities, making sound a signal: "the gathering wind, the approaching squall"; "the stove, the blankets, the old kitchen, the place." In addition, the writer repeats an article: "the." And finally, the writer repeats certain sounds, using alliteration to signal the reader concerning relatedness: "smell," "safety," "shelter." In other words, though the conventional transitional phrases (moreover, thus, and so forth) do not appear, other signals and connections provide unity, coherence.

3. You may write transitional paragraphs, sentences, or portions of sentences that carry your reader from one point to the next:

I doubt that any child I knew ever was told by her mother more than I was about babies. In fact, I doubt that her own mother ever told her any more than she told me, though there were five brothers who were born after

Mother, one after the other, and she was taking care of babies all her childhood.

Not being able to bring herself to open that door to reveal its
secret, one of those days, she opened another door.

In my mother's bottom bureau door in her bedroom she
kept treasures of hers in boxes, and had given me permission to play with one of them. . . .[1]

Welty uses a transitional paragraph to get from her point
about learning so much from her mother on the subject of where
babies come from to a story that explains why the mother told
Welty. The last paragraph goes on to tell of Welty's finding, in
the bureau drawer, a box in which lay two buffalo nickels.
Welty's mother then explains that the nickels had rested on the
eyelids of a son who died before Welty was born. And then Welty
concludes, "She'd told me the wrong secret—not how babies
could come but how they could die." So, with the transitional
paragraph, Welty moves from babies, over the "bridge" of secrets and doors, to the bureau drawer and the secret box and the
baby brother who died.

The possibility exists that college will slow you down in
the learning department. An article by Bruce Bawer issued
from the Los Angeles *Times*–Washington *Post* News Service
tells all about what students don't know. Something has
flipped. Not-knowing is the opposite of the way the educational fairy tale is supposed to turn out.

And what do these students not know? Well, for starters
these students don't know that Ireland has ever been gov-
erned by England; they don't know whether George Washington or Abraham Lincoln came first; they don't know
which countries fought in World War I; they don't know
that Robert Frost was not a contemporary of Chaucer.

Here, the transitional sentence is a question leading to a unified paragraph which might otherwise be a random collection of
facts. The question connects the two paragraphs. The writer also
uses repetition to achieve coherence: "they don't know" is repeated several times, signaling the reader again and again about
ignorance, not knowledge.

---

[1]Eudora Welty, *One Writer's Beginnings* (New York: Warner Books, 1984), p. 18.

One day twelve years ago an outraged cartoonist, four of whose drawings had been rejected in a clump by *The New Yorker*, stormed into the office of Harold Ross, editor of the magazine. "Why is it," demanded the cartoonist, "that you reject my work and publish drawings by a fifth-rate artist like Thurber?" Ross came quickly to my defense like the true friend and devoted employer he is. "You mean third-rate," he said quietly, but there was a warning glint in his steady gray eyes that caused the discomfited cartoonist to beat a hasty retreat.

With the exception of Ross, the interest of editors in what I draw has been rather more journalistic than critical. They want to know if it is true that I draw by moonlight, or under water, and when I say no, they lose interest until they hear the rumor that I found the drawings in an old trunk or that I do the captions while my nephew makes the sketches.[2]

Thurber links the anecdote to the subsequent paragraph by attaching a transitional phrase to the first part of the topic sentence: "With the exception of Ross." The transition both recalls the opening story and leads Thurber into a discussion of other editors and their reactions to his cartoons.

Transitions, then, steady the motions between paragraphs, within paragraphs, between sentences, within sentences, between phrases, within phrases, and between words (step-*and*-fetch-it types, Eat-*and*-Run Diner). Readers need clear signals, good transitions, to discover your connections, logical and otherwise.

◆

Activities

1. The following three paragraphs lack transitions, as indicated in each case by a dash. Fill in an appropriate transitional word, phrase, or sentence and justify your choice. Choose among words such as *in fact, consequently, however, but, moreover, to be sure, thus, furthermore, therefore, in addition, like, as.* Or supply your own choices.

---

[2]James Thurber, "The Lady on the Bookcase," in *Great Essays,* ed. Houston Peterson (New York: Pocket Books, 1954), pp. 409–410.

When I was growing up, I used to look with scorn upon my parents' dull routines. ———, I was highly vocal about their getting out of safe ruts and into adventure. They, ———, thought routine was fine, a safe place in which to curl up and lie down in their daily lives. Their attitude toward schedules made me sick. ———, I vowed I would never get stuck in a rut when I grew up.

———as an adult, I've changed my mind about many things, including ruts. ———, life is tough, full of tragedy, unpaid bills, doubts about the future, family quarrels, burdens. What, ———, could be better than an ordinary Tuesday, when supper is tuna, evening entertainment is television, and nothing bad happens? ———, what could be worse than never knowing what will happen next, scrambling eggs at three a.m., scrubbing the kitchen floor on Sunday morning, taking off for the beach in the middle of a work day? ———, I have changed my attitude toward ruts as I've grown older and come to see what chaos can do to human hearts, spirits, minds, bodies.

———, I have come to enjoy and find comfort in routine, just as my parents——— did. A healthy, happy life is a balance between routine and spontaneity, a comfortable rut with the occasional peak experiences to supply adventure and surprise, ——— weddings, parties, trips, dining out. I am, ———, peaceful, doing what needs doing, in good time, in good order. And ———, I find that I am, ——— my parents, able to discover great satisfaction in the simpler beauties of an ordinary day lived in the ordinary way.

2. In the above essay, the writer also uses repetition of structures and sounds as devices for transition and cohesion. Give examples of several of these transitional devices.

3. Go back through three of your past papers. Find good examples of transition. How many ways do you connect sentences and paragraphs? Find places that need better connections and add them.

8

Building Sturdy Paragraphs

Understand the function of the paragraph.

The paragraph is surely the most important unit within the larger framework of the essay, but the paragraph changes as it finds its function and placement within that larger framework.

1. *Sometimes the paragraph is a short essay, and its topic sentence is a small thesis.* You could, for example, separate this kind of paragraph from its essay and discover that it carries intention, meaning, and completion within itself. You could understand the paragraph by itself, without reference to any other paragraph. The paragraph contains a central idea, supports, and a clincher or conclusion. Generally, the topic sentence is the opening sentence of the paragraph. Whereas paragraphs drawn from the middle of an essay can sometimes function independently as complete units of thought or information, the concluding paragraphs of an essay often cannot. Notice, in the following examples, the paragraph that functions as a small essay and the paragraph that demands a context for its understanding.

I left the woods for as good a reason as I went there. Perhaps it seemed to me that I had several more lives to live, and could not spare any more time for that one. It is remarkable how easily and insensibly we fall into a particular route, and make a beaten track for ourselves. I had not lived there a week before my feet wore a path from my door to the pondside; and though it is five or six years since

I trod it, it is still quite distinct. It is true, I fear, that others may have fallen into it, and so helped to keep it open. The surface of the earth is soft and impressible by the feet of men; and so with the paths which the mind travels. How worn and dusty, then, must be the highways of the world, how deep the ruts of tradition and conformity! I did not wish to take a cabin passage, but rather to go before the mast and on the deck of the world, for there I could best see the moonlight amid the mountains. I do not wish to go below now.[1]

This paragraph stands alone, a microcosm of Thoreau's larger work, complete, unified. Its meaning is clear even to those who have not read *Walden*. It supplies its own context, carries the reader through a series of explanations, examples, details, proofs, and climaxes with a final assertion. It is, in short, an essay within an essay.

I do not say that John or Jonathan will realize all this; but such is the character of that morrow which mere lapse of time can never make to dawn. The light which puts out our eyes is darkness to us. Only that day dawns to which we are awake. There is more to day than dawn. The sun is but a morning star.[2]

This paragraph differs dramatically from the first. Though it contains a central idea and some general details and assertions, it is meaningless outside the context of the entire work. It cannot stand alone. It is not a small essay at all but, rather, a summation—the sense of which depends on many preceding paragraphs. Though the individual sentences certainly make sense and have the character of aphorism, neither insight nor comprehension can occur. The paragraph might have concluded an essay on the solar system for all the reader knows.

2. *Sometimes paragraphs have the characteristics of an essay, but the topic sentence appears midway through the paragraph, at the end, or, as in the above example, not at all.* In other words, the

---

[1] Henry David Thoreau, "Walden," in *Walden and Other Writings of Henry David Thoreau*, ed. Brooks Atkinson (New York: Modern Library-Random House, 1937), p. 288.
[2] Thoreau, "Walden," p. 297.

paragraph is an organic whole and carries complete and separate meanings, but the position of the topic sentence varies.

> We would have a similar feeling if we watched someone sailing out into the Atlantic and marking out a line of buoys to the north, east, south, and west and then proclaiming to whoever might listen, "These waves are mine. I own this piece of ocean. This water and fish therein and the plankton and the salt and the seaweed belong to me. The water is mine and the fullness thereof." *Hardly anyone would agree with him or honor his claim, no matter how much he might talk about the divine rights of man to own the ocean.*[3]

The hypothetical incident the writer describes leads, in the end, to a topic sentence—the point of the paragraph. Some of the meaning escapes the reader because the paragraph has no context, but the paragraph approaches wholeness and can be understood as a truth by the thoughtful reader.

> The years went by and I was just getting to the point where I could take it a little easy, when I was struck by an idea that was to change not only my own life but that of everyone in the entire humor business. *The idea? Fast humor.* After all, the pace had picked up a lot since my days on Delancey Street. The world was a different place; humor habits had changed. Everyone was in a hurry. Who had time anymore for a long comic essay, a slow build, a good long laugh? Everything was rush, rush, rush. Fast humor was an idea whose time had come.[4]

This paragraph contains a topic idea, not a sentence: fast humor. The main point comes in the middle of the paragraph, and the remainder of the paragraph consists of elaborations and a final reiteration. And it achieves its humorous impact even out of context. Of course, some might claim that the last sentence is the topic sentence. But, in fact, fast humor is first mentioned earlier, and is, therefore, the primary focus or concept.

---

[3]William Ryan, "Mine, All Mine," in *Equality* (New York: Pantheon-Random House, 1981), p. 91.
[4]Fran Lebowitz, "The Last Laugh," in *Social Studies* (New York: Random House, 1981), p. 113.

3. *Sometimes paragraphs have no clear topic sentence, but instead, achieve unity through theme, organization, story.*

> A man selling fence posts tarried at our place one day and told me that he had once had eighty peafowl on his farm. He cast a nervous eye at two of mine standing nearby. "In the spring, we couldn't hear ourselves think," he said. "As soon as you lifted your voice, they lifted their'n, if not before. All our fence posts wobbled. In the summer they ate all the tomatoes off the vines. Scuppernongs went the same way. My wife said she raised her flowers for herself and she was not going to have them eat up by a chicken no matter how long his tail was. And in the fall they shed them feathers all over the place anyway and it was a job to clean up. My old grandmother was living with us then and she was eighty-five. She said, 'Either they go, or I go.'"[5]

This paragraph has no topic sentence, but the story serves as the unifying device. When the story ends, the paragraph ends. The context, however, is meaningless except as it relates to O'Connor's overall theme with regard to peacocks. In other words, the paragraph is, though complete in the telling, unable to stand alone as a small essay.

4. *Sometimes a paragraph is a bridge between the preceding paragraph and the paragraph that follows* or between units of paragraphs. It is simply a pivot on which the argument of the larger essay turns. It may include very little in the way of supports, details, facts. It may or may not contain a topic sentence or central assertion, since its purpose is transition, not argument, information, or persuasion.

> I believe more good young athletes are turned off by the pressure of organized Little League than are helped. Little Leagues have no value as a training ground for baseball fundamentals. The instruction at that age, under the pressure of an organized league program, creates more doubt and eliminates the naturalness that is most important.
>
> *If I'm going to criticize such a popular program as Little League, I'd better have some thoughts on what changes I would like to see.*

---

[5] Flannery O'Connor, "The King of the Birds," in *Mystery and Manners*, ed. Sally and Robert Fitzgerald (New York: Farrar, Straus & Giroux, 1969), p. 19.

First of all, I wouldn't start any programs until the school year is over. Any young student has enough of a schedule during the school year to keep busy.[6]

The paragraph in the middle of the above example exists solely for the purpose of transition. The writer then begins to enumerate the changes in succeeding paragraphs. Certainly it would be pointless to isolate a transitional paragraph from its context, to analyze its structure.

5. *Sometimes, especially with introductory and concluding paragraphs, the content is rather general, with few specific details, facts, or examples to support.* And rather than containing a topic sentence, these paragraphs contain, instead, a thesis for the whole essay and a restatement of thesis as their unifying principles. Or perhaps, as in the example below, the introducing paragraph is simply a jumping-off place for further discussion and refutation, leading to a thesis that appears in the second or third paragraph of the essay.

There seems to be a general assumption that brilliant people cannot stand routine; that they need a varied, exciting life in order to do their best. It is also assumed that dull people are particularly suited for dull work. We are told that the reason the present-day young protest so loudly against the dullness of factory jobs is that they are better educated and brighter than the young of the past.[7]

The unifying principle of this introductory paragraph is not a thesis, but a theme: the alleged connection between intelligence and the need for vocational stimulation. Hoffer does not get to the thesis until the second paragraph, in which he asserts, "Actually, there is no evidence that people who achieve much crave for, let alone live, eventful lives." Instead, he sets up a series of general and unsupported assertions he attributes to conventional assumptions about brilliant people and work and dull people and work. The scope of the opening paragraph is wide, but the development is adequate for getting Hoffer started. In later paragraphs, he will write small paragraphs of support and refutation, with many details, facts, and examples and with topic sentences as unifiers.

---

[6]Robin Roberts, "Strike Out Little League," *Newsweek* 86, July 21, 1975: 11.
[7]Eric Hoffer, "Dull Work," in *In Our Time* (New York: Harper & Row, 1976), p. 4.

To these moral and aesthetic questions there is no answer. Meanwhile there is always, instead, *publicity*—so
easy to swallow, so difficult to remember.[8]

This concluding paragraph grows out of a previous analysis of
the risks the writer or celebrity takes by allowing his or her private reflections to be brought to public attention. The paragraph
is nothing out of context. It is also very general, and the restatement of thesis is not apparent except if one is aware of what preceded this conclusion.

So what do all paragraphs have in common?

1. They have a central idea, theme, or unifying device.

2. They serve the purposes of the longer work in which they are
    appearing, either introducing, concluding, supporting, or
    bridging ideas and information.

3. They signal to the reader that a change in direction, a shift
    in intention or content is about to occur. Their indentations
    are not arbitrary. The writer is not merely feeling the need
    for the reader to see a little white space between the dense
    passages. A paragraph is thoroughly intentional, a structural
    indication of the start of something new.

And what makes paragraphs different?

1. Some are general or wide in scope, and some are dense with
    information, details, facts.

2. They may or may not explicitly state the main idea, but
    their unifying principle will be evident, whether in theme,
    content, or direct expression.

3. They can sometimes stand alone as small essays, or they
    sometimes require a context to make clear their meanings.

◆

Activities

1. Select, either from sample essays in this book or from your
    own essays, paragraphs from beginnings, middles, and end-
    ings. Analyze their structures by first locating the topic sen-
    tence of each. If there is no topic sentence, can you state the

---

[8]Elizabeth Hardwick, "Memoirs, Conversations, and Diaries," in *A View of My
Own* (New York: Ecco Press, 1962), p. 65.

organizing principle? Note the degree of specificity within introductory, middle, and concluding paragraphs. Can the paragraphs stand alone, or do they require a context for full understanding?

2. Relate a personal incident or experience that has a central theme or point. Attach that story to a topic sentence, making the incident have a larger meaning. Write only one paragraph.

Example

My family, large on propriety, was short on pride and praise. They were trying to be good, I know, but the effort backfired, as do all observances of the letter, not the spirit, of the law. Once an old man, catching sight of chubby, eight-year-old me, stopped my daddy on the street and remarked upon my rosy pulchritude. "Hush," said Daddy. "Don't tell her. Don't tell her." He had to say it twice, as if to guarantee that my head would not further swell my fat cheeks. I 'umbly cast my eyes downward and feigned deafness like a good little girl. But I heard the old man anyway and fairly floated, or bounced, down the street.

Organize the paragraph.

The organization of a paragraph is not arbitrary, a superficial arrangement applied to the surface of an idea. Rather, the organization is organic, growing out of the needs and purposes of the preceding and subsequent paragraphs. It is an integral part of a unified whole. It is even somewhat unnatural to isolate the paragraph as a structure, to make a paragraph for practice. A single paragraph rarely serves your writing needs. Even when you write a short letter, an entry in a diary, a class assignment, you will not write one paragraph but several, touching on various points. In the first paragraph of the letter home, for example, you send greetings. In the second paragraph, you give news, gossip. In the third paragraph you ask for money and explain why you need it. And finally, in the concluding paragraph, you send love and regret and farewell. So one paragraph does not suffice, because one paragraph can seldom hold all the ritual courtesy, longing, newsy exchange, fond farewell that you are communicating.

But because the paragraph is so important as a structural component of the machinery of the whole literary work, you need to learn the various options for organization and development of a single paragraph.

How can you arrange your central thought and its logical supports, or proofs, in each paragraph? You have several choices.

Chronological organization.

The simplest organization is chronological, setting events or information within a time framework, telling what happened and what happened next. This method is very effective if the narration illustrates or supports a general assertion. Selectivity is all. If you have missed the point or meaning of an incident, then the chronological retelling will be haphazard, disjointed. The following paragraphs use chronology as the method of organization, and in each example the story proves a point which the writer states within the paragraph. The statement is the topic sentence, which is the unifying principle that gives the story meaning and purpose.

A few years ago I wrote a book which dealt in part with the difficulties of the English in India. Feeling that they would have had no difficulties in India themselves, the Americans read the book freely. The more they read it the better it made them feel, and a cheque to the author was the result. I bought a wood with the cheque. It is not a large wood—it contains scarcely any trees, and it is intersected, blast it, by a footpath. Still, it is the first property that I have owned, so it is right that other people should participate in my shame, and should ask themselves, in accents that will vary in horror, this very important question: *What is the effect of property upon the character?* Don't let's touch economics; the effect of private ownership upon the community as a whole is another question—a more important question, perhaps, but another one. Let's keep to psychology. If you own things, what's their effect on you? What's the effect on me of my wood?[9]

---

[9]E. M. Forster, "My Wood," *Abinger Harvest* (New York: Harcourt, 1936), p. 22–23.

Forster begins the paragraph with a chronological sequence of events that led to the purchase of a piece of property. The retelling of the incidents that led to the purchase expands naturally, organically, into larger meanings. The central idea, the effect of property upon the character, controls the paragraph, helping the writer, even unconsciously, to select only those events in the story that would be pertinent to the point—a little jab at American wealth, for example; a clear signal that he, too, is guilty of getting rich from the woes of the people of India. In the last sentences of the paragraph, Forster refines the point, bringing the question down, at last, to his own experience. Suppose you purchased a car, a bit of real estate, a pet, a VCR. What meanings could you derive from the small event? Could the story of the purchase serve as the support for that meaning? Could the story organize your paragraph almost without any conscious effort on your part?

> When the others went swimming, my son said he was going in, too. He pulled his dripping trunks from the line where they had hung all through the shower and wrung them out. Languidly, and with no thought of going in, I watched him, his hard little body, skinny and bare, saw him wince slightly as he pulled up around his vitals the small, soggy, icy garment. As he buckled the swollen belt, suddenly my groin felt the chill of death.[10]

White is telling the story of his son putting on a wet bathing suit. The incident may not seem significant, productive of meaning. But the chronological telling, with careful selection of chilling details, leads naturally into a concluding theme—death. There is no obvious topic sentence, but the idea, the larger meaning of the story, is clear.

> *As the factory system developed, hand-loom weaving naturally declined, and my father was one of the sufferers by the change.* The first serious lesson of my life came to me one day when he had taken in the last of his work to the merchant, and returned to our little home greatly distressed because there was no more work for him to do. I was then

---

[10]E. B. White, "Once More to the Lake," in *Essays of E. B. White* (New York: Harper & Row, 1941), p. 202.

just about ten years of age, but the lesson burned into my heart, and I resolved then that the wolf of poverty should be driven from our door some day, if I could do it.[11]

This very sketchy story settles naturally under the topic sentence, which incorporates both the development of the factory system and the changes that development brought on the father. A few details serve to recreate the scene. Carnegie then expands on the meaning of the story in the concluding sentence.

Deductive organization.

The organization may be deductive, beginning with a general premise and moving toward particular facts, details, examples that support the premise. In such paragraphs, the topic sentence appears immediately, followed by particular instances of its application, veracity, reasonableness. This method of organization is tried and true, very traditional. It is a preferred method for beginning writers who need the control that an opening topic sentence provides. All the particulars that follow the topic sentence will relate to it, prove it, steady it in the reader's mind. The following paragraphs show this organizational scheme. Note the variations in types of development and support.

> *In this way the adolescent girl, avoiding real experiences, often develops an intense imaginative life, sometimes, indeed, confusing her phantasms with reality.* Helene Deutsch describes the significant case of a young girl who imagined an elaborate relationship with an older boy to whom she had never even spoken. She kept a diary of affecting scenes, with tears and embraces, partings and reconciliations, and wrote him letters, never sent, which she herself answered. All this was evidently a defense against real experiences that she feared.[12]

The writer begins with a general assertion which requires confirmation, support, and proof. She uses one strong example to il-

---

[11]Andrew Carnegie, "How I Served My Apprenticeship," in *The Gospel of Wealth and Other Timely Essays* (New York: Century, 1900), p. viii.
[12]Simone de Beauvoir, *The Second Sex*, trans. and ed. H. M. Parshley (New York: Knopf, 1978), p. 348.

lustrate the point, with sufficient detail to convince the reader of the general truth. A summarizing sentence enlarges on the meaning and implication of the original assertion.

Cézanne realized that the act of painting is an abstract art. A realistic painting of an apple placed next to an apple would never be as "real" (physical) to the viewer as the apple itself. As one philosopher has said, you would never go to the restaurant and eat the menu. Therefore for Cézanne "realistic" painting will always be a poor imitation of reality. Painting can effectively portray the abstract principle at work behind an object and give us a truer sense of the nature of the object.[13]

The bold claim Cézanne made with regard to abstract art requires confirmation and explanation. The writer first gives an example within which is a contrast between a real apple and an apple painted in the realistic way. An apt quotation brings greater clarity to the previous example. The concluding sentences then reiterate the original assertion, and having been given an illustration, a contrast, and an appropriate quotation, the reader can now understand Cézanne's disparagement of realism in art.

The black middle class traditionally included a handful of professionals and a far larger number of working people who, had they been white, would be solidly "working class." The inclusion of Pullman porters, post-office clerks and other typical members of the old black middle class was due less to their incomes—which were well below those of whites— than to their relative immunity from the hazards of marginal employment that dogged most blacks. They were "middle class" relative to other black people, not to the society at large.[14]

The controlling topic sentence leads naturally to both classification and definition as methods of development and support.

---

[13]Roberta Vandermast, "The Search for Visual Unity," in *Mirrors of Mind,* eds. Charles Roberts, J. Louis Schlegel, and Roberta Vandermast (New York: Hunter, 1980), p. 21.
[14]Vernon E. Jordan, Jr., "The Truth About the Black Middle Class," *Newsweek* 84, July 8, 1974: 11.

The writer also uses contrast, making a distinction between the black and the white definitions and perceptions of what it means to be "middle class."

> *A very large part of hoofed mammal history has been made by members of two orders, both of which appeared in early Eocene time.* These were the perissodactyls and the artiodactyls, the odd-toed and the even-toed, so called because in the one the main axis of the foot runs through the third digit and in the other between the third and fourth, an arrangement that results in the familiar "cloven hoof."[15]

The opening topic sentence of this paragraph sets up the organizational scheme very clearly. A contrast between these two types of hoofed mammals will follow. Descriptive details fill the short paragraph, and the paragraph is clearly intended not to persuade but to inform.

Inductive organization.

The organization of the paragraph may be inductive, starting with particular facts, events, and details and leading, at the end of the paragraph, to a general topic sentence, theme, assertion, conclusion. Only the writer knows what the implications will be, having already sorted out his or her ideas and selected a scheme. The reader begins the paragraph without knowing, for certain, where the particulars will lead, what they will mean. The inductive arrangement is therefore more demanding both of the writer and the audience, requiring that the writer choose unmistakably clear and lively specifics leading inexorably to some larger meaning and that the reader wait a bit to discover it. The inductive approach is gaining popularity as educators see the need for students to draw their own conclusions, to make imaginative generalizations, about what may appear at first to be unrelated phenomena. But only the popularity of induction is new. The method has always informed good writing, scientific inquiry, speculation, debate. The ability to draw general conclusions from many particulars is the mark of a creative thinker.

---

[15]Bryan Patterson, *Prehistoric Life* (Garden City, N.Y.: Doubleday, 1954), pp. 48–49.

In the early 1920s, for example, we find Picasso painting classical Greek figures, particularly bathers by the sea. An aura of escapism hovers about these pictures in the exhibit. Was not the 1920s, the decade after the first World War, in reality a period of escapism in the Western world? Toward the end of the twenties and in the early thirties, these bathers by the sea become pieces of metal, mechanical, gray-blue curving steel. Beautiful indeed, but impersonal, unhuman. And here one is gripped in the exhibit with an ominous foreboding—the prediction of the beginning of the time when people were to become impersonal, objectivized, numbers. *It was the ominous prediction of the beginnings of "man, the robot."*[16]

Rather than beginning with a generalization that requires support, May begins with details, dates, and description from which any one of a number of conclusions could be drawn. The reader does not know, at first, where the writer is going, what will be the point of these initial particulars. Speculation enters for the first time in the question at the center of the paragraph. Chronology puts the evolution of Picasso's art in the context of historical events. Finally, the writer builds to the ominous implication of these metal, gray, mechanical bathers who replaced, in Picasso's painting, the classical Greek figures of the 1920s. The topic sentence or controlling idea gathers up the details and facts into one theme.

It's said that when Henry James received a manuscript that he didn't like, he would return it with the comment, "You have chosen a good subject and are treating it in a straightforward manner." This usually pleased the person getting the manuscript back, but it was the worst thing that James could think of to say, for he knew, better than anybody else, that the straightforward manner is seldom equal to the complications of a good subject. *There may never be anything new to say, but there is always a new way to say it, and since, in art, the way of saying a thing becomes a part of what is said, every work of art is unique and requires fresh attention.*[17]

[16]Rollo May, *The Courage to Create* (New York: Norton, 1975), pp. 52–53.
[17]Flannery O'Connor, "The Nature and Aim of Fiction," in *Mystery and Manners,* p. 76.

A particular anecdote leads O'Connor into a general assertion and then a refinement and expansion of that association. But the reader has no idea, at first, of the possible implications of the story about James. Many inductive paragraphs begin with scenes, details, and stories and conclude with the writer's interpretation of the larger meaning. In fact, much quality fiction selects and arranges the world on the page and leaves the reader to draw general truths from those events.

So he wanted another pet; and as there were starlings about the place, which could be taught to speak, one of them was caught, and he meant to treat it kindly; but in the night its young ones could be heard crying after it, and the responsive cry of the mother bird towards them; and at last, with the first light, though not till after some debate within himself, he went down and opened the cage, and saw a sharp bound of the prisoner up to her nestlings; and therewith came the sense of remorse—*that he too was become an accomplice in moving, to the limit of his small power, the springs and handles of that great machine in things, constructed so ingeniously to play pain-fungus on the delicate nerve-work of living creatures.*[18]

Again the movement in the paragraph is from several particulars to a general assertion; and the effect on the reader is dramatic, adding suspense to the incidents recounted in the paragraph, stimulating inquiry as to what meaning will derive from those details. Pater draws a parallel between the power of the boy and the "great machine in things," between the weakness of the birds and the frailty of the boy.

Pivotal organization.

Finally, the topic sentence may appear in the middle of the paragraph, creating a bridge of wider meaning between early and later particulars. The writer recounts specifics, perhaps growing out of a summarizing sentence in the previous paragraph. These particulars lead to a general assertion. More par-

---

[18]Walter Pater, *The Child in the House: An Imaginary Portrait* (Portland, Me.: Mosher, 1895).

ticulars then follow. So, in the first part of the paragraph, the organization is inductive, and in the last part, deductive. Though the topic sentence controls and unifies the paragraph, it also creates, by its position, a kind of swivel motion between two sets of particulars. In the following paragraphs, the general assertion or topic sentence links particulars, the facts and details that support the assertion.

Joan [of Arc] had three banners. The largest carried a representation of God enthroned in Heaven, holding in one hand a globe, and flanked by two kneeling angels with golden fleurs-de-lys in their hands. A smaller triangular standard showed the Annunciation, and a third small banner was emblazoned with the Crucifixion. *The Maid treasured her banners, she said, forty times more than her sword, for with the former she could wound no-one.* There is, in fact, no record that, in all her fighting, she ever herself shed blood.[19]

In the above paragraph, the writer begins with a fact, not a concept. Then follow specific descriptions of the banners. But the general assertion, Joan's treasuring the banners, does not come until the middle of the paragraph. The topic sentence contrasts her love of the banners with her feelings for the sword. And the specific proof of the latter part of the assertion, that she treasured her sword less than her banners, is the fact that she never killed anyone. Without the topic sentence, the paragraph would be disjointed, merely mentioning random facts about banners and sword with no concept or statement of their relationship and significance.

The next great development culminated in the work of Galileo. In his search for *order*, Copernicus imagined himself to be standing on the sun rather than the earth. How would the universe look to a man standing on the sun? Would the earth then appear the center of the universe? *This great leap of imagination carried man further in his search for knowledge of his world.* The Copernican theory was an abstract idea expressed in mathematical symbols until Galileo (among others) confirmed the validity of the

---

[19]Grant Uden, *A Dictionary of Chivalry* (New York: Crowell, 1968), p. 145.

theory by extending man's vision with the telescope. By re-
versing the telescopic principle, the microscope extended
man's vision of the microcosm.[20]

The central assertion—"this great leap of imagination carried
man further in his search for knowledge of his world"—links
two seemingly unrelated bodies of information. The writer
brings Copernicus's questions and Galileo's telescope into harmony by setting up a topic sentence that unites "imagination"
with the search for knowledge of the world. The reader does not
know, at first, where the paragraph is going, what the significance of the Copernican questions might be. And after the general assertion, the reader sees the connection between abstract
mathematical ideas in Copernican theory and Galileo's telescope, which brings the abstraction into the realm of the
concrete.

The playground: up from the hardball diamond, on a pla-
teau bounded on three sides by cornfields, a pavilion contained some tables and a shed for equipment. I spent my
summer weekdays there from the age when I was so small
that the dust stirred by the feet of roof-ball players got into
my eyes. Roof ball was the favorite game. It was played
with a red rubber ball smaller than a basketball. The object was to hit it back up on the roof of the pavilion, the
whole line of children in succession. Those who failed
dropped out. When there was just one person left, a new
game began with the cry *Noo-oo gay-ame,* and we lined up
in the order in which we had gone out, so that the lines began with the strongest and tallest and ended with the
weakest and youngest. *But there was never any doubt that
everybody could play: it was the perfect democracy.* Often the
line contained as many as thirty pair of legs, arranged
chronologically. By the time we moved away, I had become
a regular front-runner; I knew how to flick the ball to give
it spin, how to leap up and send the ball skimming the
length of the roof edge, how to plump it with my knuckles
when there was a high bounce. Somehow the game never
palled. The sight of the ball bouncing along the tarpaper of

[20]Lincoln Barnett, "Einstein's Universal Relativity," in *The Universe and Dr. Einstein,* rev. ed. (New York: Bantam Books, 1957).

the foreshortened roof was always important. Many days I was at the playground from nine o'clock, when they ran up the American flag, until four, when they called the equipment in, and played nothing else.[21]

This long paragraph, packed with descriptive details, explanation, definition, would seem scattered and disjointed were it not for the central, unifying assertion: "it was the perfect democracy." With this assertion, Updike unites playground, game, team, and his own expertise into one organic whole. Lesser assertions, immediately supported by facts and examples, also appear: "I had become a regular front-runner"; "the game never palled." But the central idea or theme is of democratic play, and the writer reinforces the theme by ending the paragraph with a mention of the American flag. But the first and last portions of the paragraph are specific, full of particulars that require a general statement to indicate their significance, their wider meaning.

◆

Activities

1. From your own essays or paragraphs or from samples in this book, select three paragraphs that demonstrate the three organizational schemes: an opening topic sentence followed by particulars (deductive); a closing topic sentence preceded by particulars (inductive); and an embedded topic sentence (pivotal), stating the significance of opening and closing particulars.

2. Using the three paragraphs you have selected, rewrite each, moving the topic sentence to a place in the paragraph that differs from its original position. Analyze, as you shift the topic sentence position, the different structural demands the shift places on your selection and ordering of details. Notice, too, whether your paragraph becomes more or less tight, more or less dramatic, depending on when and where the topic sentence appears. Explain your preference for the original or the altered placement of the controlling statement.

---

[21]John Updike, "The Playground," in *Five Boyhoods,* ed. Martin Levin (Garden City, N.Y.: Doubleday, 1962).

3. Using Forster's experience with acquiring property as a model, write a paragraph in which you tell the story of a purchase and its effect on you.

Develop the paragraph.

Adequate development of paragraphs has little to do with length. Very long paragraphs can be thinly developed. Very short paragraphs can, on the other hand, be sturdy and complete, the central idea having been supported sufficiently and the function of the paragraph having been fulfilled.

When your paragraphs are criticized for being inadequately developed, you need not waste time simply making them longer. The task, rather, is to make them *stronger*. This means omitting unnecessary or unrelated details and facts, providing logical transitions, adding particulars that give credibility and support, and unifying what could appear to be random information under a clear and central idea or theme. The following paragraphs illustrate the various problems of inadequate development. The examples are exaggerated, but only to make the problem of inadequate development very clear.

Example A

Football is a popular sport. Many people love it. Weekend after weekend, crowds gather at the stadium to cheer their favorite teams. In fact, football may be the most popular sport of all, having more fans than baseball, tennis, or even basketball.

This paragraph is inadequately developed, though it contains several sentences. The reason? Each sentence repeats the original assertion. Few particular details or facts appear. The paragraph is really a series of topic sentences, none of which the writer has bothered to support. In addition, the central idea, the popularity of football, is bland, conventional. Who would argue that football is popular? Of course it is. A livelier, fresher assertion might push the writer toward a fuller, stronger development.

Example B

My parents and I once stayed in a fleabag hotel. It was a nightmare. We had booked our rooms with an agent in Dubuque, my hometown. The flight to Chicago on TWA was pleasant, with food that tasted better than the cellophane-wrapped, microwave meals served on some other flights I have taken. We landed in fair weather, caught a cab, and went straight to the hotel to unpack. The lobby was dingy and dark, full of winos and people of uncertain reputation. I was getting nervous. But when my parents and I were shown to our room, we were horrified. The place was a mess, the furniture was ugly; and though the view was pretty, we could hardly see it for the dirt and grime on the windows.

This long paragraph is inadequately developed. Why? The details offer little or no support for the original assertion. And even when the writer begins to discuss the lobby and bedroom at the hotel, the discussion is general, vague: the place is a "mess"; the view is "pretty"; the furniture is "ugly." The only concrete details that relate at all to the topic sentence are those about the winos and the dirt on the windows. But what does the writer mean by the phrase "uncertain reputations"? And how dirty *are* the windows? And why does the writer include any history of the buying of tickets, the airplane flight, the taxi ride? The facts, details, specifics that would support the controlling idea never materialize. Careful selection of relevant details would improve the paragraph. The writer might also narrow the topic sentence somewhat, indicating early on whether the discussion will center on bad food, bad accommodations, or bad service. A sufficiently narrowed topic sentence offers tighter control, closer scrutiny, and greater clarity and concreteness.

Example C

The day before Thanksgiving, the temperature finally dropped below freezing. The weather had been, up to that time, soggy, humid, like the tropical climates. Mildew had flourished in the shower. Everybody in the family sweated and griped. Hopes for a white Christmas were dashed. On November 24, we were all sitting around in our shorts, drinking iced tea and fanning away flies, gnats, and mosquitoes. A few of us even went swimming in the pool, pushing away clumps of falling leaves on the surface of the water. Our electric bill was almost as low as the water bill. Usually, at this time of year, we were paying at least $100 for the month's heating.

This paragraph is fairly lengthy, full of details, but what are those details and facts supporting? Nothing, of course. There is no controlling idea or theme, no purpose, no topic sentence. The writer would not have to do much to bring the specifics into a unified whole. He or she could simply assert that this November had been the hottest on record. Or, seeking a more original slant, the writer might emphasize the eerie, unnatural feelings that come with unseasonably warm weather in November. If the writer chose this latter assertion, the facts about the electric bill would have no place in the paragraph. The writer would, instead, focus on the weird experience of paddling through clumps of wet leaves, of wearing shorts and going barefooted even as "Jingle Bells" plays on the radio. But good development very much depends on a controlling, unifying concept; and such control is clearly missing from this disjointed, pointless array of specifics.

Sturdy, adequate development, then, will result from several or all of the following conditions:

1. A fresh assertion, both logical and narrow enough for support over one paragraph

2. A careful selection of only those facts, details, and examples that support the concept or assertion

3. A clear arrangement of those supports, either above, below, or around that central idea or concept

4. A proportion of particulars far greater than the number of generalizations

5. A precise placement of the paragraph within the larger context of the essay so that the paragraph fits what preceded it and what follows it and, furthermore, fulfills the requirements of its own function, whether the paragraph is intended for introducing, concluding, supporting, or bridging ideas

The methods of development and support within the paragraph will be similar to those used within the entire essay. The writer will find that the structure of the topic sentence will often determine the organization of the paragraph. The following examples of topic sentences illustrate the way in which the expression of the concept often determines the arrangement and organization of the support.

> Love is not the result of adequate sexual satisfaction, but sexual happiness—even the knowledge of the so-called sexual technique—is the result of love.[22]

This assertion would lead naturally both to a contrast between love and sexual technique and to an exploration of cause and effect.

> The emotional impulse that moves a composer to write his scores contains the same element of poetry that incites the scientist to his discoveries.[23]

The above assertion will lead the writer into both comparing and defining. The basis of the comparison—this "element of poetry"—will, after all, require definition.

> The known facts about Chaucer's life pertain almost exclusively to his official career.[24]

The topic sentence above would lead to a paragraph packed with historical information and pertinent details about Chaucer's official career.

> Young men are lustful in character and apt to do what they lust after.[25]

The above assertion, a strong Aristotelian bias and a possibly dangerous stereotype, would require vigorous persuasion and numerous examples to convince a skeptical reader.

---

[22]Erich Fromm, "Love and Its Disintegration in Contemporary Western Society," in *The Art of Loving* (New York: Harper & Row, 1956), p. 89.
[23]Edgar Varese, "Spatial Music," in Roberts et al., *Mirrors of Mind*, p. 86.
[24]George K. Anderson, *Old and Middle English Literature from the Beginnings to 1485*, Vol. 1 of *A History of English Literature* (New York: Collier, 1962), p. 232.
[25]Aristotle, "Character of the Young," in *The Rhetoric of Aristotle*, trans. Richard C. Jebb, ed. John E. Sandys (Cambridge: Cambridge UP, 1909), p. 99.

> To know how to begin, then, is the great art—no very pro-
> found maxim—but since in any extended piece of work one
> must begin many times, this is the art which is essential to
> master.[26]

The writer of this topic sentence will go on, in the paragraph, to explain the process of beginning, its techniques and steps.

> But to continue the story of my professional experiences,
> I made one pound ten and six on my first review; and I
> bought a Persian cat with the proceeds.[27]

Narration will obviously be the organizational scheme for the paragraph that follows this topic sentence. Chronology will dominate the selection of facts and events, all falling under the heading of "professional experiences."

> Play construction can also be seen as spatial expression of a
> variety of social connotations.[28]

This topic sentence leads to a paragraph of analysis and inter-pretation of childhood play. The writer breaks down play into its component parts, focusing, in this paragraph, on social con-notations of spatial expressions.

◆

Activities

1. From your own paragraphs or sample paragraphs in this book, select topic sentences that suggest the overall struc-ture and developmental scheme in their expression. Find topic sentences that carry, within their expressions, possibil-ities of comparing, contrasting, classifying, analyzing, per-suading, defining, illustrating, proceeding, narrating, in-forming, describing.

---

[26]Jacques Barzun, "A Writer's Discipline," in *On Writing, Editing, and Publishing* (Chicago: U of Chicago P, 1971), p. 7.
[27]Virginia Woolf, "Professions for Women," in *The Death of the Moth and Other Essays* (New York: Harcourt, 1942), p. 239.
[28]Erik Erikson, "The Theory of Infantile Sexuality," in *Childhood and Society*, 2nd ed. (New York: Norton, 1963), p. 106.

2. Now select two or three topic sentences without an implied structure and revise them to suggest a developmental scheme. What are the effects of these revisions?

3. Study the degree to which the remainder of the paragraph adheres to the structure suggested in the topic sentence. Do you find mixed methods of organization within a larger structural framework? For example, does the contrast set up in the topic sentence lead to definitions of the basis of the contrast? Does the writer provide examples to clarify definitions? Is a procedural explanation part of a larger analysis? Are causes and effects explored for the overriding purpose of persuasion?

4. Go back to a paragraph on which your teacher has affixed the criticism, "inadequately developed." The marginal notation might also read "thin content" or "weak support." Using the information in this section, apply the newly acquired strategies for adequate and orderly development to the revision of one of your weak, inadequately developed paragraphs. Revise again, using different strategies. Which revision are you more comfortable with? Which is more effective?

5. Examine several essay exam questions from various academic courses to identify implied or stated developmental schemes. On essay exams, how would you handle vaguely worded questions such as the following?

Discuss the Whiskey Rebellion.

Respond to the following quotation.

Comment on the logic of X.

CHAPTER

9

Imprinting a Style

If you think for a moment about your favorite entertainers, fashions, cars, houses, friends, restaurants, movies—in short, your favorite *anything*—you will notice that each has its own flair and personality, and that your preference for one over another is based on style at least as often as substance. Faced with an array of rock groups, all of whom may display about the same level of musical competence, you pick—indeed, you *love*—the group that has imprinted its own style on words and tunes that are, after all, the same from year to year, decade to decade. Folks over 30 have lived long enough to see their favorite songs come round again, but the smart entertainer has not simply cloned an earlier version, using the rhythms, clothes, gestures, backup, lighting, makeup of the 1950s or 1960s. The singer has, with the old tune and the familiar words, transformed the song into a timely, up-to-date, stylistic achievement. And though your parents catch the substance of the tune and hum along, the style escapes them, even as it delights you.

Imprinting your writing style on content of similar meaning and form involves a similar search for natural, spontaneous, creative presentation. But the balance between substance and style, between what you are saying and the way in which you say it, is delicate. Style can easily slide into gimmickry. Style is too often a superficial mask disguising plain or conventional meanings. Style, as the image makers well know, can manipulate audiences. You end up paying more for a product that has the same ingredients and the same capabilities, because the *presentation* of the product caught your eye, not the product itself.

Then, too, very fine, substantial writing content can lose its impact and power when the presentation is inept, dull, awkward. And the loss is great. You may, after all, be the person who has the best idea, the most sensible solution, the clearest perception, but if you cannot present that content to best advantage, the reader will quickly skim, and just as quickly forget, what you have to say.

Style and substance, therefore, must come together, the idea itself and the expression of it making a dramatic impression on the reader. Alexander Pope, in *An Essay on Criticism*, put the matter nicely: "True wit," says he, "is nature to advantage dress'd, / What oft was thought, but ne'er so well express'd."

Unfortunately, you cannot just go out and get some style, any more than you can suddenly change yourself from a cowboy to a fop, a rabble-rouser to a rationalist. Style *evolves*, just as personalities, habits, and attitudes evolve—and sometimes the evolution is glacial. You may write for years, perhaps, before you find your particular voice and are confident using it, the voice that signals to the reader that a particular person, not a machine, wrote the essay. A seventh grader, intent on writing the winning essay for a contest sponsored by the Elks Club, asked the teacher what she should do about style. The teacher answered, "You just keep writing, and style will take care of itself." The teacher was only partly right. Style is, to a degree, the natural product of writing experience, writing confidence, writing maturity. But style has its techniques, tips, and shortcuts as well. And you can learn them.

What do stylish essays have in common?

Good style is, at the very least, neat. You are surprised that such a lowly consideration comes first? Well, neatness of presentation is available to everyone, whether or not he or she has writing talent. Just as you do not usually wear dirty or torn jeans to a job interview, so you do not present to your reader a smudged, scribbled, wrinkled essay. The requirement is so basic, so conducive to good communication, that it is a puzzlement more people do not take advantage of this simple stylistic device (although some students may *stop* at neatness, mistaking appearance for the completed task).

Neatness, however, is not synonymous with conventionality, obedience, or submission. A casual, off-beat, even radical appearance in fashion may be the product of hours of careful work. So it is with writing. Even a breezy, informal style does not risk sloppiness in presentation. Every writer can clean up the surface of his or her essay, without sacrificing creativity to dull convention. Legibility in handwriting, even margins, quality writing paper, clean typeface — these are the minimum stylish proprieties. (*Note:* Even if you use the hunt-and-peck method, you may want to type your papers. Your essay will seem more professional and may be taken more seriously.)

Style is pleasing to all the senses.   Even if your content is very strong and fresh, your essay will diminish in effectiveness if the sentences do not sound right, if their structures are choppy, if their words are inexact, if their descriptions are vague, if their rhythms are off.

A stylish essay hits the reader on several levels at once. The mind is delighted by the content. But the eye and ear also require attention. As you write, read the words out loud. Does one sentence jump out, breaking the flow of meaning? Do you have to reread this awkward sentence several times to understand what you yourself wrote? Smooth out the sentence. Insert a transitional word or phrase. Does one word seem inexact? Have you written "qualm" when you meant "quibble" or "quorum" or "quantum"? Check the dictionary to confirm the definition and the various uses of the words you are not sure of. Does your content produce concrete images, scenes, and sensations throughout for the reader? Are you showing and not merely telling? Follow the general assertion with an example or detail, something the reader can see in the mind's eye.

Good style is various, not monotonous.   Vary the lengths and structures of sentences. Vary word choices. You want to mesmerize the reader, not put him or her to sleep. (Be aware, however, of the danger of achieving variety for variety's sake. Effective repetition can sometimes be exhilarating, not numbing — as with a series of sentences of similar length and structure, delivered with staccato precision.)

You may combine several short sentences into one longer and more effective idea.

Don't write:

> Owning a word processor is very helpful for writers. All the editing can be done before the finished work is printed out. The writer can combine or delete paragraphs and sentences. He or she can correct errors in spelling, punctuation, and grammar.

Write instead:

> Word processors enable writers to perform important editing tasks—combining or deleting passages, correcting errors in spelling or grammar—even before the finished product is printed out.

Or dramatically vary the lengths of sentences.

Don't write:

> The shrimp boats pulled away from the dock. Their nets created a design against the pink sky of morning. I was watching from the upstairs window.

Write instead:

> The shrimp boats pulled away from the dock, their nets creating a design against the pink sky of morning. I saw it all.

Sometimes you can break the monotony by altering the order of words, getting out of the subject-verb-object pattern.

Don't write:

> The assassination of John F. Kennedy occurred on November 22, 1963. The nation watched in horror. Shots rang out. The event changed the course of history.

Write instead:

> On November 22, 1963, John F. Kennedy was assassinated. As the nation watched in horror, shots rang out, changing the course of history.

Varying word choices can also stimulate reader interest.

Don't write:

> The mechanics *ran* out to the *runway* to gas up the airplane engine because the plane was *running* late.

Write instead:

> The mechanics *raced* out to the *runway* to gas up the engine because the plane was *behind schedule.*

Now, you revise the sentences in your own way, combining short sentences, varying the lengths, altering the order, varying the word choices.

Good style is appropriate.   The language, approach, and tone will vary according to your audience, purpose, and occasion for writing. The essay leaves quite a bit of room for different styles, ranging from very formal to very light and casual. But it does not allow for impropriety, flippancy, vulgarity, undue sarcasm, pedantry, or frivolity. Good style is simple, clear, neither more nor less in the way of presentation than is called for. A research paper is intended primarily to inform, analyze, evaluate, recommend, or persuade; and extreme informality of tone and language is out of place. Slang, however, can sometimes be appropriate when you are, for example, trying to explain the language of the street or to create a believable character. Highly technical language would be suitable for an audience of experts but not for an audience of lay people, unless, of course, you include careful definitions. Humor might be inappropriate when you are treating very serious matters: famine, environmental dangers, war. Sophisticated audiences might tolerate more radical ideas and expressions, more wit and ingenuity, than would rather staid, conservative, or naive audiences. But businesslike audiences might prefer a more straightforward presentation of the facts.

As you write, you begin to sense the tension between achieving freshness and maintaining the basic proprieties. Good writers are always, in a sense, working against what they have been taught, against what is expected of them, against labels and preconceived notions. There is risk in good writing, and there is rebellion. But if a word, joke, informality, or colloquialism is questionable, you are wise to take the more cautious approach. When in doubt, leave it out. You do not want to lose your reader because you have offended or enraged him or her. You want, after all, to communicate.

Good style is genuine.   Good style has an authentic ring to it, an honesty and integrity of purpose, presentation, personality. You strike a false note when your writing strains for effects that are unnatural to you or to the subject. Are you trying to be cute and funny, but aren't? Cut it out. Are you striving to be pompous and pious when you are, by nature, irreverent? Don't. Are you writing primarily to impress rather than to inform or persuade? Stop showing off. Even if the reader does not personally know you, he or she will feel the straining after false effects, the gimmickry and manipulation. Audiences are shrewd. They will sense that you are trying to squeeze out a tear of false sentiment or produce canned laughter or convey a righteous indignation you do not feel.

The following paragraph is painful to read because it is false, overblown, seeking to apply cleverness to the surface of a banal idea.

In the lofty annals of my personal history, I discovered, to my everlasting dismay, that my mother had very cruelly destroyed my baseball cards. How, you may ask, can a mother be so insensitive, so callous of mind and heart, as to take from her dear boy the very fiber of his being, the heart of his heart? She surreptitiously snatched from my dresser drawer my Willie Mays, my Dwight Gooden, my Yogi Berra, my Steve Garvey, among others. On these cards were played out the scenes of my childhood, the stuff of my dreams. I was devastated. O, Mom. How could you?

If you are in agony as you read the above paragraph, you may have a good grasp of the importance of authenticity, genuineness in writing. An essay about a mother throwing away a kid's baseball cards could have potential. The subject is not bad and could evoke tender sympathies from the reader. Nearly everyone, after all, has been through a similar loss—a parent tosses out, without warning or permission, a love letter, a pebble, a pea shooter, a dried-up corsage, a diary, a picture of your best friend. But only a natural, unaffected rendering of the event could elicit a genuine response from the reader.

Give attention to structure and form.

Style is, in part, a matter of giving attention to the structure, the shape, and the rhythms of words, sentences, and paragraphs. Readers respond to naturalness and ease of expression, to balance and effective repetition. In earlier chapters, you considered various ways to give shape and substance to the content of your essays and paragraphs. You learned strategies for making sense of your random ideas, experiences, and information. You learned to plan ahead, to develop a thesis, to find sturdy and rational supports, to convince the reader.

But developing style leads you beyond sense into sensitivity. Many essays make sense. You can learn from them, be convinced or persuaded. But the mode and manner of expression may, nonetheless, be plodding, predictable, undramatic. And as long as you are trying to communicate an idea, you might as well strive also to please and delight the reader. Good style adds another dimension to your writing and may cause your idea to have a lasting impact on the reader.

An analysis of your writing style will lead you into more subtle and different considerations. You are thinking not only about what you write but about how you put it. You consider the texture and variety of your sentences. You note the structures, lengths, patterns of sentences and of paragraphs. You place ideas in perspective, giving some more weight, others less. You will gain more experience in constructing effective sentences in Chapter 10. But at this stage, you can nontheless learn to be attentive to the sounds of your ideas and to their placement.

Be reasonably concise.

An oft-quoted rule for good writing is "Be concise." As with most rules regarding style, the concise imperative is an oversimplification. E. B. White, in the introduction to Professor William Strunk's best-selling book, *Elements of Style*, presents a humorous anecdote about the dangers and risks of a passion for concision. When Strunk taught writing at Cornell University, he encouraged students to strive for concision, to cut the "deadwood" from their essays. But the class hour needed filling, so Strunk resorted to repetition, even as he exhorted the students to be concise. Strunk had to repeat the rule three times to top off the hour, fill it to the brim: "Omit needless words! Omit needless words! Omit needless words!" The advice is sound, even though Strunk's expression of it was, truth to tell, wordy.

The fact is, the difference between competent writing and great writing does not always depend entirely, or even in part, on severe and radical cutting, though certainly a judicious cutting can often improve the style of an essay. Though the mundane communication of an interoffice memorandum is likely to be improved by slashing, a work of art may bleed. Herman Melville's *Moby Dick* is not concise, though students skip the section on whale anatomy and go, instead, straight for the plot summary available at the campus bookstore. An article reprinted in *Reader's Digest* may be condensed almost beyond recognition, all the style of expression having been sacrificed on the altar of brevity. Though it was part of Ernest Hemingway's artistic expression to pare down sentences and meanings to the bone, for a great many fine writers the opposite is true. Dante, Dostoevsky, and Darwin are not concise. George Eliot, Henry James, James Joyce, Simone de Beauvoir, and Carl Jung are not concise. Where style coexists with substance, concision may be a strange bedfellow.

Most works of art, whether in literature or science, could, after all, be reduced to a single sentence or page if the reader sought only message, plot, and resolution. But the reader would not then feel the message along his or her pulse. The concise message of Arthur Miller's *Death of a Salesman* goes something like this: "Don't strive to be well-liked at the sacrifice of your soul. Don't be fooled by the American dream of success." The concise message of Nathaniel Hawthorne's "Young Goodman Brown" might read, "Don't leave a nice wife and go into the woods at night. The devil will get you." Student versions of novels and plays are often cut and spliced, whether to eliminate "unacceptable" parts or to simplify meanings. But the style, which is to say the "life," often goes out of the literary work.

The point, simply, is that concision for its own sake is absurd. An efficiency expert once expressed a two-point criterion for making purchases. The first was "Do you need it?" The answer was usually "No." Humans, after all, need only food, water, and primitive shelter to survive or, more precisely, to subsist. But subsistence is not everything. The second and better question posed by the expert was "Do you want it?" And here the consumer moves into style. Yes, people want more than caves, more than raw meat, more than water, more than animal skins for clothing. They want style as well, a beauty of setting, a balm to the senses. And so it is with writing. Essays that simply go straight to the point, without the pleasant detours of sound and rhythm, without the complex exploration of the nooks and crannies of meaning, are concerned only with function, not design; with sense, not sensibility.

Keep parts parallel and repeat effectively.

By all odds, the best example of concision deferring to the higher stylistic law of beauty, balance, effective repetition, and even poetry is the famous quotation that begins Charles Dickens's novel *A Tale of Two Cities:*

> It was the best of times, it was the worst of times, it was the age of wisdom, it was the age of foolishness, it was the epoch of belief, it was the epoch of incredulity, it was the season of light, it was the season of darkness, it was the spring of hope, it was the winter of despair, we had everything before us, we had nothing before us, we were all going direct to heaven, we were all going direct the other way.

Charles Dickens might have flunked composition were his teacher the sort who screams, "Get to the point!" But Dickens's crimes were petty in the light of, well, this light. The sentence is a model of wordiness. It is also a model of symmetry, parallel structure, effective repetition, beauty. Unusually rigid teachers might also mark down Dickens for his use of commas to join complete thoughts. If he wanted to join main clauses with commas, he should have inserted a coordinating conjunction between all the clauses or, at the very least, between the last two clauses, thereby creating items in a series. But you get the point, you get the point, you get the point. Style, here, is in the ascendancy, and economy must be respectful of the harmonious and sublime rendering of the idea.

Some sentences in your essays might be shorter, but they would not necessarily be sweeter. A good stylist uses symmetry and repetition to emphasize important ideas, to drill meanings into readers. And the parts of those repetitions must be parallel, following the same pattern or structure throughout the repetition. The following paragraph is stylistically weak because it does not repeat with a purpose and because the parts of the repetition are out of balance, unparallel structurally. Even if you cannot name the repeated structures, you can surely hear the errors.

Original version:

Shortly before Alfred Bernhard Nobel died, he picked up a pen, grabbing a scrap of paper, to jot down a will, establishing the Nobel Prizes. Two weeks later, Nobel himself was dead, but the prizes—in the fields of literature, chemical, physics, practicing medicine, being peacemakers—live on. Nobel, having invented and, in the end, to make millions on the deadly explosive dynamite, felt guilty, being ashamed and having the conviction, growing and huge, that he must do or try to correct, or at least wanting to ameliorate the damage to society. Nobel left nine million dollars, for the sole purpose and to see to it that the millions be invested, having earned interest and to be awarded annually to representatives of these several areas of investigating science and to write literature.

The above paragraph is full of unparallel structures and pointless repetitions. Revising the paragraph to a unified, harmonious whole is simply a matter of eliminating needless repetition, balancing the structures of effective repetition. The italicized portions of the paragraph will enable you to see and to hear the stylistic improvement.

Revision:

Shortly before Alfred Bernhard Nobel died, he *grabbed a scrap of paper, jotted down a will,* and *established the Nobel Prizes.* Two weeks later, Nobel was dead, but the prizes— in the fields of *literature, chemistry, physics, medicine,* and *peace*—live on. Nobel, having *invented and made* millions on the deadly explosive dynamite, *felt* guilty *and had* the growing conviction that he must try *to correct*, or at least *to ameliorate*, the damage done to society. Nobel left nine million dollars, money which, *having been invested* and *having earned interest*, would then be awarded annually to representatives of *science and literature*.

You will notice, in the revision, that nouns line up with nouns, phrases with phrases and that the effect is aurally and mentally pleasing when sound and sense unite.

◆

Activities

1. The following sentences and paragraphs could very likely be expressed in fewer words, but the life and liveliness of the passages would diminish as well. As you study the following examples of symmetry and effective repetition, identify the similar structures. Then revise each sentence or paragraph solely on the basis of concision. Can you effectively retain the meaning as you tighten the expression? Why or why not? What happens to each passage when concision is the only criterion for evaluation?

    a. All of our lives are filled with examples of this seeming effortlessness, this airy result. The trumpet on which you've wasted your hot breath for hours suddenly emits a round, sweet note. The problem you carried heavily to bed, with sighs and tears, miraculously sinks in the cradle of night, and you awake with the answer on your lips. The bike you couldn't ride suddenly swings onto the sidewalk of its own accord and carries you, weightless and free, into the wind.

    b. All my life I've tried to build a fool-proof library. I was greedy. I wanted what I wanted, not what somebody else thought I should have: my favorite poems, my perfect art books, my best literary lights, my kind of trivia, my recipes with no more than two ingredients and two steps, my wisdom of the ages, my quotable quotations, my impeccable sources.

    c. Pedantry effectively clips the wings of all life-changing experiences. The body of true believers forms over the kitchen table, then meets in a mobile home, then builds a wooden church, then gets a budget and new pews, then builds a brick church, then goes on Christian television to cry and plead for money. The minister begins in overalls, then ends up in a three-piece business suit, white collar, rep tie, with a ten-point program for salvation in his hip pocket.

d. Most people would rather take wide swings at life: they'd rather punch than spar, demolish than win, knock out than daze, draw blood than defend, kill than compromise.

e. Declarations of independence take plenty of courage. More than courage, they require measured thought, careful preparation, philosophical conviction, and in the end, just plain outrage.

f. The world needs all kinds, but lovers of mountains are better for daily life. From them we get memories of home, shelter from storms, warmth against dark, order against chaos.

g. But there I was, deep in sand, my hand sifting through cool, clean mud; the whitecaps building toward tomato sandwiches and afternoon naps.

h. I used to want everybody to like me; now I'm satisfied if nobody hates me.

i. Once at home, I fix my coffee, do my work, and late in the evening, when midnight's all aglimmer, sit in my aluminum lawn chair and smile and smile.

2. Revise the following sentences, making the related portions parallel. You will notice that cutting unnecessary repetition will help you revise more effectively. If you cannot locate the unparallel structures, read the sentences aloud and let your ear tell you what is wrong.

Example:

Flannery O'Connor said that the secret of living well is to mind your own business and having plenty of business you are minding.

Revision of faulty sentence:

Flannery O'Connor said that the secret of living well is to mind your own business and to have plenty of business to mind.

a. Having graduated from college, Elizabeth had set out to find an apartment and getting a job.

b. The task proved harder and most difficult than she was to believe.

c. All the personnel people had a litany of questions: Can you type? Take dictation? Do you file? Are you able to make coffee? How's your telephone voice?

d. Since Elizabeth majored in French and having taken a minor in psychology, she was confused and being dismayed over her inability to be hired for what she could do, not what she hadn't the slightest idea how to do.

e. Elizabeth spent week after seven days, pounding the pavement and having knocked on every door of opportunity, but the doors were closed, even having been locked.

f. Finally, in a burst of ingenuity and being desperate, Elizabeth signed up as a cruise director on an ocean liner, owned and to be managed by a French company.

g. Her psychology helped her understand the passengers, and her knowledge of French aiding her in communicating.

h. Some courage, confidence, and being willing to travel helped Elizabeth embark on a different kind of career and having kept her from the unemployment office.

i. A healthy salary and getting a chance at adventure made Elizabeth happy and a success at her work.

Use irony and satire responsibly.

Irony and satire are kinfolk because both carry double or multiple meanings or intentions. They both are the offspring of wit. They both look at life, customs, tragedies, human foibles with a wry eye. The eye is winking. *Clever ironists always mean the opposite of what they are saying.* Irony is just your mother saying, with tongue in cheek, "Yeah sure, my kid's at the top of his class. He's so high he could float to the top of anything." She does not mean it, of course. Or does she? The thrill of irony is in the chase for the real meaning. You probably have friends who are ironists. They are the ones who are always muttering absurd and dramatic comments, to which you invariably respond, with a shiver of doubt, "You *are* kidding, aren't you?" Only the ironist knows for sure.

Satire is also witty, though its bite is often literal and more painful than is irony's. Skilled satirists jab and poke at human error, social ills, using humor and exaggeration to expose and deflate all that is pompous, pious, or evil in humankind. The satirist preaches the gospel of fitness, thereby exposing and deflating the American obsession with both health and overnight religious conversions. The satirist fantasizes about a cute, sexy male secretary, with a great telephone voice and a talent for making coffee, thereby exposing sexist stereotypes of women around the office. But the satirist does not require a double meaning to make his or her killing point.

Both the satirist and the ironist have serious intentions, but they are moralists in clown's clothing. They want to change human behavior by coming at conventional thinking and behavior in circuitous ways. Rather than clubbing society over the head for injustice and cruelty, they tease evil into submission and cajole good into power.

Irony may be satirical, but satire is not always ironic. If, for example, you say one thing and mean quite another, you are being ironic; you may also be satirical or mildly critical or even sarcastic, depending on the seriousness of the foible you seek to expose. The reader has to understand that your tone is ironic, your meaning opposite to what is being stated, or he will actually believe that he is God's gift to women when he is, in reality, the wimp of the century. But satire need not necessarily carry double meanings, though it sometimes achieves its effects through irony. A good satirist may simply describe what is, in fact, going on in society, and the arrangement of the details will be satirical. Political satirists often do not use irony to make their satirical points. They simply place the actual events in unusual combinations, tell the truth, and the satire emerges in the telling. Why does truth rise to the level of satire? Because people seldom tell it. So literalness can produce effective satire, though irony cannot, by definition, be literal.

But both irony and satire are similar in tone. Both are, to varying degrees, mean. Both are, at times, very funny. Both eschew earnest and frumpy moralizing in favor of sophisticated banter, clever ripostes, subtle intimations of virtue and vice.

Rather than stating directly and pedantically that most presidents of the United States are ill-prepared and inadequate for the task, Clarence Darrow comes at the issue with a wry, satirical jab, saying, "When I was a boy I was told that anybody could become President; I'm beginning to believe it." And rather than directly attacking excessive American sentiment toward the institution of motherhood, Noel Coward satirizes the problem, using heavy irony: "Mother love, particularly in America, is a highly respected and much publicized emotion and, when exacerbated by gin and bourbon, it can become extremely formidable." The piety and sentiment fall prey to the ironist's powerful weapons of exaggeration and surprise.

Writers have a long history of being ironic and satirical, having recognized that exaggeration and indirectness often effect change more swiftly than does straightforward didacticism.

The following examples show the differences and similarities between irony and satire: Dorothy Parker is being satirical when she says, "Men seldom make passes / At girls who wear glasses." Here, Parker means *exactly* what she says. There is not a trace of irony in this statement, though there is an implicit, gently satirical criticism of male attitudes toward women. But Groucho Marx is being "purely" ironic when he says, "I've worked myself up from nothing to a state of extreme poverty." James Baldwin is being satirical when he says, "It is a great shock at the age of five or six to find that in a world of Gary Coopers you are the Indian." He surely means what he says, though the expression of the meaning is both exaggerated and bitterly comic. But Brendan Behan is being both ironic and satirical when he says, "I always say that a general and a bit of shooting makes you forget your troubles." He does not literally mean that war is a wonderful leisure activity. He means the opposite, but he also is satirizing the passion, among some, for warfare. And Robert Benchley is being both ironic and satirical when he says, "Even nowadays a man can't step up and kill a woman without feeling just a bit unchivalrous." Benchley, in this example, uses irony and understatement to increase the impact of the satirical jab at male and female role stereotypes.

If irony and satire are both mean, to varying degrees, why do writers use them as persuasive devices? The answer is simple. With irony and satire, a writer can sidle up to touchy social issues—to hypocrisy and prejudice and poverty and inequity and ignorance—without getting punched in the mouth and often, paradoxically, without hurting others. Ironic or satirical portrayals often miss their mark even while hitting the mark. The great human protection we all share is the armor of arrogance, the conviction that the ironist or satirist is talking about everybody *except* us. Irony and satire, therefore, lock the writer and the victim in an intimate, snickering embrace. The joke, with irony and satire, is always private, an inside matter going on between writer and reader, and the victim seldom feels the pain, even as the small poison dart is being quietly planted in his heart. But later, in the darkness of his little bedroom, the victim may suddenly realize that the poison dart was directed at him, not everybody else.

Irony and satire are stylistic and tonal modes that do not come naturally to everyone. Irony is figurative, for example; and the figurative always carries risk. Some people might not get the joke. Some people might be offended by harsh satire about serious issues. The satire may, in fact, be so heavy that an earnest reader may swing over to the victim's side, a kind of sympathy vote. Using satire and irony, then, depends on a delicate balance between not going far enough (being merely blandly silly or cute) and going too far (being ruthless and decidedly unfunny). Satirist Jonathan Swift, in "A Modest Proposal," repeatedly recommends that Ireland solve the problem of poverty by serving up stewed babies to the rich. Such bitter satire sometimes spoils the appetites of more serious and straightforward citizens. Ironic or satirical quips about the pope, motherhood, the sanctity of the family, or the American flag can often produce a nation of religious, flag-waving, Mother-loving zealots, the opposite of what the satirist intended.

But a writer who makes good use of these devices, who has a clear sense of audience and purpose, can woo and win the crowd to a new way of thinking and seeing. The writer must be considerate of the audience, finely tuned to what the crowd will or will not tolerate. Stand-up comedians, who often use humorous irony and satire to make their serious points, know when they have gone too far. A growl of protest begins in the audience, laughter turns to hissing, and the comedian backs off, sweating and saying over and over, "Just kidding folks. I love you all. Really, you're beautiful." The tension subsides. The audience smiles again. And the bold comedian sneaks up for another ironic jab, calling east St. Louis the garden spot of the world, praising Rotarians for their sweeping social reforms, expressing dismay over the increasingly socialistic bent of the American Medical Association, recommending that we solve the problem of overpopulation by sending all city kids to play on the expressway.

The following essay uses irony and satire to make several observations about American values and attitudes. The tone is inflated, mocking, humorous, but the underlying message is serious. As you read and study the essay, analyze the portions that are ironic, satirical, or both. Were the thesis presented straightforwardly, how might it be expressed? Why does the writer use irony and satire to persuade and influence the audience? Why would the straightforward approach perhaps be less successful?

MY SON, THE CAPITALIST

It's so nice to have a capitalist around the house, especially at Christmas. You need somebody whose ruling passion is money, somebody whose values are shallow and materialistic, somebody who shamelessly hawks greeting cards in the church lobby just prior to worship service. You need somebody like my teenaged son.

My son is an American dream. He could teach Willie Loman a thing or two about getting ahead and being well liked. He is a dedicated label aficionado, a canny financier, a barterer, a risk taker, a status seeker. He will do anything for money, even work. He will clean a neighbor's house, have a yard sale, cat sit, babysit, trade up or down. He is counting the days until he can be independently wealthy and free of his low-life mother.

If you wonder how the parents produced this fine figure of a wheeler-dealer, I'll tell you. We kept him slightly deprived for years. Give a child the best of everything, and you'll wind up with a slob or a socialist. You've got to underfeed and underclothe a budding capitalist. The best way to guarantee that your child will get rich and stay rich is to keep him poor.

Poverty was the only thing we could give the boy. We made him wear jeans with holes in the knees, tennis shoes with broken shoe strings, loafers with soles flapping in the breeze. We never let him have the roast beef sandwich at the fast-food restaurant. He had to get the plain hamburger and small fries or nothing at all. We never let him order dessert or took him to fancy restaurants. We left him home, eating frozen fish sticks. He never got a pool table, a ten-speed bike, or a checking account of his own. He was forbidden to go down to the drug store to hang around and buy grape bubble gum. The minute we caught him having any fun whatsoever, we made him stop. All the efforts have paid off. My son is the greatest little free-enterprise capitalist this side of Milton Friedman. Let them eat dirt is his motto. He plans to go to Harvard. He wouldn't soil his shoes by stepping on the campus of a state-supported school, unless, of course, it has a good football team.

Most of the time I feel duty-bound to portray his financial orientation as being mildly reprehensible. I say a little greed goes a long way. I preach to him about sharing. I remind him that love of money is the root of all evil. I say it's easier for a camel to go through the eye of a needle than for a rich man to enter the kingdom of heaven. But I never nag him at Christmas. When the big bucks are rolling and the pocketbook is empty, my son's financial wizardry comes in very handy.

My son took over the Christmas shopping operation after I resigned. I was too soft-hearted and too prideful for the job. Anybody who wanted a weed-eater, I got her one. Anybody who fleetingly longed for a sterling silver salad fork, I bought it for him. And even when the relatives were nice, saying I should just send them a card, I couldn't obey. I had to scotch-tape the card to a thirty-dollar box of Godiva chocolates. I didn't want anybody to think I was tight.

My son took to Christmas shopping like Ronald Reagan takes to defense spending. First he got a clean sheet of notebook paper on which he recorded, in ink and in cursive, the fifty-two people we had to buy something for. Then he and I descended on the nearest shopping mall. In just two whirlwind nights, we had all the relatives wrapped up and were well on our way to finishing the friends.

While we shopped, my son looked neither right nor left: no exclaiming over the Christmas decorations, no idle chatter, no humming of carols, no visit with Santa, no stopping for peppermint ice cream, no nonsense. He wanted to get the whole thing over with so he could go home and watch some sex and violence on TV.

And he was no sappy, sentimental liberal either. He was generous but not too generous. He had a shrewd sense of just how much we should spend on Aunt Ethel vs. Cousin Ernest. Aunt Ethel is blood, and Cousin Ernest is by marriage. My son carried a felt-tipped pen with which he blackened each name on the list as he finished with it. When the shopping was all over and we had necklaces, earrings, sweaters, wallets, tie racks, pajamas, and woks all paid for, he took the whole load to gift-wrapping, handed the woman our receipts, and asked for the free wrap. It was wonderful.

My son has put new meaning back into capitalism for me. We had enough money left over after the holidays to start his trust fund and buy six new tapes for his collection. He saved a considerable amount by giving me a hot plate he made in shop class.

I'm sorry I can't give you a capitalist of your very own for Christmas. But I can't. You'll have to raise your own capitalist because I won't share mine. That's the good old American way.

Questions for discussion

1. How would you describe the tone of this essay? Is it light, sarcastic, humorous, bitter? Which portions are more or less humorous, more or less caustic?

2. Where, in the essay, does the writer mean exactly what she says, and where does she not mean what she says?

3. What is being satirized besides the son's values? What does the writer think of capitalism, of Christmas, of the American dream?

4. Does the writer make herself a target of the satire? Where? In what ways?

5. What developmental schemes and methods of support does the writer use to make the satirical point?

6. The writer alludes at various points to the Bible, to Milton Friedman, to Willie Loman. Milton Friedman is a conservative economist. If you are not familiar with his philosophy, you can consult the reference department in the library. You may, perhaps, recognize the reference to Willie Loman, the central and tragic victim of the American dream in Arthur Miller's *Death of a Salesman*. Miller, however, does not use humor, satire, inflated language to convey meanings. Study Miller's play to discover how the theme of that work relates to the message of this essay.

7. What is the central idea in this essay, sans satire and irony?

◆

Activities

1. You can test your ability to recognize the similarities and differences between irony and satire by studying the follow-

ing sentences. Ask yourself whether the passage simply means the opposite of what it is saying (irony), seeks to expose folly or wickedness (satire), or both. Consider also the tone of each sentence. Is it mildly amusing, very funny, sarcastic, bitter? How, in each example, does the arrangement of details contribute to the surprise and humor of the sentences?

a. Southerners never get mixed up about what's important: Daddy's family tree comes first; God comes second.

b. I just loved camping. There was so much to do. I could sit in a chair and swat bugs. I could walk in the woods and watch for snakes. I could build a fire and watch it go out. I could hike a mile to the bathroom. I could get in a canoe and row to the other side of the lake. Then I could row back.

c. College students come by their vagueness naturally. They have learned from politicians, preachers, educators, and parents how to say nothing in 2,000 words or more.

d. Christmas is the good-works season. Everywhere I look I see another good work. Just yesterday I saw a shiny-faced minister pat several old people on the heads as he left the nursing home. He had only one hand free for patting. The other hand was filled with a brand new Bible. And I myself have been doing some good works. So far I've dropped one dollar in the Salvation Army bucket.

e. As Gloria Steinem (or was it Abraham Lincoln) once said, "Progress is going where you haven't been before."

f. I am a graduate of the Cereal Bowl School of Hair Design, with high honors in hacking and chopping.

g. Nothing can drive a child to a life of filth and degradation faster than growing up in a houseful of righteous indignation.

h. Skillful procrastinators lead lives of ease, privacy, and peace. Nobody calls up procrastinators and asks them to serve on committees because procrastinators are irresponsible. Then, too, procrastinators won't be bothered by visitors. Who wants to visit somebody whose house is filthy and who never reciprocates? Procrastinators can even, if they play their flaws right, surround themselves with saintly, long-suffering types who will do the work the procrastinators were supposed to do but never got around to doing. If you must have a tragic flaw, procrastination is a good one. It's not illegal; it's only passively, not aggressively, cruel; it eliminates the possibility of failure since nothing ventured is nothing lost; and it is a real time-saver, leaving the procrastinator free to swing in the hammock, drinking a Pepsi Cola and dreaming about what he's going to accomplish tomorrow.

2. Write a short essay in which you satirize one of the following notions. Be certain that irony—saying one thing and meaning another—operates either throughout the entire essay or at least in some portions of it.

Cleanliness is next to Godliness.

Clothes make the man (or woman).

Stop and smell the roses.

Something *good* is going to happen to *you*.

Have you hugged your child today?

Put on a happy face.

It's always darkest before the dawn.

Every cloud must have a silver lining.

Children are to be seen and not heard.

Save for the future.

If you haven't got anything nice to say, don't say anything at all.

A friend in need is a friend indeed.

Have a nice day.

Let figurative language convey literal meanings.

In the section on defining as a developmental scheme, you learned that words carry denotative (literal) and connotative (figurative) meanings. The word "figurative" means, literally, "not literal," "metaphorical," "symbolic." A sophisticated writer learns to use figurative language to make literal meanings. Writers seek fresh and arresting ways to express old ideas or to introduce new ones. Sometimes writers use figurative language to express the inexpressible. And sometimes they want to layer meanings, to make the textures of their essays dense with images, symbols, words that give color, depth, and richness to plain expression.

You do not have to be a poet to make use of figurative language. In fact, you and your friends use figurative language every day, though perhaps you are not aware of the terminology of those uses. You say your buddy is lower than a snake's belly, but though your meaning may be literal, your expression of it is clearly figurative. Then, too, the songs you hum, the television programs you watch, the advertising jingles you remember are all supercharged with the figurative use of language. A perfume is the essence of springtime. A lover builds a fortress around the heart, or the heart is in a total eclipse. A dishwashing detergent is Joy or Dawn. A car is a Bronco. If commerce uses figurative language to sell products, why can't you put figurative language to work as well, using it to sell an idea or a thesis?

Some may say that figurative language has little or no place in essays intended primarily to inform. But even scientific writers can find ways to put the figurative use of language to work for them, clarifying and explaining what is difficult or impossible to understand. Anthony Cerami, professor of biochemistry, says that the "immune system forms a sort of surveillance and combat patrol, ready to fight foreign substances in the body's defense." And Galileo describes the moon's surface as being "spotted as the tail of a peacock is sprinkled with azure eyes." And in a chapter from *The Evolution of Physics*, by Albert Einstein and Leopold Infeld, the authors use the figurative language of the detective story throughout, following the plot, solving the mystery of motion, velocity, and mass in relation to each other. The scientific expert knows that figurative language can often convey meanings to lay readers who would not otherwise comprehend vastness, implication, information, or complexity.

But figurative language, when it is not fresh, is often a hindrance to clear and effective writing. Cliché is the culprit, but cliché may have taken a worse rap than it deserves. A cliché is like old money: once the dollar was crisp; once the coinage was shiny. But overuse has wrinkled the dollar, tarnished the coin. It is true that the trite, the tired, and the overworked expression can often lessen the impact of good writing. But cliché, when it works against itself, can be an effective device both for humor and persuasion. The comedian says, "A day without sunshine is like—pause—night," and the audience roars with laughter. What makes them laugh? The cliché turned on them and offered a twist on old meanings, standard expectations. Even an entire cliché, unrevised, can elicit strong reactions when it turns up in an unusual setting. "What's a nice girl like you doing in a place like this?" is not funny when a bar hopper puts the question to a good-looking and curvaceous customer. But pose the question to a Girl Scout, selling cookies door to door, and even the Girl Scout may snicker. In other words, when you trot out over-worked expressions, do so in crazy, improbable places, and the old workhorse will be a stallion.

Of course, if your writing purposes are purely practical—a memorandum, a company report, the minutes of the last meeting, a short news story about a business promotion, a letter of application—you will want to eschew the figurative and get to the point. Sometimes plain speaking and plain writing are best. You do not want to cast the pearls of figurative language before the swine of daily life.

But sometimes, both in subject matter and purpose, you want to move beyond the literal into the figurative, the creative, the dynamic, the artful. Figurative language does with words what artists do with paint. And the more vivid the picture, the clearer the meaning. The best figurative language leaves the reader, paradoxically, figuratively, speechless.

You are moving toward the imaginative use of the figurative when you ask yourself what hate looks like; why Monday is condemned, always, to being blue; how come envy is invariably green; why ships are female, homes are castles, boys are young bucks, gossip is backstabbing, honor is tall, happiness is rosy. Maybe Monday is purple, envy is yellow, happiness is green as a new leaf. Maybe ships are cats, boys are birds, gossip is luscious and satisfying as a double-dip cone of strawberry ice cream. Home may be jail; honor may be fat; hate may be hot as a romance or icy as a judgment. You are in charge of the fresh images and symbols you create for each writing occasion. You are likewise in charge of making certain the image or figurative expression is exact, poignant, lively, arresting.

Create fresh similes.

A simile is a short comparison using "like" or "as." The great thing about similes is that they are short. The dangerous thing about similes is that they are simple. And when they are simple, they are not always sweet. Their simplicity derives from their ease of construction. Similes are, after all, the most frequently used figures of speech. We use them to explain colors, exotic and alien people, places, behaviors, tastes, abstract ideas, concepts of depth and space, moods, time periods. We use them to clarify what is unknown or intangible or unfamiliar by comparing it to what is recognizable and real.

But similes are often carelessly constructed, tiresome, predictable. You may tend to grab the nearest simile, the one that pops immediately into your head; and the image loses its impact on the reader. You have to spend several minutes, sometimes even hours, looking for ways to confound triteness, cajole originality. And temptations abound to do neither. The old similes will do: red as a rose, happy as a lark, dead as a doornail, skinny as a rail, tall as a tree, deep as the ocean, wise as an owl, dumb as a post, ugly as a mud fence, crazy like a fox, tight as a tick, meek as a lamb, ran like the wind, slept like the dead. These similes will do because they are familiar, handy, close as your next breath.

But similes can be fresh, clarifying, if you spend the time necessary to think in a new way about old comparisons. Similes must be striking to succeed. They will juxtapose unlikely combinations in logical ways. They will then sneak up on the reader, eliciting delight, alarm, understanding.

One of the easiest ways to freshen similes is to substitute a slight variation on an old comparison. No need to travel very far from the tried and trite. The following simile is a slight variation on the motherly admonition, "Eat your spinach like a good girl."

So I picked up the children from kindergarten and went home to fix pot roast for supper, like a good old woman.

You can also achieve freshness by placing very unlikely combinations in proximity. Nobody has ever thought that a moon might be like a stomach, right? Well, the following simile sets the unlikely pair side by side, making a new meaning with an entirely original simile.

My stomach rolled over and sank like a big, pale moon in a shaky sky.

And sometimes the freshness derives from humor. A completely outrageous comparison may elicit a guffaw from bored readers. But humor is hard. You may need to pause and ponder for quite a while before you arrive at the pinnacle of absurdity. Is the filter on your air conditioner dirty? Well, how dirty is it? Is it dirty as a kid's knees at the end of a summer day? Is it dirty as the unspeakable region beneath the refrigerator? No. The filter is worse. You might, if you push yourself to the limits of folly, come up with the following simile:

The filter on my air conditioner was as filthy as a flasher's imagination.

Here are some more similes, all of which achieve their freshness by appearing in unusual or unexpected combinations, by being highly descriptive and concrete, or by varying slightly the typical and trite wording of a standard simile.

Sickness is like patriotism: a little of it can't hurt, but too much of it will kill you.

The excellent reasons for hating line up like crisply attired soldiers at a dress parade.

A childhood fort is like home: it is where, when you go there, they may or may not take you in.

The horizon is blue; the air is cool as a mother's palm on a fevered brow.

The shadows are long and blue, the grass green as creation.

Only the small photograph remains: my mother and I, close as breath, on a soft May morning.

She held the secret as tightly as a child clutches the best, shiniest marble.

◆

Activities

1. Similes are not meaningful out of context, but you can appreciate the difficulty of creating fresh ones when you practice writing them in isolation. Complete the following comparisons in as original a way as possible. Keep in mind, however, that the content of what you are writing usually informs and enhances your use of figurative language.

    The librarian looked like ———.

    The city dump smelled like ———.

    The airplane passenger was as sick as ———.

    The latest hit record was as popular ———.

    Taking the mid-term was like ———.

    Losing my job was like ———.

    Arguing is like ———.

    Studying is like ———.

    Finding something to do in my hometown is like ———.

    Going out on a blind date is like ———.

    My spirits were as low as ———.

    Now, having completed the above similes, select one and let it serve as the topic sentence of a paragraph in which you develop the idea, using similes as the primary method of describing.

2. In the following paragraph, spaces are provided for you to supply your own similes. Do so, striving, of course, for freshness, concreteness, humor, or surprise. When everyone in your class has completed the paragraph to his or her satisfaction, compare the results. Do the different similes make for very different paragraphs? Did other students create similes exactly like or similar to yours? What was the effect of these different similes on the tone of the paragraph? Do fresher similes make for better paragraphs? Why or why not? (*Note:* Remember that your paragraphs would not, as a rule, contain such a large number of similes. Use the device sparingly to achieve dramatic stylistic and descriptive effects.)

The first day I arrived on this campus is as vivid in my memory as ———. My roommate had already settled in like ———, and I could barely find room to store my trunk, hang my posters, set up my records and tapes. I felt like ———. And the roommate was about as friendly as ———. Her (his) face was hostile, the lips tight and thin as ———, the eyes narrow as ———. And the room was equally depressing. The window looked out on the Dempster Dumpster, the walls were painted a vile, indescribable color that looked like ———. The beds were as lumpy as ———. I could see this semester was going to be as awful and endless as ———. I flung myself on the mattress, like ———, and surrendered to a good, long afternoon of self-pity. My roommate had no use for my petulance. She (he) grabbed a jacket and sauntered out of the room, like a ———. When the door closed behind her (him), I forced myself to get up and arrange the room in a manner more to my liking. I took down all of my roommate's pictures, hung curtains at the windows, filled the shelves with my books, played my favorite tapes, and began to feel better. But I knew, as surely as ———, that when the roommate returned, she (he) would be mad as ———. The thought made me smile like ———.

Use unmixed, arresting metaphors.

A metaphor, like a simile, is a comparison, but the comparison is not explicit and the words "like" or "as" do not link the things being compared. Does that definition sound confusing? Well, metaphors are a bit more complicated than similes, and often more effective. Metaphors, for example, may be short, but they may also run on over several sentences or paragraphs. Here are two examples of metaphors. One is very short, and one extends over several sentences.

When you are happy, the world is home, and you are easy in it.

Notice that the comparison is not literally true. This short metaphor provides a figurative way to explain and define one of the effects of happiness. The world is not, in reality, home, but happiness makes for cozy comfort, safety, security, peace. So the short metaphor explains a feeling.

The next metaphor extends over several sentences, but the language of the metaphor is consistent.

Procrastination and sloth are not the same as not trying. The person who dares to trust and wait on his own creative sparks, his special epiphanies, is neither inert nor lazy. He is a poised cat, waiting to strike, to alight nimbly on the right moment, the best opportunity, the choicest morsel of experience. He always lands on all fours and, without a sound, walks off with the prize in his mouth, as if it were his due.

This extended metaphor compares a confident, relaxed person to a cat. The metaphor runs through the paragraph consistently, using only the language of catdom—poised cat, waiting to strike, alighting nimbly, taking the choicest morsel, landing on all fours, soundlessly and a bit arrogantly walking off with the prize. What would be the effect on the paragraph if the writer began by comparing the confident person to a cat and then, without warning, turned the cat in mid-metaphor into an eagle, making the cat soar and swoop, snatch the prize of luck in its beak, fly off in grand style? Cats don't swoop, don't have beaks, can't fly. So the metaphor would be illogical if any figurative language, other than that which relates to cats, made a sudden appearance.

Metaphors set up connections between unlikely pairs: government is the ship of state; the crowd is a thundering herd; life is a bowl of cherries. These metaphors are, of course, clichés, but they enable you to comprehend more readily what metaphors are all about and how often you use them. Government is not really a ship. Crowds are not cattle or sheep. And life, on a bad day, is hardly a bowl of cherries; very likely, it is a bitter brew.

Metaphors must be logical, consistent, unmixed, pure. The *New Yorker* carries an amusing feature called "Block That Metaphor." Subscribers send in *mixed metaphors* they have read or heard, and often the mix is very funny, as well as enlightening, to those of you who have trouble understanding and using metaphors effectively. Sometimes the way to learn how to do something well is to see examples of how *not* to do it. Here follows a badly mixed metaphor, both illogical and possibly hilarious:

> We can't lick the monster of inflation unless we can carry the ball of fiscal responsibility over the goal line and corral the public into some serious belt-tightening.

The language of this sentence is entirely figurative, metaphorical, but the metaphor is not sustained logically throughout. How could you unmix the metaphor? You would need to select one metaphor among the four that appear in this illogical sentence and stay with your choice throughout. What are the four metaphors in this sentence? Inflation is a monster that needs killing. So the language of monster and hunter, of sword and spear, of victor and victim, could explain the danger in the economic arena. Or you might choose the sports metaphor, writing about economic problems and solutions in terms of fouls, goals, touchdowns, victory. Or perhaps you like the metaphor of the Wild West and choose to discuss economics by using the language of the rodeo: corralling, riding out, wearing down, and subduing the bucking bronco of uncontrollable inflation. Or you might put government and consumers on a diet, trimming excess fat, tightening belts, striving for lean spending, eliminating waste, using up leftovers. The point, however, is that you must choose one metaphor, one implied comparison, and stay with it to the end of the thought.

Metaphors, like similes, can be very helpful in explaining or describing what is difficult for the reader to understand or see. And their effective use can also add vitality and sophistication to many kinds of writing, even writing that is decidedly unliterary in purpose and tone. A scientific book may bear the title *Frontiers of Science,* for example, and the metaphorical language would perhaps be of pioneers, exploration, discovery, the subduing of the wilderness of ignorance about scientific advancements. And metaphors can also clarify psychological or philosophical meanings. Psychiatrists may speak of the "mirrors of the mind." Philosophers and educators may speak of "the royal road to learning." Clerics may describe conversion as a "mountaintop experience," though the conversion took place in the flatlands of depression or the ruts of daily life. In other words, metaphors use other words to explain this word, other objects to explain this object, other images to explain this image.

◆

Activities

1. In the following examples, you will see metaphors used in logical, unmixed ways. As you study these examples, identify the things being compared and the related words that sustain the metaphor over several words or sentences.

   My body is my house. Every now and then, I get busy and clean it up, knowing very well that some wear and tear are unavoidable. I claim my right to some depreciation and decay. My body can't last a lifetime without accumulating some nicks, scratches, leaks, and dust, the effects of living all the way and hard.

   The way to happiness is absolutely blocked for the depressed person. This person is at the bottom of a mine shaft, a wall of rocks between him and the dim voices, the lanterns, the human concern on the other side.

   Tips, if you aren't careful, have a way of getting into your blood and ruining your health. The tip bug can even be fatal.

   I collect properly prideful people and their grand accomplishments and put them on the shelf of my mind, along with my own special trophies.

   The difference between me and Pammy Lou is that her religious conversion "took," and mine eased off after a few days of bed rest and plenty of fluids.

   Looking back over the family tree, I could see some skewed branches here and there, some fig trees that sprouted bananas.

   In life, all of us like to know where we are, how many steps to take, what direction to follow, what obstacles block our paths. We don't want always to be groping along dark corridors, feeling our way for the light switch, cracking our shins against the furniture, monsters and demons close behind us, nipping our heels and breathing down our necks.

2. The following list provides both sides of the comparison: the literal meaning and the figurative treatment of it. Select one, and write a paragraph in which you sustain the suggested metaphor over several sentences. You will need, of course, to develop a topic sentence or controlling idea for the paragraph, but the suggested metaphor may provide direction and focus.

post—holiday bargain-seekers—tigers and sheep

inability to make decisions—house of mirrors and mazes at the fair

making a good life for yourself—sewing a quilt

falling in love—illness

getting caught up on work and chores—war

taking a trip—eating

caring for your car—psychotherapy

perfect people—machines

first date—clown act

liberal arts and science—ballet

estrangement from close friend—winter

winning an election—sports

debate—boxing or fencing

writing a poem—jigsaw puzzle

3. Look for examples of metaphors and similes in three ads for the same product (for instance, cat food, cars, perfume). Write a paragraph analyzing the effective and ineffective uses of the figurative devices.

Personify ideas, abstractions.

Being human, we all to varying degrees like to re-create the world in our own image, to give human characteristics and actions to ideas, inanimate objects, or natural phenomena. Every time we name a hurricane "Ada" or "Albert" and analyze her or his temperamental streak, we are personifying. Personification differs from metaphor in this crucial way: with metaphor, we establish an implicit comparison between objects or ideas that does not derive from human behavior or physical appearance. A metaphor may turn a person into a machine, but personification turns a machine into a person. The washing machine flirts with the dryer. The blender winks at the can opener.

As with simile and metaphor, personification offers ways to see and understand, to describe and particularize what is hard to express. Personification is the mainstay of love songs. If we cannot see, taste, or touch love, we can give love human characteristics and capabilities: love walks right in and drives the shadows away; love heaves and sighs and weeps and teases and plans and daydreams. Love often has lips (red), flowing hair (golden), hands (tender).

But personification is not merely a way of communicating ideas that are hard to express. It is also a way of discovering connections and remembering them. The Greeks and Romans, for example, personified tendencies in the human spirit through divine myths. Gods and goddesses are, after all, abstractions given psychic reality through personification: the concept of war finds its expression in the humanized form of Ares; the sun finds its expression in the humanized form of Helios; the idea of heaven finds its expression in the god Uranus, who mated with Gaea, the goddess of Earth. Why did the Greeks and Romans create deities who behaved in all the complex, turbulent, specific ways humans behave? Because personification provides a way to externalize inner emotions, thoughts, impulses.

Of course, personification has stepped down in recent times from its ancient throne of meaning. Now, the figurative device shows up in mundane, absurd settings. The cleanser talks to the toilet bowl. The margarine snaps at the butter. America is a top-hatted Uncle Sam. Love is sexy and whimsical, not stately and devoted. But though times have changed, we continue to use personification to convey meanings that would otherwise leave us tongue-tied, fumbling, inarticulate.

The following examples show personification at work in excerpts from essays, making abstract ideas concrete, establishing connections between the tangible and intangible worlds, providing a way to express the inexpressible—to touch, taste, smell, feel, and see what would otherwise remain hidden. Notice how, in each example, the personification is specific, the results fresh, the image clear. Personification is an excellent descriptive device, especially when the figure of speech appears in an unlikely setting. When you do not know what to do with a feeling, frustration, or idea, make it walk, talk, strut, dance, cry, pout. The reader will catch the meaning in the concrete and human rendering of it.

But Nature is smart. Nature has a warped sense of humor. Sometimes Nature is downright malicious.

On July 4, 1776, America, a rebellious teenager, stalked out of the House of England and got her own apartment.

Spring fever is tender, lilting, sexy. The sap is very pleased to be up and at your service.

I never met a number I could trust.

Sleep and I have had a long, disquieting relationship. Sleep is a strange bedfellow.

If you dread the passing of each minute, you might as well relax and acquaint yourself with Time's affable, companionable side. Time will get you out of a tight place. Time will teach you a thing or two. If you cooperate, Time may even favor you with gentle smiles and graceful gestures.

After you have found the fear, you have to wrestle it to the ground and lick it good. Or you have to stare it down. Or maybe you have to live with it until the fear turns into an old, mildly disagreeable friend. But, in any case, you won't be able to pull the covers over your head and pretend it isn't there. That's a child's way of handling fear. You know better. You know too much.

◆

Activities

1. Turn the following inanimate objects or ideas into people, making them do, in one sentence, anything a person might do.

Examples:

Local bar—The joint was jumping.

Four-leaf clover—The four-leaf clover hid in the grass, winking its good luck to the gloomy child.

Scissors—"Apparently the scissors just got up and walked off all by themselves," said the irate mother to the children.

Now you try it.

Laundry	Car
Juke box	Horizon
Hate	Cloud
Sloth	Hope
Lust	Linoleum
Dust	

Note: As you create examples of personification, be aware of certain risks in using the device. Sometimes personification can produce absurd or sentimental images—as when a student wrote, "The trees held hands around the pond." Or a bad poet might write, "The sun kissed the blushing face of the tulip."

2. Now, choose one of the sentences you created and let it serve as the topic sentence for a paragraph in which you continue to discuss the idea or object in human terms.

10
Revising the Essay

Take a professional approach to revision.

When you roll your first draft out of the typewriter or affix the last period to the concluding sentence, you may think you have finished the writing assignment. But you have only begun. The first draft was very likely composed in confident haste or tentative exploration. You were intent primarily on getting your overall organizational scheme in order. Your mind was busy with theme and thesis, not with refinements and subtleties. As you wrote, you may have noticed that in certain places in the essay the tone shifted, the energy flagged, the point veered off unexpectedly. But you shrugged your shoulders and pressed on, not wishing to quibble with yourself and your meanings until you had first set down that initial draft.

Though everyone's writing approach varies somewhat, most people in the first draft are simply trying to get down the whole argument or body of information. And they are right to move quickly. Too much pausing and pondering at this early writing stage could block creativity, could cause the writer to lose the thought even as he or she is starting the next sentence. You are wise, at this point, not to agonize over a word choice, not to worry that the source for the quotation escapes you at the moment, not to panic when an appropriate example does not come to mind. Writing offers multiple opportunities to polish, refine, and change both the content of the essay and the expression of it.

But having completed the whole essay, you are then ready to do the highly disciplined work of revising and editing what is, in fact, a rough draft. Professional writer Elizabeth Hardwick once commented that her rough drafts looked like "chicken scratch." Perhaps yours is not as primitive. Certainly, some drafts are rougher than others. Some students express their ideas rather easily and produce, with only a little revision, creditable essays. But most students—and experienced writers as well—may re-write an essay several times before they achieve the desired effect.

If you approach your writing tasks with the respect and care an editor or a professional writer displays toward a prospective manuscript, you will see surprising results. You may even achieve a remarkable union of idea and form. We call that union "art." Writer Raymond Carver understands the relationship between creation and revision. In his essay "On Writing,"[1] he cites a quotation from a story by Isaac Babel: "No iron can pierce the heart with such force as a period put at just the right place." Carver admires writers who shun tricks—glitz, if you will—and rely, instead, on careful revision, ordinary words, precise punctuation, and sound logic to achieve sublime effects. He reminds us that all we have are "the words, and they had better be the right ones, with the punctuation in the right places so they can best say what they are meant to say." Carver concludes, "If the words are heavy with the writer's own unbridled emotions, or if they are imprecise and inaccurate for some other reason—if the words are in any way blurred—the reader's eyes will slide right over them and nothing will be achieved." Carver is correct. And his message is inspired as well. It should come as no surprise that Carver's favorite phase of writing is revision and that he is happy tinkering with a manuscript until it behaves exactly as he envisioned it would.

Perhaps, as you proceed through the important steps following the initial draft, you will come to understand what fine writers already know: the tension between invention and rigorous control, between getting your ideas down and getting them right, is, well, fundamental to writing well. Don't settle, simply, for pricking your readers' minds. Go on. Pierce their hearts.

---

[1] If you wish to read further, see Raymond Carver, "On Writing," in *Fires: Essays, Poems, Stories* (New York: Random House, 1984).

Make several drafts.

Revising means, literally, "looking back" or "looking again." Between the first draft and the second, you pause an hour or a day for reflection about what you have written, where it succeeds, how it fails. Good writers let the rough draft rest for a while, until they have had time to ponder what they wrote and to return to the first draft with greater objectivity and detachment. It is odd that standing back a bit would help you to "see" better. But such is the case, whether in writing or life. The problem that gnawed at you for hours suddenly resolves itself simply because you busied yourself by chewing on somebody else's problem. So, too, with the rough draft. Standing up too close and too soon may deceive you. The rough draft you just wrote looks super, fantastic, when it is brand new. A day later, a blush may come to your cheek as you reread the fantastic essay and find that it is merely foolish. Or the reverse may occur. You may think the rought draft you just finished is awful, but discover, upon returning to it later, that it's not bad, not bad at all.

But after you have given some distance to the initial draft, you will need to begin the tinkering and fine tuning that will make the essay hum, not clank. The following questions will lead you to effective revision.

1. Is my central theme or thesis clear, and does it appear early enough in the essay to alert the reader to my overall purpose?

2. Do all the supporting paragraphs relate to, defend, prove, or inform my thesis or central idea?

3. Does each paragraph have a central idea or a structural purpose (for example, providing necessary transitions)?

4. Are phrases, sentences, and paragraphs properly connected by appropriate transitional words and phrases?

5. Are the examples, details, facts, anecdotes, procedures, comparisons, contrasts, causes, and effects vivid, concrete, appealing as often as possible to the five senses, creating clear mental pictures for the reader?

6. Are all the details and proofs in the paragraphs relevant to the central idea in the paragraph and to the overall theme or thesis?

7. Does the argument or development move forward climactically? Do I save my best arguments, examples, and anecdotes for last?

8. Are there gaps in meaning, illogical assertions, requiring the addition of further explanatory material?

9. Does the introduction entice? Does the conclusion wittily or tidily sum up the central idea in the essay?

10. Is the tone even, appropriate for the subject and the audience, and natural to me and my personality?

11. Is the language fresh and clear, free of cliché, jargon, slang, colloquialisms? (Of course, slang and colloquialisms are sometimes appropriate in certain writing contexts—perhaps in fiction, poetry, humorous essays.)

12. Are the sentences varied in structure and length, pleasing to the ear and eye?

Here follows a very short essay, undergoing revision from the first to the second draft.

Rough draft:

Nobody would argue that shyness is a crippling social and professional ailment; nobody would deny that shy people painfully stumble through their days, unable even to rap with close friends, to make a simple purchase in a department store, to summon the courage to answer the telephone. There is surely debate about the cause of the shy person's inability to interface with people on a basically intimate and relaxed level. Could it be that shy people are really egotists at heart, more obsessed with themselves than with others?

Study the personality behind the docile exterior of a shy person, and you will detect an awesome preoccupation with himself or herself. Shyness does not spring from a desire to defer to and respect the other person. It is the offspring of pride. The shy person is seldom interested in what the other person has to say. When a shy person hears somebody tittering nearby, he assumes the other person is laughing at him. When a stranger looks at a shy person, the shy person thinks the stranger actually notices an unattractive hairdo, a pimple, an ill-fitting outfit. When shy people get up to address an audience, they quiver and shake primarily because they are anxious to impress the audience, not deliver information. In short, a shy person thinks, though his or her self-esteem may be low, though his or her confidence may be zilch, that the eyes of the world are trained on him and him alone.

Shy people could begin to cure their illness if they would only swallow a dose of genuine modesty. Reason would teach them that most people are not looking at them, not listening to them, not judging them harshly or favorably. The task at hand, the problems of others, the beauty in a sunset, the vast and various world beyond the narrowly absorbed shy person would change the focus considerably. If the shy person looked outward rather than inward, became lost in the things and chores and people Out There, he or she would very likely begin to feel more relaxed, more confident, more outgoing. In fact, the word "outgoing" is perfect for describing what happens when a formerly shy person finally stops thinking only about himself.

You begin to re-see the rough draft, which is to say revise it, when you critically evaluate the first attempt. What are the problems in this essay? Where does it succeed? You can carry on a critical conversation with yourself in the following way.

1. Where's the title?

2. The thesis is clear, but the expression of it is awkward, too tentative for forceful writing.

3. Though the introduction moves, as it should, from more general assertions to a particular point, the beginning is not lively, arresting.

4. The middle is muddled. Do I need to break up the central paragraph into two or three ideas? The arrangement is not climactic. Few concrete images, details.

5. The language could be fresher, more appropriate. Have I eliminated cliché (metaphor of shyness as illness), slang ("rap," "zilch"), jargon ("interface"), overworked expressions ("basically intimate and relaxed level")?

6. Is the conclusion memorable, snappy? Probably not. Can I find a new way to restate thesis and expand meaning?

7. Sentences are too long and involved. I'll try to vary lengths and structures, alternating between more involved sentences and short, crisp ones.

8. Dominant developmental scheme okay. Causes and effects. But do I need to use other methods of development and support? More description. Some definition.

Revision:

SHY PEOPLE: SELF-EFFACING OR SELF-ABSORBED?

Take a survey on the causes of shyness, and the responses would likely be predictable as the knocking knees, trembling lips, and sweaty palms of a shy person being introduced at a cocktail party. Shyness, most people assume, is related to modesty, low self-esteem, humility. Shy people are even believed to be selfless, given to sacrifice, willing to place themselves last in the queue of life. Shy people are often called introverts. But what is introversion, after all, but a turning inward, a concentration on the self? Shyness may, in reality, be a form of pride; and shy people may be, in reality, egotists at heart.

Look behind the docile exterior of a shy person, and you may be surprised to encounter the roaring monster of "me, me, me." All the questions shy people ask focus directly on them, and no one else: "What will I say?" "How will I act?" "Do you think anybody will notice my tie's crooked, my hem's pinned up, I've gained five pounds?" The harsh reality is, of course, that nobody does. Shy people forget the paradox—namely, that the less they think about themselves, the more they will be noticed, appreciated, admired.

Shy people fail in social and professional situations because they cannot admit that failure is fine. At a party, they cannot listen to the conversation, so busy are they trying to formulate their next witty remark. At a committee meeting, they can sacrifice the entire business project solely because they mispronounced a word or dropped a page of the feasibility study on the boardroom floor. Shy people do not recover well from errors because they assume, in their fantasies, that they must be perfect.

How does the shy person rid himself or herself of egotism? The solution is, of course, selflessness, not the kind that is sacrificial but the kind that is self-forgetting. The personality that is pleasing to most folks is outgoing, not inward turning. And to be outgoing is to give little or no thought to the impression, image, or impact we have on friends and strangers. Piling paradox on paradox, shy people will discover, to their amazement, that the less attention they pay to themselves, the more attention they will be paid by others.

The revision is an improvement. The thesis is tighter, more forcefully presented. The writer has included more details, a few direct quotations. And the middle paragraphs now fall into two categories: a paragraph of analysis, followed by a paragraph of examples of shyness in social and professional settings. Sentence lengths and structures are more varied. The introduction is tighter, the conclusion a bit snappier. Of course, the second draft is not perfect, but it is better than the first.

Omit unnecessary words.

You may be surprised to learn that the word "edit" literally means to cut or to delete. In fact, this rather narrow definition of one important phase of revision describes a professional editor's task. She will apply her blue pencil to a prospective manuscript, but the pencil might well be a scalpel, expertly excising any word, phrase, sentence, or paragraph that seems redundant, irrelevant, gratuitous, or inappropriate. Sometimes the cuts make a writer bleed.

Critical Cuts

Over the years, my pride has occasionally been wounded by the surgical removal of what I considered to be my best sentence, my cleverest example, my most vivid detail. Then I learned from a fellow writer—a poet—that judicious cutting and tightening can strengthen my meanings. She said, and I have not forgotten the advice, that a good writer learns to toss out a jewel of a sentence as if it were nothing but a dime-store bauble. Why? Very simply, in trying to preserve and showcase what the writer believes to be a perfect gem of a sentence, he or she may sacrifice or cheapen the larger context of the whole essay. The advice was good, and I continue to remember it each time a cut hurts.

Remember that a word, phrase, or sentence is not valuable or essential simply because you wrote it. It is useful only to the degree that it enhances your meaning, adds to your argument, clarifies your intention. As you learn to tighten your writing, you will develop the confidence and maturity to let go of any part of the essay that detracts from or mars the overall impact. The following guidelines will help you decide what to omit and what to retain.

Delete irrelevant words, sentences, or paragraphs.

Did you find yourself, midway through the essay about the importance of quality day care for youngsters, making an impassioned plea for better nursing homes for the elderly? Did you find yourself, midway through the paragraph describing the coins in your collection, suddenly mentioning the butterflies you have netted? Obviously, these unrelated passages have got to go. The clarity and purpose inherent in your thesis and topic sentences will usually keep you from wandering over alien country.

In the following paragraph, what details, facts, and examples would you cut?

> Generalizers are made, not born. The best quality about little children is their wonderful capacity for the concrete, though children are certainly cute and cuddly as well. Toddlers aren't vague. If they want water, they ask for it. If they think you're ugly, they kick you in the shins. And if you're smart, you'll run the other way. Usually, when babies are allowed to get away with kicking and biting, the parents have not disciplined them. Children's questions are as straightforward and specific as the ones great scientists have always asked: Is the earth flat or round? Why does an apple fall? Where does the sky get its blue? Do I have to go to bed now? Then society gets hold of them and before you can say blah, blah, blah, the children are talking and writing like grown-ups.

And which details or facts are irrelevant in the next paragraph?

> My grandmother taught me the proper way to weed a garden. In the early morning, when the ground was moist with dew, the birds were chirping, the breakfast dishes were done, the front hall swept, she led me into the yard and placed in my small, chubby, waiting hand—the one with the bitten fingernails and the chipped red nail polish—a tool of some sort. The tool might be a stainless steel spoon from the kitchen or a trowel from the greenhouse. She then showed me how to get all the way down underneath the dandelion plants covering the yard like millions of tiny suns glistening in the universe. She said, "Don't just yank up the dandelion. You've got to get all the way underneath it and take it up by the roots." After promising me a

penny a weed, money she suggested I put in a savings account for college, she left me to my weed-digging task. This small chore taught me responsibility and helped me, when I grew up, to be a better lawyer.

Eliminate redundancies.

A redundancy carries repetition to the point of absurdity. Repetition in writing is often a fine stylistic device, a way to emphasize meanings. But redundancy is unnecessary repetition. It is silly, like somebody's saying, "I'm traveling on a trip to Los Angeles out west because my sister is pregnant and is going to have a baby and I'll be an uncle and have a nephew or niece."

Major redundancies, the unnecessary repetition of whole sentences or paragraphs, are usually the result of careless thinking and careless editing. You endlessly reiterate the point when you should be proving or developing it. The content is "tautological" or "circular." The redundancies are unmistakable in the following paragraph.

   Vandalism is the willful and malicious destruction of private or public property. When people vandalize, they go around defacing statues and buildings. They often also tear up houses and yards that belong to other people. Sometimes vandals even destroy their own property. To vandalize is, therefore, both vicious and mean. And vandalism is, furthermore, intentional, not accidental.

Though the above paragraph may look as though it is going somewhere, giving examples, it clearly is not. Each sentence is simply a reiteration of the topic sentence. The transitional words create a comic effect, giving the impression that the writer is drawing conclusions, arriving at meaning.

But sometimes redundancies are minor, having to do with individual words, often containing prefixes with meanings the writer does not comprehend. In such cases, the single word contains the complete meaning, but the writer relentlessly attaches one more prefix or whole word to the complete word. The following list of small redundancies may amuse you out of context. But they sometimes slip into the essays of even very good writers, and, in revision, must be deleted. Find the redundancies in the following list.

new innovations	open up
revert back	empty out
irregardless	advance forward
raise up	set down
unite together	maximize to the fullest
connect up	link up
in the final conclusion	at the original beginning
long ago in the past	in the future ahead
at the lowest nadir	at the highest zenith
the reason why	the resulting effect
the fundamental basics	the central core
in the modern world today	in today's modern society

Combine phrases, clauses, and short sentences.

You can attach less important ideas to main ideas, incorporate separate but equally important ideas into a list, let one verb or one subject do the work of several, or change a complete thought to a phrase and attach the phrase to another complete thought.

Don't write:

I like to go fishing. The activity calms me. I sit beside the pond, and I watch the birds flying overhead. They make fantastic formations. Every now and then, a fish tugs at my bait, and I am stirred out of my revery. I don't much care, however, whether the fish gets away. It is enough for me to watch the birds and wait for another bite. I can doze beside the pond all day. I am very good at doing nothing.

Write instead:

Going fishing calms me. I sit beside the pond, watching the birds flying overhead in fantastic formation. Now and then a fish tugs at my bait, stirring me out of my revery. But I don't much care whether the fish gets away, since I'm very good at doing nothing. All day I doze, watch the birds, wait for another bite.

The writer has cut 22 words from the above paragraph, simply by combining sentences, phrases, and clauses. Yet no detail or assertion is lost in the revision.

After you have followed the appropriate editorial guidelines through at least two drafts, you may assume that the essay is as tight and compact as the pantry in a Winnebago. But an essay is seldom as snug and concise as you think. Even in as advanced a writing stage as the third draft, you will discover loose or nonessential cargo. Good writers are boldly battening down their meanings until the last moment. They follow the sound editorial procedures that result in tighter, stronger essays: deleting irrelevant details, eliminating redundancies, combining smaller elements into more effective sentences. Can they toss out certain relative pronouns? Should they let one adjective do the work of two? Is there yet another subordinate clause that could just as easily be a phrase? The editor's pencil is always poised above words that add nothing to the content.

The third draft may be simply a matter of tightening. Good editors know that what you leave out is as important as what you put in. If you are uncertain about what to keep and what to throw away, you might learn from a sculptor's analogy. Asked how he approached a shapeless rock and transformed it into a magnificent stallion, the sculptor said that he just kept on chipping away at the rock until the horse emerged. The artist knew the horse was in there. His task was not to make a horse out of a rock but to find the horse that was inside the rock all along. The artist just kept working until everything that was not a horse was gone. In much the same way, you will be chipping away at your early drafts until everything that is not your idea is gone.

In the third draft of the essay on shyness, the writer has tightened the content, using the guidelines for effective editing discussed in this section.

Third draft:

SHY PEOPLE: SELF-EFFACING OR SELF-ABSORBED?

Take a survey on the causes of shyness, and the results would be predictable as the knocking knees and sweaty palms of a shy person at a cocktail party. Shyness, people assume, is related to modesty, low self-esteem. Shy people are selfless, sacrificial, willing to put themselves last in the queue of life. They are introverts, but introversion is, after all, a turning inward, a concentration on the self. Shyness is, in reality, pride; and shy people are egotists at heart.

Look behind the docile exterior of a shy person, and you will encounter the roaring monster of "me, me, me." Shy people think only of themselves: "What will I say?" "How should I act?" "Do you think anybody will notice I've gained five pounds and my tie is crooked?" The harsh reality, of course, is that nobody does.

Shy people fail socially and professionally because they can't admit that failure is fine. At a party, they're so busy formulating their next witty remark that they don't listen to the conversation. At a committee meeting, they sacrifice a fat business deal over a mispronounced word or a page of the feasibility study they clumsily dropped on the boardroom floor. Shy people don't recover well from errors because they fantasize that they must be perfect.

How do shy people rid themselves of egotism? The solution is selflessness, not sacrificial but self-forgetting. Pleasing personalities are outgoing, not inward turning. To be outgoing is to give little or no thought to the impression, image, or impact we have on friends or strangers. Piling paradox on paradox, shy people are amazed to discover that the less attention they pay to themselves, the more attention they are paid.

Avoid common mistakes.

Go into any bookstore in America, and you will find, lined up like grandiose promises of instant success, a whole series of *Made Simple* books, dealing with everything from patio building to trigonometry to physics. Well, grammar is not simple. But neither is it mysterious, illogical, or a matter of personal preference or opinion. The more you learn about eliminating distracting errors from the surfaces of your essay, the more you will be impressed with the certainties and consistencies of clear, correct writing. Grammar, after all, is a systematic study of language that operates according to regular principles and practices. Arrangements of words, arrangements of those words into sentences, punctuation of those structures, and standard usage—all constitute *grammar*.

As you are revising your initial draft, after you have omitted unnecessary words, you are then ready to scrutinize your writing, looking for common errors and finding ways to correct them. Become familiar with the particular flaws that recur time and again in your own writing. Understand the solutions to these problems. You will be rewarded with an essay that displays, in the words of poet William Butler Yeats, both "passion and precision."

Be aware of grammatical trouble spots.

As you examine your second or third draft, consider the following general rules.

Make subjects and verbs agree in number. If your instructor has, at some stage of the writing process, made the marginal notation "agr," then your essay contains an agreement error. You have placed a plural verb with a singular subject or a plural subject with a singular verb.

I suppose you could go through life not encouraging a subject to agree with its verb, but the racket these two make disagreeing would often disturb the tranquillity of your communication. In song lyrics or casual conversation, you might hear the following subject–verb disagreements (the parenthetical elements contain the appropriate agreement):

We has been had. (instead of "we have")

He weren't going to Abilene. (instead of "he wasn't")

There is some pickles in the barrel. (instead of "are pickles")

Weren't it heaven last night? (instead of "wasn't it")

It don't matter. (instead of "it doesn't matter")

You was mean to me, baby. (instead of "you were")

But what is fine in everyday speech or on the stage of the Grand Ole Opry will not be appropriate in this particular writing context. Here are some reminders of ways to avoid agreement errors.

Make certain that you have identified the correct words as subjects. Words like "there" or "here" are never subjects, though they may deceive you by appearing just before the verb. These words are, in fact, adverbs and never determine the number of the verb. The single line indicates the subject(s) and the double lines indicate the verb(s).

There <u>are</u> (not "is") two <u>captains</u> on each team.

Here <u>come</u> (not "comes") <u>Ruth</u> and <u>Naomi</u>.

Sometimes compound subjects joined by the word "and" may require singular verbs because the compound subject is being treated as a single unit.

<u>Dessert</u> and <u>coffee</u> <u>is</u> the fitting conclusion to a fine meal.

The <u>producer</u> and <u>director</u> of the show <u>is</u> a former actor.

(Compare: The <u>producer</u> and <u>director</u> <u>are</u> former actors.)

School subjects that end in "s" are treated as single units. But the same words are plural when they are not naming courses of study.

<u>Genetics</u> <u>involves</u> (not "involve") the study of the transmission of inherited traits.

The veterinarian said that the <u>genetics</u> of the pigs <u>were</u> (not "was") <u>being</u> closely <u>monitored</u>.

When compound subjects are joined by dividing words like "or" rather than combining words like "and," let the subject nearer the verb determine its number.

Bed <u>rest</u> or <u>fluids</u> <u>are</u> the typical prescriptions for a virus.

<u>Fluids</u> or bed <u>rest</u> <u>is</u> the typical prescription for a virus.

Make pronouns refer unambiguously to a specific antecedent.   Perhaps, at some point in your writing, the instructor may have circled a pronoun (very likely a demonstrative pronoun) and scribbled "ref" above it. Your problem is vague or ambiguous reference. Because pronouns are, after all, noun substitutes, they must have a clear antecedent. Remember that pronouns cannot refer to groups of words, only to individual nouns or pronouns.

Unclear reference:

> The tractor trailer and the car collided, but its driver was not charged with a safe-moving violation.

Revision:

> The tractor trailer and the car collided, but the driver of the Oldsmobile was not charged with a safe-moving violation.

Vague or ambiguous reference:

> I lost my job, which disappointed my family.

Revision:

> The loss of my job disappointed my family. (relative clause with reference error eliminated)

Vague or ambiguous reference:

> We were underpaid, and this made us angry.

Revision:

> We were underpaid, and this injustice made us angry. (demonstrative pronoun transformed into a demonstrative adjective)

As you check your draft for correct pronoun usage, pay special attention to sentences beginning with any of the demonstrative pronouns (this, that, these, those). These pronouns are most likely to create reference problems. You can easily solve the problems by making certain that you change the demonstrative pronouns into adjectives. Simply add an appropriate noun for "this," "that," "these," or "those" to modify.

Put pronouns in the correct case form.   Do not rely on your ear to detect errors in pronoun case. The error in correct use of the objective case forms is so common that your ear will deceive you. What seems right is actually wrong. Only a clear understanding of all pronoun case forms will remedy these particular errors. Oddly enough, if the pronoun sounds right, it is probably wrong. So be wary of assuming that your pronouns are in the appropriate case. The following examples are correct. Compare them to the pronouns in your own essay.

> The students and <u>we</u> (not "us") gave Hal and <u>her</u> (not "she") high praise.

> The gift was for Mabel and <u>me</u> (not "I").

> Liz said the secret was just between <u>her</u> (not "she") and <u>me</u> (not "I").

> The boss is fussier than <u>I</u> (not "me").

> I will select <u>whomever</u> (not "whoever") I prefer.

> Invite <u>whoever</u> (not "whomever") wants to come.

Eliminate double comparatives or double superlatives. Adjectives, after all, have specific forms to indicate the degree of comparison (positive, comparative, and superlative). When you double the degrees, you needlessly repeat yourself.

> more astute (not "more astuter")
> smartest (not "most smartest")
> more friendly or friendlier (not "more friendlier")

Do not use adjectives that denote one of a kind or absolute concepts as though these adjectives had degrees. Careful writers avoid giving degrees to words such as "perfect" or "unique."

> He had a unique idea. (not "the most unique")

> Her holiday was perfect. (not "more perfect" than she expected)

Eliminate the awkward use of nouns as adjectives. If an appropriate adjectival form is available, use it.

> Executives studied the <u>industrial</u> report. (not the "industry" report)

The senator entered the <u>presidential</u> race (not "president" race)

(Compare <u>football</u> field, <u>police</u> department)

Use the possessive forms of nouns and pronouns before gerunds.

<u>Estelle's</u> constant studying made me feel guilty.

The coach applauded the <u>players'</u> having a mature attitude toward losing.

I objected to <u>their</u> (not "them") arriving late.

<u>My</u> (not "me") being punctual is something of an obsession.

None of us liked <u>his</u> (not "him") assuming that we would take on the kitchen duties.

Clear up confusing punctuation signals.

A professional writer knows that marks of punctuation provide excellent ways to clarify meanings and define grammatical structures. They, therefore, do not feel they are wasting valuable time when they check and recheck these marks for placement and accuracy. One writer commented that he knew his writing effort was nearing completion when he began to go through the essay, scrutinizing each comma and deciding whether or not there was a valid reason for its presence in the sentence. Similarly, punctuation revision is an important step in the finishing and refining of your content. As you go through your draft, use the following guidelines to resolve questions about tricky or confusing placement of these useful marks.

Insert commas before coordinating conjunctions joining main clauses.

Compare:

The neighborhood <u>citizens</u> <u>protested</u> the construction of a four-lane highway; but <u>they</u> <u>discovered</u> the city council had already decided in favor of the thoroughfare. (conjunction joining main clauses)

The neighborhood <u>citizens</u> <u>protested</u> the construction of a four-lane highway but <u>discovered</u> <u>the</u> city council had already decided in favor of the thoroughfare. (conjunction joining predicates)

Adults learn quickly that they will repeat the mistakes their parents made and that they will make new ones as well. (conjunction joining subordinate clauses)

The dandelion is a common perennial plant, and its young leaves are edible. (conjunction joining main clauses)

Insert a comma following a short introductory phrase if it is needed to prevent misreading.

Compare:

<u>Around</u> <u>town</u> Joe was known as quite a social butterfly. (no comma necessary)

<u>Flying</u> <u>around</u>, the pilot hit an air pocket. (comma needed to prevent misreading)

Place commas both before and after nonrestrictive modifiers, parenthetical expressions, and adverbs appearing in the middle of the sentence.

Don't write:

Buffalo Bill, whose real name was William Frederick Cody toured with a Wild West Show.

Then too, you must learn to be patient.

Write instead:

Buffalo Bill, whose real name was William Frederick Cody, toured with a Wild West Show.

Then, too, you must learn to be patient.

Compare:

> The boy who cried the loudest got the most attention. (restrictive)
>
> Sammy, who cried the loudest, got the most attention. (nonrestrictive)

Insert a comma correctly between coordinate adjectives. You can double check on the necessity for placing a comma between coordinate adjectives by asking yourself whether or not each adjective modifies the noun following. If the first of the modifiers does not, then it is an adverb, not an adjective, and no comma is necessary.

Compare:

> the rather tall fellow (not "rather, tall fellow")
>
> the agile, tall fellow (not "agile tall fellow")
>
> ("Rather" modifies "tall," not "fellow," and is therefore an adverb.)

Replace confusing commas between larger elements with semicolons. Sometimes a sentence may be so overloaded with commas that readers have difficulty making sense of the structures the commas are defining. Here is an example of comma overload:

> Finally, after hours of moaning about how incredibly bored he is, a gleam will settle in Joe's eye, the doorbell will, at last, ring, Billy will stand outside, wanting to get up a neighborhood basketball game, an uncontrollable urge for Sweet Tarts, grape bubble gum, and Mello Yello will overtake the guys, and the boredom will be gone once again, at least until tomorrow.

You may think this sentence is awkward and unclear. But substituting semicolons for certain of the commas between the larger items in a series would instantly clarify it.

Revision:

Finally, after hours of moaning about how incredibly bored he is, a gleam will settle in Joe's eye; the doorbell will, at last, ring; Billy will stand outside, wanting to get up a neighborhood basketball game; an uncontrollable urge for Sweet Tarts, grape bubble gum, and Mello Yello will overtake the guys; and the boredom will be gone once again, at least until tomorrow.

Colons should not separate verbs from objects and complements or prepositions from objects.

We brought tents, food, and clothing. (not "brought: tents, food, and clothing")

We were thirsty, hungry, and weary. (not "were: thirsty, hungry, and weary")

I sat among counselors, campers, and parents. (not "among: counselors, campers, and parents")

Compare:

My motives for crossing the Alps were a desire for glory, a curiosity about the unknown, and a yearning for adventure.

My motives for crossing the Alps were several: a desire for glory, a curiosity about the unknown, and a yearning for adventure.

A colon should set up quoted material and establish the meaning or use of the quoted passage. All quoted passages need elaboration or comment as to their significance: too often, the quoted passage is merely tossed into the essay, without signals to the reader about the statement it is supporting or to which it is connected. Here is an example of a confusing use of a quoted passage.

Confusing use of quotation:

Writer Henry Miller was clearly pleased about being over forty. "It was only in my forties that I started feeling young." With this comforting remark, Miller takes the sting out of that dreaded fortieth birthday.

Revision:

> Writer Henry Miller was clearly pleased about being over forty: "It was only in my forties that I started feeling young." With this comforting remark, Miller takes the sting out of that dreaded fortieth birthday.

> or

> Writer Henry Miller was clearly pleased about being over forty. "It was only in my forties that I started feeling young": with this comforting remark, Miller takes the sting out of that dreaded fortieth birthday.

Use quoted passages responsibly and correctly. Remember that the quotation must be exactly worded and punctuated as you found it. If you alter the quotation in any way, include a bracketed explanation. If the quotation contains an error, you insert *[sic]*, a signal that you are aware that the person being quoted is in error. If the direct quotation contains an unclear pronoun reference, you may insert the name following the quotation, again in brackets.

Direct quotation containing errors:

> The student's paper read, "*Paradise Lost* is about a war between Satin [sic] and the Angles [sic]."

In typewritten papers, prose quotations of more than four lines and poetry of more than three lines are indented 10 spaces from the left margin and double-spaced. Indented quotations are not set off by quotation marks. The indentation indicates that the passage is a direct quotation.

In "Self-Reliance," philosopher Ralph Waldo Emerson exhorts readers to bold nonconformity and comprehends the risk of intellectual and spiritual isolation:

> A foolish consistency is the hobgoblin of little minds, adored by little statesmen and philosophers and divines.

With consistency a great soul has simply nothing to do. He may as well concern himself with his shadow on the wall. Speak what you think now in hard words and to-morrow speak what to-morrow thinks in hard words again, though it contradict every thing you said to-day.—"Ah, so you shall be sure to be misunderstood."—Is it so bad then to be misunderstood? Pythagoras was misunderstood, and Socrates, and Jesus, and Luther, and Copernicus, and Galileo, and Newton, and every pure and wise spirit that ever took flesh. To be great is to be misunderstood.[2]

The long indented passage is not set off with quotation marks, but the direct quotations integrated into the body of the paragraph are. Notice, too, that the direct quotation is rendered exactly, including variations of spelling and punctuation that would not follow today's standard usage.

Don't overuse quotation marks. Though words used in a special sense are generally supposed to be set off with quotation marks, sometimes you may tend to overdo this use, placing quotation marks around words that are not at all special, fresh, clever, or enigmatic.

Compare:

The employer delicately referred to the firing as a "voluntary resignation." (appropriate)

His "logic" was a reasonable person's lunacy. (appropriate)

My mother is a real "winner." (inappropriate)

She was "busy as a bee." (inappropriate)

Don't write:

The teacher said John wouldn't "catch on" unless John had the meaning all "spelled out" for him.

---

[2]Ralph Waldo Emerson, "Self-Reliance," in *The Selected Writings of Ralph Waldo Emerson* (New York: Modern Library–Random House, 1950), p. 152.

Write instead:

> The teacher said John wouldn't catch on unless John had the meaning all spelled out for him.

Or better yet, don't write a sentence like this one at all. Even the elimination of quotation marks cannot improve it. Usually, in fact, when you overuse quotation marks around allegedly special words, you are trying to disguise the thinness of your assertion.

Watch for awkwardly juxtaposed punctuation marks. It is usually a mistake to place punctuation marks adjacent to each other, with the exception, of course, of quotation marks with other marks of punctuation.

Errors:

> "What is the meaning of life?," the philosopher asked.
>
> The plane will arrive at 3:00 p.m..
>
> "Out! Out!," said Lady Macbeth to the spot.

Revisions:

> "What is the meaning of life?" the philosopher asked.
>
> The plane will arrive at 3:00 p.m.
>
> "Out! Out!" said Lady Macbeth to the spot.

Insert apostrophes where they are needed and eliminate them where they are not. Ride down the nation's highways, and you will notice an endangered species. It is not the American bald eagle. It is the apostrophe. Here is how the billboards read:

> Joes Place
>
> Discount City, Its the One to Visit
>
> Welcome to the Bluebird Motel, the Nations Finest

Rays Bar-B-Q Villa

Whos Going to Stop Abortion?

The apostrophe is nearly extinct in regions where it should appear. And it proliferates in areas where it should not. Many people, for example, like to insert an apostrophe in plural nouns, where it has no function, no purpose. So the person who is insecure about correct apostrophe use ends up writing a sentence like this one:

> Lily Maes biscuit's are so good its a shame she doesnt sell them to restaurant's and hotel's.
>
> (*Correction:* Lily Mae's biscuits are so good it's a shame she doesn't sell them to restaurants and hotels.)

The apostrophe seems to cause needless confusion. It has, after all, only two major uses: to indicate omitted letters (contractions) and to show ownership for nouns and indefinite pronouns. Be certain that you check for common mistakes in using apostrophes, especially with pronouns: "its" (a possessive personal pronoun) versus "it's" (a contraction for "it is"); apostrophes incorrectly inserted in nouns to show plurality; apostrophes incorrectly inserted in personal pronouns. These errors appear quite frequently in writing and are the result of illogical thinking about punctuation marks.

Why are apostrophes in possessive personal pronouns *always* incorrect? Possessive personal pronouns have their own case form to indicate ownership, and an apostrophe would, therefore, be redundant. Indefinite pronouns, however, do not have nominative, objective, and possessive case forms. They are like nouns in that respect. Personal pronouns, on the other hand, change their forms: I, me, my; he, him, his. And so the only way an indefinite pronoun or noun can show ownership or possession is with the addition of an apostrophe and the letter "s." The following examples show possessive case forms of personal pronouns:

> The house is *hers.*
>
> The dog loves *its* bone.
>
> The mortgage is *theirs.*

Ours is an impossible situation.

The problem is *yours*.

Contractions may also present problems. An apostrophe, for example, can indicate the omission of more than one letter. And if the omitted letters are separated by other letters, you may need an additional apostrophe. Remember, too, that contractions must be appropriate to the writing occasion. Use contractions sparingly in very formal writing. The following list will show you the contraction and its more formal translation, so to speak.

wouldn't—would n*ot*

weren't—were n*ot*

what's happenin'—what *is* happenin*g*

it's—it *is* (Don't confuse with "its," which is a possessive personal pronoun.)

must've—must *ha*ve

they're—they *a*re

Twist 'n' Turn Disco—Twist *and* Turn Disco

y'all come—y*ou* all come

make 'em hush—make *th*em hush

class of '87—class of *1*987

o'clock—o*f the* clock

Be careful not to overuse exclamation points.   As with quotation marks around words that are intended to be special but are not, you may tend to place exclamation points at the end of bland, obvious, or sentimental assertions. Exclamation marks should be used sparingly. Otherwise, the emotion may be strained. Too many exclamation points create a rather hysterical or sprightly effect that is wearing to the reader. Generally, it is wise not to manipulate the reader's responses with marks of punctuation. Let the content carry the emotion or meaning.

Don't write:

Oh! What a lovely morning! How joyful is springtime!

Write instead:

Oh, what a lovely morning. How joyful is springtime.

(Or better yet, don't write either.)

Be careful not to rely carelessly or haphazardly on the dash. Sometimes you may use the dash simply because you are uncertain about using the punctuation mark that would define the grammatical structure more precisely. In other words, you are not sure whether a comma or a semicolon would be appropriate, so you simply insert a freewheeling dash and avoid the problem altogether. Take the time to find the mark that would serve your writing purposes exactly. Overuse of the dash, as with the exclamation point, can give a frantic, breathless quality to your writing and, therefore, be distracting to the reader.

Don't write:

The evening had all the makings of a disaster—a noisy restaurant—tasteless food—microwaved—of course—and a singer called Johnnie Melodie—whose voice was somewhere between bad and awful—whose neck was weighted down with several gold chains—and whose shirt was—what a Las Vegas cliché—unbuttoned to the waist—and the bill came to a mere $100 per couple.

Write instead:

The evening had all the makings of a disaster: a noisy restaurant; tasteless food—microwaved, of course; and a singer named Johnnie Melodie, whose voice was somewhere between bad and awful, whose neck was weighted down with several gold chains, and whose shirt was—what a Las Vegas cliché—unbuttoned to the waist. And the bill came to a mere $100 per couple.

Eliminate sentence faults.

One of your persistent writing problems may be your inability to sense when one sentence ends and another begins. You may not feel the completeness of the idea or thought and, therefore, might punctuate an unintentional fragment as though it were a sentence, join complete thoughts with a comma (comma splice), or run on for several sentences without supplying necessary end punctuation (fused sentence). But the overall misunderstanding from which these errors derive is the same: you don't recognize a complete sentence when you write one. And sentence faults may muddle meanings. As you revise, follow these guidelines:

Eliminate comma splices and fused sentences. When you join main clauses, certain formal connections are necessary. These clauses cannot be joined by commas except in very specific grammatical circumstances. For example, you may join main clauses with commas when those clauses are being treated as items in a series. You would not hesitate to write "apples, bananas, and oranges." Nor should you hesitate to write "I like apples, I hate bananas, and I have no opinion about oranges." In these examples, you are joining main clauses as though they were single words. The final connecting word, "and," signals to the reader that you know very well what you are doing structurally and why. But suppose you write:

Sentence fault:

I like apples, I hate bananas.

The comma alone is inadequate to connect these two main clauses. Firmer and more formal connections are necessary.

Revision:

I like apples, but I hate bananas.

I like apples; I hate bananas.

You may feel this distinction to be arbitrary or whimsical. The reader would, after all, have no difficulty understanding the meaning of this simple assertion. But the formal connections between main clauses are both logical and clarifying. Each punctuation mark in a sentence has a purpose, a function, all its own. The marks may signal phrases, subordinate clauses, or main clauses. The marks may signal the end of one thought and the beginning of another. The marks may establish equal and unequal relationships between sentence parts. Therefore, each punctuation mark you use is to be thoroughly intentional, the reason for its placement as clear to you as your thesis—your purpose in writing. When you write, you will use standard punctuation just as you use standard language, so that universal communication is possible.

One comma splice is not detrimental to clear communication. But recurring comma splices can destroy the force and logic of your written communication. Why? Because commas alone do not effectively signal the end of one thought and the beginning of another. I knew a spacey, splicey woman who used to write letters like this one:

> Dear Mary, I just got back from Disney World, it was fantastic, gee, you should have seen Mickey Mouse, Donald Duck, Goofy, and all the rest, even though I must have walked fifty miles, I wasn't tired one minute, all those gorgeous flowers, the shops, Tomorrow Land, Jungleland were great, I just couldn't believe how beautiful everything was, I spent a hundred dollars, the trip was worth every penny, Love, Colene.

I am sure you are as relieved as I to arrive, finally, at a period. This breathless rendering of Colene's trip to Disney World might be called a trip to Comma World. There are several comma splices in this paragraph. There are also several correct uses of commas. But how can you tell the difference? Colene will communicate clearly only when she learns that commas define structures—as do all punctuation marks. And commas are inadequate to the task of defining main clauses.

To unsplice Colene's cheery epistle, you would need to understand how each comma is used. The following revision will explain each punctuation change or comma use in parentheses:

> Dear Mary, (after informal greetings)
> I just got back from Disney World. (comma splice replaced by end punctuation) It was fantastic. (comma splice replaced by end punctuation) Gee, (interjection) you should have seen Mickey Mouse, (item in series) Donald Duck, (item in series) Goofy, (optional comma for item in series)

and all the rest. (comma splice replaced by end punctuation) Even though I must have walked fifty miles, (comma after introductory adverb clause) I wasn't tired one minute. (comma splice replaced by end punctuation) All those gorgeous flowers, (item in series) the shops, (item in series) Tomorrow Land, (item in series) Jungleland were great; (comma splice replaced by semicolon) I just couldn't believe how beautiful everything was. (comma splice replaced by end punctuation) I spent a hundred dollars; (comma splice replaced by semicolon) the trip was worth every penny. (comma replaced by end punctuation)

> Love, (comma after informal closing)
> Colene (no period)

Fused, or run-on, sentences are like comma splices in that fused sentences hint at the writer's inability to detect the end of one thought and the beginning of another. But the problem is somewhat more serious. With comma splices, you at least indicate some sense of a shift in thought or meaning, though the comma splices are surely distracting. But when you write fused sentences, you give no signal of having completed one thought and begun another. You are running on, sometimes over several sentences, with no sense of having written several main clauses. Here is a paragraph that proves the problem:

> When I was a young kid, money was scarce and entertainment was even scarcer so when my mostly broke parents suggested a fun evening, my brothers and I felt an anticipation comparable to the arrival of Santa Claus on hot summer nights, sitting at the supper table, Mother would announce "Let's go to the drive-in" squeals of delight followed the announcement we children ran upstairs, climbed into our pajamas, and piled into the back of the 1956 Chevy station wagon then my parents wheeled us through the hot summer night, into the drive-in theater, up to the loudspeaker on the post and there we watched Jerry Lewis stumbling over his own feet or Doris Day getting teary-eyed over Rock Hudson it was bliss it was Christmas, Saturday, and summer vacation all rolled into one we watched the couples necking in the car beside us and the night fell over us like a dark coverlet of peace and joy.

Of course, the example is extreme, but you can see how fused or run-on sentences can interfere with clear written communication. How can you be certain, for example, whether the writer meant that Santa Claus arrived on hot summer nights or whether Mother sat at the supper table on hot summer nights? Correct end punctuation—the placement of periods, question marks, exclamation points—is basic to good written communication. And though the patterns for connecting main clauses may be a bit complicated, those patterns, too, are essential to clarity and logic in writing.

Here is a revision of the paragraph, in which all fused sentences have been eliminated. Notice the options available to you.

> When I was a young kid, money was scarce and entertainment was even scarcer. So when my mostly broke parents suggested a fun evening, my brothers and I felt an anticipation comparable to the arrival of Santa Claus. On hot summer nights, sitting at the supper table, Mother would announce, "Let's go to the drive-in." Squeals of delight followed the announcement. We children ran upstairs, climbed into our pajamas, and piled into the back of the 1956 Chevy station wagon. Then my parents wheeled us through the hot summer night, into the drive-in theater, up to the loudspeaker on the post; and there we watched Jerry Lewis stumbling over his own feet or Doris Day getting teary-eyed over Rock Hudson. It was bliss. It was Christmas, Saturday, and summer vacation all rolled into one. We watched the couples necking in the car beside us, and the night fell over us like a dark coverlet of peace and joy.

Eliminate unintentional fragments. Fragments are sometimes fine, sometimes not so fine. What is the difference? Fragments are sentence faults when they are not intentional. You want your grammatical choices to be conscious, not the result of intuition, whim, or doubt.

But first, what is a fragment? A fragment is a subordinate clause or a phrase punctuated as a complete sentence. Here are several examples of sentence fragments:

> Although you would like to stay. (subordinate clause)
>
> Jogging up the road. (phrase)
>
> Since Mary moved out. (subordinate clause)
>
> Why John is hard of hearing. (subordinate clause)

Sometimes writers use fragments for creative and stylistic purposes, wishing to give immediacy to a novelistic moment, using phrases to convey complete descriptive meanings. In the following passage from James Joyce's novel *Ulysses*, several fragments mimic the mind's and the eye's random observations:

> Sardines on the shelves. Almost taste them by looking. Sandwich? Ham and his descendants mustered and bred there. Potted meats. What is home without Plumtree's potted meat? Incomplete. What a stupid ad![3]

Only two complete sentences appear in this passage. Can you find them? The rest of the phrases are punctuated as complete sentences, though not one of the fragments contains the three structural essentials for a complete sentence: a subject, a complete verb, and a complete thought. But these fragments are consciously wrought, a part of the author's artistic purpose.

Sometimes fragments answer questions, as in the funny title of a book by Robert Paul Smith: *Where Did You Go? Out. What Did You Do? Nothing.* And surely most of you have heard fragments effectively used in this typical exchange with Mother:

KID: "Can I go to the movies?"
MOM: "No."
KID: "Why?"
MOM: "Because."
KID: "Because why?"
MOM: "Just because."
KID: "Just because why?"
MOM: "Just because I said so."

Only one sentence in this clipped conversation is complete, but the meaning is certainly clear. And the fragments effectively replace complete questions and complete answers.

But even in writing intended primarily to inform, the intentional fragment is stylistically useful. Here are several examples of intentional fragments:

> What kind of draft? More than anything else, a fair one, with as few holes as possible to wriggle through.

> —James Fallows

---

[3]James Joyce, *Ulysses* (New York: Vintage Books, 1961), p. 171.

What bird? Which branch? What leaf? Which shadow?
These question-boundaries . . . are ours, not of reality.

—John Fowles

Not too low, not too high; not too simple, not too hard—an
easy breadth of idea and vocabulary.

—Sheridan Baker

But what of unintentional fragments, the kind that reveal the
writer's confusion about the completeness of thoughts? Unintentional fragments are sentence faults, indicating the writer's inability to distinguish between phrases and clauses, to punctuate
main clauses or complete sentences correctly. The following
paragraph contains several unintentional fragments:

Original version:

I think of the telephone. When I think of it at all. As an
instrument of function, not of pleasure or aesthetics. When
I went to buy my first phones at the phone store. I ordered
the cheapest, most untechnologically advanced, utilitarian
machines I could find, I didn't want a phone fit for a princess, I didn't want a phone shaped like Donald Duck, a
Model T, or a gumball machine I preferred dials to buttons,
I didn't want a phone with little red lights. That could put
human beings on "hold," I wanted a real phone, the kind I
could cradle on my shoulder. While I filed my nails or fixed
myself a Mello Yello on ice, the only curtsy I made to the
refined tastes of Ma Bell was to buy a beige phone instead
of a black one. On the theory that a phone that blends in is
better than one that stands out.

Revision:

I think of the telephone, when I think of it at all, as an
instrument of function, not of pleasure or aesthetics. When
I went to buy my first phones at the phone store, I ordered
the cheapest, most untechnologically advanced, utilitarian
machines I could find. I didn't want a phone fit for a princess. I didn't want a phone shaped like Donald Duck, a
Model T, or a gumball machine. I preferred dials to buttons. I didn't want a phone with little red lights that could
put human beings on hold. I wanted a real phone, the kind
I could cradle on my shoulder while I filed my nails or fixed

myself a Mello Yello on ice. The only curtsy I made to the refined tastes of Ma Bell was to buy a beige phone instead of a black phone, on the theory that a phone that blends in is better than one that stands out.

Avoid awkwardness.

Some problems in revision could not strictly be categorized as errors. Rather, they are problems with style, with the mode and manner of your expression in writing. Although awkwardness in sentence structure and in overuse of the passive voice are not officially mistakes, they nonetheless interrupt or block the free flow of your ideas. You should be aware of why these issues of style matter and of how you can revise your essay to give greater sophistication and clarity to your meanings. Be alert to the following principles:

Revise to avoid oversubordination or overcoordination.

Sometimes, in writing the first draft of your essay, thoughts do not come easily, your expression of them is tentative, and the sentences seem awkward and difficult to understand. You may find, upon looking at the rough draft, that *oversubordination* is the problem. Your sentences are literally packed with noun, adverb, and adjective clauses. Some of your most important ideas, observations, or facts are buried in subordinate clauses when those ideas and facts deserve prominence. Perhaps the reader cannot locate your main idea because of these many modifying or noun clauses. Your instructor may make the marginal comment that the sentence needs breaking up, but he or she may not explain why.

You can learn to revise such unwieldy sentences by using one of the following techniques:

1. You may transform a subordinate clause into a phrase.
2. You may bring an important idea into prominence by placing it in a main clause rather than in a subordinate clause.
3. Or you may simply break the sentence into two or three shorter sentences.

Here is a sentence that needs revision to correct the problem of oversubordination.

Mosques, (which are buildings used by worshippers) (who are members of the Moslem faith), (which was founded by the prophet) (who was named Mohammed), display certain essential elements of design (that include a maksoura or prayer hall with a mihrab or prayer niche) (that indicates the direction of Mecca), a dikka [(that functions as a platform for services) and (which is near the mimbar) (that is also referred to as a pulpit)], and a large court (that has minarets).

The main clause in this sentence is almost impossible to locate because of the numerous relative clauses, most of which could easily be transformed into short phrases. The writer has tried to pack too much information into one sentence. Here is a possible revision, though you may think of other ways to improve the sentence:

Members of the Moslem faith, founded by the prophet Mohammed, worship in mosques, which are buildings displaying certain essential designs, including a maksoura or prayer hall with a mihrab or prayer niche facing Mecca, a dikka or platform for services, a mimbar or pulpit, and a large court with minarets.

The revision has tightened the sentence and clarified its meaning. Only one relative clause remains. The rest are now phrases. Here is another example of oversubordination:

[(Although administrators were angry) (when the government cut back on funds for public education) (because citizens had complained) (that educators simply believed) (that throwing money at education would solve its problems)], the tightened educational budget forced educators to be more efficient and more cautious (when they hired new teachers) and to behave more responsibly [(when they discussed purchasing new equipment or planned new facilities) (which, in more prosperous times, seemed essential) but (which, in reality, had not significantly improved the quality of education)].

Can you find the main clause in this awkward sentence? Do not be surprised if you cannot. The sentence contains nine subordinate clauses, relative and adverbial. Most of the subordinate clauses could be transformed into phrases. The main clause is, in fact, as follows: "The tightened educational budget forced educators to be more efficient and more cautious and to behave more responsibly." Now, you attempt a revision, giving prominence to the main idea and eliminating subordinate clauses. Compare your revision to the example following:

[(Although administrators were angry) (when the government cut back on public-education funds) because of citizen complaints about throwing money at education], the tightened educational budget forced educators to be more efficient and more cautious about hiring new teachers and to behave more responsibly about purchasing new equipment and planning new facilities (which, in prosperous times, seemed essential but, in reality, had not significantly improved the quality of education).

The revised sentence, though it is still rather complicated, now contains only three subordinate clauses. The other subordinate clauses are now phrases of various types. And the sentence is structurally defined as being complex. The sentence, however, probably needs further revision. You could, perhaps, break up the sentence in the following way:

Administrators were angry (when the government cut back on funds for public education) because of citizen complaints about throwing money at education. However, the tightened educational budget forced educators to be more efficient and more cautious about hiring new teachers and to behave more responsibly about purchasing new equipment and planning new facilities (which, in more prosperous times, seemed essential, but, in reality, had not significantly improved the quality of education).

Just as oversubordination may muddle meanings, so overcoordination may confuse the reader. *But, in a certain sense, overcoordination is worse than oversubordination, if only because the writer displays no sensitivity to the relative importance of details, ideas, and facts.* The stylistic impression made by overcoordination is of a young child, breathlessly relating the plot of a grade-B Western: "I went to the picture show, and then I got some popcorn, but the theater was real dark, and I got scared, and the cowboy shot all the people in the saloon, and the horse ran up on the bar, and he broke all the glasses, and I was so scared, and Mama said not to cry, and I didn't, and I really don't like shooting and breaking things." As you can see from this example, the child gives equal weight to all ideas and observations, even though buying popcorn is certainly not as important as being scared.

When you overcoordinate, you have not placed less important details, facts, and ideas in phrases or subordinate clauses or deleted them; nor have you brought the central idea(s) into prominence. And overcoordination produces more than confusion about what matters: overcoordination is also stylistically monotonous, creating a sing-song, chanting effect that gets in the way of communication.

Here is an example, somewhat more sophisticated than the child's breathless plot summary but nonetheless stylistically and conceptually weak.

Colette was a French novelist, (and) the critics called her "incomparable," (but) the "legend of her excellence is not quite consonant with her real excellence," (and) her best books have been somewhat neglected, (and) these most beautiful books are about the countryside and animals, (for) in them Colette is actually a part of nature and the world of childhood, (and) she creates a magical world, (and) she is a part of flowers, animals, her mother.

This awkward sentence contains eight main clauses, though not all the information in these main clauses deserves equal weight. The connections are repetitious, drearily predictable (a comma and a coordinating conjunction, usually "and"). And the reader has no sense (because the writer conveys none) of which observations merit more and which less emphasis.

Here is a revision of the sentence, in which certain of the main clauses have been transformed into phrases or subordinate clauses. The writer also strives in the revision for variety in patterns of connection between complete thoughts (main clauses) and incomplete thoughts (subordinate clauses).

Critics called French novelist Colette "incomparable," (but) the "legend of her excellence is not quite consonant with her real excellence"; (in fact), her best and most beautiful books, though somewhat neglected, are about the countryside and animals, a world of nature and childhood (in which Colette is a magical part of flowers, animals, her mother).

The first portion of the revision now sets up the critical dispute, which, in fact, is the central idea of the sentence and deserves emphasis. The second part of the sentence, following the semicolon, explains and defends the earlier assertion. Minor bits of information—that Colette is a French novelist, for example—have been transformed from main clauses to phrases or subordinate clauses.

Be careful not to rely on the passive voice.   Though either the active or passive voice is certainly correct, there are advantages in using the active voice whenever possible or appropriate.
  1. *The active voice often shortens sentences.* Compare:

Passive voice:

The rock star was applauded by thousands of adoring fans.

After the test was over, the papers were collected by the teacher's favorite student.

A Boeing 707 was hijacked today by international terrorists and the pilot was forced at gunpoint to land in the desert.

Revision to active voice:

Thousands of adoring fans applauded the rock star.

After the test was over, the teacher's favorite student collected the papers.

International terrorists today hijacked a Boeing 707 and forced the pilot at gunpoint to land in the desert.

You will notice that a shift to the active voice has eliminated the underscored words.

2. *The active voice brings the subject into its exact relationship with the action or expression of the verb.* In recent years, the overuse of the passive voice has deadened the impact of many assertions, blurred or disguised the culprit in many situations. You need to be aware of this habit, a favorite among those who wish to make fuzzy what should be clear, who know very well the person or thing at fault but prefer to avoid the issue of responsibility. Compare:

The decision to place a nuclear waste dump just outside the city was arrived at yesterday. (passive voice)

Yesterday, the mayor and city council members decided to place a nuclear waste dump just outside the city. (active voice)

There are advantages, however, in using the passive voice:

1. *Use the passive voice when you are unsure about who or what is carrying out or expressing the action or being of the verb.*

Appropriate use of the passive voice:

The last cold chicken leg was stolen from the refrigerator last night.

I went out this morning and discovered that the tires on my car had been slashed.

The decision about whether or not the space program should be expanded will surely be made in the next several years.

2. *Use the passive voice when the focus of interest is on the act, not the do-er or be-er.*

Appropriate use of the passive voice:

The best-selling novel <u>Lost Innocence</u> has been hailed as the love story of the century.

Mighty oaks, towering elms, and voluptuous magnolias were uprooted by the raging hurricane.

The Potato Queen has been invited to ride in the parade.

Always consider your uses of the active and passive voices when you are revising your work. As a general rule, prefer the active voice—unless, of course, you can find a good reason for using the passive voice. The passive voice is, after all, sometimes both vague and wordy.

Maintain consistent logic.

As you read and reread your essay, do you notice confusing or inconsistent words, phrases, or sentences? You can spot problems with logic or clarity simply by noticing places in which you yourself have to pause, ponder, and discover what it was you intended to say. After all, you are only the first among the readers of your essay, and you enjoy a status as audience as well as author. Certain grammatical and stylistic issues are frequent deterrents to clear communication: shifts in point of view or grammatical constructions and dangling or misplaced modifiers are among the most common. As with errors in punctuation or spelling, these problems of logic or clarity need to be addressed to remove distracting inconsistencies and to protect your meanings.

Revise any illogical shifts in point of view or number. Once you have decided on your perspective toward a subject, your obligation is to stay with that perspective throughout the sentence, paragraph, or sometimes even the entire essay. And if you use, for example, a singular indefinite pronoun such as "anybody" or "everyone," your subsequent pronouns or nouns must also be singular.

Original versions:

One is miserable until *they* stop looking for happiness.

Harry is furious because *you* can't receive *your* tax fund earlier.

Everybody has *their* faults.

A *person* needs to keep *their* wits about them.

Revisions:

One is miserable until *one* stops looking for happiness.

Harry is furious because *he* can't receive *his* tax fund earlier.

Everybody has *his* faults.

Everybody has *her* faults.

A *person* needs to keep *his* wits about *him.*

A *person* needs to keep *her* wits about *her.*

Avoid pointless or illogical shifts in verb tense, mood, or voice.

Illogical shift in verb tense:

William Hazlitt directly *contradicts* the process-mongers of this century when, in his essay "On Prejudice," he *wrote,* "We never do anything well until we cease to think about the manner of doing it." And Hazlitt *was* right. Though our generation *learns* much about how to do everything, we *accomplished* little. (shift from present to past to present to past tense)

Note: When writing about literary works, remember always to refer to them in the eternal present—that is, as though the writer and work were contemporaneous with your own time.

Revision:

William Hazlitt directly *contradicts* the process-mongers of this century when, in his essay "On Prejudice," he *writes,* "We never do anything well until we cease to think of the manner of doing it." And Hazlitt *is* right. Though our generation *learns* much about how to do everything, we *accomplish* little.

Illogical shifts in mood:

It is important that she *be* on time and *is* well *prepared.* (shift from subjunctive to indicative mood)

I suggest that the student *call* her parents and *invites* them in for a conference with the teacher. (shift from subjunctive to indicative mood)

Revisions:

It is important that she *be* on time and that she *be* well *prepared.*

I suggest that the student *call* her parents and *invite* them in for a conference with the teacher.

Illogical shifts in voice:

Richard[s] sang[v] tenor, and the soprano[s] was sung[v] (by Marian[op]). (active to passive voice)

When the club[s] meets[v] in September, the plans[s] for the banquet will be made[v] (by the members[op]). (active to passive voice)

Revisions:

Richard[s] sang[v] tenor, and Marian[s] sang[v] soprano.

When the club[s] meets[v] in September, the members[s] will make[v] plans for the banquet.

Modifiers should clearly indicate what they are modifying and have something to modify. Nobody likes to be left hanging. And neither does a modifier. Modifiers are words or groups of words that give information about or describe other words or groups of words. These modifiers need to be placed as close as possible to what they are modifying.

But sometimes modifiers get misplaced. Then there is nothing to do but run all over the sentence looking for the words they modify. For example, if you have a father and a pot in one sentence, you had better make clear which one is boiling.

Boiling, Father turned down the pot.

The participle "boiling" is misplaced, but only, of course, if Father is in a good mood. He may, in fact, *be* boiling. But the writer surely intended to convey the meaning in any one of the following ways:

The pot having boiled, Father turned it down.

Father turned down the boiling pot.

Father turned down the pot after the water was boiling.

Father, the pot having boiled, turned it down.

You can see from the above examples that many choices are available to you in placing modifiers.

Misplaced modifiers:

She fell down *almost* with exhaustion.

She will not *even* budge an inch.

The students *hardly* pay any attention to the boring lecturer.

Revisions:

She *almost* fell down with exhaustion.

She will not budge *even* an inch.

The students pay *hardly* any attention to the boring lecturer.

Misplaced prepositional phrase:

The politicians spoke to the crowd in the mall *off the top of their heads.*

Revision:

The politicians spoke *off the top of their heads* to the crowd in the mall.

Misplaced participial phrase:

The man chased the hat *running down the street.*

Revision:

Running down the street, the man chased the hat.

Misplaced relative clause:

The quarterback passed the football across the goal line *which hit the referee in the head.*

Revision:

The quarterback passed the football, *which hit the referee in the head,* across the goal line.

Split infinitives and squinting constructions may also be confusing or awkward. A split infinitive is certainly no great writing crime, but it can be offensive to the eye or ear. And squinting constructions leave the reader confused as to whether the modifier is describing the words preceding or the words following.

Split infinitives:

I wanted *to,* above all, *succeed.*

To, in contradiction of all the evidence, wrongly *convict* someone is irresponsible.

Revisions:

I wanted, above all, *to succeed.*

To convict someone wrongly, in contradiction of all the evidence, is irresponsible.

Squinting modifiers:

Will realized *at noon* the meeting would begin. (Did Will realize at noon that the meeting would start, or would the meeting start at noon?)

Why Elizabeth disappeared *completely* bewilders me. (Did Elizabeth completely disappear, or was I completely bewildered?)

Revisions:

At noon, Will realized that the meeting would begin.
or
Will realized that the meeting would begin *at noon.*

Why Elizabeth *completely* disappeared bewilders me.
or
Why Elizabeth disappeared bewilders me *completely.*

Dangling modifiers are not the same as misplaced modifiers. When a modifier is misplaced, it at least has something to modify, even though what it modifies is unclear. But a dangling modifier has nothing to modify. And what logical reason could there be for giving information about nothing?

Dangling modifiers:

Splitting hairs, the committee decision wasted a sunny afternoon.

Getting married for the third time, the white wedding dress and elaborate ceremony caused either great consternation or amusement among the guests.

Recuperating nicely, the desiccated liver and vitamin C were having excellent effects.

The dangling modifiers need something or someone to modify. Buildings and April 1 cannot hope. Decisions cannot split hairs. Wedding dresses and ceremonies cannot get married. Desiccated liver and vitamin C cannot recuperate at all, much less "nicely." You can revise these sentences in several ways.

Revisions:

The construction workers *hope* the building will be completed by April 1.

The building, *architects hope*, will be completed by April 1.

Splitting hairs, the committee members wasted a sunny afternoon, trying to come to a decision.

The committee members were *splitting hairs* over the decision, thereby wasting a sunny afternoon.

Because the bride and groom were each getting married for the third time, the white wedding dress and elaborate ceremony caused either great consternation or amusement among the guests.

The bride and groom, *who were each getting married for the third time*, caused great consternation or amusement among the guests because of the white wedding dress and the elaborate ceremony.

Recuperating nicely, the patient said that the desiccated liver and vitamin C were having excellent effects.

The patient was recuperating nicely, due to the excellent effects of desiccated liver and vitamin C.

Note: Do not confuse dangling or misplaced modifiers with absolute elements. Absolute elements are not intended to modify anything in the sentence. Compare:

Absolute element:

The book having been published, the author celebrated with an autograph party.

Dangling modifier:

Having been published, the author celebrated with an autograph party.

Misplaced modifier:

Having been published, the author celebrated the book with an autograph party.

Diagnose and remedy spelling errors.

No matter how well you write, you may nonetheless be plagued by spelling problems. You have tried to memorize words; you struggle to improve the "guess" factor. But nothing has made a difference. Diagnosis may be 90 percent of the cure. Often your spelling errors follow a predictable pattern, and you can trace the pattern in your essays. You may have problems with one or several of the following:

Do you have trouble with "ance" versus "ence" endings?

assurance

attendance

confidence

prevalence

Can you remember when to double consonants?

occur	occurrence
win	winning
vote	voting

Do you, despite frequent nagging from the authorities, continue to write "a lot" as one word?

Do you get mixed up about apostrophes or about hyphens in compound words?

its	or	it's (meaning "it is")
ladykiller	or	lady-killer
full-back	or	fullback

Do certain combinations of letters come out all wrong?

> recieve (instead of "receive")
>
> neice (instead of "niece")
>
> situashion (instead of "situation")
>
> presense (instead of "presence")

Do you find it easy to spell big words and hard to spell little words?

> psoriasis
>
> to (instead of "too," meaning "also" or "as well")

Do you wrongly assume that sound is a reliable indicator of spelling?

> xylophone
>
> phloem

Does your mispronunciation of words lead you to spelling errors?

> goverment (instead of "government")
>
> liberry (instead of "library")

Your first task, then, is to diagnose your particular kind of spelling problem. Even if you have several such problems, the diagnosis will lead you to a more specialized treatment of only those errors that plague you.

Note: If your spelling problems are insurmountable, if you consistently transpose letters or syllables, you may be learning disabled, perhaps dyslexic. If you suspect that you might have this "word blindness," you would be wise to have the problem diagnosed by reading specialists and, of course, to alert your teacher.

People who write often and conscientiously—whether for personal, professional, or academic purposes—rely on the dictionary to solve small problems and large ones. You will learn to do the same. Do not take chances on spelling or word usage: when in doubt, even if the doubt is the merest flicker across the surface of your mind, look up the word. You will be surprised at how much you will learn. (Of course, if you are not in doubt, if you are convinced that your spelling of a word is correct when, in fact, the spelling is incorrect, only humility can save you. Learn to distrust your spelling impulses if words you consistently assume are right are, in fact, wrong.)

A thesaurus can be a useful reference source when you want to vary word choices. But there are risks in relying too heavily on the thesaurus. Beware of subtle variations in meanings. Remember, too, that you may be tempted to use a word with which you are not familiar. Verify a word you select in the thesaurus with the dictionary definition. Compare:

Some thesaurus synonyms for the word "cry" as a verb:

cry, roar, shout, bawl, bellow, halloo, halloa, whoop, yell, howl,
  scream, screech, shriek, squeak, squeal, squall, whine, pipe,
  call, caw, bark, bray, mew, mewl, ululate, weep

So then, seeking to vary the word "cry," you write the following:

The little boy cried when the crow ululated and the dog mewed, but his mother squalled when the pig brayed.

Dictionary synonyms for the word "cry" as a verb:

weep, wail, keen, moan, whimper, sob, blubber

So then you write:

The little boy blubbered when the crow cried and the dog whimpered, but his mother wept when the pig moaned.

Referring to the dictionary often and using (with caution) the thesaurus to vary word choices may not be sufficient to cure your spelling problems. Study the following groups of words to discover why you misspell and to warn yourself of special spelling difficulties. And when you revise your essay to eliminate spelling errors, be certain to read through the essay several times. Question any word, no matter how apparently simple. Remember, you may be the kind of student who can spell "hors d'oeuvre" but cannot spell "a lot."

Mispronunciation may cause you to misspell words:

You may be adding unnecessary letters.
athlete (not ath-*e*-lete)
mischievous (not mis-chie-*vi*-ous)
realtor (not real-*i*-tor)
Worcestershire sauce (not Wor-c*h*est-er-shire sauce)
Westminster (not West-min-*is*-ter)

You may be dropping necessary letters.
arctic (not ar-tic)
boundary (not bound-ry)
everyone (not ever-one)
government (not gover-ment)
literature (not liter-ture)
probably (not prob-ly)
reference (not ref-rence)
sophomore (not soph-more)
temperature (not temper-ture)

You may be altering letters.
Fayetteville (not F*ed*ville)
gratitude (not gra*d*itude)
himself (not hi*s*self)
hundred (not hun*ne*rd)
nuclear (not nuc*ula*r)
sherry (not *c*herry)
should have (not should *of*)
themselves (not the*ir*selves)
Wimbledon (not Wimble*t*on)

You may be transposing letters.
perhaps (not p*r*ehaps)
pervade (not p*r*evade)
prescribe (not p*er*scribe)

Some words sound alike but have different meanings, and you must check the dictionary to find the word you actually want.

already	all ready
assistance	assistants
bored	board
complement	compliment
dam	damn
everyday	every day
hoard	horde

instance	instants
into	in to
it's	its
lesson	lessen
passed	past
patience	patients
pin	pen
stationary	stationery
there's	theirs
you're	your

Use the appropriate manuscript form.

Presentation is all, as any good host or hostess will tell you. And when you arrive at the stage of typing the final manuscript, you will want to give careful attention to its appearance and form. Your instructor may offer you a required format of her own, or she may suggest that you follow the suggested manuscript form in your handbook or in such books as the *Chicago Manual of Style* or the *MLA Handbook.* For less formal papers, matters of form may be as simple as taking care with margins, writing legibly, affixing a title, and numbering the pages. When you write a research paper, you will, of course, want to follow scrupulously the recommended format. But for a weekly composition assignment, simply observe the basic requirements for producing an attractive final manuscript.

Whether you type your essay or write in longhand, certain proprieties and rules apply.

1. Use blue or black ink for all handwritten papers and black ink for all typewriters. (Typewritten essays are preferable. They are more professional, and your reader will take your work more seriously.)

2. Use good quality paper, sturdy, not flimsy. If you use notebook paper, choose wide-lined paper, white. Do not use a yellow legal pad or pages ripped from a spiral notebook.

3. The appropriate page size is 8 1/2 inches by 11 inches.

4. Always double-space in typewritten essays.

5. Type or write on only one side of the page.

6. Leave margins on all sides, about 1 1/2 inches at the top and an inch on the sides and bottom.

7. Number all pages except the first—which bears the title— using Arabic, not Roman, numerals and placing the number in the upper right-hand corner of the page.

8. Indent five spaces for the first line of each new paragraph. If you are writing in longhand, be certain that the indentations are very clear.

9. Affix your title to the top of the first page and leave at least two lines of space before you begin the actual essay. Center the title, and do not place quotation marks around it. The placement indicates that you have written a title. If, as with a research paper, you prepare a separate title page, center the title a little less than halfway down the page, and include beneath it your name, the course title and number, the instructor's name, and the date. Capitalize the first and last words of the title, all important words, and all other words except conjunctions and prepositions of less than five letters, articles (a, an, the), and *to* as a sign of the infinitive.

10. If you quote more than four lines of prose or two or three lines of poetry, indent each line of the quotation 10 spaces on the left side and double-space. Do not set off the quotation with quotation marks. The placement indicates that the passage is being quoted.

11. If you are writing your paper, write legibly and in cursive. If you are typing your paper, your typing ribbon should be clean and sufficiently dark. The point of your pen should be neither too fat, as with some felt-tipped pens, nor too narrow; the ink should flow steadily, not producing unsightly blobs, as with some ballpoint pens.

Proofread carefully.

Proofreading is a term used in the publishing world to describe a very important task: the checking of the typeset material against the author's manuscript. But the word "proofreading" is often used somewhat loosely to describe your final task in writing: the last-minute corrections of grammar, punctuation, fact, and form. At this final stage, you probably have neither the time nor the energy to undertake additional major revisions. The essay is finished, if indeed, any piece of writing is ever finished; and even though you may wish that you had an extra hour or day to rearrange a paragraph or delete a large section, you do not. But you can, in these final moments, give the essay a few more readings before you submit it to the instructor.

You may believe that a single, thorough reading of the finished work will suffice. But the evidence shows otherwise. Professional writers check and recheck their work and find, each time through, that another error jumps out at them. Careful writers give each essay a minimum of three readings. Even then, books and articles are published with several typographical errors, with words or entire paragraphs omitted.

Unfortunately, errors often jump out at your reader, even as they escaped your careful attention. After you have written the second or third draft, you may have looked at the content so long that you can no longer see the spelling error or the dangling modifier. But readers, uncomfortable with your content or resisting your opinion, may use pesky errors to dismiss you from their minds. Even readers who are normally unable to write error-free compositions seem unusually skillful at detecting your mistakes. If the readers find your presentation to be sloppy and careless, then they will tend to disparage or ignore your message.

How do you catch your errors before the instructor catches them? Read the essay through several times, each time with an eye to a particular problem. Let one reading focus entirely on punctuation, another on spelling, another on grammatical constructions, another on word choice. If necessary, read the essay backward, thereby forcing yourself to ignore the sense of what you are writing and to concentrate solely on the individual words. Sometimes you may miss a typographical error simply because you are lost in the meaning.

You are also wise, if you still have time to spare before the deadline, to put aside the final manuscript for a while and then return to it. For some reason, the "n" you omitted from "idicate" will suddenly be noticeable.

If you think you do not have the time to proofread several times over, think again. Most compositions have assigned lengths of only two or three pages. In the time you need to walk to the front of the room and put the paper on the instructor's desk, you might notice the apostrophe you mistakenly inserted in the personal pronoun. And, like all good writers, you will run back to your desk, grab the liquid paper, and remove the offending mark. Only an amateur would let the error go by—as if writing did not matter. You know it does.

PART

IV

Special Assignments

IV
Special Assignments

CHAPTER

11

Writing Essays About Literature

In the early stages of freshman composition, you are invited to
write essays about yourself and your perceptions of the world,
about science, business, social customs, campus life, technology.
But sooner or later, you will move into another kind of writing:
literary analysis. Even if you are not majoring in English, literature will comprise at least a portion of your required freshman
and sophomore courses. And papers will be due, all of them
about the literary staples: poems, novels, short stories, essays,
plays.

Though you learned in Chapter 6 about analysis as a way of
thinking, as a way of developing and supporting your ideas,
opinions, and information, you will need more specialized instruction in this particular analytical mode. Literary analysis
has certain conventions, proprieties, and approaches that are
similar to scientific analysis or political analysis but not identical. If you have difficulty understanding or appreciating literature, you will need friendly advice about how to write about fiction or poetry. You may feel uneasy, confused, about literary
interpretation. This chapter, therefore, is intended to give you
the confidence and the necessary techniques to look at a literary
work in a new way, using the same speculative, objective approach that a scientist uses when she sets forth an hypothesis
and tests its validity in a laboratory.

At some point, your teacher will almost certainly assign a
poem or story, a novel or play, and ask you to take it apart, look

at it, and make some sense of it. You will find yourself staring at Matthew Arnold's "Dover Beach," John Milton's "Areopagitica," Virginia Woolf's "Kew Gardens," or Marianne Moore's "Silence." What do you do? How do you look? Where do you go?

When you analyze a literary work, you are developing the same mental skill, using the same coolly rational approach that a doctor gives to the anatomy of a disease, a mechanic gives to the operation of an engine, a historian gives to the framework of the Constitution. You are attempting to understand the whole by gazing attentively at the various parts. But in literature you are not gazing at xylem or phloem, blood count or pulse rate, carburetor or spark plugs. You are gazing at character, setting, theme, figurative language, plot, dialogue, climax, denouement, meter, rhyme.

Literary criticism may focus on only one or two aspects of the work: one scene, two characters, plot defects. But *explication* is a line-by-line textual reading of a poem or story. After reducing the work to its smallest components of language, expression, composition, you then reassemble or synthesize the individual components, relating the smaller parts to the larger parts, the larger parts to the work as a whole, and then relating that whole work to the entire body of literature of that genre.

Your purpose is enlightenment, not indoctrination or propaganda. You are not trying to make the reader like or dislike the work. You are trying, very simply, to help him or her see it. In other words, you stride up to the poem, pick it up, turn it over, run your fingers across its surfaces, check the label on the bottom, ask its price, get its dates, examine its fingerprints, in much the same way you would examine an antique vase. Whether you buy it or not—the final judgment—is irrelevant. You are, as you frequently say to clerks, "Just looking, thank you."

But how do you get at the inner workings of what may well be a complicated intellectual and artistic piece of writing?

1. You begin by reading and rereading the literary work. The point seems obvious, but it is often lost on those who do not enjoy reading or have trouble reading or fail to appreciate literature. Close reading leads to close analysis (though rereading is not necessarily close reading).

2. Read carefully. Do you see recurring images, themes, possible symbols? When you read the work aloud, do the lines

sing? Do certain parts of the literary work strike you as being familiar, false, overstated, or just right? Are there words or references you do not understand? Look them up. Are there footnotes that provide additional information? Attend to them. In other words, bring to the reading of the work all of your own powers of discipline, interpretation, imagination.

3. Ask questions as you read. Why did the author juxtapose these two characters? Why is the season spring? How does the author make a character believable?

4. The questions that occur to you as you read and study the work will lead you to possible thesis statements. Are you particularly struck by the author's handling of weather, conversation, personality? Does the plot seem suspiciously like a message, not just a vehicle for carrying the action of the novel or drama?

5. After the work is very familiar to you, not by hearsay or by studying scholarly interpretations or by relying on "ponies"—plot summaries available in most book stores—but by actual reading, you may be ready to begin analyzing how the novel or poem or story works in terms of setting, characterization, handling of dialogue, credibility of plot.

6. Divest yourself of preconceived notions, of personal preferences about types of literature, of the current reputation of the author, of glib or sweeping assertions others may make about the work under consideration. Approach the writing coolly, intending to foster greater understanding of the work, not to heap gratuitous praise on the author or to advance your own literary career or to use the criticism for personal propaganda about morality.

7. Let the length, scope, and complexity of the work guide you to a manageable thesis. Literary works can be deceptive. A very long work may lend itself to a very simple critical treatment, the work being unsophisticated, easy to understand, even somewhat banal. On the other hand, a poem or even one verse may be rich in meaning, complex, very dense, requiring lengthy analysis. As a rule, however, a long work such as a novel will require that you single out a particular aspect of the novel for analysis—perhaps a character, perhaps one scene. And a short poem or story may make possible a close textual reading, even a line-by-line treatment.

8. Having developed a supportable thesis, look for support mainly within the primary source—that is, the work itself.

(However, you may refer occasionally to secondary sources—scholarly criticism, letters, journals, diaries, other works of the author that contain similar themes.) Use direct quotations to support your assertions, providing appropriate documentation for each source (see Chapters 10 and 12).

9. Finally, remember that you are just looking, thank you, and you want the reader to look as well. As you write, suspend judgment until you have first displayed the work and its component parts in the clear light of analysis, of objective and courteous treatment. Then, if you still "hate" the poem, you can very delicately hint of your displeasure. But you will have reasons for the judgment, not merely self-indulgent, lazy reactions.

The following essays demonstrate the techniques of development, support, and organization in literary analysis.

A DECADE

Amy Lowell

When you came, you were like red wine and honey,
And the taste of you burnt my mouth with its sweetness.
Now you are like morning bread,
Smooth and pleasant.
I hardly taste you at all, for I know your savor;
But I am completely nourished.

"A DECADE": AN EXPLICATION

In the poem "A Decade," the speaker is tracing the change in a relationship over several years. The speaker sets up a contrast between the tastes and sensations evident at the beginning of the passion and the tastes present after the long and familiar association has undergone the subtle alterations to which love is subject. The metaphor is food, illustrating how intimately connected the passions are with the bodily appetites. And yet the metaphor works as well on a deeper level, giving some sense of the keenness and complexity of early love and the quiet simplicity of the mature relationship.

Amy Lowell, "A Decade," in *The Complete Works of Amy Lowell* (Boston: Houghton Miflin, 1955).

The speaker begins by comparing the initial passion to red wine and honey. The comparison illustrates both the tartness and sweetness of early love. The speaker captures the paradox of mixed and seemingly conflicting sensations when she says, "The taste of you burnt my mouth with its sweetness." She calls up for the reader that deliciously painful experience of raw passion, when all the senses are heightened and everything awaits the pleasures of the lovers. The wine is "red," for red is the symbol of passion, a hot color, a rich color. The honey is smooth and sweet, thick and rich, perhaps like the amber skin of the beloved, perhaps like the feeling the lovers would experience in a first long embrace.

But love changes; and the change, in the speaker's view, is not loss but gain. Wine and honey have their pleasures, but bread is life-sustaining, pure, nourishing, and hearty. Wine and honey cannot, in the speaker's view, be the steady diet of mature lovers. Drunkenness and satedness would result. And "morning bread" is fresh as well, suggesting that even as the relationship deepens and strengthens it does not lose its "savor." There is a newness in bread, which is more satisfying than aged wine, mellow honey, the metaphors, paradoxically, of a new love.

The poet does not grieve over or yearn for the end of the sharp, sweet poignancy of the lover's first coming. After a decade, the lover is familiar as morning bread, a presence so all-encompassing that sharp tastes and sensations are gone. It is as though the lovers have arrived at the comforting, warm place of not-seeing, not-thinking, not-pining and yet continue to sense each other's presence as fully as if they spent hours gazing at each other. The speaker is "completely nourished" in this new and deeper stage of loving. The bread works as an effective symbol of perfect communion, of strength, of familiarity. The reader knows very well how bread tastes, its powerful fragrances; and that "savor," in the end, is how true love tastes.

Questions for discussion

1. Does the writer agree or disagree with the poet's description of love's alterations. Why are you not sure?

2. How does the writer of the literary analysis support assertions about the meaning of the poem?

3. Does the writer, at any point in the analysis, assume too much or too little about the poet's purposes? Explain.

4. What is the primary method of development and support used in the poem itself? In what ways does the poem demonstrate the same characteristics and techniques discussed in freshman composition courses? What have a "good" poem and a "good" essay in common? Be specific.

5. Is the literary analysis thorough, or are there meanings and dimensions in the poem that the critic missed?

LOVE

Guy de Maupassant

I have just read a drama of passion among the general news items in one of the daily papers. He first killed her and then committed suicide, showing that he must have loved her. What matter who the actors were? Their love alone interests me—not because it moves or surprises me, or because it softens me or makes me think, but because it recalls to my mind a remembrance of my youth, a strange recollection of a hunting adventure where love appeared to me as the cross appeared in the sky to the early Christians.

I was born with all the instincts and the senses of primitive man, tempered by the reasoning power and the feelings of a civilized being. I am passionately fond of shooting, and the sight of the wounded animal, with blood on its feathers and on my hands, affects my heart so that it almost stops beating.

That year the cold weather set in suddenly toward the end of autumn, and I was invited by one of my cousins, Karl de Rauville, to go with him duck shooting on the marshes at daybreak.

My cousin, a jolly fellow of forty, with red hair, very stout and bearded, a country gentleman, an amiable semi-brute, with a happy disposition and endowed with that Gallic wit which makes even mediocrity agreeable, lived in a house, half farmhouse, half chateau, situated in a broad valley through which a river ran. The hills right and left were covered with woods, old seignorial woods where magnificient trees still remained, and where the rarest feathered game in that part of France was to be found. Eagles were shot there occasionally, and birds of passage,

---

Guy de Maupassant, "Love," in *Short Stories of the Western World*, eds. Eugene Current-Garcia and Walton R. Patrick (Glenview, Ill.: Scott, Foresman, 1969).

those which rarely come into our over-populated part of the country, almost infallibly stopped amid these branches, which were centuries old, as if they knew or recognized a little corner of an ancient forest which had remained there to serve them as a shelter during their brief nocturnal halt.

In the valley there were large meadows watered by trenches and separated by hedges; farther on, the river, which up to that point had been canalized, expanded into a vast marsh. That marsh, which was the best shooting ground I ever saw, was my cousin's chief care; he kept it like a park. Among the rushes that covered it and made it a living, rustling, noisy spot, narrow passages had been made, through which flat-bottomed boats, impelled and steered by poles, passed along silently over the stagnant water, brushed up against the reeds, and made the swift fish take refuge among the weeds, and frightened the wild fowl, whose pointed, black heads disappeared suddenly as they dived.

I am passionately fond of the water, of the sea, although it is too vast, too restless, too impossible to hold; of the rivers which are so beautiful, but which pass on, flow away, and are gone; and above all, of the marshes, where the whole unknown existence of aquatic animals palpitates. The marsh is an entire world to itself on this earth, a different world, which has its own life, its settled inhabitants, and its passing travelers, its voices, its noises, and, above all, its mystery. Nothing is more disturbing, nothing more disquieting, more terrifying occasionally, than a fen. Why should this terror hang over these low plains covered with water? Is it the vague rustling of the rushes, the strange will-o'-the-wisps, the profound silence which envelops them on calm nights, or is it the strange mists which hang over the rushes like a shroud? Or else is it the imperceptible splashing, so slight and so gentle, and sometimes more terrifying than the cannon of men or the thunders of skies, which makes these marshes resemble tne lands of one's dreams, fearsome countries concealing an unknown and dangerous secret?

No, something else belongs to it, another mystery, more profound and graver, floats amid these thick mists, perhaps the mystery of creation itself! For was it not in stagnant and muddy water, amid the heavy humidity of moist land under the heat of the sun, that the first germ of life stirred, vibrated and expanded to the day?

I arrived at my cousin's in the evening. It was freezing hard enough to split stones.

In the large room whose sideboards, walls, and ceiling were covered with stuffed birds with extended wings, or perched on branches to which they were nailed, hawks, herons, owls, night-jars, buzzards, tercels, vultures, falcons, my cousin, who himself resembled some strange animal from a cold country, dressed in a sealskin jacket, told me during dinner what preparations he had made for that same night.

We were to start at half-past three in the morning, so as to arrive at the place which he had chosen for our watching place at about half-past four. On that spot a hut had been built of pieces of ice, so as to shelter us somewhat from the terrible wind which precedes daybreak, that wind which is so cold that it lacerates the flesh as if with a saw, cuts it like the blade of a knife, and wounds it as with a poisoned dart, twists it like a pair of pincers, and burns it like fire.

My cousin rubbed his hands: "I have never known such a frost," he said. "It is already twelve degrees below zero at six o'clock in the evening."

I threw myself on my bed immediately after we had finished our meal, and I went to sleep by the light of a bright fire burning in the grate.

At three o'clock he woke me. In my turn, I put on a sheepskin, and found my Cousin Karl covered with a bearskin. After having swallowed two cups of scalding coffee apiece, followed by two glasses of brandy, we started, accompanied by a gamekeeper and our dogs, Plongeon and Pierrot.

From the first moment that I got outside I felt chilled to the very marrow. It was one of those nights on which the earth seems dead with cold. The frozen air becomes resistant and palpable, such pain does it cause; no breath of wind moves it, it is fixed and motionless; it bites, pierces through you, dries and kills the trees, the plants, the insects, the small birds themselves, that fall from the branches on to the hard ground, and become hard themselves under the grip of the cold.

The moon, which was in her last quarter and was inclining to one side, seemed to be fainting in the midst of space, and so weak that she was unable to take her departure, and thus remained up yonder, also overcome and paralyzed by the severity of the weather. She shed a cold, mournful light over the world, that dying and wan light which she gives us every month, at the end of her resurrection.

Karl and I went side by side, our backs bent, our hands in our pockets, and our guns under our arms. Our boots, which were wrapped in wool so that we might be able to walk without slipping on the frozen river, made no sound, and I looked at the white vapor of our dogs' breath.

We were soon on the edge of the marsh, and we went into one of those lanes of dry rushes which ran through this low forest.

Our elbows, which touched the long, ribbon-like leaves, made a slight noise, and I was seized, as I had never been before, by the powerful, singular emotion which marshes cause in me. This marsh was dead, dead from cold, for we were walking on it, amid its population of dried rushes.

Suddenly, at the turn of one of the lanes, I perceived the ice hut which had been constructed to shelter us. I went in, and as we had nearly an hour to wait before the wandering birds would awake, I rolled myself up in my rug in order to try and get warm.

Then, lying on my back, I began to look at the misshapen moon, which had four horns through the semi-transparent walls of this polar house.

But the frost of the frozen marshes, the cold of these walls, the cold from the firmament penetrated me so terribly that I began to cough.

My Cousin Karl became uneasy. "It will be bad if we do not kill much to-day," he said. "I do not want you to catch cold; we will light a fire." And he told the gamekeeper to cut some rushes.

We made a pile in the middle of our hut, which had a hole in the middle of the roof to let out the smoke, and when the red flames rose up, the clear crystal chunks began to melt gently, imperceptibly, as if these stones of ice were sweating. Karl, who had remained outside, called to me: "Come and look here!" I went out of the hut, and remained struck with astonishment. Our hut, in the shape of a cone, looked like an enormous diamond with a heart of fire, which had been suddenly planted there in the midst of the frozen water of the marsh. And inside we saw two fantastic forms, those of our dogs, who were warming themselves at the fire.

But a peculiar cry, a lost, wandering cry, passed over our heads, and the light from our hearth showed us the wild birds. Nothing moves one so much as the first clamor of life which one does not see, and which is passing through the sombre air so quickly and so far off, before the first streak of the winter's day appears on the horizon. It seems to me at this glacial hour of dawn, as if that passing cry which is carried away by the wings of a bird is the sigh of the soul of the world!

"Put out the fire," said Karl. "It is getting daylight."

The sky was, in fact, beginning to grow pale, and the flights of duck made long, rapid streaks on the sky, which were soon obliterated.

A stream of light burst out into the night. Karl had fired, and the two dogs ran forward.

And then, almost every minute, first he, then I, aimed rapidly as soon as the shadow of a flying flock appeared above the rushes. And Pierrot and Plongeon, out of breath but happy, retrieved the bleeding birds, whose eyes, occasionally, still looked at us.

The sun had risen; it was a bright day with a blue sky, and we were thinking of taking our departure, when two birds with extended necks and outstretched wings glided rapidly over our heads. I fired, and one of them fell almost at my feet. It was a teal, with a silver breast, and then, in the blue space above me, I heard a voice, the voice of a bird. It was a short repeated, heart-rending lament; and the bird, the little animal that had been spared, began to circle round in the blue sky, above our heads, looking at its dead companion which I was holding in my hand.

Karl was on his knees, his gun to his shoulder, watching it eagerly, until it should be within gunshot. "You have killed the duck," he said, "and the drake will not fly away."

He certainly did not fly away; he circled over our heads continually and continued his cries. Never had any groans of suffering pained me so much as that desolate appeal, as that lamentable reproach of this poor bird which was lost in space.

Occasionally he would fly off, under the menace of the gun which followed his flight, and seemed ready to continue his flight alone; but, as he could not make up his mind to this, he soon returned to find his mate.

"Leave her on the ground," Karl said to me; "he will come within gunshot by and by." And he did indeed come near us, careless of danger, infatuated by his animal love, by his affection for that other animal which I had just killed.

Karl fired, and it was as if somebody had cut the string which held the bird suspended. I saw something black descend, and I heard the noise of a fall among the rushes. And Pierrot brought it to me.

I put them—they were already cold—into the same game bag, and I returned to Paris that evening.

SETTING AS PLOT IN GUY DE MAUPASSANT'S "LOVE"

Guy de Maupassant's "Love" scarcely seems a story at all, at least in the conventional sense: two cousins on a hunting trip; minimal description of the characters; a bit of dialogue; and two dead ducks, matter-of-factly bagged by the narrator and taken back to Paris. But great meaning rides on the broad backs of de-

scriptive passages, of settings so detailed, so intricate and passionately mobile, that the reader fairly races over the action-
packed terrain of the human heart. The French countryside, the
hunter's lodge, and the frozen marsh reveal the cursed conflict
between primitive and civilized man, between warmly palpitat-
ing and frozen hearts.

The narrator and his cousin Karl are torn between primitive,
natural passions and an insatiable quest for power. Describing
his cousin and the countryside in which he lives, the narrator
calls Karl "an amiable semi-brute," whose love of nature is tempered by his need to keep the marsh, that place of "mystery," the
"land of one's dreams," "like a park." Cousin Karl has made the
teeming marsh into the "best shooting ground" the narrator has
ever seen. Karl has fashioned "narrow passages" through the
fen, "through which flat-bottomed boats, impelled and steered
by poles," can make the "swift fish take refuge among the weeds"
and frighten the "wild fowl." The marsh, a "lively, rustling,
noisy spot," is, in fact, the setting for man's sabotage of nature
and his inevitable dominion over its creatures. The reader gradually comes to recognize what the narrator cannot, namely that
the terrors of the marsh derive from civilized man, with his burgeoning indifference toward the passion within his breast.

Cousin Karl's lodge reveals the distance humankind has trav-
elled from "that first germ of life" that "stirred, vibrated, and expanded to the day." The contrast between the house itself and
the inhabitants of this unnatural country is ironic. The "sideboards, walls, and ceilings were covered with stuffed birds with
extended wings . . . perched on branches to which they were
nailed," and Cousin Karl resembles "some strange animal from
a cold country, dressed in a sealskin jacket." Both the narrator
and his cousin are often described as being wrapped in animal
skins, usurping the bestial for their own comforts, using the
creatures of nature to promote unnatural civilities and artist-
ries.

The wintry marsh, on the day the hunters will murder the
duck and the drake, symbolizes the ominous threat of civilization: the cold, cold hearts of humankind. The frozen marsh, normally "living," "noisy," "rustling," "splashing," is, on the morning of the hunt, cold enough to "split stones." The biting,
piercing cold foreshadows the heartless assassination, cousin
Karl's doing, of the passionately grieving drake, lamenting and
groaning for his mate.

Even these two men, however, carry within their breasts some
stirrings of passion and compassion until the moment that the

shots are fired and the winged lovers fall from the sky. The narrator, though the "drama of passion" in the daily newspaper neither "moves" nor "surprises" him, is nonetheless "passionately
fond" of "shooting," of "the water, of the sea." But though he
loves the water, it is "too vast, too restless, and too impossible to
hold." And, in the narrator's words, there is "nothing more disturbing, nothing more disquieting, more terrifying occasionally,
than a fen." He has channelled his passion, therefore, into what
is possible, finite, subject to control—shooting birds, watching
them fall heavily at his feet, there to turn as cold as the narrator's indifference to human love.

Karl's heart is likewise kindled for a moment when he expresses compassion for his Parisian cousin's cough and builds a
fire in the ice hut. It is Karl who calls the narrator outside to see
"the enormous diamond with a heart of fire . . . suddenly
planted there in the midst of the frozen water of the marsh." But
it is also Karl who suggests that the fire be extinguished when a
"peculiar cry, a lost, wandering cry" passes above the hunters.
The only way to stop this passionate movement, so terrifying to
the narrator, is to take aim and fire at these restless, vast
flocks—"the first clamor of life," "the sigh of the soul of the
world!" Only when the fiery gleam of the hut is dead, only when
the sky grows "pale," do the hunters end as well the love that
flies unfettered and boundless across the heavens. The narrator
murders the duck just as he will soon murder whatever flames
of sympathy, curiosity, or compassion he will feel toward lovers.
Then Karl, a conspirator in these crimes against passion, waits
to take aim at the grieving drake who inevitably returns, "careless of danger, infatuated by his animal love."

Neither the narrator nor his cousin escapes responsibility for
the death of love; but the narrator, for a split second, feels his
stony heart break with grief for the wrenching loss the drake
feels for his lover: "Never had any groans of suffering pained me
so much, as that lamentable reproach," says the narrator, with,
for once, a "heart of fire." But the moment of passion flies quickly, and when Karl shoots the drake, the narrator says, simply,
coldly, "I put them—they were already cold—into the same
game bag, and I returned to Paris that evening."

The descriptive passages, meticulously detailed, artfully craft-
ed, show the narrator's true heart, the icy heart of an articulate,
highly intelligent being who is, in the end, a dispassionate Parisian, "chilled to the very marrow." The paradox, breaking the
cold hearts of our civilized, rational, sophisticated natures, is, of
course, that the primitivism of the birds is the highest form of

sensitivity, delicacy, refinement. And the "fearsome" country of the human heart conceals the "unknown and dangerous secret": the inability of civilized humans to love passionately, or even, perhaps, to love at all.

Questions for discussion

1. How does the thesis statement control the topics of the three supporting paragraphs?

2. Is the introductory paragraph funnel-shaped, beginning generally and narrowing to a single intention?

3. How do the direct quotations lend support to the writer's argument?

4. How does the restatement of thesis go beyond the original thesis?

5. Can you identify several literary conventions and proprieties in the analysis?

6. Having read the story "Love," develop other thesis statements the writer omits, dealing with characterization, use of the first person, or other aspects of description.

7. Do you agree with the writer's thesis? Could you argue that the narrator is, in fact, a tender man, merely hampered by the trappings of polite behavior rather than being, in some way, dead?

8. Why does the story end so abruptly? Is the abrupt ending an artistic coup or a flaw? Explain.

Certain conventions and proprieties apply when you are analyzing all types of literature. The following reminders will add greater sophistication and professionalism to the presentation of your critical insights.

Be objective.

Though you surely have opinions about a literary work, hold them in abeyance. Focus, instead, on what the author is trying to do in terms of the work itself. Keep some distance; maintain some propriety and discretion; develop a critical, dispassionate eye. Literary analysis will, after all, continue to be a part of your life, even after you complete the required freshman and sopho-more courses. Movies are fictional works which elicit from you and your friends various critical discussions, reactions. So are television programs. Though you may sweepingly assert that you loved or hated a movie, astute friends will want to know on what basis you formed your opinion. At that exact moment, analysis steps in to save your point. You perhaps respond that the plot was not believable, that the characters were flat, that the sets and lighting were unimaginative. And you base your opinion on a careful analysis of what did or did not work. Liter-ary analysis is the mainstay of everyday conversation. Great meanings derive from entertainment, from books, magazines, music video, situation comedies, soap operas. You, then, already have some experience with literary analysis, and the essays you write about literature will inform and enhance your critical pre-sentation and perception in other areas as well.

How do you achieve the necessary distance and objectivity to write effective literary analysis? First, you do not confuse the teller of the tale, the speaking voice in the literary work, with the poet or author. Call the narrator in the story "Mr. Faulkner," and the teacher will quickly correct your perspective. Narrator and author are not the same. The narrator may be an actual character in the literary work. Herman Melville, for example, is not Ishmael, the narrator in *Moby Dick*. And even if the narrator bears a striking resemblance to the author, respect the author's right to wear a thin literary mask, the one behind which he or she can hide, or even cower.

Confusing the persona, narrator, or speaker with the author can produce outrage and can muddle meanings. When Thomas Wolfe wrote about his hometown, Asheville, North Carolina, the folks back home were hopping mad. They could not see the ob-jective world of art, so blinded were they by personal, intimate considerations. But the voice in *Look Homeward, Angel* is not Thomas Wolfe. And the town is not Asheville. The voice is a nar-rator, telling a tale that contains, perhaps, elements of realism but that has been reshaped into art, into a newly created world. The central character is Eugene Gant, certainly Wolfe himself but also every sensitive, different young person on a pilgrimage in search of an "unfound door." Asheville is the universe, as is Sherwood Anderson's *Winesburg, Ohio*, as is Africa in Joseph Conrad's *Heart of Darkness*, as is Emily Brontë's *Wuthering*

Heights. Fiction writers use the worlds they actually live in to inform their writing. But the fiction, though real in the sense of being authentic or genuine, is a figurative, stylistic creation.

Observe protocol.

So how do you refer to the author, poet, or dramatist as you discuss his or her artistic creation? You mention the author's full name immediately (spelled correctly and in the conventional form: T. S. Eliot, Edna St. Vincent Millay), often in the opening sentence of the literary analysis. And when you identify the author, you also identify both the genre and the title of the work under consideration. Your opening sentence might therefore read, "William Faulkner's Gothic tale 'A Rose for Emily' centers on necrophilia." Or you write, "Death is the theme of Christina Rossetti's poem 'Song.'" Then, throughout the remainder of the analysis, you refer to the author by last name only, and exclusively when you are discussing matters concerning the author's life, philosophy, and reputation, not the central voice in the literary work. Furthermore, you treat both male and female authors with the same detached courtesy. You do not refer to Amy Lowell's poem "Patterns" and, in subsequent references, call her "Miss Lowell." Why should she be "Miss Lowell" when male writers are not "Mr. Chaucer," "Mr. Shakespeare," and "Mr. Updike"?

And how do you distinguish between the voice in the literary work and the author himself or herself? In poems, you usually refer to the voice as "the speaker" or "the persona." In stories or novels, you usually refer to the voice as "the narrator" if he or she has no name. Robert Frost probably did not stop by woods on a snowy evening. And even if he did, you are not to let on that you think so. Give a literary person some privacy, as well as his or her fantastical powers of invention.

Avoid plot summary.

Your instructor may, at times, assign essays to check your understanding of the plot, the action of the fictional work. A book report, for example, usually contains some description of the plot, along with an opinion about the possible appeal of the literary work both for the reviewer and for the audience. But literary analysis is not the place for plot summary. Why? Because analysis is, by definition, an interpretation of how a book, poem, or play works. Analysis is neither judgment nor summary. It is a study, not a recapitulation.

The surest way to avoid plot summary is to return to the fundamentals of good essay writing. Plot summarizers invariably begin their paragraphs with facts about the plot, not concepts or interpretations. The plot summarizer writes, "After the heroine divorces Sir Cedric, she then marries Lord Watlington." Having begun the paragraph with a factual statement, the student then has no choice but to relate the next fact or incident in the plot: "But the heroine is miserable with Lord Watlington, so she runs off with the stable boy." One fact leads yawningly to another; and by the time the reader finishes the "analysis," he feels as though he has been reading a condensed version of the novel.

If every paragraph begins with a bold assertion, a concept, a slant, an angle, then profundity may lead to profundity. The statements about the heroine seem to center around marriage and divorce, infidelity and class. The student might write: "The novel seems to mock God-ordained monogamy." Or the student might write: "The heroine flaunts social and moral convention by choosing, in the end, happiness with a stable boy." Or the student might write: "This novel, as evidenced by the whimsical and fleeting alliances, makes a mockery of marriage, devotion, fidelity." All of the above hypotheses might be wrong in the analytical sense, but they would be right in the conceptual sense. They force the critic to put plot in its place, underneath meanings, themes, characterization, and setting.

Note: It is important, here, to make a distinction between setting forth a critical hypothesis about a literary work and passing judgment on it. Certainly, your thesis needs a fresh slant, an angle. Judgments, however, are attempts to manipulate the reader's thinking even before you have engaged his or her respectful attention. Your critical perception in literary analysis will focus on *what is* or *what might be*, not *what should be*. The thesis statements set forth earlier could all slip into judgment with only the insertion of a word or phrase. In the statements that follow, the italicized portions indicate the point at which the writer veers from analysis into preaching and propaganda.

The novel seems to mock God-ordained monogamy *by glamorizing reckless and indiscriminate adultery, surely the path to destruction.*

The heroine *wisely* flaunts *dreary* social and moral convention by choosing, in the end, happiness with a stable boy, *a life that will surely afford her greater freedom and choice than would life with Lord Watlington.*

This novel, as evidenced by the whimsical and fleeting alliances, makes a mockery of marriage, devotion, and fidelity, *all cornerstones of a healthy, responsible, Godly life.*

Ask the appropriate analytical questions.

But if you are not called upon to summarize the plot, then what is your task in literary analysis? As discussed earlier, certain questions lead you to analyze rather than to summarize or pass judgment. In novels, stories, or plays, you ask yourself the following: What is the theme? Why do the characters act as they do? What is the significance of their names? How do the diction, tone, and plot carry meaning? How does the setting relate to theme? How does the literary work fit into its era? What are the images and symbols and how do they support or relate to theme and character?

In poetry, you ask all those questions and more. You speculate on the way in which rhyme or meter supports or enhances the artistry of the poem. You analyze the logic behind the figurative language and imagery, explaining the poet's use of metaphor, simile, personification, symbol. You consider the voice, the persona. You note the punctuation in the poem—or the lack of it—as it relates to the overall aesthetic purpose of the poem. You explain the allusions or references in the poem. The poet may allude to myths, events of the time, biblical passages, famous people. If you do not catch the allusion, the meaning of the poetic line or verse will escape you. For example, you cannot analyze W. H. Auden's poem "Musée Des Beaux Arts" unless you are familiar with both the myth of Icarus and Breughel's artistic depiction of it.

You will analyze with greater skill and accuracy if you remember that the effects in literary works are not whimsical, accidental. In fact, the definition of good or great literature may be simply that the desired effects are intentional, conscious. Implicit meanings derive from setting, character, imagery. Why is the season winter rather than summer? Why are there recurring images of circles—suns, moons, cycles, droplets of water? Why does the heroine wear red? Why is the garden formal? Your task, in analysis, is to get beneath the surfaces of the poem or story and explore the country of imagination, significance, symbol.

Stay in the eternal present.

Literary works exist in the eternal present and, therefore, must be discussed as though the works were contemporaneous to you and your era. Even though Chaucer's *Canterbury Tales* is a fourteenth-century work, you are to write about it as though the action were in progress at this moment. You assert, "The Wife of Bath *says*, 'But yet I hadde alwey a coltes tooth. Gat-toothed I was, and that bicam me weel.' " And you write as well, "Chaucer *creates*, in *The Canterbury Tales*, witty, amusing, endearing, believable characters, much like many of the characters of this modern world." Or you write, "In the 'Prologue,' the speaker *says*, 'He was a verray parfit gentil knight.' "

Does this mean that every verb in literary analysis must be in the present tense? Certainly not. But the overriding time is the present, and when you are quoting from or referring to the literary work, you treat the action as though it were now, adjusting the time sequences accordingly. Even when you are writing about what is happening at this very moment, you need other verb tenses to clarify relationships in time. For example, I *am writing* about this chapter on literary analysis, and it *will be* useful, if only because you *have* never *learned* how to handle special techniques that *apply* only to literary analysis. I begin with the now and slip into other time frames as they relate to the now.

And the same applies to references to critical articles about the literary work. You write, "In the May 1977 issue of *College Composition and Communication*, Hugh Rank *claims* that Orwell's essays are weak because they 'end with a vague, shoulder-shrugging attitude.' " Critical articles, culled from scholarly journals, are called *secondary sources*. The *primary source* is the literary work you are analyzing. But whether the work being cited is primary or secondary, written last year or five centuries ago, it is referred to in the eternal present.

Quote from primary and secondary sources.

Because the story or poem comes first in literary analysis, you will want to use direct quotations from it to support your theories and assertions. Effective use of quoted material is, of course, important in all kinds of writing. But quoting directly is perhaps of even greater significance in writing about literature. You are, after all, looking in two directions when you analyze literature. The work itself stands before you, demanding your constant attention. And simultaneously you are writing an essay about that literary work—in other words, creating a literary work of your own. And so both you and the reader must always have before the mind's eye the object of art and the analysis of it.

Literary analysis, then, requires that you have an excellent grasp of how to quote, how often to quote, and how much to quote. Usually, you may quote only a piece of a line or a single word. Other times, you will quote longer passages. You will want to study Chapter 10 (pages 337–340) even as you consider the importance of direct and reasonably frequent quoting in your analytical essay. (See also the sample research paper in Chapter 12 for examples of effective quoting.) Most, or even all, of your supporting paragraphs should contain one or several direct quotations (though not necessarily *long* ones), either from the primary source or from secondary sources—journals, letters, diaries, scholarly articles. Why? Because a literary analysis without apt quotations is like an accident with no witnesses. How will the reader feel confident of your interpretation if he or she sees no concrete examples from the work itself? Nothing is more concrete than a quotation of support and verification. (And nothing is worse than a naked quotation expected to prove itself or make its own case.) Paraphrasing—rewording an idea or description from the literary work—is fine, and often preferable, but the *occasional* direct quotation will carry weight with the reader. Quoting occasionally, directly—and smoothly integrating the quotations into the pattern of your interpretation—will be a great convenience to the reader. He should not have to read your critical analysis with a copy of the book or poem at his side.

Of course, when you quote directly, either from primary or secondary sources, you will need to acknowledge the source of the quotation. Indicate the author and/or title within the body of the essay, or indicate the author, title of the work, and page number in parentheses. (See Chapter 12.) Supply for the reader a list of works cited. After all, the interpretation may be so interesting or original that the reader may want to pursue your idea further. Or if your theory about some aspect of a literary work is controversial, the reader may want to double-check the accuracy of your reading of the work.

When you use critical, scholarly articles, you will want to choose strong comments that offer opportunities for vigorous critical debate. Why should you quote a critical opinion that no one would dispute? There is no need, for example, to quote a scholar who asserts that the letter "A" in Nathaniel Hawthorne's *The Scarlet Letter* stands for "adultery" or that John Keats's Grecian urn is from Greece. Seek provocative, challenging quotations, and use them either to support your views or to enhance the liveliness of your systematic refutation of the critic's idea.

Vigorous critical comment is available to you. You may write, for example, "Kenneth Rexroth, writing in the July 1, 1967, issue of *Saturday Review*, says of Henry Fielding's *Tom Jones:* 'Tom Jones has been compared to Ulysses and Huck Finn. Huck Finn he somewhat resembles; Ulysses not at all.' " You can then go on to argue that Rexroth is right or wrong, basing your agreement or disagreement on your own critical analysis of Tom Jones's character.

Remember, too, that each time you quote from the work itself or from a noted authority on the literary work, you must comment on the quotation. You have troubled yourself to locate an apt quotation. Why would you then think the quotation unworthy of explanation, rebuttal, defense? The reader needs to understand why and in what context you are using the quotation.

You may choose your quotations more effectively by asking yourself the following questions:

1. Do I know what the quotation really means? Do I understand its context, implications?

2. Does the quotation exactly prove what I am asserting? Or does the quotation set up a provocative critical dispute between the authority and me?

3. Does the quotation say better than I could say what needs to be said?

4. Is the authority I am quoting respectable, the best in his or her field? Should I verify the reliability of the source by asking the instructor or professor, by checking the credentials of the critic (for instance, graduate degrees, previous publications, reputation of the school at which she teaches)?

5. Will one word, one phrase, one sentence, or perhaps an entire quoted paragraph be necessary to support my assertion?

6. Does the quotation flow smoothly into the structure and development of my own ideas, or does it feel "stuck in," abrupt?

If you know the answer to all these questions, then you can feel confident that the quotation will serve to enhance, not detract from, your analysis. You might agree, perhaps, with novelist Henry James's assessment of the critic's role: "Just in proportion as he [the critic] is sentient and restless, just in proportion as he reacts and reciprocates and penetrates, is the critic a valuable instrument." And so you will want also to choose quotations just in proportion to whether or not those quotations cry out for reaction. And you will then be quoting effectively. A quotation is useful only when it relates to your thesis, your topic sentence, your analytical, critical view.

Understand literary terminology.

Every field, whether science, history, politics, commerce, or art, has its specialized language. You may struggle with literary analysis not because you do not understand the literary work but because you do not have the language to write about it. You have to know what to call things, or you will be left with the frustrating feeling of wanting to respond without knowing how to frame the response.

The following glossary will supply you with the language of literature, with the correct terms and labels for the structures, devices, and philosophies that run through literature. The glossary is not all-inclusive, certainly. But it will serve as a quick reference when you suspect that something intentional and artistic is occurring but you have no words to express that intention.

And the glossary will help you talk about literature as well as write about it. Your instructor, for example, may use a language that is, at times, incomprehensible or confusing to you. Then, too, the meaning in scholarly articles may elude you because the technical language of literary analysis is unfamiliar. So this short glossary will help you in writing about literature, in researching literary authorities, and in classroom lectures and discussions about literature.

Understand literary terms: A glossary.

alliteration: The repetition of initial sounds—goodly, gracious, and grand; wicked witch of the West; frenzied, frantic friars

anthropomorphize: giving human traits to animals or inanimate objects, as with the rabbits in Richard Adams' *Watership Down* (Compare *personification:* giving human traits to abstract ideas or inanimate objects as when *houses groan* and *sigh* or *pride struts* and *preens*)

apostrophe: a turning away from discourse to address an absent or imaginary person—"What boots it, Shelley! that the breeze/ Carried thy lovely wail away" (Matthew Arnold, "Stanzas from the Grande Chartreuse")

assonance: an almost-but-not-quite rhyme, echoes of vowel sounds—opens/rose; equals/breathing; hill/wilderness

blank verse: unrhymed lines of iambic pentameter (see **metrical feet** and **metrical patterns**)

caesura: a natural break in a poetic line, signified by two parallel slanted lines—"That sunny dome! // those caves of ice" (Samuel Taylor Coleridge, "Kubla Khan")

classicism: aesthetic principles from the ancient Greeks and Romans emphasizing form, simplicity, balance, and restraint in art and literature

couplet: two successive lines of poetry with the same end rhyme and the same meter—"True ease in writing comes from art, not chance, / As those move easiest who have learned to dance." (Alexander Pope, "Essay on Criticism")

denouement: literally, the "untying"—the solution or resolution of the plot, sometimes ending in "happily ever after," usually not

elegy: a mournful poem, often expressing grief over a death

epic: a very long, narrative poem, celebrating a heroic tradition or a specific hero, as in Virgil's *Aeneid*

epigram: a short, witty poem or observation expressing a single thought—"Some good, some so-so, and lots of plain bad: That's how a poem is made, my friend." (Martial)

existentialism: a philosphy or system of ethics, prevalent in the twentieth century, emphasizing the unique and particular in human experience and rejecting general or abstract laws and meanings; individuals, therefore, struggling to give meaning to existence, freely choosing and accepting responsibility for their actions

explication: a close textual analysis of a literary work (usually a poem) (see explication of Lowell's poem on pages 376–377)

free verse: poetry that has no set rhyme and no set meter

hyperbole: an exaggeration—"No spring, nor summer beauty hath such grace, / As I have seen in one autumnal face" (John Donne, "Elegy IX, The Autumnal"); "She is all states, and all princes, I, / Nothing else is" (Donne again, "The Sun Rising").

imagery: using figures of speech or vivid description to produce mental images

juvenilia: literary works written in childhood

metaphor: a comparison, not using "like" or "as," between two unlike things—"War is a contagion." (Franklin Delano Roosevelt)

meter: the beat or rhythm of a poem—ta-DAH, ta-DAH, ta-DAH or, perhaps, TA-dah-dah, TA-dah-dah, TA-dah-dah (Compare the beat of " 'Twas the night before Christmas" with the beat of "Hickory, dickory, dock.")

metrical feet: the number of times a metrical pattern repeats itself (see **metrical pattern**)

    dimeter: twice, as in spondaic (spondee) dimeter—bíg, táll / milkmán

    trimeter: three times, as in trochaic (trochee) trimeter—Kiśś thĕ / giŕl ŏn / Chŕistmăs

    tetrameter: four times, as in iambic (iamb) tetrameter— I seńt/ mў lóve / ă kiśś / oŕ twó

    pentameter: five times, as in iambic pentameter— I seńt / mў lóve / ă kiśś / oŕ twó / oŕ thŕee

hexameter: six times, as in anapestic (anapest) hexameter—
'Twăs thĕ níght / of thĕ yeár / thăt I dréad / ĕd thĕ móst, /
aňd I féared / thăt thĕ míst

metrical pattern: the several or various ways the beat can fall
   anapest: short, short, long (or soft, soft, hard)—mĭs-ăl-ly
   dactyl: long, short, short (or hard, soft, soft)—coúr-tĕ-oŭs
   iamb: short, long (or soft, hard)—pŏ-líce
   spondee: long, long (or hard, hard)—slám-baňg
   trochee: long, short (or hard, soft)—wín-soṁe

motif: a recurring thematic element, as in Chancery in Charles
   Dickens's *Bleak House,* the river in Mark Twain's *Huckleberry
   Finn,* or the moors in Emily Brontë's *Wuthering Heights*

narrator: the speaker or teller of the tale in a novel, story, or
   play; may or may not be an actual character and is distinct
   from the author himself or herself (generally, in poems, the
   speaker or persona)

naturalism: explanations for humanity found in science, not the
   supernatural; humans depicted as helpless in an indifferent
   world, as victims of things they cannot control; outgrowth of
   realism; "survival of the fittest," a Darwinian concept; biolog-
   ical determinism

ode: a lyrical poem, full of praise for a person, quality, or thing
   and usually rhyming, as in Percy Bysshe Shelley's "Ode to the
   West Wind"

onomatopoeia: a word that sounds like the sound it makes—
   crack, thud, thump, buzz, whir, fizz, hiss, cuckoo, bang, whine,
   and *whimper*

pastoral: a literary work that conveys rural life in an ideal
   manner

pathos: subjective, emotional elements in a work of art, in contrast to the objective, rational elements; specifically, a quality
   in something or someone that arouses feelings of pity or
   sympathy

persona: the speaking voice in a literary work, as distinct from
   the author or poet, also called the *speaker* (generally, in novels
   or stories, the *narrator*)

personification: giving human characteristics to abstract ideas
   or inanimate objects, as when Love weeps, Hate frowns,
   clouds dance (see **anthropormorphize**)

point of view: perspective from which a literary work is conveyed
  first-person point of view: uses "I" and is limited to seeing events only through that "I"
  third-person point of view: sees events through the eyes of "he" or "she" or "they" and is limited to seeing events only through those characters; other-oriented
  omniscient point of view: sees all, knows all, sees events from the perspective of all, moving freely in and out of the minds of all the characters

realism: a quality of or effort in literature toward what is literal, observable through the senses, pragmatic, actual (not theoretical and ideal); an authentic and complete report of human experience with an emphasis on character over plot; (usually capitalized) beginning in the late nineteenth century, a rebellion against Romanticism

review: a critical report on a particular literary work or performance leading to an evaluation or appraisal of its artistic success or failure

rhyme: repetition of sounds within words, whether exact (life/rife) or approximate (shines/tides); exact rhymes also called end rhymes; approximate rhymes also called *slant rhymes*

romanticism: (usually capitalized) a break from classical forms, beginning in the late eighteenth century and giving rise to exotic subjects, rural themes, intervention of supernatural forces in human affairs, Gothic tales, an emphasis on the common man, an intensity of feeling and imagination; (usually lower-cased) making the ordinary extraordinary, insisting that everything is a fit subject for literature and, more particularly, for poetry

simile: a short comparison using "like" or "as"

soliloquy: a monologue in which a character converses with himself, a kind of thinking out loud

sonnet: fourteen rhymed lines of iambic pentameter, the first eight of which (octave) state the problem and the last six of which (sestet) bring the resolution, or alternatively, the first twelve of which (three quatrains) state the problem and the last two of which (couplet) bring the resolution

symbol: a word that conveys several meanings or associations; an object (rose, moon, circle) used to suggest intangible or invisible meanings (passion, femininity, perfection)

synecdoche: a word that broadly serves as a substitute for a more specific term or vice versa—policeman also called "the law"

the unities: from Aristotle's *Poetics*, the idea that drama requires a singleness of time, place, and action—one plot, the action of which occurs in one day and in one locality

◆

Activities

1. Poetry need not be the mysterious, befuddling experience you may, thus far, have expected. It may come as a surprise to you that a poem has an implicit thesis, logic, content, development, methods of support, descriptive details, and figurative language that are similar to the techniques and devices you use to create an essay about stamp collecting or ecology. Select a short poem, and using the techniques explained in this chapter, recast the poem as an essay.

2. The glossary contains general literary terms and philosophies. But it omits much specialized language about the theater, about drama. Write a short essay in which you use definition as the primary method of development and support and in which you discuss the specialized language of the theater, the dramatic arts. You will likely need to research the topic somewhat, seeking explanations and definitions of technical terms. Assume that your audience is not familiar with the world of the dramatic arts.

3. Now that you have seen how to approach literary works, you may wish to transfer that skill to other disciplines. Select a scientific article, and analyze it as you would a literary work. You may analyze a highly technical scientific work or a popular source, perhaps a magazine dealing with scientific subjects for the general public. Similar principles apply, after all, in the writing of all good analysis.

4. Choose one of your favorite songs, and explicate the lyrics as you would a poem, paying attention to the use of figurative language, the rhyme, the meter, the characters or conflict in the song. Rock songs, for example, often employ devices and techniques similar to those of poetry or drama. Country-Western songs often contain the same elements as novels or stories: plot, character, setting, conflict, and resolution or denouement.

5. Review a movie of your choice, including both your opinion about the quality of the movie and your analysis of why it succeeds or fails, of how it works.

12

Writing the Research Paper

If you thought of doing all the myriad small tasks of daily life at one time—making your bed, flossing your teeth, paying your bills, preparing your food, getting the oil changed in your car— you would very likely crawl under the covers and stay there forever, paralyzed by all the work to be done. But you do not. You break down the responsibilities of your life into manageable chunks, allocating each task to minutes, hours, days, or weeks. Look too far ahead, think too often about how much there is to do, and you will freeze.

The research paper may seem to be an imposing task. But it is not. When you break down the task into small parts handled daily, you find that the process goes smoothly and that the product—a fine piece of well-documented writing—is a source of pride. "I wrote that?" you find yourself saying, as you flip through the final manuscript and discover, to your surprise and delight, that the content is clear, authoritative, original, and professional-looking.

The approach to the research paper is, in some ways, the same approach you use in the writing of an in-class assignment or a weekly composition. The research paper is not really harder than other kinds of writing. It is simply longer. Two tasks, however, make the research paper different from a personal essay: learning to use the library and understanding how and when to document your sources. The principles of good writing, the same ones you have learned in earlier chapters, will apply to every writing task, including this one.

The Chronology of a Research Paper provides you with a daily agenda that you may follow in your own quest for information and documentation. Though this chapter provides models and explanations for this special writing task, it seeks, also, to reassure and guide you as you begin your own first day of research and conclude, some weeks later, with a final research paper that equals or even surpasses your initial expectations. And once your paper is nearing completion, you can then use the checklist (pages 420–422) to test the quality and professionalism of your research and writing effort.

Chronology of a research paper.

First day: Receive the assignment.

The instructor today announces in class that you will be writing your first research paper. A groan goes up around the room. After all, for several weeks you have been writing paragraphs and short essays. You are nervous about the huge writing task you face. The instructor assures you that a *research paper is simply a very long essay written on the basis of library materials.* She says you will be *using the techniques for writing good essays that you have already studied:* choosing a topic, developing a thesis, preparing an outline, finding materials that will best support your theory and assertions. The reminder is only a little comforting. After all, even before you write the research paper, you will need to learn how to use a library.

The instructor then describes the requirements of the assignment: the research paper can be on a topic of your choice (sighs of relief), *but,* she adds, the topic must relate in some way to current fads, trends, modes of thought, technology. And the topic must relate to your experience as well. She does not want you simply to patch and piece together other people's ideas and facts. She wants you to use your own voice in the paper. And the library materials will simply provide support for what is, in fact, your own opinion. Furthermore, she thinks the thesis of the research paper can be as fresh, as original or controversial, as the thesis statements for your routine compositions.

You hear the usual speech on *plagiarism.* She reminds you that you must cite any ideas, opinions, theories, or information that is not generally known or not your own. Some students are surprised. They think plagiarism simply involves not putting quotation marks around direct quotations and citing their sources. Wrong, says the teacher. Even if you paraphrase or re-word another person's idea, you must give credit to that person.

You wonder how you can avoid plagiarism, even though you would never knowingly copy or steal another person's idea. The instructor advises that as you find each source, you quickly read the passage and then close the book before setting down notes. That way, you will be forced to use your own words when summarizing the material you have just read. She also discourages relying too much on only one or two sources; doing so, she says, will tempt you to copy long passages. For that reason, the instructor reminds you that the encyclopedia offers perhaps the strongest temptation to plagiarism, since the subject under consideration might be treated over only one or two pages. You laugh, remembering high school research papers that sprang full-blown from the pages of *World Book* or the *Encyclopedia Britannica.*

Finally, the instructor lays out the requirements for form and length. The paper should be approximately 10 typewritten pages, double-spaced. Notes must be taken on three- by five-inch cards. You complain that notecards are a nuisance, but she says the notecards will be very useful later, in the organizing and writing of the paper. You can, she says, spread out the cards and restack them according to subject headings. You will then be less likely to rely too much on one source, and your research paper content will easily fall into place.

The instructor places no limit on the number of citations and list of works used, saying that the citation numbers will vary, depending on the scope and topic of each person's paper. But she does advise that too few citations will indicate an overreliance on unsupported personal opinions. And too many citations will suggest that you are not really thinking on your own, relying instead almost entirely on the ideas of so-called authorities.

She also hopes your sources will be varied, including citations from magazines (both popular and scholarly), reference books (easy on the encyclopedias), newspapers, books by one author, edited anthologies, books in several volumes, maybe even personal interviews and television programs. She will be looking for variety, she says, in works consulted and cited.

Then the bad news comes. The research paper will be due in four weeks. You beg for extra time, but she says something about how "work expands to fill the time available" and that the longer you are permitted to work on the research paper, the longer you will need to complete it. She wants to see the rough outline, thesis, and the notecards in a couple of weeks, the rough draft by the end of the third week, and the revised and final paper at the end of the month. A little scary.

Second day: Use the library.

Today you spend the class period talking about how to use the library. The instructor assures you that the reference librarians are there to help you and will direct you to the appropriate initial sources. But the instructor warns you not to waste your time cruising through the library until you have first thought about your topic. How do you decide on a possible topic? You ask questions: Is there a book you have been reading that makes you want to know more about the author, characters, period in which it was written? Is there a course that excites you? Is there a recent assignment that seemed a pleasure, not a duty? Do you have special talents, hobbies, experiences that might generate a topic? "Brainstorming," says the instructor, "comes first."

After you have settled on a possible topic for research, you can begin by going first to the reference desk for information about the location of the stacks—the shelves where the books are kept. In some libraries, researchers may go directly into the stacks. Other libraries have "closed stacks," meaning that the researcher must fill out a *call slip* and give it to the librarian, who then goes into the stacks and brings out the necessary material. Let us assume that your campus library has open stacks.

The reference librarian will first direct you to the *card catalog*, where sources are arranged alphabetically in filing drawers, by subject, author, and title. If you do not know enough about the subject to be searching for a particular book, you can look under the general category, say "computers" or "Congress," and find all the books in the library that deal with those subjects. Each file card will contain, as well, a call number, the length of the work, and perhaps a bit of information about the contents of the work. So you can rule out certain sources even as you flip through the

Figure 12-1   A Sample Catalog Card

```
616.89
B192      Baldwin, Christina.
             One to one : self-understanding through journal
          writing / Christina Baldwin. New York : M. Evans,
          c1977.
             xvi, 186 p. ; 22 cm.
             Bibliography: p. 181-186.


             1.   Diaries--Therapeutic use.
          2.   Self-perception.   I.   Title
```

files. Figure 12-1 is an example of a catalog card. Your library may have replaced the card catalog with a *microfiche catalog*, which contains the library's listings on film. The microfiche catalog is simple to operate, but if you are having difficulty, just ask the librarian for assistance.

The library may also have an *on-line catalog*, which uses computers to catalog all of the library's books. The on-line catalog, like the card catalog, lists books by title, author, and subject. But the on-line catalog may offer additional information. Some systems will indicate whether a book is checked out or on reserve or how many copies of the book are available. Most on-line catalogs are user friendly, a reassuring thought to a nervous researcher. Again, the librarian will help if you find the on-line catalog to be user hostile.

For *magazines* (called "periodicals"), you can go to the *Readers' Guide to Periodical Literature.* There you will find articles listed under subject headings, with title or author and including the date, month, or year the article appeared. Your library will have a listing nearby of all the magazines to which it subscribes. No need to search for an article you remembered reading in *Architectural Digest* if the library does not subscribe to the magazine. The instructor tells you that some magazines are bound and placed in the *periodical room.* Other magazines might be stored on microfilm. You can ask. Figure 12-2 contains a sample entry from the *Readers' Guide.*

Figure 12-2   A Sample Listing from the *Readers' Guide to Periodical Literature*

DIARIES
Dear diary: putting your life into words. J. Marks. Teen 25:8-9 N '81
Dialogue journals:
  Counselor responds. M. Wall. il Todays Educ 70:36 S/O '81
  First step in helping troubled students. M. M. Potts. il Todays
    Educ 70:34-5 S/O '81
Diary writing turns a new leaf. P. Huyghe. N Y Times Mag p 98+ N
  8 '81
Journey with a journal [camping trips] M. M. Kuehn. il Sierra
  66:76-7 My/Je '81
1964. B. Greene. il Esquire 96:17-18 N '81
Way of the journal [Intensive Journal workshops; views of I. Pro-
  goff] R. B. Kaiser. bibl il Psychol Today 15:64-5+ Mr '81

Newspaper articles are now often stored on microfilm as well. The librarian will show you how to flash on the screen an article from, say, the June 27, 1962, issue of the *New York Times*.

But suppose you are interested in consulting sources other than magazines of general interest, newspapers, and books. You can rely on indexes. Each field is represented by an index: for example, *British Humanities Index, Arts and Humanities Citation Index, Chemical Abstracts, Business Periodicals Index*, and so forth.

And, of course, you might explore the reference room for encyclopedias, atlases, collections of quotations, biographical information.

Some of the professors put sources on a *reserve shelf* to prevent students from checking out a source and taking it back to the residence hall for two or three weeks. The reserve shelf is behind the reference desk. Placing books on reserve may make gaining access to those books a little more complicated, but that way one student cannot check out every available source on, say, the Monarch butterfly, and deny all the other students access to those materials. *If there is a run on a certain research paper topic and you cannot find any books on that topic in the stacks, you should check the reserve shelf.* Another professor or instructor may have assigned the same topic to his or her students and gathered the available materials in advance.

Third day: Track down trivia.

The instructor wants you to be thinking about your topics. But she is more concerned, at this point, that you become comfortable with the library and with what is available to you. She proposes a trivia game, full of questions that will lead you to a variety of sources. The detective game will be fun, and you will learn better how to track down obscure or exotic information. The assignment, then, is to answer the questions that follow and to document informally where you find the answers. Even if you already know the answer to a question, you must nevertheless provide specific documentation. The winner gets an extension on the research paper deadline.

1. Why is the sky blue?

2. In 1973, what college had the highest tuition rate in the United States?

3. Of what is Teflon made?

4. Who solved the problem of the seven bridges of Königsberg?

5. What golfer has won more titles and more money than any other player in the history of the sport?

6. What state caused the Equal Rights Amendment to be defeated?

7. What percentage of sleeping hours does a person spend dreaming?

8. How many babies were born at Woodstock?

9. What pigment in the skin is responsible for protecting the body against radiation?

10. Define a "villanelle," and give one example of a twentieth-century poet's use of the form.

11. As of 1985, which three cities in the United States were considered the best places to live?

12. What poem caused philosopher Simone Weil to have a conversion experience?

13. What was the artistic philosophy of the Dadaists?

14. What was the headline for the May 16, 1932, issue of the New York Times?

15. What is the primary cause of most traffic accidents?

Fourth day: Choose a topic.

You think you have a topic. You want to write about street people. You figure the topic is certainly relevant. All kinds of homeless people are wandering around the city. They worry you. Where do they come from? Where are they going? You have read that some of them have been released from institutions— ex-mental patients, for example. Of course, there are all kinds of street people out there: alcoholics, drug addicts, prostitutes, un- employed people hanging around on street corners, homeless elderly who cannot afford nursing homes and have no families to take them in, battered or abused women who have left home, runaway teenagers, mentally incompetent or disturbed people.

You are pretty pleased with your topic choice, but when you tell your instructor, her only comment is "What about them?" Well, you do not exactly know. The variety of reasons why peo- ple are homeless is endless. And do you want to focus on the problem, on the solution, or on one particular type of street per- son? And what sources will you use? You cannot seem to settle on a thesis. Though you see these people all the time, you guess you know absolutely or almost nothing about where to begin and what to say about them.

After the instructor and you chat a minute, she suggests you mull over your topic choice a bit more. Here is some good ad- vice: she says you will do better to *select a subject about which you are already reasonably well-informed and will feel comfortable about exploring it further.* "Build on what you know," she says. "No need to start from zero, in a field about which you know noth- ing." Hmm, you have never taken a sociology course, and you do not even know a street person. More thought.

Fifth day: Change the topic.

You have changed your mind. You look over your books at home and notice that you are forever buying and reading pub- lished journals, diaries, and collections of letters, especially by writers. And in your psychology class, the professor has been talking lately about how journals are being used, these days, in therapy groups. You do not know anything about the history of journal keeping, but certainly you are interested both in writing and in psychology. Maybe you can write about how or why the journal has changed. When did journal keeping come into vogue? Why do so many writers keep journals? Why the sudden and recent popularity of journal writing in the field of psycho- therapy? The topic is certainly relevant.

The instructor agrees with you. When you talk about the subject, she says she can detect more than passing curiosity. She sees that you can build on prior knowledge, draw from material that relates both to literature (your primary interest) and psychology (certainly one of your favorite subjects). But what is your thesis? Not yet sure. You will go to the library and do some reading.

Sixth day: Begin research.

You pick up some notecards and pens at the bookstore and head for the library. The reference librarian points you to the card catalog, and you already know some books by title and author that you want to check out. These books will be your *primary sources*, the journals themselves. You find *The Diary of Alice James*, edited by Leon Edel; two journals by May Sarton; another called *The Measure of My Days* by a woman named Florida Scott-Maxwell; Anne Morrow Lindbergh's *Gift from the Sea; Journey Around My Room*, by Louise Bogan (edited by Ruth Limmer). You notice that all these journals have been kept by women. Perhaps you will focus primarily on why journal keeping seems to be more important to women. Or maybe it is not. Anyway, you have read all or portions of these books and think a thesis may emerge as you study their motives for writing in journals.

You jot down the *call numbers* (determined by the Library of Congress) and head for the stacks. *As you locate each book, you write on a notecard the call number, author, title, city of publication, publisher, and copyright year.* The instructor has advised that, for each source consulted, you set down every bit of available information about the work. Then, later, you will not have to return to the library to find the copyright or get the publishing company. Good advice: *never handle a source more than once.* After all, you are not sure yet which sources will be useful and which will not. Figure 12-3 shows what source cards look like.

You gather up these books and go to the circulation desk to check them out. They will require careful reading to discover the writers' motives for keeping journals and diaries. Today, you do not check other sources. You are more interested in getting a general view, in getting in the right frame of mind for thinking about journals and their uses.

Figure 12-3 Sample Source Cards

Article

Book

> Rainer, Tristine
> "The New Diary—Where Anything Goes"
>   pp. 57-61
> Writer's Yearbook
> 1979

> 616.89
> B192
> Baldwin, Christina
> One to One: Self Understanding Through Journal Writing
> New York: M Evans and Co.
> 1977

You return to your room and begin perusing the books, looking particularly for the writers' statements about why they keep journals. You record their reasons on individual notecards, putting quotation marks around parts you quote exactly. *The content card contains, in each case, the author's last name, the page or pages from which the idea is taken, the central idea of the note, and the quoted or paraphrased passage.* Of course, you have two journals by May Sarton, so you must distinguish which idea comes from which journal by including the title as well. Figure 12-4 displays a sample content card.

Seventh—fourteenth days: *Look for secondary sources and review and analyze all research materials.*

Last night's reading has led you to several motives for keeping journals: self-definition, self-understanding, a way to sort out

Figure 12-4   A Sample Content Notecard

> Evolution of Journals   Huyghe
>   p. 102
>
> "Diaries gradually became less a spiritual tool and travelogue and more an instrument of release."

feelings and opinions. Your thesis, then, will assert that the journal leads inward, in pursuit of the Self, of identity, transforming its creator into a work of art. You can then tie in the use of the journal as a psychological exploration. You can expand the meaning and importance of the journal, not simply as a way of recording events but of shaping one's destiny. But you are still ignorant of the history and various uses of the journals.

Another trip to the library leads you to different and *secondary sources:* articles and books *about* journals. This time you return to the card catalog, not to search for specific works by specific authors with whom you are already familiar but to find other books that might deal entirely or in part with journal keeping. You find only one, under the subject heading "Journals": a book by Christina Baldwin called *One to One: Self-Understanding Through Journal Writing.* As before, you go to the stacks, find the book, and immediately prepare another bibliography card.

You then return to the reference room and head for the *Readers' Guide to Periodical Literature.* Because you want to include the latest views and attitudes toward journal keeping, you begin with the most recent installment and work backward. The softcover editions contain the most recent magazine articles and will be bound, as time passes, into hardcover collections. You look under several headings: "Diaries," "Journals," "Letters." One of your best sources turns out to be listed under the "Diary" heading, an article by Patrick Huyghe from the 1981 *New York Times Magazine.* You also see possible articles from *Psychology Today, Today's Education, The Writer,* and *A Writer's Yearbook.* You are sure the library subscribes to the first two magazines, but you are not certain that *Today's Education, The Writer,* or *A Writer's Yearbook* will be on hand. You find the librarian and ask where to check for a list of the magazines the library carries. She directs you to the appropriate listing, and you find that the library does, indeed, have both magazines on the shelves of the periodical room. Since the *New York Times Magazine* will be on microfilm, the librarian directs you to a small room filled with an imposing machine. Simple instructions enable you to locate the article on the screen. The article is very long, and there is no surface space on which to spread out your materials and take notes. So the librarian makes a copy for you to read at home.

You pick up still another valuable source from a friend's home library. You are chatting about your research paper topic, and she recalls a very witty passage from Jane Austen's novel *Northanger*

Abbey, in which journal keeping is satirized as being a frivolous female pastime. Even better, her copy of *Northanger Abbey* is part of *The Oxford Illustrated Jane Austen,* in six volumes. Your citations, therefore, will have an example of an edited series.

You spend additional days in the library, reading the magazine articles, making bibliography cards for each, and filling notecards. The book by Christina Baldwin you save for later, sensing that it will be completely pertinent because its title focuses on the idea in your thesis. None of the articles is very lengthy, and you find it easier to take notes immediately than to check out each magazine.

Patterns are beginning to emerge as to how you can incorporate this varied information into a unified whole and use it to support your thesis: the development of the journal, changing attitudes toward journal keeping, the artist as journal writer, women as journal writers, the journal as therapeutic tool.

Fifteenth day: Hand in working materials.

The instructor had asked you to hand in a thesis, a rough outline, bibliography cards, and content cards by this day. She wants to check on your progress, to make certain that you are working regularly and systematically. Your thesis has changed as you have done more research. You initially intended to explore why writers keep journals. But you have since learned that the journal provides a way for all kinds of people to discover who they are, what they think and know. So your emphasis will be on how the journal defines the Self. Your outline falls into three broad categories: the evolution and history of the journal; the reasons for keeping a journal; and the dangers and risks in journal writing. The introduction will set up a contrast between other literary genres and this particular and highly personal mode of expression.

Sixteenth day: Understand form and air complaints.

You continue reading and taking notes, grouping the information you find under the broad headings of your outline. You also purchase, in booklet form, the *MLA Handbook,* the source that explains the form your instructor wishes you to follow in manuscript preparation and bibliography. She says consistency is the key in matters of form. Other teachers might recommend models in various handbooks. But the model must be followed throughout.

The instructor lectures briefly in class about the purpose of citations and about their correct form. *She advises that you follow exactly and precisely the MLA format, right down to the last punctuation mark.* A danger exists, for example, that you will follow the overall form but will not notice that the bibliography is alphabetically arranged, by last names of authors. She points out that preparing a list of works used in research is a matter, very simply, of plugging new information into old models. If your source is a book with one author, you simply look for the model that illustrates that source and replace the information in the model with the information about the book you are citing in our research paper.

In class, the students have a chance to air their particular difficulties with their research papers. In some cases, they have selected a topic that is so new, so timely, that there are, as yet, no books written on the subject, only magazine and newspaper articles. Other students have developed a thesis that is too broad, and the abundance of material on the broad subject is intimidating and disheartening. The instructor suggests that these students revise and narrow their topics to bring them in line with a tighter range of sources and materials.

Of course, other students are simply procrastinating. They have not, as yet, even decided on a topic or visited the library. The instructor warns that *a research paper is not an overnight project,* that even the best researchers need to keep pace with the various stages of research writing: planning, researching, writing the rough draft, revising, and correcting the final manuscript.

Seventeenth day: Organize the notecards and begin the first draft.

You have finished taking notes and have a bibliography that is sufficiently varied and lengthy to prevent undue reliance on (and therefore possible plagiarism from) one source. Your ideas have been growing, taking shape. You flip through your note-cards and arrange them in logical order, grouping the main and related ideas under the broad headings of your outline and then further arranging those three piles into groupings that correspond to the subheadings in your outline. For example, all your notecards about the reasons for keeping journals are in one pile. You then divide that pile into smaller piles: one consisting of the writer's motives for keeping journals; another, of women's motives for keeping journals; still another, of psychologists' reasons for encouraging people, especially women, to keep journals.

Having arranged your notecards, you are ready to begin the first draft. *You write this draft exactly as you would any essay, but you place formal citations in parentheses.* You try to create an interesting, enticing introduction; you develop the middle, using comparison, contrast, example, definition, cause and effect, process, description, fact, or narration; you struggle to produce a memorable conclusion, remembering to restate the thesis and expand the meaning of it.

Eighteenth day: Finish the rough draft.

You finish working on the rough draft, confident that your introduction and conclusion are clear and that your organization of the middle is sound.

Nineteenth day: Take a break.

You put the rough draft aside for a day so you can gain some objectivity and distance from it.

Twentieth day: Receive critical comment.

You submit the rough draft to the instructor who is pleased with it in several ways: she likes the timeliness of the topic, the variety of sources cited, the balance between your voice and the authoritative voices of other sources. She dislikes the conclusion, though, feeling that it does not fulfill the promise of the thesis, that it is weak.

Twenty-first day: Revise the rough draft.

You begin a major revision. Some paragraphs you combine; others you delete; still others you strengthen with better examples and proofs or with a stronger topic sentence. You look particularly at the conclusion, which the instructor thought weak. In other words, you use all the techniques for revision suggested in Chapter 10, "Revising the Essay."

Twenty-second day: Edit and correct.

You begin editing and correcting the second draft. First you cut unnecessary words and sentences. Then you check and recheck bibliography form, making certain that you have not inadvertently omitted the year of publication or a punctuation mark. You also double-check the spellings of authors' names, the page numbers cited, and the accuracy of direct quotations against notecards. You find, in rechecking, that you have omitted one piece of information on a notecard that would greatly strengthen one of your assertions. You integrate that information into the body of the research paper and cite the page number in parentheses.

Twenty-third – twenty-sixth days: Type the final manuscript.

You spend the next several days typing the final draft, formal outline, title page, and list of works cited. Though in the *MLA Handbook* there is neither a separate title page nor a formal outline, your instructor favors both. She says that the title page gives a more professional look to the manuscript and that the formal outline offers both writer and reader a quick summary of the paper's contents. The instructor reminds you that you are to type your own papers, thereby guarding against the tendency among hired or biased typists (family members, spouses, friends) to correct your errors. The paper must be entirely your own. You do not type well; you use the hunt-and-peck method and take your time.

Twenty-seventh day: Proofread the final manuscript.

You read the finished research paper several times over, checking first for grammatical errors, then—on successive readings—for punctuation, spelling, and finally manuscript form. You find some errors, naturally, and correct them neatly with a fine-point black pen. A couple of pages have too many errors: they look messy after you make the corrections, so you retype them carefully. You put the final paper into an attractive cover and submit it to the instructor on that twenty-seventh day.

Document your sources carefully.

When you begin writing your paper, remember that you must give credit within the text of your paper to those people whose ideas and words you are using. Until recently, citations were made by supplying the reader with consecutively numbered notes placed within the paper and explained either at the bottom of the page or on a separate sheet at the end of the essay (footnotes or endnotes). The *Modern Language Association Handbook*, however, now recommends a new system calling for citations to be placed in parentheses immediately following borrowed material. These parenthetical citations are meant to refer the reader to the list of works cited that appears at the end of your paper and supplies complete bibliographical information on each source. Because the bibliographical material appears in this list of works cited, the parenthetical citations in the paper need give only enough information to point the reader to the correct volume and page; the works cited list does the rest. This system is simpler and less bulky than either footnotes or endnotes, and if used correctly and with a little common sense, accomplishes the same end in just as clear a manner as the old system.

The most basic elements in this citation system are the author's last name and the page numbers of the reference. If your list of works cited contains more than one work by the same author, you should add to the text reference a shortened but clear title of the work. Similarly, if an author's work is in more than one volume, you should list the appropriate volume number in the text. You will find, however, that you will rarely need to put this much information into your parenthetical references, as you will see by the following examples. For instance, if you have clearly identified the author in introducing your quotation, the author's name need not be repeated in your citation. If you have made it clear which of the author's works is being cited, do not bother to give the title in your citation.

Sample citations

A work by one author: The following example is from the sample research paper.

> The journal has evolved, over a long period, into what Patrick Huyghe has called "a psychological tool, an instrument for self-understanding" (102).

Because Huyghe's name is clearly identified in the introduction to the text and only one of his works appears in "Works Cited" in the sample term paper, only the page number needs to be provided. If you were to rearrange the wording only slightly, however, the citation would be different:

> The journal has evolved, over a long period, into what has been called "a psychological tool, an instrument for self-understanding" (Huyghe 102).

Notice that the abbreviations "p." and "pp." are not used, and there is no comma between the author and the page number. The object is to keep these notes as short as you can, while still directing the reader to your source. Also observe the punctuation of the quoted material. Never place your parenthetical citations within your quotation marks. (After all, they do not appear in the original quotation.)

Moving on to another example, suppose you were quoting from an author who had several entries in your list of works cited. You would have to supply enough information to identify which entry the reader needs to consult:

> May Sarton's two published journals, *Journal of a Solitude* and *The House by the Sea,* rival in popularity many of

her poems and novels, rising to art through the unlikely regions of the personal. She cites depression as a major motive for producing *Journal of a Solitude*, but surely she aspires to art as well. The first sentence of the journal reveals the two-fold purposes: "Begin here. It is raining" (11).

Here, the reference is clearly to *Journal of a Solitude*, but later in the sample paper the following reference appears:

As Sarton says, "A journal cannot be planned ahead" (*House* 11).

In this case, it is necessary to provide a shortened version of the title to refer the reader to the correct work.

Works by different authors with the same last name: Of course, if you cite works by authors with the same last name, you must include their first initials within your citations unless you have clearly identified the author in the introduction to your quotations. Although this case does not occur in the sample term paper, it does in the following examples:

It has been said of Defoe that "From boyhood his most cherished belief was that most of mankind's problems could be solved by the ingenuity of man" (J. Moore 283).

Crusoe's desire for Friday's salvation may be seen "as a symbol of civilized man's potential for good" (C. Moore 117).

The above examples clearly refer the reader to two different sources:

Moore, Catherine. "Robinson Crusoe's Two Servants: The Measure of His Conversion." *A Fair Day in the Affections: Literary Essays in Honor of Robert B. White, Jr.* Ed. Jack Durant and Thomas Hester. Raleigh: Winston, 1980. 111–18.

Moore, John Robert. *Daniel Defoe: Citizen of the Modern World.* Chicago: U of Chicago P, 1985.

Identification of volumes: Occasionally you may need to refer the reader to one volume from a multivolume work. Do so by providing the volume number, followed by a colon, followed by a space, and then provide the page numbers:

> Certainly no high spiritual motive is accorded women in this sprightly exchange between Catherine Morland and Henry Tilney in Jane Austen's novel *Northanger Abbey:*
>
> "I see what you think of me," said he gravely—"I shall make but a poor figure in your journal to-morrow."
> "My journal!"
> "Yes, I know exactly what you will say: Friday, went to the Lower Rooms; wore my sprigged muslin robe with blue trimmings—plain black shoes—appeared to much advantage; but was strangely harassed by a queer, half-witted man, who would make me dance with him, and distressed me by his nonsense." (5: 26–27)

The above citation is to *The Oxford Illustrated Jane Austen*, a six-volume work; *Northanger Abbey* is contained in volume 5.

The following examples show how to handle works that are written by more than one author, using works documented in the samples of bibliographic form:

A book by two authors:

> The problem with some autobiographical material is that "We delude ourselves if we read everything written in the first person by, say, Rudyard Kipling, H. G. Wells and George Orwell himself as being literally true" (Coppard and Crick 11).

A book by three authors:

> Financial mix strategies are said to "involve the selection of means for financing company projects, inventories, production operations, and various other activities" (Anderson, Sweeney, and Williams 194).

A book by more than three authors: When citing a book written by more than three authors, merely follow the first author's name with the abbreviation "et al.": (Busse et al. 11).

Citing poetry, drama, and the Bible.

When quoting from poetry, drama, or the Bible, you should give line numbers, act and scene numbers, or chapter and verse numbers instead of page numbers, for they allow the reader to check your source in an edition other than the one from which you are quoting. (In your list of works cited, however, you must identify the edition you use.)

Poetry:

> The narrator of "The Chimney Sweeper" by William Blake exemplifies the cruelty which often confronted poor children in eighteenth-century England:
>
> > When my mother died I was very young,
> > And my father sold me while yet my tongue,
> > Could scarcely cry weep weep weep.
> > So your chimneys I sweep & in soot I sleep. (1–4)

Notice that in the case of block quotations, the parenthetical reference should come *after* the period. The parenthetical reference means that the first four lines of the poem are being quoted.

Drama:

> In William Shakespeare's *Richard III*, Richard complains that he is "so lamely and unfashionable / That dogs bark at me when I halt by them" (1.1.22–23).

The above citation identifies the quotation as being from Act 1, scene 1, lines 22–23. The largest unit, the act, comes first, followed by the next largest, the scene, followed by the smallest, the line. These numbers are separated by periods, and Arabic numbers are used rather than Roman numerals. (The slash within the quotation is necessary because this play is written in verse; it indicates the end of the first line.)

The Bible:

Ernest Hemingway drew the title of *The Sun Also Rises* from the Bible (Ecc. 1.4).

The above citation refers to Ecclesiastes, Chapter 1, verse 4. Names of books of the Bible are neither underlined nor put in quotation marks, and long names should be shortened.

Prepare a final list of works cited.

Use the bibliographical material from your notes to prepare your final list of works cited. The first page bears the centered heading "Works Cited." As with the body of the research paper, the bibliographical entries are double-spaced throughout, with the first line of each entry touching the left margin and the subsequent lines of the entry indented five spaces. Arrange your entries in alphabetical order, by the author's or editor's last name. For more than two authors or editors, give the last name of the first person credited with authorship or editorship, followed by "et al." If you use more than one work by the same author, do not repeat the author's name in subsequent entries; substitute three hyphens followed by a period.

The following examples show some of the more common types of text references: a journal article with continuous pagination, a citation from an introduction, one author of two books cited, a two-volume novel with a translator, and a work with two authors. Notice that the broad divisions within each entry are separated by periods and that each entry ends with a period.

Note: If your list of works cited includes several books by the same person functioning sometimes as author, sometimes as editor, always cite last the works that the person edited, even if the edited work precedes the authored work either alphabetically or chronologically.

Works Cited

Bogel, Fredric V. "The Rhetoric of Substantiality."

Eighteenth-Century Studies 12 (1979): 457-480.

Fuller, Edmund. Introduction. Lives of the Poets. By

Samuel Johnson. New York: Avon Books, 1965.

9-14.

Sarton, May. The House by the Sea: A Journal. New

York: Norton, 1977.

———. Journal of a Solitude. New York: Norton, 1973.

Tolstoy, L. N. War and Peace. Trans. Rosemary

Edmonds. 2 vols. Middlesex: Penguin Books,

1978.

Trimmer, Joseph F., and C. Wade Jennings. Fictions.

San Diego: Harcourt, 1985.

Checklist for a research paper.

This checklist is designed to help you look analytically at the structure, style, and conventions necessary to all research papers. As you read the research paper model, measure it against this checklist, and note the degree to which the examples you discover in the model adhere to these proprieties and structures.

1. The research paper, as with all good essays, contains a thesis, topic sentences, an introduction, a well-developed middle, and a conclusion with a restatement and expansion of the thesis.

2. The research paper includes a title page, outline, the paper itself, and a list of works cited. (**Note:** Though the *MLA Handbook* suggests that the title and class information appear on the first page of the text and that no outline be included, many other handbooks suggest otherwise. Follow your instructor's preference in this matter. The research paper model includes both a title page and an outline as examples of the more traditional format.)

3. The citations within the research paper also appear as a complete listing within the works cited and vice versa. In other words, every text citation appears within the list of works cited, and every entry in the list appears in the research paper.

4. The text references and the list of works cited follow exactly and consistently the recommended models found in the *MLA Handbook* or in the source the instructor recommends.

5. There is good integration of sources. The writer does not cite the same source several times in a row.

6. There is neither too much nor too little reliance on source material. The writer's voice is strong, but the writer gives a clear voice as well to other sources and authorities, using primary and secondary sources to bolster his or her assertions.

7. The quoted passages are appropriate to the purpose and context (some merely a word or phrase, some a sentence, some a longer passage that is indented), the quotations are integrated into the flow of the writer's ideas, and the writer comments on the significance or purpose of each quoted passage, leaving no doubt as to how the quoted passage fits into the context of the whole paper.

8. All or most paragraphs contain citations in sufficient numbers to prove the truth of the writer's assertion, and all citations are calculated to support the thesis or topic sentence. But the citations do not outweigh the writer's assertion: the proportion is appropriate.

9. The writer quotes neither more nor less than is necessary to make his or her point, using only the telling portion of the quotation.

10. Some ideas are paraphrased, but the idea is carefully cited just as a direct quotation would be.

11. The pagination is correct, with Arabic numerals correctly placed.

12. The authors in the list of works cited are arranged alphabetically, by last name; the first line of the entry begins at the margin, and all subsequent lines are indented five spaces.

13. Each entry in the list of works cited contains all information appropriate to the genre being cited:

    Books: author(s) and/or editor(s), title (underlined), city of publication, publisher, year of publication

    Periodicals: author, title of article (in quotation marks), title of magazine or journal (underlined), date of publication (month, date, and year; or month and year; or year), the pages of the article.

14. Each work cited follows the punctuation exactly as it appears in the *MLA* model or in the recommended model.

15. The research paper title on the title page follows the correct rules for capitalization, but it is neither underlined nor in quotation marks.

16. The writer discusses books and articles in the present tense, as if the work were contemporaneous to his or her time period.

17. The quotations are exactly as the writer found them. All changes are indicated with bracketed explanations. When a pronoun reference is unclear in the quoted passage, the writer inserts the name or thing in *brackets* to clarify the reference. Brackets also appear around the symbol *"sic,"* which means that the quoted passage contains a factual or spelling error, and the writer is aware that the fault is there but does not intend to tamper with the quoted authority's words.

18. When words are omitted from the middle of a direct quotation, the writer has inserted *ellipses* (three spaced dots) to indicate the omission. When the omission falls at the end of a sentence, the writer includes a fourth dot, which represents the period or end punctuation.

19. The outline structures are parallel within each category.

20. The manuscript is free of errors in punctuation, grammar, spelling, fact, and form.

◆

Activities

Using the checklist, examine the research paper that follows for examples of each consideration. In other words, evaluate the research paper as a model. As you go down the checklist, make notations and suggestions for improving the research paper model. Then discuss your conclusions with other members of the class who have made their own analytical comments about the model. Is there general agreement or disagreement? Why or why not? Even though the content or subject matter may not appeal to you, can you imagine using similar techniques and approaches with an interest or specialty of your own? Would, for example, a research paper on the uses of chemistry in the home be effectively evaluated on the basis of the same criteria? Why or why not? **Note:** In the following model, the thesis statement, topic sentences, and restatement of thesis are underscored to aid in the critical evaluation of the model.

The Art of Survival: Journal Writing

by

Anne Howell

English 112, Section 3

Ms. Simpson

April 29, 1985

Outline

Thesis: The contemporary journal leads inward, in pursuit of the self, of identity.

Introduction: Journal writing differs from conventional literary genres in its audience, its purposes, and its effect on the individual.

I. The evolution and history of the journal

    A. Spiritual journeys

        1. Puritans

        2. Quakers

    B. Feminine diversion

II. Reasons for keeping journals

    A. For the writer/artist

    B. For women

        1. The search for self

        2. The journal as companion/audience

        3. The journal as metaphor

III.   Dangers and risks in journal writing

    A.   Inhibitions

    B.   Circularity

    C.   Judgment

    D.   Stasis

Conclusion: The journal—a loose, subjective,
personal literary creation—requires that
its creator surrender to its flow and ebb,
allowing himself or herself to be swept
along on tides of meaning. The risk is
great, but a paradox emerges. The more the
individual yields himself or herself to the
flow of the journal, the more he or she will
regain control over self, personal destiny,
life. The journal writer becomes, in a
sense, a work of art.

The Art of Survival: Journal Writing

Countless motives push people to put pen to
the page: the impulse to create a work of art; the
desire to instruct and delight; the yearning,
insatiable in humans, to achieve immortality.
But these creative impulses move outward,
engaging the reader, enlisting the reader's
support for participation in and affirmation of
the artist's efforts. As poet Louise Bogan puts
it, "the heart's cry" lies behind poetry, "the
mind's search" behind "speculation" (97). In
the conventional literary genres--poetry,
novel, story, drama--the consideration of
audience is primary.

But there is another kind of writing, a
conversation with one's self, that, though it
does not ignore the audience beyond the writer's
room, nonetheless places the audience in a

Howell 4

secondary role. It is, of course, the journal,

or "flow writing" as some have called it (Baldwin

15), a looser, odder, far more personal and

subjective creative effort. In the journal, the

human heart cries out to itself; the journey is

inward; the activity is solitary; the audience is

shadowy, distant, uninvolved. The journal may

or may not find its place in the world, may or may

not become fair and public game for the cruel or

kindly pen of the critic, may or may not fly from

the secret drawer onto the published pages of

books, magazines, newspapers. Though the

journal is often great literature, its greatness

is often a literary accident of sorts, deriving

from a freakish combination of events and

circumstances that were never the journal

keeper's original intention. Whereas in other

literary genres the writer shapes the work, in

journals the work shapes the writer. The

Howell 5

contemporary journal leads inward, in pursuit of

the self, of identity.

The journal has evolved, over a long period,

into what Patrick Huyghe has called "a

psychological tool, an instrument for

self-understanding" (102). Says June Singer, a

Chicago psychotherapist, "We really find out who

we are through journals" (Huyghe 102). What one

puts into a journal is not likely to find its way

into John Bartlett's Familiar Quotations. It

may be that no one will ever read the journal,

save the journalist himself. Huyghe, quoting

Henry David Thoreau, reminds us of the

distinction between journals and other literary

forms: "The journal is a record of experience and

growth, not a preserve of things well done or

said" (100). It is precisely this fluidity, this

privacy and intimacy, that has propelled the

journal into its present popularity. In a sense,

Howell 6

the journal keeper shapes himself, not public

opinion, thumbing his nose at literariness,

seeking those "subtle intimations of truth"

that give direction to his life. These

unliterary musings are, in Huyghe's words,

"frequently attempts to fend off . . . chaos, to

bring order, coherence and purpose to one's

subjective world" (104).

    In earlier centuries, however, the journal

was not always a "theraput," an "attendant or

midwife . . . who made way for Psyche's head"

(Balwin 5). The Puritans, says Huyghe, were

"prolific diarists," who used the diary as a

"hedge against despair . . . based on the belief

that salvation could be attained through

self-examination" (102). And Robert Kaiser

cites, in a similar vein, the way in which Ira

Progoff, New York psychologist and popular

creator of the "Intensive Journal," suggests the

Quakers used journals. Progoff says the goal of

Quaker journal keepers was "self-measurement,"

rather than self-understanding. The Quakers

were attempting, in their journals, to "keep tabs

on their consciences," a motive that might lead

them, and dangerously, to making the journal

"static," merely an "instrument for

self-justification" (Kaiser 76).

   In the eighteenth and early nineteeth

centuries, journals were often popular modes of

female expression, perceived therefore, and

rather condescendingly perhaps, as being

frivolous, light, gossipy in tone and purpose.

Certainly no high spiritual motive is accorded

women in this sprightly exchange between

Catherine Morland and Henry Tilney in Jane

Austen's novel Northanger Abbey:

         "I see what you think of me," said

Howell 8

he gravely--"I shall make but a poor

figure in your journal to-morrow."

"My journal!"

"Yes, I know exactly what you

will say: Friday, went to the Lower

Rooms; wore my sprigged muslin robe

with blue trimmings--plain black

shoes--appeared to much advantage;

but was strangely harassed by a queer,

half-witted man, who would make me

dance with him, and distressed me by

his nonsense."

"Indeed I shall say no such

thing."

"Shall I tell you what you ought

to say?"

"If you please."

"I danced with a very agreeable

young man, introduced by Mr. King; had

a great deal of conversation with

him--seems a most extraordinary

genius--hope I may know more of him.

THAT, madame, is what I WISH you to

say."

"But perhaps, I keep no journal."

"Perhaps you are not sitting in

this room, and I am not sitting by

you. These are points in which doubt

is equally possible. Not keep a

journal! How are your absent cousins

to understand the tenour of your life

in Bath without one? How are the

civilities and compliments of every

day to be related as they ought to be,

unless noted down every evening in a

journal? How are your various dresses

to be remembered, and the particular

state of your complexion, and curl of

your hair to be described in all their

diversities, without having constant

recourse to a journal?--My dear

Madame, I am not so ignorant of young

ladies' ways as you wish me to believe;

it is this delightful habit of

journalizing which largely

contributes to form the easy style of

writing for which ladies are so

generally celebrated." (5: 26-27)

Austen's delicious satire aims at eighteenth-

century views of journal keeping, keenly

exposing the male perception of writing in

general and of journal writing in particular.

Women's journals--surely an unfit pastime for

wise and worldly. intellectual males--were to

serve as monuments to female vanity, as records

of female conquests of suitors, as nothing more

substantial, really, than the modern adolescent

girl's anguished entry in her five-year diary of

Billy's unwillingness to escort her to the prom.

This view of journal keeping is a far cry both

from the spiritual explorations of the Quakers

and of the Puritans and from the recent

renaissance of journal keeping as therapy or

psychological journey.

The motives for keeping journals in this

century, though nearly always related to growth

and personal insight, are nonetheless varied, as

varied as the thousands upon thousands of people

who keep them. No longer is journal keeping a

mere scribbling of surface days and petty party

encounters. No longer is journal keeping merely

a pious attempt to justify the ways of man to

God. Journal keeping has become a serious

business, both in the literal and figurative

senses. Huyghe says, "Diaries gradually became

less a spiritual tool and travelogue and more an

instrument of release" (102). He adds that

nearly 50,000 people, up to the year 1981, had

participated in Ira Progoff's "Intensive

Journal" workshops and that more than 5 million

blank books or diaries are sold each year. How

and why are people filling the pages of these

books, and what patterns emerge from group to

group?

Writers, according to Mary Phraner Warren,

use journals for purposes subtly or boldly

different from the more than fifty thousand

people attending Progoff's workshops. The

journal can increase the writer's powers of

observation, break stereotypes, improve the

writer's style, produce raw material for later

literary efforts, relieve the system of what is

ultimately unpublishable, and stimulate the

creative juices (19-20). Many famous novelists

and poets have used the journal as an adjunct to

their more formal creative productions, among

them Virginia Woolf, Katherine Mansfield,

Bertolt Brecht, Henry James. The journal is, for

these writers, the field in which the seeds of

creation take root.

And for some writers, the journal has been

the primary genre in which they operated, such

writers becoming famous primarily, not

secondarily, for their journal entries. Anaïs

Nin is one such writer. Nin is quoted, in Robert

Kaiser's article "The Way of the Journal," as

saying, "The lack of intimacy with one's self,

and consequently with others, is what created the

loneliest and most alienated people in the

world. . . . The process of growth in a human

being, the process out of which a human being

emerges, is essentially an inward process"

(72). The journal, then, even when it strives

Howell 14

for artistic integrity, is still intimately

bound up with discovery.

May Sarton's two published journals,

Journal of a Solitude and The House by the Sea,

rival in popularity many of her poems and novels,

rising to art through the unlikely regions of the

personal. She cites depression as a major motive

for producing Journal of a Solitude, but surely

she aspires to art as well. The first sentence of

the journal reveals the twofold purpose: "Begin

here. It is raining" (11). It is, of course,

"raining" on several levels, as the reader soon

discovers. Sarton further explains herself to

herself--and indirectly to the reader--in the

following passage:

I am here alone for the first time

in weeks, to take up my "real" life

again at last. That is what is

strange--that friends, even

Howell 15

passionate love, are not my real life

unless there is time alone in which to

explore and discover what is happening

or has happened. (11)

But Sarton begins to hint at the wider scope of

journals, the movement toward the psychological,

when she cries out, frightened, "I had made an

open place, a place for meditation. What if I

can't find myself in it?" (12). Here Sarton

bridges the gap between the journal as art and the

journal as self-revelation.

Christina Baldwin perhaps best explains the

modern, psychotherapeutic function of journals

when she says, "The journal illuminates the

self. And the self illuminates the collective

self" (28). For this reason, though begun in the

personal, though grounded in the particular, the

journal can rise to the universal. Anne Morrow

Lindbergh, writing in the introduction of her

Howell 16

best-selling book, <u>Gift from the Sea,</u>

illustrates very well this movement from the

particular to the general, from the self to other

selves:

> I began these pages for myself,
> in order to think out my own particular
> pattern of living, my own individual
> balance of life, work, and human
> relationships.   And since I think best
> with a pencil in my hand, I started
> naturally to write.   I had the
> feeling, when the thoughts first
> clarified on paper, that my experience
> was very different from other
> people's.   (Are we all under this
> illusion?) (9)

Though the average journal keeper may not begin,

as does the artist, with an eye to the universal,

the universal may loom before her in the end, an

unexpected and happy sunrise of meaning, far more

glorious than she ever intended.

   If the discovery of self is a modern motive

for the journal writer, that motive gains even

more significance for women, who have had,

perhaps, a vaguer sense of self, a blurry,

discomfiting amorphousness, lost, as they have

often been, in the needs and demands of other,

external selves. The journals of women, whether

famous or unfamous, reveal an urgency, a longing,

an insatiable need to discover who they are and

what they think. Alice James, for example, began

her journal as a commonplace book, into which she

merely "copied verses, aphorisms, passages from

novels, sentences culled from her wide and

ever-curious readings" (1). But a few years

later, what had begun as a commonplace book, a

receptacle for the ideas of others, became a

personal journal: "I think," wrote James in 1889,

Howell 18

"that if I get into the habit of writing a bit

about what happens, or rather doesn't happen, I

may lose a little of the sense of loneliness and

desolation which abides with me" (25). The

journal becomes at this point, "a companion," in

the words of Baldwin, "someone patient and

involved who would never tire of my changing

views and location" (xv). The journal becomes,

in short, a person. The conversation is between

the non-self and the self. The outcome is

identity.

Florida Scott-Maxwell felt a similar need

welling up in her, pushing her to discover

herself within the journal even though, or

perhaps especially because, she was already

old. She, like Baldwin, also characterizes the

journal as a person, a friend to her passionate

old age:

Now that I am old something has

Howell 19

begun . . . to make me start this note

book. When I was sewing, or playing a

soothing—boring game of patience, I

found queries going round and round in

my head and I began to jot them

down. . . . The queries were

insistent, and I began a game of asking

questions and giving answers. . . .

My answers must be my own, years of

reading now lost in the abyss I call my

mind. What matters is what I have now,

what in fact I live and feel.

It makes my notebook my dear

companion, or my undoing. . . . When I

play that grim, comforting game of

noting how wrong everyone else is, my

book is silent, and I listen to the

stillness, and I learn. (7—8)

And another journal writer, Tristine

Rainer, sums up the search for self in this way:

"In the pages of that blank book, without

divisions and without instructions, I began to

discover and create the rules of my own being"

(58). Rainer describes a painful transition,

similar to the shift for James, from being the

keeper of other people's ideas to being the

keeper of her own. Rainer began writing a

journal with her beloved as audience. Even when

she was no longer involved with him, she

continued to "address" him, as though he

controlled her perceptions even from a

distance. But one day, in an epiphany of sorts,

she wrote in her book, "Let my page be a woman for

the first time." Says Rainer, "In that moment, on

that page, I met myself as the audience of my own

diary" (58). That women gradually see

themselves as selves in journals, and therefore

as fit audiences for the play of their ideas, is

an important psychological breakthrough,

dramatically surpassing the inanities and

banalities so bitingly satirized in Austen's

novel.

In poetically metaphorical language,

Baldwin describes the yearning of women toward

light. Speaking of counseling women, she

describes herself as a page on which they keep

their verbal journals: "I hear stories from the

sea-bottom, neon-eyed from years of dark

swimming where no light penetrates" (xiv). This

kind of enlightenment, achieved through

self-definition, is not so much an education

about the self as a seeing of the self.

Ruth Limmer, writing on Bogan, uses a

similar "seeing" metaphor, a moment when light

falls on meaning: "That winter of her depression,

a small camera eye opened and shut in her memory

and suddenly a scene would be disclosed with

Howell 22

terrific clarity" (Bogan 27). That "clarity"

brings out sharp, well-defined shapes; bounded,

and paradoxically liberated, selves, capable of

shedding, not merely reflecting, light. It is

the journal, then, that may give the woman, any

woman, the self she has always possessed but

never truly owned.

But journals are not always shedders of

light, shapers of personality. Dangers exist in

this highly subjective, loose genre. There is

the problem, first of all, of getting started.

Baldwin cites two major inhibitions to journal

writing: (1) "the perception of life as static

instead of dynamic" and (2) "the denial of

introspection as a meaningful function in our

society" (27). Huyghe, echoing Progoff,

similarly states that journals are too often

wrongly used, aiming toward stasis rather than

growth, locking people into "circular attitudes

Howell 23

and behaviors" (106). Progoff stresses in his workshops that the journal writer is not to think, not to judge, but, rather, simply to write. Kaiser provides us with a metaphor for this not-thinking, not-judging stance:

> He [Progoff] says there's an underground stream of images and recollections within each of us. The stream is nothing more or less than our interior life. When we enter it, we ride it to a place where IT wants to go. (67)

That the journal carries us along on the tide of itself is very different from the artistic creation, in which the artist, not the work, controls.

An unwillingness or reluctance to go to places within the self we would sooner not visit is at the bottom of journal failures. Meta

Potts, an English teacher who initially used the
journal with her high school students in
conventional ways—to react to current events or
literary works—discovered this resistance
among her students to the free flow of creation.
Their initial entries were trite, stilted. And
only with great difficulty did the students learn
"to vent their frustrations, divulge fears, and
reveal traumas" in their lives. The journal
became a "dialogue," first with the teacher and
then with the journal's primary audience, the
journal writer himself (34). Rainer sums up the
overcoming of these problems with inhibitions,
circularity, stasis: "For some people learning
to be free in their diaries is a way of learning to
be free with themselves" (57).

There is risk in keeping journals, and great
danger as well, in being swept along on the tide
of the subjective, interior ocean. Rainer

advises that journal keepers "write fast, write everything, include everything, write from your feelings, write from your body, accept whatever comes" (58). As Sarton says, "A journal cannot be planned ahead" (House 11). The accepting of whatever comes is perhaps the hardest and riskiest aspect of this fluid literary activity, in which survival depends not on grabbing the nearest branch of another person's idea, theory, or technique but, rather, on swimming vigorously and courageously over the blank pages of ourselves, with no land in sight.

But if the journal writer takes the risk of surrendering, a paradox may result: the more the journal writer forgets himself or herself, yielding to the creative and psychological journey, the more the journal writer will discover about the elusive self. It is odd that by relaxing control the journal writer could

Howell 26

regain control over self, personal destiny,

life. But such is the promise of both

psychologists and writers who use journals to

bring personalities, emotions, ideas, and fears

into being and who courageously dare to confront

these hidden thoughts and feelings. The journal

writer becomes, in a sense, a work of art.

Works Cited

Austen, Jane. The Oxford Illustrated Jane

Austen. Ed. R. W. Chapman. 6 vols.

Oxford: Oxford UP, 1983.

Baldwin, Christina. One to One: Self-

Understanding Through Journal Writing.

New York: Evans, 1977.

Bogan, Louise. Journey Around My Room: The

Autobiography of Louise Bogan: A Mosaic.

Ed. Ruth Limmer. Middlesex: Penquin, 1980.

Huyghe, Patrick. "Diary Writing Turns a New

Leaf." New York Times Magazine 8 November

1981: 98–108.

James, Alice. The Diary of Alice James. Ed.

Leon Edel. Middlesex: Penquin, 1964.

Kaiser, Robert Blair, "Way of the Journal."

Psychology Today March 1981: 64–76.

Lindbergh, Anne Morrow. Gift from the Sea. New

York: Pantheon, 1955.

Howell 28

Potts, Meta. "Dialogue Journal: A First Step in

   Helping Troubled Students." Today's

   Education 70 (September–October 1981):

   34–35.

Rainer, Tristine. "The New Diary––Where

   Anything Goes." Writer's Yearbook 1979:

   57–61.

Sarton, May. The House by the Sea: A Journal.

   New York: Norton, 1977.

–––. Journal of a Solitude. New York: Norton,

   1973.

Scott–Maxwell, Florida. The Measure of My

   Days. Middlesex: Penquin, 1968.

Warren, Mary Phraner. "A Writer's Journal."

   The Writer June 1982: 18–20.

Copyrights and Acknowledgments

Index